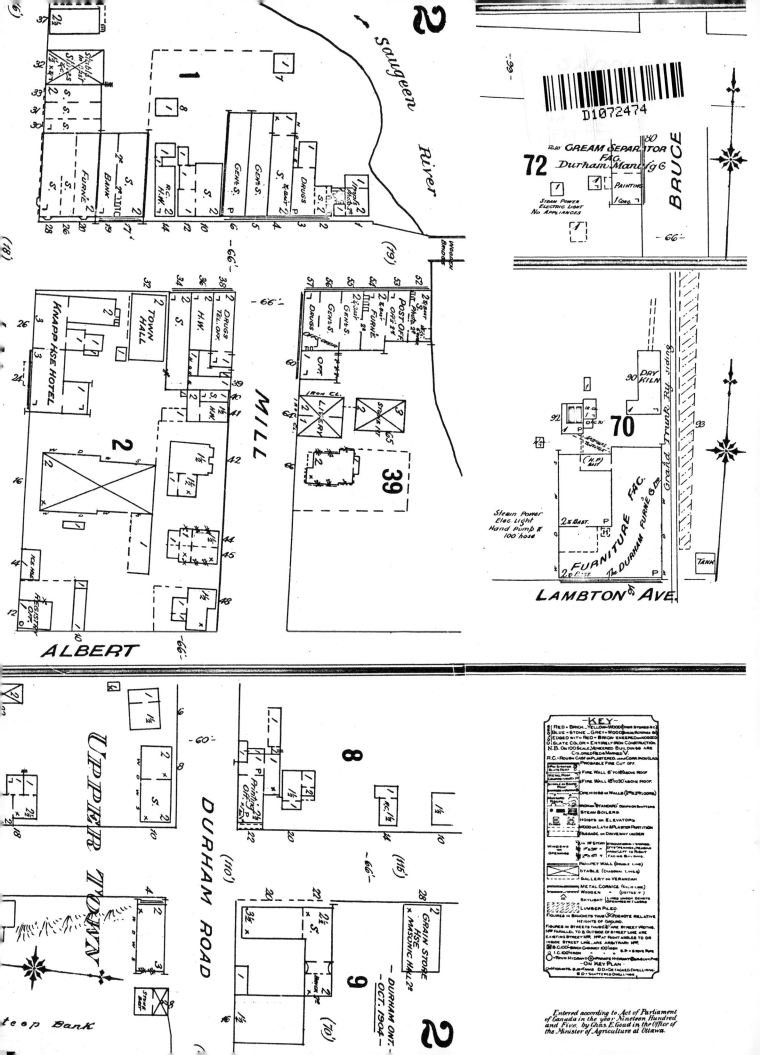

A History of the Town of Durham 1842-1994

compiled by
The Durham Historical Committee

Copyright © 1994

EDITING COMMITTEE
Thos. Firth, Mrs. Donald (Betty) Corbett,
Mrs. Donald (Betty) Pust, Mrs. Thos. (Vera) Firth

DURHAM HISTORICAL COMMITTEE

Chairman
Thos. Firth

Secretary
Mrs. Donald (Betty) Corbett

1st Treasurer
Ina Milne

Treasurer
Mrs. Donald (Betty) Pust

Directors
George Prew
Albert Reay
Charles Watson
Dr. J. Bruce
Gordon MacLean
Charles Moffat
Carol Lawrence

For many years it has been said that George Jackson had conferred the name of Durham on this community in honour of his English birthplace. However, descendents of the Jackson family report that this statement is an error because George Jackson was not born in Durham, England. A perusal of the George Jackson family tree confirms this statement. In 1838 the British government appointed John George Lambton, the Earl of Durham, Governor-General and High Commissioner of British North America. He was responsible for preparing a report on the Canadian rebellion of 1837. Lord Durham's report recommended the joining of Upper and Lower Canada and the establishment of a democratic government, something the colonies had never possessed before this time. Unquestionably, this is the source of the name for the Town of Durham.

ISBN: 0-9699201-0-5

Printed by
Stan Brown Printers Limited
Owen Sound, Ont.

The Wood Show

MEMORIES OF HOME

If you've ever lived in Durham
Then you'll know the crystal streams
That come bubbling down the rocky hills of home
To the millponds and the water wheels
That slumber now, serene,
In the valley of the beautiful Saugeen.

You'll remember graceful willows
And the fragrant evergreens,
Stately maples, and their crimson leaves in fall,
Velvet sumacs, red as rubies,
Lighting up the long ravine
In the valley of the beautiful Saugeen.

You've accepted, as your birthright,
Air and water — fresh and clean —
And the parklands in the rolling hills you love;
All these precious things you'll know about,
This fair and pleasant scene,
As you walk beside the beautiful Saugeen.

You have known the changing seasons,
Autumn colours, sparkling snow,
And the lacy greens of springtime in the glen,
Rushing waters, summer sunsets —
All these lovely sights you've seen
In the valley of the beautiful Saugeen.

  Wilma Coutts

Heritage Walkway Bridge

While I was not born here, I was brought here at such an early age that Durham is in my earliest memories. I can remember no other place. Therefore, to me, it is my hometown.

I left in 1943 at the age of 20 years to join the Canadian Women's Army Corps — the first time that I had ever been away for any length of time.

The following spring I got my first extended leave and headed for home. I was unprepared for the tidal wave of emotion and memories that engulfed me as the bus crested Cork Town hill and the whole valley was laid out before my eyes. My Durham! Home! The familiar sight started a flood of tears and renewed love for the dear town I had left only a few short months before. Until you have left it you can never really appreciate the homecoming as I did.

Do you appreciate the beauty of this town? Snuggled in a lovely valley, the beautiful river at its centre, the surrounding hills encircling the whole as in one enormous hug. Wherever I went in the years that followed, Durham stayed clearly in my memory, sometimes to the point of homesickness. When retirement time came I found there was no other place I'd rather be than right here, at home, in Durham.

June (Elvidge) Baynes

FORWARD TOGETHER

FOREWORD

The Durham History Book Committee presents for your enjoyment a new extended and comprehensive History of the Town of Durham. Three Historical Reviews have already been published. The first review was edited by Dr. J.F. Grant in 1935, the second by Isabelle McGirr and Hector Mac-Donald in 1958 and the third by I.B. Sharpe and J.B. Duffield in 1972. The committee has used these reviews extensively as a starting point and has done a great deal more primary research on the life and development of the town of Durham. This history was never intended to be an academic work but rather a warm social history of Durham. The committee's number one objective was to present as many interesting facts as accurately as possible. If we have failed, or made errors in this objective, we apologize.

The committee wishes to thank all those who have contributed time and material to this project, with special thanks to the Hunter family for permission to use the aerial colour photographs of Durham taken by A.K. Hunter. This includes those who edited the book, the proof-readers, the keyboard operators, the researchers, the generous contributors of pictures and the paste up artists. It would be impossible to name all those who have made contributions but a few people not on the committee will be mentioned. We thank Marlaine Elvidge and Dorothy Mead who did research and writing, Helen Hopkins for the art work, Narda Elvidge, photographer, who supplied present day pictures of Durham, Mrs. Ottilie McGowan, who provided a vast amount of information, and our resident author and poetess, Wilma Coutts, who furnished some memories of former years and gave us permission to use her poem "Memories of Home."

This book would not be complete without recognizing the unnamed citizens who make any community a reality. They are the majority who do the work, raise the children, buy the goods, attend the social functions, play the games, enjoy the scenery and create the personality of loyalty, pride and love which is very special to the town.

ACKNOWLEDGEMENTS

We gratefully acknowledge the contributions made to this project by:

The Government of Canada: Department of Health and Welfare
New Horizon Programme
Durham Public Library
Owen Sound Public Library
The National Public Archives, Ottawa
The Ontario Public Archives, Toronto
The National Postal Museum, Ottawa
The Presbyterian Church in Canada Archives, Toronto
The United Church of Canada Archives, Toronto
The Roman Catholic Church Archives, Hamilton
St. Mary's Rectory, Owen Sound
Grey County Registry Office, Owen Sound
Saugeen Valley Conservation Authority
The Durham Municipal Council Office

The Directors of the History Book wish to pay special tribute to Tom and Vera Firth.

Tom initiated the idea of this book and has worked ceaselessly and diligently using his vast knowledge of historical facts to realize its completion.

Vera, his wife, has spent many hours daily at her computer preparing diskettes for the printer.

To Tom and Vera we offer our sincere thanks.

MESSAGE FROM THE MAYOR

As Mayor of Durham I bring greetings from our Town to all those who read this book.

It is an excellent history covering all facets of the town from its founding to the present.

On behalf of the Citizens of Durham I wish to express appreciation and congratulations to the committee and to those who contributed the many hours for work and research.

Yours sincerely,

Floyd Lawrence, Mayor.

CONTENTS

THE PHYSIOGRAPHY OF THE TOWN OF DURHAM

by Clark Armstrong

(Information for this article is taken from
The Physiography of Southern Ontario, 3rd Edition, by L.J. Chapman and D.F. Putnam,
published by Ontario Ministry of Natural Resources, 1984.)

The economy of an area, and the nature of its people, are largely determined by the environment of the region. History and Geography influence each other. In order to have a good understanding of the history of an area or people then, some knowledge of a region's geography is desirable.

The formation of the Earth's crust occurred about three and one-half billion years ago when molten materials cooled. So the bedrock of any place on the earth's surface consists of Precambrian rocks, such as granite. These Precambrian rocks were formed between one billion and three and one-half billion years ago.

On some parts of the earth's surface, including Southern Ontario, large seas of warm water covered the land for long periods of time. Aproximately 425 to 500 million years ago, the sediments on the bottom of these seas, including fossils, cemented themselves under their own weight into solid rock and were deposited on top of the Precambrian rocks. These Paleozoic rock layers consist of relatively soft limestones, shales and sandstones. They are exposed at places such as McGowan's Falls.

The bedrock of the Durham area is relatively higher in elevation compared to the rest of Southern Ontario. Durham is part of the region known as the Huron Uplands. The higher elevation of the Huron Uplands means the area experiences slightly cooler temperatures, and slightly heavier precipitation than the rest of Southern Ontario. These climatic characteristics affect the natural vegetation of the area, as well as the agricultural potential of the Durham region.

The major factor affecting the landscape of Durham is that of Continental Glaciation. The continental ice sheets have advanced from the polar regions at least four times in the last million years. The present landscape is the result mainly of the last ice sheet, called the Wisconsin Glacier, which left Southern Ontario only about 10,000 years ago.

Glaciers generally acted on landscapes in two ways. First, the tremendous weight of the ice sheets (more than half a kilometre thick) and the rough nature of the ice, resulted in a "sandpapering" effect as the ice sheet advanced and retreated over the land. This action resulted in a lowering of the elevation of an area, and a generally smoother, rounded appearance. Secondly, when the ice sheets melted, the materials embedded in the ice sheets (rocks, sediments, soils, etc.) were deposited on the landscape to an average depth of 30 metres. These deposits are generally known as glacial till.

When the glaciers melted and retreated, huge amounts of meltwater were released which also affected the landscape. In some areas the meltwater carved out drainage channels called spillways. In other areas the meltwater spread out and/or rearranged the glacial till into various unique shapes.

Looking at a map of the Physiography of the Durham area, several general patterns emerge. Most of the lower areas of the town and surrounding region, such as the Saugeen River Valley and downtown Durham, are classified as spillways. The higher areas of the Durham region tend to be of two types. First are the drumlinized till plains. Till plains are usually relatively flat areas of land. Drumlins are elongated, whale-shaped hills. Examples of this landscape are found: north of town on the east side of Highway No. 6 (present-day Eccles farm); in the south-east part of town including the gravelly area around the Curling Club; and in the area west of Durham south of Highway No. 4. The area west of Highway No. 6 and generally north of the Rocky Saugeen River is another good example of the drumlinized till plain.

The other areas of higher elevation are classified as Kame Moraines. Kames are more conical-shaped and smaller than drumlins. When several kames are joined together, the result is a ridge-type of feature called Kame Moraine.

"Within the Saugeen basin between Wingham and Flesherton the Georgian Bay (ice) lobe left scattered groups of kames within a drumlin field. Quite often these sandhills are found along the shoulders of the river valleys. Associated with them are great quantities of coarse pitted outwash. The Saugeen Kames exhibit some of our roughest morainic topography and consist of unusually coarse material."

1

These features are located slightly further from the town proper. Kame Moraine tends to dominate the landscape towards the hilly areas of Priceville, and the hilly, stoney areas near Edge Hill.

In summary, Durham, along with the townships of Bentinck, Normanby and Glenelg, are covered by a complex of till ridges, kame moraines, outwash plains, and spillways, interspersed with more smoothly moulded till plains and drumlinized areas. The area also contains many small lakes and streams, and numerous swampy areas.

The dominant "stream" in the Durham area is the Saugeen, including various tributary streams such as the Rocky Saugeen. The Saugeen River system drains an area of 1,565 square miles including some of the highest land in south-western Ontario. The main branch travels a course of 115 miles from the Dundalk area, through Durham to Lake Huron. The headwater areas contain much rough and rocky land and farm lots there have between 30 to 35 per cent of their acreage in woods and swamp. In addition, a large part of the cleared land is used as permanent pasture. The soil is loamy or gravelly, and the streams run clear even after heavy summer showers.

To some extent, the Saugeen was used as a transportation route in the early days of settlement. More important have been the power sites which permitted the establishment of grist mills, sawmills and wood-working plants. Settlements, such as Durham, were originally located near power sites. The growth and importance of these settlements, in turn, were the cause of the development of the pattern of railways, provincial highways and country roads. These transport systems served to connect the settlements with their surrounding areas, and with more distant parts of Southern Ontario. Another feature of the Saugeen River not to be overlooked is that the tributaries are known to be among the best trout streams in Southern Ontario. This fact has helped Durham and "Saugeen Country" in its efforts to promote tourism.

As has been previously mentioned, the land in and around Durham is hilly and contains gravelly and sandy soils to various degrees. This has led to mostly extensive pasturage rather than cash crops. Nevertheless, the moraine and spillway systems of the area provide large workable areas for farming. The size and prosperity of settlements such as Durham have been, at least in the past, a reflection of the intensity of the agricultural activity in the surrounding countryside.

The declining relative importance of agriculture in the twentieth century has had an impact on the population distribution of the Durham area. For example, between 1901 and 1961 Glenelg and Bentinck Townships lost 47 per cent of their population, while Durham doubled in size. From 1961 to 1981, however, the townships' population increased by 35 per cent, while Durham's population increased by 17 per cent. This may be attributed partly to the attractiveness of the townships as residences for both local and retiring urban people. Durham at one time was larger than Hanover, and in pre-railway times had closer connections with Southern Ontario. This could have been due in part to the central location of Durham in regard to its ability to serve four townships.

Final evidence of the environmental effect on the history and economy of the Durham area can be found in the importance that the wood and wood products industries have long had for the town. This tradition is still celebrated, as the highly successful Annual Wood Show attests. Because the agricultural potential of the area has been limited compared to other areas of Southern Ontario, this left large areas of land not cleared for farming. Combined with the availability of several streams with good power sources, it is not difficult to understand why sawmills and furniture industries developed in this area.

In sum, the Durham area has been blessed with natural resources. The presence of wood, water, gravel, fertile soil and attractive scenery will ensure the economical viability of its people for generations to come.

Looking south from George Street circa 1900.

Early Days In Durham

In 1837 Charles Rankin, Public Land Surveyor, was commissioned to survey and blaze a road from Garafraxa Township north of Fergus to Sydenham (now Owen Sound). He completed the line in June, 1837. Due to the Upper Canada rebellion all work on finishing the survey and clearing the road of trees was suspended. In 1840 John MacDonald, Public Land Surveyor, was commissioned to finish the project. He was instructed to lay out a row of lots on each side of the road, 150 acres in size, each divided into three equal parts. The settlers received 50 acres free when they had completed the settlement agreement, and they could purchase the adjoining 50 acre lot which was held for them. MacDonald followed Rankin's line from Garafraxa to the Long Swamp north of Mount Forest, where he deviated around this area as far as possible to avoid the swamp quagmire. However, many of the early settlers still found this section of the road at times very difficult to negotiate.

Samuel Edge, who immigrated to Durham in 1844 from Ireland with his father, mother, sister and brother, wrote an account of their journey to Durham. When they disembarked at Toronto they bought a yoke of oxen and a wagon and piling all their belongings on the wagon, set out for their new home. The road to Fergus was rough but passable; however, from Fergus north the travelling was difficult. Great ingenuity was needed to drive the wagon around stumps on the so-called road, or over the corduroy, which consisted of logs laid side by side crosswise over the boggy part of the road, and the oxen hauling the wagon were driven over the logs which were extremely rough. Sometimes evergreen boughs were cut and thrown over the logs to cushion the bumps. The travellers proceeded slowly until they came to the Long Swamp north of Mount Forest where the oxen and wagon became completely mired in the mud but they were able to get the oxen unhitched and back on drier land. They then set out to seek a way to avoid the swamp, if possible. A path of drier ground was found where others (possibly Indians) had walked around the bog.

Dalglish Hall and two private homes corner Queen Street and Durham Road. Hall no longer there; homes now owned by L. & D. Bristow and Grant Greenwood. First house was built for Presbyterian Manse circa 1860.

Since there seemed to be no other way, they went back to the wagon, carried their belongings to higher ground, then took the wagon apart and carried it wheel by wheel, axle by axle, plank by plank, to the other end of the bog, which, by the trail followed, was a matter of two or three more miles. The wagon was put together again and their belongings were carried to the vehicle. The oxen were finally hitched to the wagon and the party proceeded to Durham. This account is very briefly mentioned in the Belden Atlas of Grey County, 1880. This family settled just north of what became the town of Durham, but the Edges played an important role in the town's early development.

The site of the town of Durham was marked in the early maps by Charles Rankin, P.L.S., when he surveyed the Garafraxa Road in 1837. This site was later defined by John MacDonald, P.L.S., in 1840, and in 1841 David Gibson, P.L.S., surveyed the site into streets and lots. It appears that Gibson was a true royalist because he named several of the streets after royalty well known at that time. Some of the streets in Durham so named were: Victoria, Albert, George, William, John, Bruce, Countess, Queen, Elizabeth, Elgin and Kincardine.

Arch.d Hunter
The Founder of Durham
ONT.

The following account of the first settler in Durham is taken from A History of Grey County by E.L. Marsh, 1931:

"The first settler in what is now the town of Durham was the late Archibald Hunter, who "located" there on May 1st, 1842. The manner in which he was led to settle here is of considerable interest. Emigrating from Scotland to America in 1841 he spent one year in New York State. Hearing, however, of the free homesteads to be obtained in Canada, and no doubt impelled by the love he had for the old flag, he, with a party of four others decided to make a home for themselves in the "Queen's Bush." The party consisted of Mr. Hunter and his son, William, a Mr. Jamieson and his son, and a man by the name of Wm. Pullin. The party proceeded first of all to Oakville, where one of the surveyors who had assisted in surveying the Garafraxa Road was then staying. Upon their inquiring of him in which part of the newly surveyed country he would advise them to "locate," he told them that if they followed the survey until they came to the Big Saugeen River and took the farms immediately north of the townsite, they would, in his opinion, get as good farms as could be had between Fergus and the lake.

"Leaving Oakville they proceeded to Guelph, walking the entire distance from Guelph up. Frequently they passed small clearings with their little log shanties. The nearest one to what is now the town of Durham was a mile or two to the south, at what was later known as McClinton's Corners. Here a Mr. Vollet had "located."

Cairn at the Anglican Church where A. Hunter spent the first night in Durham.

"Reaching the Saugeen River they crossed, and found a deserted Indian wigwam near where the Church of England now stands. Here they passed the night. In the morning there was some difference of opinion as to whether they should go on farther, which Mr. Hunter settled in his characteristic way by saying, "Well, men, you can do as you like in the matter, but I go no farther. I'll take this farm for myself and the one opposite for my son." Mr. Jamieson and the others took farms close by. Mr. Pullin did not stay long, and his claim was taken by Mr. Alexander Hunter, brother of the founder of the town. The first building erected in Durham was a log house built by Mr. Hunter on the Glenelg side, north of the Durham road. Mr. Hunter passed the winter here and the following year went back for his family. (The late George Skene of Latona related that when he was coming in to take up land, he saw this shanty with a note on the door which read, "Gone to the United States to bring back my family.")

"On his return he immediately commenced the chopping and clearing process, and as settlers began to move northward past his door to locate on the Free Grants on the Garafraxa Road between there and Sydenham (now Owen Sound), he opened his house to the public, which proved a great advantage to settlers, as there was no other inn between Mount Forest and Syndenham. Closely following Mr. Hunter came Mr. John Davidson and family, whose son, Archibald, was the first white child born in the town."

In 1840 all the land north of Fergus to Owen Sound was put into the District of Wellington. It was the year 1848 before a representative was sent from this district to the Wellington Council. In 1849 the west part of what is now Grey County was attached to the County of Waterloo and a provisional county council was established in Grey in 1852. Thus, for the first few years of what is now Durham there was no municipal government, and there were no municipal laws and no taxes. In 1852, when the townships were organized, the east side of Garafraxa Street was part of Glenelg and the west side was part of Bentinck. Thus the village was governed by two separate bodies with different by-laws and different enforcement officers until Durham became a town in 1872.

When the early pioneers arrived they would acquire a lot and immediately commence to clear the property of trees and build a log house to protect their families. The following spring the earth would be dug up between the stumps in the yards and a garden would be planted, usually consisting of potatoes and turnips because these two crops would provide the most food per square yard. If the pioneer possessed a young family, the next requirement would be to purchase a cow from the older settled areas in southern Ontario in order to supply milk and butter; the cow would be driven to Durham on foot. A few hens would also be bought and a log barn on the back of the lot would then be needed to house the stock. At a later period accommodation for a horse, to provide transportation, and a pen to house two or three pigs raised for meat, would be necessities. As there would not be enough grass on a town lot to supply pasture for a cow, a bell would be tied around the cow's neck and the animal would be allowed to forage for food wherever it might be found. All the lots with clearances were fenced — not to keep animals in, but rather to keep stray animals out. Beaver grass, which grew to a height of 3 feet, was often stored as winter feed for cows. The townships passed by-laws with regard to the impounding of animals wandering at large and these seemed to be revised every few years. Cows were generally exempted.

Garafraxa Street circa 1904.

Durham Dry Goods Store circa 1900.

The April 7th, 1875 issue of the *Durham Chronicle* reports on the review of impounding by-laws. The council accepts the recommendation of the by-law committee "so much of the By-Law as prohibits the running at large of cattle of either sex except bulls, should be appealed [sic] and also so much thereof as refers to sheep. In reference to horses, hogs and geese the law prohibiting them running at large should be strictly enforced, but it is worthy of consideration whether it would be better instead of impounding the animals to impose a fine or penalty on the owner for every offence and enforce payment by a summary process. The impounding is attended with great difficulty."

In 1848 the land office was moved from Owen Sound to Durham and as a result the area around Durham was very quickly settled. Those who settled in and around Durham came almost entirely from England, Scotland and Ireland, and were predominantly Protestant.

There appears to be no record available as to whether the new settlers had any dealings with the Indians. But it is known that Indians did travel back and forth through the village following the Saugeen River, and that they were friendly to the settlers.

The oldest house in Durham on Durham Road West built as the Land Office in 1848.

There existed two Negro groups, who were runaway slaves and had come to Canada by the underground railway. One group settled at the Rocky but soon moved to Williamsford and Owen Sound. The other group settled east of Durham at a place which is still called Darkies Corners. This group moved to the Priceville area; they were hard-working honest people. Gypsy caravans, whose occupants originated in continental Europe, came to Durham annually for many years. They squatted on private property at the edge of town and as one pioneer said, "Their business was dealing and stealing." After about a week they moved their caravans to another community.

With the rapid influx of new settlers to what is now Durham came many skilled craftsmen who practiced their trades and opened small shops to sell their goods. At any given time there were three or four blacksmith shops in Durham. Another small business was that of the tinsmith — one of these was Parrotts Metal Iron Works, that had a huge tin tea pot hung over the door which swayed back and forth in the wind. Before the introduction of granite cooking wares, many utensils

McFarlane's Blacksmith Shop.

Group in front of store on West Garafraxa Street south of Lambton Street.
Front Row: Robinson, ? , Peter Patterson (sleeve coverings)
little boys: Lorne Smith, Harry Kress, Tip Smith.
Back Row 4th from left: Bob Hughes, Alex McLachlan wearing straw hat.

were made locally of tin. Another industry was cabinet making. J.W. McDonnell made furniture and employed two or three man. He advertised "finest furniture sold here, no cheap imported trash." Two other cabinet makers were J. Shewell and Geo. Kraize. In Durham's early days it was not uncommon for the spelling of names to change. An advertisement in an 1865 edition of the *Durham Standard* gives the name Geo. Kraize, later the name was Geo. Kriss, and finally the name was spelled Geo. Kress. Both J. Shewell and Geo. Kress made coffins, and both men later added undertaking to their furniture business. Other early local businesses included R.P. and Mrs. Warner's Weaving Works, dress shops where clothing was made on the premises and men's suits made in the local tailor shop priced five dollars and up. There was an apple processing shop that made cider and apple butter for half a century. The last operator of this establishment was Robert Smith. There were many other craftsmen such as shoemakers, wooden pump and pipe makers, coopers, saddlers, etc.

As soon as the new settlers had provided shelter and food for their families, their next priority was to establish a school, where their children might be educated, and a church, in which they could worship.

Joe Snell's house.

Garafraxa Street.

Storrey's Wagon Shop ....Blacksmith.

The following is taken from a booklet Poetical Directory of Businesses in Mount Forest, Neustadt, Durham, Owen Sound, written by A. G. Churchill. It was printed at the Comet Office in Owen Sound in 1863. Mr. A. G. Churchill wrote and published several poetical directories of communities across Southern Ontario.

INTRODUCTION
Durham, November 25, 1863

The above title-claim tells a village of fame
In changable paintings and gay;
Where commercial trade, and Mechanical aid,
Shops, Dwellings and Stores in array.
Teams laden with freight on two Gravel Roads great
Through Town at right angles they pass;
Four Stages that hail, carry light freight and mail,
And travelling public each class.
Two villages join, where the hill does incline,
The table-land, Town; and the low;
Where the powerful Saugeen drives the Mills and
   Machine,
Swift Cards, Shears, and Spindles that go.
Two Mills saw each kind, and two Grist Mills that
   grind,
Two Factories Full, Press, and Card;
One Foundry does cast, that is daily in blast,
Best Leather is tanned in one yard.
Twelve Stores up and down, five Hotels in Town,
And also two Drug Stores are there;
Two Harness Shops in, and two Stores that sell Tin,
Two Shops that make Cabinetware.
Three Doctors in skill, two Butchers that kill;
To heal and to furnish fresh meat;
One Clerk tallies down, eight Squires in town,
Three Coopers in barrels they beat.
Six Shops that Shoe-make, and one Oven to Bake,
One Artist takes likenesses for all;
One Post Office stand, where the letters do land,
And also one Orangemen's Hall.
One Member they send, the people's best friend,
One Agent of Lands for the Crown,
The Churches are five, and the Clergymen strive,
To establish Religion in town.
Two Lawyers make plea, and Carriage Shops three,
Three Tailors that make men's attire;
One ample Brick-yard, well stocked and prepared,
Four Blacksmiths that heat in the fire.
One Agent of Bank, and one Printer of rank,
One smith that works silver and gold;
Two houses for school, two Teachers that rule,
In branches of science untold.
Six Carpenters' build, five Painters that gild,
Five Wards in location laid down,
And five Councilmen with their ink and their pen,
To estimate jobs for the town.
One Bailiff dwells here, and one Brewer of Beer,
One oven in Durham that Pearls,
One Milliner's room like roses in bloom

To illustrate the beauty of girls.
The soldiers in red that their enemies dread
And Captain in splendor appears,
Front centre he, stands as a Monarch commands
The valiant and brave Volunteers;
They mark time in fact to the music exact,
On drill they're a beautiful show,
They are Great Britain's pride, to their country
   allied,
If invaded they're ready to go.

JOSEPH, ALLEN, Waggonmaker.
   Gears, Rim, Hub and Spoke, of seasoned White Oak,
   Joints solid, well finished, and all,
   Hinged barrows he makes and Patent horse Rakes,
   To order as customers call.
   Fine carriage spring seat, and Buggies that's neat,
   Strong waggon, wheelbarrow and cart;
   Bobbs, cutter and sleigh he will make for the pay
   Enamelled and painted in art.

WILLIAM ANDERSON, Lieutenant in the Light
   Infantry, Blacksmith, Horse and Cattle Farrier.
   Lieutenant on drill and Blacksmith in skill,
   The race horse can shoe very neat,
   Can make the mill pick, cure horses that's sick,
   Botts, spavin, hip, stifle, and feet.
   Makes linchpins and skeins, rings, staples and chains,
   Bolts, washers, band, tire, and sleigh shoes;
   Spikes, nails small and great, pins rivet and plate,
   Will hammer, file, drill, and cut screws.

MARTIN BEGG, Cabinetmaker.
   Keeps fine fancy chairs and cabinetwares
   And ready-made bedsteads to sell;
   Splendid Bureaus, for ladies fine clothes,
   And coffins, if ordered, made well.
   Makes frames every class, for the fine looking-glass
   And portraits will keep in his stock;
   Desk, table and stand keeps constant on hand,
   And beautiful cradles to rock.

CAMERON & ROSS, importers and general dealers
   in Dry-Goods, Groceries, Crockeries, Hardware,
   Boots and Shoes, Ready-made Clothing, &c.; keep
   assortment and salesmen at Priceville and Durham.
   Mr. Wm. Ross is Agent for the assurance of prop-
   erty against fire on all descriptions of buildings and
   their contents, on as reasonable terms as any other
   responsible Company.
   Call on William Ross, for fear of great loss,
   Make all that's in danger secure,
   Barn, shed and household, with their contents
   untold,
   For thousands by fire are made poor.
   Keep goods in their stores from all foreign shores,
   Glass, dry-goods and groceries too,
   Keep crockeries there, shelf and heavy hardware,
   Goods countless, the boot and the shoe.

HENRY COLE, keeps Royal Exchange Hotel,
   best stable in town.
   There the weary can rest on a bed of the best,
   There the hungry can get their supply,
   Of good bread to eat, fish, fowl or fresh meat,
   Buns, biscuit, good sweet cake and pie.
   There the teams are well fed in a competent shed,
   And a tempting show case in the bar,
   It glitters within with whiskey and gin,
   Ale, Brandy, soft drinks and cigar.

A. & A. COCHRANE'S Foundry, established in 1851,
   manufactures Threshing Machines eight and ten
   horse power each; Ploughs, Fanning Mills, Waggons
   and Carts of oak, cast Stoves in great variety, of
   every description; and all other kinds of castings; 12
   horse power boiler propels the Lathes and machinery; employ 20 men on an average; the main large
   three story stone building is 90 feet by 50; with bell
   to call the men.
   Their Foundry bell large volumes will tell,
   Bids men of great genius appear,
   Build mills that will clean, and threshing machine,
   Strong waggons of white oak made here;
   Ploughs, stoves every kind, mill gearings that grind,
   And models abundant appear;
   They turn every class, wood, iron and brass,
   Old metal is daily brought here.

JAMES DONALDSON, Agent for Leeming & Patter-
   son, wholesale dealers in confectionaries, biscuits,
   and cigars, Colborne-street Brantford.
   Carries biscuits afar, mint sticks and cigar,
   He sells at wholesale and retail;
   To hotels and shops and all where he stops,
   He deals on a liberal scale.
   His appearance in town speaks a man of renown,
   And trader with ample supplies
   Of cigars for to sell, soda biscuits baked well,
   Sweet candies, mint sticks and bulls-eyes.

F. H. EDWARDS, Clock and Watchmaker.
   He will make and mend all the jobs that you send,
   Your clocks and your watches will clean,
   Fine breast-pins for girls, gold amber and pearls,
   And safety chains fit for the Queen.
   The clock and the watch he will make them to talk,
   And tell the true time of the day,
   Gold beads in fine strings, clasps, lockets and rings,
   Rich pen-knives and scissors that's gay.

JAMES EDGE, J. P., and Councillor, has been Reeve for
   many years.
   Let the millions that read, remember indeed,
   And ages unborn understand;
   The Judges admire his seat as a squire,
   And Reeve for five years in the land.
   He is held in renown as a Councillor in town,
   In talent that great nature wills,
   His standing is great, in church and in state,
   And official investments he fills.

CHARLES FOREMAN, Bailiff and County Constable.
   He is bound to collect without fail or neglect,
   And entry of credit will make,
   And then will report to the Clerk of the Court
   Who is ready to render and take.
   This officer's ride through the county is wide
   With summons, subpoena and sale;
   While the robber and rogue and thieves that's in
      vogue,
   He will shackle and take them to jail.

J. W. GALBRAITH, Albion Hotel, Durham.
   His house is a home for he public that roam,
   The teamster the drover and all;
   His hostler indeed, will curry and feed,
   And water your team at the stall.
   His maids cook and bring, and his bell it will ring,
   Good eating and lodgings are there,
   His bar it does shine with rum, brandy and wine,
   Beer, whiskey, soft drinks and cigar.

A hitching post in front of the Middaugh House.

Second oldest house in Durham built by George Matthews at the corner of Garafraxa and Chester Streets.

SAMUEL HARVEY, Butcher, Horse and Cattle dealer.
  Let the public endorse, in cattle and horse
  This gentleman daily does deal,
  And also fresh meat, that is dressed very neat,
  Beef, mutton, pork, poultry or veal.
  The tenderest lamb, good bacon and ham,
  And sparerib to roast or to bake,
  Good sirloin to fry, and the rounds for to dry,
  Lard, tallow, beef's heart and beef steak.

J. H. HUNTER, dealer in Staple and Fancy Dry Goods,
  Groceries, Hardware, Boots and Shoes, Ploughs and
  Shares.
  Importer in store, from many a shore
  With staple and fancy does fill,
  Dry goods every class, nails, hardware and glass,
  And groceries are there in the bill.
  Keeps very good teas from over the seas,
  Molasses, fish, sugar and rice;
  Tobacco, cigar, and soap in the bar,
  Cloves, ginger, and pepper and spice.

GEORGE ISAACS, Saddle and Harness maker; was
  attached to the Royal Artillery in the Crimean War,
  and for some time in the Royal Arsenal, Woolwich,
  England, made litters to carry the dead and
  wounded, and sponges for the cannon, straps, belts,
  and equipage for the army.
  Side-saddles that's neat, with fine quilted seat,
  Men's saddles to trim off the nags,
  And trunks that are fine in brasslets they shine
  Valises and fine carpet bags.
  Makes collars the best for saving the breast,
  And harness both mounted and plain,
  Both single and sett, spurs, whip and flynet,
  Hook, buckle the snap and the chain.

GEORGE JACKSON, M. P. P.
  Let the county of Grey give attention I pray,
  And village of Durham give ear,
  The bright safety chain, money safe in check-rein,
  And the hope of the Province dwells here.
  A fine little joke, as ever was spoke,
  The Sheriff jumped out for to win,
  Resigned serving writs, in miserly wits,
  And got shackled too close to jump in.

Harness Shop Pasco Saunders.

WILLIAM JACKSON, Crown Land Agent.
  The maps of crown land are found at his stand,
  Of townships both far and the near,
  The dimensions all round, location and bound,
  Terms, prices, the cheap and the dear.
  Of lands to be sold of the scenery bold,
  Grove, forest, the hill and the vale,
  Runs, rivers and rills, and sites for the mills,
  That are in land market for sale.

THOMAS JONES, Boot, Shoe and Leather Store, and
  Findings; home-made and imported work in great
  variety.
  The boot and the shoe, in fashions that's new,
  He keeps in abundance on hand,
  Keeps upper and sole the best Spanish roll,
  Sells pattern or piece on demand.
  Just choose for yourselves, his store full on shelves,
  Holds gaiters and slips ready-made,
  Men's coarse, kip and fine, and children's that shine,
  And ladies' all classes to trade.

JAMES JONES, Carpenter and Joiner.
  Can build you a frame and finish the same,
  In tasty and fine architect,
  The square roof that's tall, cottage, Gothic and all,
  As owners may please to direct.
  Roof, clapboard and floors, fine mantle and doors,
  Will finish of good pannel pine,
  Stairs, base and surbase, lath, closet and case,
  Rake, cornice in moulding that's fine.

Rob Roy Dam 1910.

JAMES KOILEY, keeps Durham Hotel and Livery Stable.
His furniture grand in that elegant stand
His lodgings are fitted all fine,
Delightful his bar, tobacco, cigar,
Beer, brandy, gin, whiskey and wine.
There the townsmen will call the transient and all,
At his splendid tables will dine,
While their teams are well fed in the stable or shed,
Take notice, his name's on the sign.

JOHN KELLY, Manager of the Edge Mills, carries on Farming, Cloth Dressing, Grinding Wheat, three run of stone, Sawing with upright and circular saws.
Is making good flour, by water-wheel power,
And also is carding the wool,
Will color and dress, shear nicely and press,
And Flannel to order will full.
It's a great business stand in this glorious land,
A lavish of blessings on all,
His flour is so nice it brings highest price,
In the village and in Montreal.

MATTHEW FRASER'S Cheap Cash Store.
Pure Liquors, Teas, Groceries, and Dry-Goods, Crockery, Hardware, will pay cash for wheat, and goods for all kinds of produce.
Pure liquors and teas that came over the seas,
And dry-goods are all rank and file,
Shelf and heavy hardware and crockery is there,
Boots, shoes, and good clothing in style.
His stock is complete, he will pay cash for wheat,
For other produce he will trade,
Goods heap upon heap that he sells very cheap,
There are bargains indeed to be made.

THOMAS GRAY, Carriage-maker and general Blacksmith.
Makes carriages good, both iron and wood,
Strong waggons, wheelbarrow and cart.
Gears, hub, spoke and rim, are finished in trim,
By workmen of science and art.
Good cutter and sleigh, and buggies that's gay,
Ploughs, harrows, farm implements all,
Shoes, horses, makes bobs, and all other jobs,
In order to meet public call.

JAMES RENWICK, esquire, sets sleigh shoes and tire.
On most that James Sutherland makes,
Wm. Dargavil will aid, he is learning the trade,
And L. McKinnon boys that he takes.

S. L. M. LUKE, publisher of the *Durham Standard*.
Wakes, weddings will tell and how items sell,
Prices current, and news of the day,
Fairs, lectures and balls, show, sermon and all,
Fine letters that's done for the pay.
Sales, hand-bill and card, and books for the bard,
Advertises all classes and ranks,
Reporters best notes, and fine anecdotes,
Both sheriff and constable's blanks.

McKENZIE & BROTHER, keep general store; they are just opening a splendid assortment of Dry-Goods, Groceries, &c., &c., in their new three story brick store.
Imported goods grand, to furnish the land,
They are selling at prices that's low,
Not wanting their pay, the very same day,
That they pack up the goods for to go.
Shawls, hoops, ladies skirts, and stuff for fine shirts,
Prints, bread-cloths and carpet and silk,
All groceries there and crockeryware,
And cambric as white as the milk.

JOHN MILLER, General Merchant.
Keeps goods rank and file, in elegant style
All splendid in shining array;
Dry-goods every class, nails, hardware and glass,
And groceries he sells every day.
Boots, shoes by the pair, fine crockeryware,
And clothing that is ready-made;
Cloves, pepper and spice, teas, coffee and rice,
Molasses and sugar to trade.

H. J. MIDDAUGH, keeps Livery Stable, Stage proprietor from Durham to Collingwood.
His great business stand, in this glorious land,
His livery is nimble and good,
His stage is the pride of gentry that ride,
From Durham to Port Collingwood.
Rich tables do stand, and good meals demand,
Like a room full of roses his beds,
His dazzling bar holds drinks and cigars,
And his hostler you find at the shed.

HUGH MACKAY, keeps Argyle Hotel, buys cattle, sheep and stock of all kinds, auctioneer.
He keeps the Argyle in excellent style
His bar with good liquors does shine,
His tables well spread from the foot to the head,
His lodging room furnished all fine.
His hostler will serve, his steward carve,
His porter goes ringing the bell,
Bids parties appear, Mackay is auctioneer
To the highest, best bidder will sell.

House on Durham Road East built by Archibald Hunter Jr. Home of Margaret and Oliver Hunter.

PARKER & CATTLE, Druggists and Wine merchants, Durham, Owen Sound & Dornoch.
  Drugs, medicine line, whiskey, brandy and wine,
  Prescriptions for healing disease;
  Cuts, fevers and cramps, coal oil and fine lamps,
  Lacquers, paints, coffees and teas.
  Bar larder for rooms, essential perfumes,
  Good books for to read and believe,
  All colors and shade of dye stuffs to trade,
  And all the materials to weave.

PETER PATERSON, Manufacturer of Woolen cloth, Sattinets, Tweeds, Flannels, makes Flour and Oatmeal, Saws Lumber, Lath, &c.
  Will make cloth of wool, card, spin, weave and full,
  Pleat neatly and color and press,
  All the flannels he gets, men's tweeds, and sattinet,
  And women's wear also will dress;
  Makes superfine flour, by water-wheel power,
  For custom and also to pack,
  Every grist that you bring please sew on a string,
  And brand your full name on the sack.

DONALD ROSE, keeps General Store.
  An establishment all new, just open to view,
  With staple and fancy does fill,
  Keeps groceries there, dry-goods and hardware,
  And ready-made clothes in the bill.
  Good shoes in the list, pins, ribbons and twill,
  Fine crockery stands on the shelves.
  Keeps teas in his store, and a thousand things more,
  All parties can choose for themselves.

Treasurer of Durham.

THOMAS SMITH, Tanner, keeps Upper and Sole Leather for sale, pays cash for hides.
  He keeps stock on hand, for belt, strap and band,
  For harness and saddles in sides;
  Good kip and calf-skin, for boots thick and thin,
  And will pay the money for hides.
  Keeps upper and sole the best Spanish roll,
  And leather to make saddle seat,
  He will tan upon shares, William Gray is up stairs,
  And will curry his leather complete.

JOHN R. SMITH, Saddler and Harness-maker, has been in California, Australia, New Zealand, all gold diggings, also the South Sea Islands, Fejee and Navigator's Isle; crossed the Isthmus of Darien, about 50,000 miles in all.
  Jas. Crittenden's skill and Chas. Leavens' will,
  Make harness for Smith, and perhaps,
  Sleighs, buggies and all, they will draw to the ball,
  That's laden with lasses and chaps.
  He keeps harness for sale on a liberal scale,
  And trunks that in brasslets do shine,
  Men's saddles to ride, and long skirts on one side,
  For ladies that's quilted all fine.

JOHN SHEWELL, Cabinet-maker.
  Makes cradles and chairs, for young wedded pairs,
  And large chairs all ready to rock,
  And lovely bureaus to hold ladies clothes,
  With drawers all ready to lock.
  Makes fine sofa seat and lounges complete,
  And bedsteads all ready to sleep,
  Makes frames every class for the fine looking-glass,
  And portraits forever to keep.

JOHN SHEPARD, Brewer.
  Where beer is made best, in Canada West,
  To furnish the taverns and shops,
  In town and without, and the regions about,
  With pure extract of barley and hops.
  Barrels, gallons and jugs, not poisoned with drugs,
  Is constantly made and sold here,
  Grand gentry that dine, if their tables lack wine,
  Can send to John Shepard's for beer.

J. G. WILLEY, Boot and Shoe-maker, Compositor and Poem writer.
  Makes boots coarse and fine, with the peg and the twine,
  And boot for the ladies that's gay,
  With rows of eyelets clinched closely and set,
  On the ankle in brilliant array,
  Will make and will mend, as customers send,
  In fashions that's tasty and new.
  He can fancy fit, is nimble with kit,
  To model the boot and the shoe.

THOMAS WALTON, General Blacksmith.
  Shoes mares and mules, and makes farming tools,
  Will iron the cutter and sleigh,
  Pins, rivets and screws, sets tire and sleigh shoes,
  All broken utensils will mend,
  Bolts, linch-pins and skeins, rings, staples and
    chains,
  And all other jobs that you send.

JOSHUA WOODLAND, Importer, keeps General
  Store.
  Just step in and buy of his splendid supply,
  Where the public can choose for themselves
  Of his groceries there, nails, glass and hardware,
  And dry-goods delightful on shelves.
  Keeps the boot and the shoe, and tobacco to chew,
  And groceries plenty to sell,
  Sugars, teas in his store, and a thousand things
    more,
  It would puzzle the author to tell.

GEORGE WATTERS, Farmer, formerly a Miller.
  Has bought him a farm, though new it's a charm,
  In the wild virgin forest its fine,
  Has the title, full claim, and is clearing the same,
  To farming does seem to incline;
  For land that he tills, is equal to mills,
  His crops they will grow when he sleeps,
  When the mill he does tend, he has no time to spend,
  On duty must constantly keep.

This house on Durham Road East was built possibly in the 1870s by Henry Parker, Druggist and Businessman in Durham for many years. Later it became the Presbyterian Manse, the home of Robert Smith and Jack Coutts; and is now owned by James E. Parker. Mrs Robert Smith in front of house.

Thomas Lauder House — north end of town — unfortunately burned by intruders 1993.

DURHAM ASSESSMENT ROLL — 1880

The names on this list are the property owners in Durham in 1880. The names are spelled the same way as they appeared on the assessment roll and may not be correctly spelled. A summary of other facts from this roll appears below.

Edwin McClocklin, Butcher
Alma W.S. Scott, Plasterer
George Privalt, Sawyer
Thos. Harris & Co., Tinsmith
Wm. H. Anderson, Blacksmith
Joseph Townsend, Printer
Robt. McFarlan, Wagon Maker
John Gibbons, Hotel-keeper
John H. Hogan, Hotel-keeper
James H. Hunter, Merchant
James H. Hunter, Hotel-keeper
Arch. Hunter, Farmer
James Gunn, Doctor (MD)
Geo. Woodland, Merchant
Duncan McDonnel, Clerk
Dr. Jamieson, MD
James Burnett, Merchant
Thos. Derby, Blacksmith
Allen McFarlan
English Church
James Edge, Farmer
Henry Young, Constable
Alexander Robertson, Tailor
Town Hall
Welby McAllister, Hotel-keeper
Registry Office
Thomas Carson, Baker
John A. Munn, District Registrar
Ira Tike, Machinist
John Stuart, Agent
Moore Armstrong, Teacher
Geo. Whitmore, Wagon Maker
Wm. Whitmore, Blacksmith
Zenus Clark, Miller
Lorenza Hagerman, Baker
Thos. Meredith, Bailiff
Jas. McGirr, Carpenter
W.B. Vollet, Carpenter
Wm. Saunderson, Machinist
Merv. Warner, Hostler
Thos. Lauder, Registrar
Alex Stuart, Minister
Wm. B. Swinburne, Watch Maker
Charles Brown, Trader
Wm. Jas. Hughson, Merchant
A.C. McKenzie, Merchant
Hugh Rose, Blacksmith
Henry Storry, Wagon Maker
Norman McIntyre, Teamster
Geo. Buillic, Blacksmith
John A. Johnstone, Printer
James Brown, Merchant
Thos. Brown, Clerk
Wm. W. Gray, Tanner
Henry Cole, Farmer
F.N. Warner, Carpenter
John Chaffy, Miller
Thos. Easton, Wagon Maker
Geo. Barnaby, Painter
Robt. Austin, Miller
Christopher Leopart, Labourer
H.C. Havens, Teamster
Philip Fox, Plasterer
Thos. Fox, Carpenter
James Ritchie, Carpenter
James Geo. McKinzie, Cooper
Wm. R. Rambough, Farmer
Thos. Sanders, Stage Driver
Charles Wilkinson, Labourer
Robt. Andrews, Shoemaker
Wm. Burl, Moulder

Wm. Stuart, Labourer
Michael Bray, Labourer
John Wells, Labourer
John Stuart, Labourer
Francis Buckingham, Farmer
Walter Tucker, Farmer
Thomas Brown, Shoemaker
Wm. A. Vollett, Finisher
Nelson Leopart, Farmer
Wm. Irvin Innes, Machinist
Edward Ferrier, Carpenter
David Allen, Sawyer
John Rowland, Constable
Mrs. Crawford, Widow
Isaac Potter, Shoemaker
James McGirr, Farmer
Thos. Smith, Farmer
Robert Prosser, Trader
Chas. Gray, Farmer
Jas. Wyllic, Shoemaker
John Morrow, Temperance House
Thos. Arrowsmith, Labourer
Wm. Fox, Plasterer
John Campbell, Carder
Duncan Cambell, Carder
Rod McKinzie, Carpenter
James Woodland, Merchant
Dr. Kernan, MD
John Brown, Merchant
Geo. Russell, Merchant
James Paterson, Carder
Philip Eva, Mason
Geo. Waters, Farmer
Alexander Rose, Tailor
John Cambell, Labourer
Hugh MccQuarrie, Labourer
Dowl McDonald, Farmer
Wm. Wilson, Labourer
Thos. Barclay, Machinist
Sam Gamble, Labourer
Wm. McClaughlin, Mason
Agriculture Grounds (Fall Fair)
John A. Johnstone, Printer
H.S. Middaugh, Gentleman
Geo. Krase Sr., Cabinet-maker
Wm. Henderson, Labourer
G.S. Evans, Barrister
Wm. Laidlaw, Plasterer
Jas. Davidson, Carder
Geo. Warner, Carpenter
Robt. Bull, Carpenter
Mrs. Kelly, Widow
John Kelly, Banker
Arch. McLellan, Land Agent
Wm. Dawson, Farmer
Alex Struthers, Carpenter
John Millar, Carpenter
Geo. Krase Jr., Carpenter
John Carson, Trader
James Lawson, Book Agent
James Southerland, Sawyer
Arch. McKenzie, Postmaster
Wesleyan Methodist, Parsonage
Rev. Wm. Godfrey, Minister
Bennet Paterson, Clerk
Wm. Slatcher, Miller
John McLean, Carpenter
Walter Hastie, Clerk
O.B. Walker, Clerk
Wm. Ferrier, Carpenter
Wm. Williams, Plasterer

Wm. Caldwell, Shoemaker
John Sanders, Labourer
John Dunsmore, Hotel-keeper
Wm. Lambston, Labourer
Charles Foreman, Farmer
John Moore, Farmer
Wm. Sanders, Pensioner
James Spence, Gentleman
Franklin Bavick, Labourer
Ed. McAllister, Finisher
Thos. Vollett, Carpenter
Wm. Mitchell, Labourer
David McIntyre, Tailor
William Johnstone, Constable
Walter Douglas, Labourer
Samuel Keys, Labourer
Charles Vollett, Farmer
John Fagan, Farmer
John Baldwin, Carpenter
Stephan Cocken, Plasterer
Charles Levens, Saddler
Wm. Larter, Butcher
Hugh McKay, Auctioneer
Owen Gainoss, Contractor
John Sack, Painter
Oliver Ferrier, Tanner
Francis Porter, Farmer
Jabes Stephen, Merchant
Jas. Davidson, Clerk
Thos. Devlin, Carpenter
Norman Kelsey, Farmer
Wm. Boulden, Harness Maker
D. McKenzie, Tailor
Wm. Boyle, Farmer
Samuel McCracken, Carpenter
Lockwood Elvide, Livery
George Privatt
David McKee, Merchant
Charles Fletcher, Farmer
Jas. Laidlaw, Mason
Malcolm McIntyre, Photographer
Amos Palmer, Baker
Mathew Scott, Farmer
Rev. Wm. Wray, Minister
John Stuart, Agent
Alexander Cochrane, Foundry
Robert McFarlan, Waggon Maker
Gib McKecknie, Merchant
John McKecknie, Merchant
Nicholas Shaver
Nicholas Fagan
John Gordon
Rev. I.C. Dunlop
Anna McNab
George Mighton

Thos. Mighton, Farmer
Geo. McFarlan, Druggist
Thos. S. Mowat, Iron Monger
Norman McIntyre, Iron Monger
C.B. Sackes, Barrister
Adam Cochrane, Iron Monger
John Parrott, Tinsmith
Richard Horn, Blacksmith
Robert Maitland, Minister
John Moodie, Auctioneer
John Shewelle, Cabinet Maker
Old School House
Geo. Mathews, Cabinet Maker
Thos. Jones, Stationer
John A. Warren, Machinist
Henry Parker, Druggist
David Derby, Tailor
Alex Gordon, Watch Maker
Geo. Donnelly, Hotel-keeper
A.W. Mockler, Merchant
Geo. Rowsell, Merchant
David Jackson, Land Agent
Charles L. Grant, Merchant
Robert Daglish, Merchant
Mrs. W. Scott, Widow
Rev. Wm. Park, Minister
John Robertson, Tailor
Archibald Davidson, Merchant
John Cameron, Merchant
Finlay MacRae, Warden
Thomas Donaghy, Photographer
E.D. McMillan, Barrister
Robt. McCracken, Blacksmith
John A. Hunter, Clerk
Samuel Arrowsmith, Contractor
Mrs. Jas. Burns, Widow
James Hunter, Shoemaker
Mrs. McLean, Widow
Mrs. Rutherford, Widow
Jas. Crawford, Saw Mill
Henry Davis, Butcher
Albert McCutcheon, Labourer
Anthony Jamieson, Carpenter
Geo. Jackson, Gentleman
Mrs. Wm. Jackson, Widow
Jabez Banks, Farmer
David Jackson, Land Agent
Neil McKecknie, Merchant
Thomas Scarf
Rev. Wm. Davis
George Elvidge
David Derby
Colin McDougald
Flora McKenzie
George Mitchell

Children between 5 and 16 - 237
Children between 7 and 13 - 114
Children between 16 and 21 - 62

Religion in Durham 1880
Roman Catholic - 34
Presbyterian - 425
Church of England - 224
Methodist - 220
Baptist - 71
Congregationalist - 5

Animals in Durham
Bitches - 1
Dogs - 70
Hogs - 31
Sheep - 72
Cattle - 114
Horses - 77
Number of days statute labour - 685
Gardens with orchard - 19 acres
Wooded land - 31 acres
Swamp - 42 acres
Fall Wheat - 17 acres

Frank Lenahan's Store.
Frank Lenahan and Bob Lindsay.

Interior of Webster's Jewellery Store.
Mr. Percy Webster and Zetta Marshall, Clerk.

Education

2

DURHAM PUBLIC SCHOOL

Although the first settlers came to Durham in 1842, and Durham was incorporated as a town in 1872, the first written school records were dated January 18, 1877. Fortunately, Dr. J. F. Grant recorded what he had learned by talking to older residents. His diary tells us that four different school buildings were used between 1842 and 1877, as well as two other buildings to accommodate the overflow students. The first school was built of logs on the north bank of the Saugeen River near where the Town Hall now stands.

At the Wellington District Council meeting in Guelph on February 5th, 1848, a petition was presented by Bentinck and Glenelg representatives for the Council to establish three union school sections along the Garafraxa Road. This petition was granted; Durham was designated as Union School Section No. 1, U.S.S. No. 2 was at the Rocky and U.S.S. No. 3 was at Latona. Since the people from Durham were pressing for a school, it is almost certain that the log school was built during the spring and summer of 1848.

We do not have a description of this school, but other early log schools in this district have been described in detail and they all follow a certain pattern. The ends of the building usually faced north and south; the sides faced east and west, and each side had two windows thus making the room as bright as possible.

A short distance in from the door was a fireplace. On both sides of the door a shelf was fastened to the wall about four feet from the floor where students would place their mitts or lunch. Beneath the shelf was a row of wooden pegs on which to hang coats and caps. A shelf was attached the full length of the side walls, then a wide board was placed slanting slightly downward from the shelf with a cap at the bottom to hold books and papers. This served as the larger students' desk. The shelf gave them a place to store books not in use. The students sat facing the wall on a backless bench which ran the full length of the wall. There were long lower tables made from dressed lumber with low benches across the middle of the room on which the little children sat. At the front of the school was a one or two step platform on which the teacher's table and stool stood; from this vantage point the teacher was able to see everything that was happening in the classroom. Hanging on the wall beside the teacher's table was a blackboard about four feet square made from dressed lumber, and possibly painted. Chalk on the blackboard could be wiped clean with a damp cloth.

When a class was to be taught a lesson, the teacher would call the pupils in that class to the front of the school where they would stand in front of the platform until the lesson was finished and work had been assigned to them. Then the pupils would return to their desks to finish the assignments, and another class would be called to the front for a different lesson. At first the subjects taught consisted of Reading, Writing and Arithmetic; Reading also included Spelling, Grammar and Sentence Structure. After the first year or two, depending on the teacher's ability, the subjects taught would include Geography, History, maybe even good morals, and studies which develop good character. There were few, if any, good teaching aids so the instructor had to improvise.

The second school building was a frame structure, larger than the log school, erected on the west side of Garafraxa Street half way up the hill. A few years later a third stone shcool was built a little farther north of the frame school.

The September 23, 1859, *Durham Standard* published the following notice: **"School Examination** — A public examination of the pupils of the senior and junior Durham schools will take place on the 29th instant, at 10 o'clock A.M. Parents, guardians, and all others interested in the cause of education, are respectfully invited to attend." This afforded an opportunity for any one to go to school and examine all the pupils' workbooks, and to ask any pertinent questions of the pupils, as well as of the teacher. Grey County divided the county into three areas and appointed a school inspector over each area. The first inspector mentioned is Mr. William Ferguson. At the board meeting of January 17, 1887, Mr. N. W. Campbell, who had received the appointment of county school inspector, was appointed inspector for the town of Durham at a salary of $20 per annum. In the board's estimates for 1893 an increase of five dollars is noted in the inspector's salary. This was the last time that the inspector's salary appears in the yearly estimates.

In 1862 these two schools became overcrowded, and overflow classes were held in the Orange Hall across the road from the frame school. Mrs. Mockler taught in this school and had up to 90 students. In the minutes of the Board meeting of April 3rd, 1877, it was noted that there were 209 pupils on the roll with three teachers as instructors — 70 pupils in Mr. Cushnie's room, 79 in Miss McArthur's, and 60 in Miss McMillan's.

At Durham Town Council meeting of March 19, 1874, a communication from the Board of School Trustees was read requesting council to acquire the building known as the Agriculture Society Hall, and to repair same so that it may be used by the said Trustees for school purposes until other premises are procured. This hall was on the east side of Bruce Street north of Lambton Street and was used as a school for a short time. On January 22, 1875, Trustees notified council that they had contracted for a new four-roomed brick school on Elgin Street at the end of Mill Street for $3,500.

In the early 1870s the Anglican Church decided to construct a rectory on Kincardine Street at Durham Road East. The minister, Rev. Wm. Evans, included accommodation for a parochial school in the plans for the rectory. Mr. Evans left town before the project was completed, and as the town had started to build a school, the school part of the rectory was taken down.

On January 19, 1881, the town council passed a resolution, "That the Board of Works be requested to examine the old Stone School House with a view to making it a Lock-up House (jail) and report at the next meeting of Council the probable cost of fitting it up for that purpose and to contact the School Board concerning the same." Possibly some of the students who attended that school would think that a jail would be a very appropriate use for the building.

Mary Gray, a student in the junior school in 1875, related that the teachers of the junior and senior schools lined up all the students and every one marched to the new brick school in a body.

From the early years until the mid 1930s students who completed Senior Fourth Grade (equivalent to Grade 8 today) were required to write an Entrance examination. These were a series of written examinations on subjects completed at public school, and were held in a central location in the inspectorate.

On April 14, 1888, the Board Secretary laid on the table a letter received from Mr. Gordon, Chairman of the Education Committee, Owen Sound, stating that unless the Durham Board would pay the examiners' fees for holding the examination, there would not be

Public School 1913.

one in Durham that year. The Board decided to pay the examiners' fees and also supply paper, pen and ink for the pupils writing the entrance examination. The students paid one dollar to write the exams, and they were required to receive a passing grade in order to gain access to a Continuation or High School.

In January, 1890 the county council decided that the entrance examinations formerly held in Durham would be held in Hanover. When this notice was received by the Durham School board, a special meeting was immediately held and a resolution was passed asking Hon. Mr. Ross, the Minister of Education, to appoint an entrance examination to be held at Durham in July, the said board engaging to meet the necessary expense. This request was granted.

THE MODEL SCHOOL

The first teachers were usually persons living in the community who possessed some formal education. As the demand for teachers increased, the Department of Education decided to set up an Examining Board in both Owen Sound and Collingwood. The candidates appearing before the Board were questioned with regard to their knowledge of the required subjects; those most knowledgeable were granted teaching licenses. But after a number of years the Department

of Education realized that those teachers with the most subject knowledge might also have few teaching skills, which would prove disastrous for the students. Therefore, at the Public School Board meeting on July 23, 1877, it was moved by Adam Cochrane, and seconded by Dr. Gun that the "nomination of Durham Public School as a County Model School made by the Lieutenant Governor in Council of the Province of Ontario be accepted." From 1877 until 1885 the principal of the Public School, Thos. Allen, supervised the Model School for four months each year, along with his regular duties. In 1885 it was decided to allow the principal full time with the Model School, and an assistant was engaged for the public school fall term. Enrolment in the school ranged from 25 to 50 teachers-in-training. Many of these students came from communities all over Western Ontario as far away as Sarnia. This school operated for 37 years. In 1913 Hanover was successful in having the school moved away from Durham to that town, but the next year all Model Schools were closed.

The entrance requirement to the Model School was Grade 10. Those Model School students who were successful would receive a 3rd Class Certificate which was good for three years. This certificate could be renewed if the school inspector deemed the teaching methods satisfactory during that time. Many teachers

Junior Leaving Durham School 1903 (Grade 10).
Back Row: E. Brooker, Jno Bachus, Lyal Ireland, Thos. Allen, Principal, Thos. McDonald, Binnie McGirr, Alex McComb
Centre Row: Clara Aljoe, Laura Hutton, Minnie Andrews, Miss Lick, teacher, Jewel McComb, Grace Everitt, Susie McClocklin.
Front Row: Bertha Wilson, Ethel Ryan, Mabel Hunt, May McClocklin, Maggie Colwell, Ethel Limin, Alie Blackburn, Margaret Hutton.

from Durham went to the Owen Sound Collegiate and Vocational Institute and completed Grade 12; this would allow them to upgrade their certificate to 2nd Class. If they completed Grade 13, and attended Normal School for a year, they would receive a 1st Class teaching certicate.

In 1890 a four room addition was added to the Public School at Elgin and Mill Streets — the desks for the new addition were made in the Durham Foundry. The September 5, 1904, Durham Review stated that "the school had an attendance of 330 this year, of which 58 were enrolled in the High School, and they expected at least 12 more in that department. Miss Forfar, B.A., and Mr. J. H. Smith, B.A., were the teachers in the High School. The Model School attendance the first day was quite low due to the severity of the Provincial exams last summer." The Continuation and Model Schools regularly advertised for students. The following notice is from the *Durham Chronicle*, November 24th, 1910:

DURHAM SCHOOL
Staff and Equipment

The school is thoroughly equipped in teaching ability, in chemical and electrical supplies and fittings, etc., for full Junior Leaving and Matriculation work. The following competent staff are in charge:

THOS ALLAN, Principal, 1st Class Certificate. Subjects: Science, Euclid, English Grammar, Book-keeping and Writing.

MISS DONALDA McKERRACHER, B.A. Graduate of Queen's University. Subjects: Latin, French, Algebra, Arithmetic.

MISS AMY EDGE, Graduate of the Faculty of Education. Subjects: Literature, Composition, Geography, History and Art.

Intending students should enter at the beginning of the term if possible. Board can be obtained at reasonable rates. Durham is a healthy and active town, making it a most desirable place of residence.

Fees, $1.00 per month in advance.

J.P. TELFORD   C. RAMAGE
Chairman.   Secretary.

The February 23rd, 1911, Durham Review reported that a delegation consisting of school board members, councillors and others, went to Queen's Park to request that an Agriculture School be established at Durham. The request was not granted. Also, in the same year a Durham District Continuation School, High School grades, was organized in the Public School. Now the school housed the Elementary, Continuation and Model School classes, and soon overflow classes were held in the Armoury, Town Hall and the Old Library. When the Model School and High School vacated the Public School, there was considerably more room for the Elementary pupils. However, in

1954 a new school was built on Kincardine Street south of Saddler Street, and named Saugeen Valley Elementary School.

The old brick school built in 1875 was sold to Durham Chair and Store Fixtures as a storage depot, and was consumed by flames in the early 1970s. The Principals at this school were:

William Cushnie, 1877	Thomas Allen, 1888-1916
R.N. Carr, 1878	A. Morton, 1916-1919
M. Armstrong, 1879-81	John A. Graham, 1919-1935
C. McCabe, 1882	George Noble, 1935-1944
J. Winterbourne, 1883-6	Robert Christie, 1944-1950
A. Wherry, 1887	J.C. McKechnie, 1950-1954

The grounds surrounding the old school on Mill Street were meticulously groomed, with a flower garden at the front, and another around the flagpole. The pupils played in the large field behind the school. Directly to the north was a terraced slope which provided wonderful ice slides in winter for many generations of children. Just when these slides became swift and smooth and attracted the biggest crowd, they would be mysteriously covered with ashes to the children's chagrin. Year after year the slides were made and just as faithfully the ashes appeared. How all the pupils bemoaned that fact! Just behind the school was a rusty tool shed which, because of its colour, was called the "Red House." When school reconvened in the fall, the toughness of boys' and girls' feet was tested by accepting the dare to run across the cinders

Teacher's Contract with School Board 1888.

20

behind the "Red House." By spring there would be a huge pile of furnace ashes there, but only a very few accepted the dare after wearing boots all winter. Many who attended that school can recall "skinning the cat" on the outside railing at the front door, or the frenzied excitement when some one had his or her tongue stuck to that same railing on a frosty day. Teachers weren't usually supervising the play ground as they do today, but nothing seemed to occur that a good argu-ment or a wrestling match couldn't settle. Corporal punishment was in vogue, however, and was a reminder to all to shape up. When some unfortunate, usually lad, received the strap, one could hear the whacks in the classrooms. Like the tolling of a bell, the whacks were counted and the number indicated the seriousness of the crime, or the mood of the person administering the punishment.

School Certificate.

Mary Morton Retirement Party, Saugeen Valley Public Elementary School, June 1960.
Miss Morton taught 11 of the 12 Aljoe children.
Left to Right Standing: Beatrice, Helen, Arthur, Vernon, Ada, Murray, Sharon, Evelyn
Seated Left to Right: Doreen, Miss Morton (teacher), Lorna.

Inside the Continuation School, Third Form (Grade 11), 1912.

School children ready for parade 1900.

Local school children boarding train to Guelph to see
King George VI and Queen Elizabeth 1939.

Durham Public School Board 1930.
Back Row: Stewart McIlraith, Guy Kearney, John McGowan, W.J. McFadden
Front Row: Sam Chapman, John Graham (Principal), Bill Hunter.

Staff Durham Public School 1933.
Back Row: Myrtle Mortley, Emily Clark (Hunt), George Noble, Norah McIntyre (Stewart), Jean Harding
Front Row: Elizabeth Schaefer, John Graham (Principal), Mary Morton.

Durham Public School, Jr. Third Bk., 1933.
Back Row: Margaret Derby, Vera Lauder, Florence Martin, Clara MacDonald, Mamie Thompson, June Elvidge, Emily Whitmore, Emily Hunt (Teacher)
Second Row: David Rowland, Hector Deware, Bill McGirr, Donald Kennedy, Gordon Armstrong, ? Caswell, Jamieson Watson, Ivan McEachnie, John Collier, Hammell McCaslin
Third Row: Anna McLean, Agnes Atkinson, Isabel McCormick, Gladys Gray, Elvyn Becker, Sadie Osborne, Jean Town, Irene Atkinson, Bertha Glass, Mary Noble
Front Row: Harry Schenk, Harry Falkingham, Ronnie Watt, Jack Ashley, Keith Greenwood, Ralph Wilson, Stanley Greenwood, Abi Tinianovi, Lorne Long.

Grade 1, 1947 Durham Public School.
Back Row: Alice McCormick, D. Lunn, S. Atkinson, G. Falkingham, Gary MacDonald, D. Graham, F. Kingston, K. Whitmore, D. Lawler.
Second Row: J. Gardiner, ? Torrie, M.L. Graham, Virginia, ? , Mary Padfield, B. Campbell, ? , N. Wood.
Third Row: June Cook, C. Armstrong, Edna Sills, M. Lloyd, K. Connor, L. MacDonald, E. Ritchie, L. Johnson, M. Fisk.
Front Row: M. Aljoe, H. Miller, C. Goldsmith, D. Spiez, B. Thompson, R. Murdock, J. Gray, D. Morton.

SAUGEEN VALLEY ELEMENTARY SCHOOL

On October 22, 1954, Miss Mary Morton, a long time staff member, laid the cornerstone for the new school. The bell, which was purchased in 1885 and used at the school on Mill Street, was taken to the grounds of the new school and hung in a place of honour. On April 1, 1955, the students, along with their principal J. C. McKechnie and staff, paraded from the old building on Mill Street to the new ten-room school led by a band composed of school children under the direction of John Jarratt. The staff members at this time were: J.C. McKechnie, Principal, Margaret Hopkins, Mabel (Sharp) Alles, Myrtle Mortley, Mary Morton, Hazel Ritchie, Marjorie McKechnie, Jean Cuyler and John Jarratt. Donald McQueen was custodian. The school inspector was W.G. Rae. J.C. McKechnie was Principal until his resignation from that position in 1967. Allan Carpenter was Principal, 1967-1968; Kees VanGeen, 1968-1969; John Bell, 1969-1970; and Harry M. Leatham, 1970-1978; followed by LaVerne Francis, Willard Foster and Margaret Moore. Marnie Coke is the present principal.

In 1971 a classroom for the Trainable Mentally Retarded (now known as Developmentally Challenged) was opened at Saugeen Valley. This was a pilot project initiated by the Ontario government. Prior to this time, these children had been sponsored by parental associations and housed mostly in former country schoolhouses. Durham was the first elementary school to have such a classroom integrated with it. The school was undergoing renovations at this time and plans included a fine facility for this special education room. The enrolment in the first year was 11 pupils ranging in age from five to 21. They were taught by a special education teacher, Betty Corbett, until her retirement in 1989. Joan Fennell was hired at that time as an assistant and is presently still working in that capacity. Since there were no actual ministry guidelines and no curriculum had yet been published, the preparation of each child's individual programme was the responsibility of the teacher. The Principal, Harry Leatham, was extremely interested in this project, and devoted much time ensuring that these children were well received and welcomed by the rest of the school, and that they had the best facilities, equipment and educational tools available. Superintendent Stuart Foden and School

Pupils moving from the old Public School to the new Saugeen Valley School April 1, 1955.

Cutting the ribbon at Saugeen Valley Public School 1955.
Ralph Wilson, Elda Cadogan, Rev. Gorman, Clare Hutchinson, Art Adlam, Inspector Wm. Rae, J.C. McKechnie, Principal,
Fred O'Brecht, Frank Irwin.

Saugeen Valley Public School Staff 1957.
Back Row: Hazel Ritchie, Margaret Hopkins, Joyce Meads, Amelia Peart, Mabel Sharp, Betty Corbett, Emily Mc-Naughton
Front Row: Don McQueen, Myrtle Mortley, Mary Morton, John C. McKechnie (Principal) Marjorie McKechnie, Clara Neff.

Board member James Sullivan were also strong supporters. During the first years of this class, Camp Oliver, a minimum security facility for young offenders, was situated just out of town in Glenelg township. These boys proved to be of great assistance. Each week they accompanied the class to Owen Sound and worked one-to-one with the children at the Holiday Inn swimming pool, and helped out with skating at the arena. Because of the school's unique situation, educators from other counties and government officials, as well as county staff, were among the many visitors who frequented the classroom on a regular basis. In 1980 Grey county provided education for the older children in the secondary schools. At the present time there are six students in the Developmentally Challenged class.

Saugeen Valley Public School 1962, Grade 5.
Back Row: Janice Watt, Jane Lawrence, Dianne MacDonald, Ken Noble, Dennis Caswell, Wayne Vollett, Richard Cordick, Sheila Christie, Denise Awrey, Suzanne Calder
Second Row: Donna Nixon, Bert Koeslag, Eleanor Fenton, Steven Kerr, Brenda Ewasick, Tim Budd, Gertrude Grein, Jim Atkinson, Brenda Sweeney
Third Row: Grant Robertson, Albert Koeslag, John Player, Richard Kerr, Brock McDonald, Terry McFadden, Peter Taylor, Peter Jamieson
Front Row: Linda Smith, Eileen McAfee, Cheryl Arnett, Mary Lee Clutchey, Grace Lamberts, Sheila Londry, Lynda Greenwood.

Saugeen Valley Public School, Grade 8 Graduation, 1953-1954.
Back Row: Larry Awrey, Nathan Gardiner, Don McNaughton, Bob Becker, Bruce Cordick, John Longworth, Lorne Pust, Keith Hastie, Don Adlam, Edward Middleton, Dennis Noble, Don Collier
Centre Row: Faye Arnett, Barbara Philips, Evelyn Watson, Gwyn Vollett, Shirley Cook, Marilyn Dickson, June Sleeper, Margaret Misener, Judy Renwick
Front Row: Dorothy Rogers, Judy Campbell, Catherine Glass, J.C. McKechnie (Principal), Wilma Clark, Diane Becker, Joan Griffin, Sandra McClyment.

Mary Morton Retirement Night 1960.
School Board Members: Bowman Jamieson, Ralph Wilson, Elmer Clark, Jack Atkinson, James Sullivan, Art Adlam, Wm. Rae, School Inspector, Mary Morton.

Saugeen Valley Public School 1968.

Myrtle Mortley at her retirement party in 1970 with former students L. Vollett, D. Pust, D. Campbell and A. Schenk. Miss Mortley taught 38½ years in Durham schools.

First graduating class from Grade 13 in Durham High School. *Back Row:* Donald Young, Harry Tinianovi, Sandy Mc-Culloch, George Hay, Irvine Matthews, Stewart McIlraith *Front Row:* Mary Beaton, Myrtle Mortley, Dorothy Ritchie, Eleanor Marshall, Ina Milne, Margaret Arnill, Florence McDonald.

DURHAM HIGH SCHOOL

For several years before the organization of the Durham District Continuation School in 1911, there had been an agitation to build a High School in Durham. The Durham Public School was so vastly overcrowded that the complaints of the ratepayers finally convinced the Durham council of the urgent need for a high school. In 1915 the Council passed a by-law allotting $15,000 to construct a high school; a site was chosen on the Edge property on the banks of the Saugeen River facing George Street East. A four room, two-storey red brick school was erected and opened for classes in the spring of 1916. Thomas Allen, principal of the public school since 1888, brought his staff, consisting of Misses Julia Weir and May Criderman, and pupils with him to the new building. Mr. Allen remained as principal until 1919 when he retired after serving the community for 31 years. From 1919 to

1923 there were five principals, and discipline was a real problem in the school. Mr. J.A.M. Robb became principal in 1923, a position he held until 1953. He was followed by Mr. Irvin B. Sharpe, who was principal until his retirement in 1967.

In 1926 two classrooms, a science room, office and staff rooms were added, and soon a full curriculum for University entrance was established. Home Economics, taught by Miss H. Gerrie, and Manual Training, taught by Mr. I. B. Sharpe, were introduced in 1939. Vocal music was introduced in 1946 when Mr. John Jarratt was engaged as Music Instructor.

The school became the Durham District High School in 1951, and bus service was provided for rural students; this increased attendance and necessitated expansion.

A major renovation of the school was undertaken in 1952, and a gymnasium, stage, change rooms, cafeteria, new Manual Training shop, Home Economics room, offices and other auxiliary rooms were added. In 1954 the cafeteria was completely equipped, and Mrs. Bert Cross and Mrs. Velma Vollett served full course noon meals to some 150 students. The next year a Commercial Department was organized with Miss M. Hetherington as teacher. In 1963 the attendance had climbed to over 300 students and a new addition was necessary. The school had grown from four rooms and three teachers in 1916 to 14 rooms and 18 teachers in 1963.

In the early 1960s the Federal and Provincial governments realized that there was absolutely no equality of educational opportunity between the urban and rural students. Students in urban centres had access to technical, vocational, commercial and other specialized schools, which were totally non-existent in rural areas. To assist in rectifying this situation, the Federal government agreed to pay for constructing, equipping and setting up a technical, vocational addition to an academic high school. These schools were called Composite High Schools. The new high school areas had to be large enough to supply approximately 1,000 students to the high school. On January 1st, 1966, the South East Grey Board of Education was established; this was the first Rural Board of Education in Ontario. The following year a South West Grey Board of Education was set up consisting of Durham, Hanover, and Bentinck and Normanby Townships. This Board decided to build an addition to the Hanover High School to accommodate Business and Commerce, Science, and Trades and Technology departments, despite the fact that there was a Composite School at Walkerton just six miles west. This decision effectively sounded the death knell for the Durham High School.

Douglas Smith became Principal from 1967 to 1970 when the Durham High School closed and became the Durham District Community School.

Durham High School, Grades 11 and 12, 1946.
Back Row: Jean McArthur, Shirley Neilson, Bob McRonald, Don Miller, Gord Raeburn, Vic Thompson, Jim McLachlan, Charlie Pratt, Bob Ray
Second Row: Verna Crutchley, Isabel Hastie, Jean Gray, Mary McGowan, Mary Mead, Helen Knisley, Norma Gagnon, Doris Klein, Grace Darling
Third Row: Madeline Catton, Wilma Watson, Pat Kress, Jessie Lou Moran, Isabelle Marshall, Ellen Roberts, Muriel Jack, Marianne McGillivray
Front Row: Clare Elvidge, Jim Duffield, Richard Cammidge, Bob Hunter, Ken McGillivray, Doug Falkingham.

Grade 10, 1946 High School.

Back Row: Bev Cole, Leonard Dinger, Mel Barfoot, Don Schenk, Art Wilder, Oren Noble, Don Corbett, Bill Roberts, Ken Reaburn, Wes Kellar, Tom Barker.

Second Row: Mr. J.A.M. Robb (Principal), Marion Patterson, Jean Roseborough, Del Chapman, Lois Torrey, Betty Ledingham, Joyce Jacques, Blanche Ray, Audrey Lennox, Muriel Miller, Edna Noble, Beatrice Marshall.

Third Row: Joyce Henry, Evelyn Cross, Sally McInnis, Jean Brocklebank, Audrey Whitmore, Myrtle Mortley, Jean McQueen, Marjorie Wolfe, Peggy Schenk, Lenora Lizotte.

Front Row: Ken Kress, Brad Armstrong, Bob Thompson, Wally Pratt, Don McGillivray, Howard McRonald, Bob Johnston, Denton Kinnee.

Durham District High School 1967, now Durham District Community School.

Durham District High School Staff 1967.

Back Row: Donna Reay, P. Mathieu, K. Lucier, J. Robb, Norman Marshall, Mrs. B. Cross, Mrs. A. McGirr
Centre Row: Mrs. V. Arnett, Miss M. Cullaton, Mrs. M. Partridge, Vern Rolufs, Mr. Walden, J. Pout-MacDonald, Mrs. M. Fisk, Stewart Ogg
Front Row: P. Moran, Roger Renton, I.B. Sharpe, Mr. Woollatt, J. MacKay.

Durham District High School Grade 11B 1967.

Back Row: Brenda Wright, Doug MacMillan, Donald Firth, Don Hill, Angus Roseborough, Karen Cragg, Doreen Monk, Cathy Schafer
Centre Row: Lloyd Wilton, Don McLean, Joe Smith, Roger Baskerville, Jutla Schleehahn, Paul Wettlaufer, Paul Luckhart
Front Row: Warren McDougall, Louise McTavish, Joan McGowan, Debbie Rahn, Bill Gordon, Norma Hill, Elaine Caldwell.
Absent: Geoff. Glass.

D.H.S. Grades 11 and 12, 1950.
Back Row: Bill Knisely, Andy McAuliffe, Charles Jarratt, Jack Underwood, John Bell, Don Boyce, Alex Robertson, Mary Mortley, Jessie Bell
Third Row: Jean Roseborough, Sheila Darling, Betty McGowan, Jessie Crutchley, Mary Carol Baird, Janet Leonard, Mary Miller, Dorothy Smith, Flora Marshall, Janet Cross
Second Row: Nora Darling, Jean Weir, Darlene McCracken, Lorna McFarlane, Marie Riddell, Lorna Peart, Jean Morrison, Louise Armstrong, Marilyn Wilson, Marion Marshall.
Front Row: Bob Renton, Ron Doney, Harvey Ellis, Bill Marshall, Morris Tschumi, Gordon Manarey, Edward Sweeney.

Durham High School 1916.

JAMES A.M. ROBB

Mr. Robb was born in the Pickering area east of Toronto. He was a graduate of Queen's University. He came to Durham from Sault Ste. Marie in September, 1923, to be principal of the high school. At that time the school was feeling the adverse effect of having had four principals in as many years.

Mr. Robb soon established a positive rapport with the students and an excellent school spirit prevailed. Physics, chemistry and geography were well taught with his "hands on" experiments and down to earth explanations.

After thirty years as principal, Mr. Robb retired in 1953. He continued to live in Durham spending much time with his dogs, his hunting and his cars.

Mr. J.A.M. Robb died in 1979.

Grade 8 Graduates of Durham District Community School 1977.

Back Row: Darren Dupont, Rick Marshall, Craig Scales, Jeff Meads, Janis Nearingburg, Patti Schleehahn, Lowell Johnston, Craig Corbett, Kelly Clutchey, John Burnett, Kevin Falkingham, Jeanette Jende, Gwen Ferguson, Deanna Irvin, Wendy Hardy, ?
Fourth Row: Tammy Watson, Dianne Thompson, Alisa Bray, Wally Meyerink, Patty Thompson, Lori Talbot, Geoff Bovingdon, Laurie Eckhardt, Denise Johnston, Debbie Fleischmann, Lyle MacArthur, Peter Munro, Jo-Anne Warren, John Johnston, Patti Hastie, Laurie Livingston, Cheryl Hiltz, Freda Lekx
Third Row: Linda Jeffries, Kathy Tiffany, Jo-Anne Lawrence, Ricky Huellemann, Jean McGowan, Deanna Little, Wanda Holley, Debbie Tiffany, Sarah Baxter, Debbie Bannister, Sherry Rydall, Steve Clark, Ricky Reay, Leonard Locke, Caroline Peitz, Linda Ellis.
Second Row: David Bittles, Scott Foster, Steve Watt, Allan Zettler, Edith Anderson, Kevin MacGillivray, Bob Sullivan, Larry Newell, Sharon Mountain, Garry Laughlin, Randy Oetelaar, Scott McLean, Andrea Petersen, Doug Bell, Steven Fennell, Brad Marshall, Anne Marie Drost
Front Row: Ricky Stere, Bob Storrey, Wendy Hand, Bernice Hiltz, Susan Marx, Gordon Hammer (Teacher), John Bell (Principal), Arvid MacPherson (Teacher), Larry Hastie (Teacher), Cindy Campbell, Joyce Hopkins, Debbie Sulkye, Bob Hewer, Peter Hooey.

DURHAM DISTRICT COMMUNITY SCHOOL

With the closing of the Durham High School, the building was extensively renovated, and Grades five to eight were accommodated in the building to be known as Durham District Community School. Because of the existing well-equipped Home Economics and Industrial Arts rooms, pupils from Egremont Central School and St. Peter's and St. Paul's are transported to this school for Family Studies and Design and Tech. The school also has a well-equipped cafeteria where students may purchase hot lunches. John Bell was the first Principal, followed by A. Ritchie, and Valerie Brodrick; the present Principal is Rick Henry. The gymnasium is used extensively by community groups for recreation and instruction. Many night courses are offered through the Community School programme.

Another branch of education which served young people for several years was a private business school conducted by Mrs. Sadie Dargavel in the 1930s and early 1940s.

ST. PETER'S & ST. PAUL'S SCHOOL

The land where St. Peter's & St. Paul's School is located was sold to the Separate School Board of Trustees in 1963 by Helen Jean Watson — parts of lots 4 and 5, east of William Street and north of John Street in Durham.

St. Peter's & St. Paul's School, 190 John Street West in Durham was established August 21, 1963, with only two classrooms. Initial enrolment figure is unavailable, but by September, 1968, there were 83 students enrolled — using the two classrooms and one portable.

Prior to the second addition being added to the school, it was again necessary to use a portable. The current enrolment of St. Peter's & St. Paul's is 103 students.

The first addition was made to the school in 1970, and the second addition completed in 1991, to give the school five classrooms at the present time.

Principals:

1963-66 —	1979-81 —
Mr. J. Rier	Mr. Dave Slosser
1966-67 —	1981-83 —
Mrs. Jessie Mortley	Mr. Pat Cureton
1967-69 —	1983-88 —
Sister M. Michaela	Mrs. Sandra Lang
1969-70 —	1988-90 —
Mr. J.O. MacSweeney	Dr. Gino Ferri
1971-74 —	1990 — Present
Mr. Vern Batte	Mrs. Dolores McNamara
1974-79 —	
Mr. Patrick Morneau	

Saint Peter and St. Paul's School.

MEMORIES OF A RURAL HIGH SCHOOL STUDENT

In 1951 the Durham High School became the Durham District High School, and one result of this change was the inauguration of busing for all rural high school children. Prior to this, it was very difficult for students living long distances from the school to receive a secondary education. Some came by horse and buggy, if a stable or shed could be found in which to tie the horse during the day, a few came by bicycle, the rest walked miles every day carrying their books and lunch. From Christmas to Easter all students coming over three miles roomed in Durham. This meant that they would rent a bedroom, usually shared with another student. and a small room for eating and working. Sometimes there would be as many as four students in one house. The student would bring in enough food from home on Sunday night to last all week. If oatmeal and potatoes were brought, the lady of the house would cook them for the student along with her own meal, but all the rest of the cooking and heating up was done by the students on the kitchen stove. Clean up was communal. Students living more than five miles from town usually roomed for the entire school year. Some students stayed with grandparents or other relatives in town. The writer recalls one early spring day when, beginning the long walk home with a fierce east wind and piercing sleet to face, a car pulled up beside him and the driver — a fellow student, Starr Jamieson — opened the door and said "Get in, it isn't a decent day to walk anywhere. I'll drive you home." That kindness has been long remembered.

The fees, prior to 1951, for rural students attending the Durham High School were set at the average daily cost per student including debenture interest. This was paid by the township to the County Council and then forwarded to the Durham High School Board.

J.A.M. Robb, Principal of Durham High School for 30 years.

NURSERY SCHOOL

During the early 1970s Mrs. Erica Bruggemann started a private Early Childhood Programme for pre-schoolers ages two and a half to five years.

This school has operated over the years from the Durham Presbyterian Church, the Durham Arena, Saugeen Valley Public School, and is presently in the Town Hall. It has proven to be very popular, with attendance ranging from 20 to 30 chldren. Mrs. Bruggemann usually has one paid assistant as well as parent volunteers.

THOMAS ALLAN

Thomas Allan was born in Scotland in 1852 and came with his family to Egremont Township in 1856. In 1877 he started to teach school and in 1888 he became principal of the Durham Public School as well as the Model School. For eight years he had the added responsibility of teaching the Model School without any increase in salary or an additional assistant. After 1895 the school board hired an extra teacher for the fall semester which left Mr. Allan free to spend all his time with the Model School. When the Continuation School was established in 1911, he became the principal and teacher of science. He accompanied the students to the new high school in 1916 and remained principal and teacher until 1919 when he retired. Mr. Allan had the rare ability to win the respect and trust of his students both in the classroom and on the street. He was active in the community and after retirement he was Mayor of Durham for two years. He was active in church affairs and was an elder in Knox church and Sunday School superintendent for many years. He was an ardent sportsman and fisherman. Thomas Allan died in 1932.

ARTINA GUN

(From the Durham Centennial Historical Review by I.B. Sharpe)

Artina Gun, a sister of Dr. James Gun, was born in Scotland in 1853 and came to Durham with her family in 1862. She became a teacher and taught in several rural schools before joining the staff of the Durham Public School. Miss Gun was a typical school "marm." She wore her hair in a "bun" on the back of her head. Her black sateen dress, protected by a white apron, rustled as she moved up and down the rows of seats, peering at work slates through small steel-rimmed glasses and rapping imperiously with her pointer to emphasize a point.

Although the 3 R's received a large proportion of attention, there were many other ingredients required to fit boys and girls for adult life. Rote singing was part of the daily routine. Sunday School hymns such as "Yield not to Temptation" and "Work for the Night is Coming" revealed her deep religious convictions and devotion to the work philosophy. Most of the memory work was taken from the Bible with the "Ten Commandments" and "The Lord's my Shepherd" being the favourites. She taught for over 40 years and died in 1935.

JOHN A. GRAHAM

John A. Graham was born on the family pioneer farm in Glenelg on July 4, 1868. In 1885, at seventeen years of age, he became a teacher. Mr. Graham taught school at Edge Hill, Proton township, Paisley and Hutton Hill. In 1905, while at No. 9 Glenelg, he resigned to become a bookkeeper at the National Portland Cement Company where he remained for the next six years.

An article in the *Durham Review* of June 1905 deplored the low salaries of public school teachers which forced talented, devoted and successful teachers of Mr. Graham's calibre to leave teaching for a more remunerative occupation.

Returning to teaching in 1912 Mr. Graham was a teacher at the Rocky Saugeen and other schools in the area. During the period of the Great War Mr. Graham's patriotic activities were notable as he sparked fund raising projects for soldier comforts.

It has occasionally been wondered out loud why Mr. Graham had not come on the staff of the Durham Public School earlier, but there is no answer available to that query. Suffice it to say that he did become the principal of Durham Public School in 1919. He held this position until ill health forced him to resign in 1935.

Mr. Graham was married to the former Adeline Burgess and had four children: Donald, Adeline (Mrs. A. Morrison), Annie (Mrs. Stanley Pust), and Gordon.

Mr. Graham died in April 1935.

Irvin Sharpe

IRVIN SHARPE

Irvin Sharpe was born and grew up in Durham and attended its schools and churches. He graduated from Fourth Form Durham High School in 1924 and from Fifth Form of the O.S.C.V.I. in 1925. He attended

Miss Julia Weir, a teacher at Durham High School from 1912 to 1939, with former students at the Old Home Week 1958.
Some in picture from left: Jim Morton, Christine McIlraith, Perc Willis, Elsie McGowan, Miss Weir,
Jerry and Oliver Sibbald, Jessie Darling.

Toronto Normal School and became teacher at S.S. No. 3 Bentinck Township in 1926. During the five years he taught there, and a final year at the University of Toronto, he completed his B.A. degree. He came on the staff of the Durham High School in 1932 and remained on that staff until his retirement in 1967. On the retirement of Principal James Robb of the Durham High School in 1953, Irvin became principal at a time of rapid expansion of facilities, staff and courses. During his lifetime in Durham Mr. Sharpe has been active in church, Rotary, hospital, local history groups and community affairs. For 16 years he was a member of the Grey Simcoe Foresters Reserve Army and was local commander for most of that time.

JULIA WEIR

Miss Julia Weir was born in Glenelg township in 1878. In 1894 she attended Model School in Durham and taught until 1900. She attended Ottawa Normal School in 1901 and then taught in Alliston until 1911. In later years one of her Alliston students, Dr. Frederick Banting, came to visit her in Durham. In 1912, having completed her university degree, she joined the staff of the Durham Continuation School and in 1916 she moved with her principal, Thomas Allan, to the Durham High School. Her special teaching interests were Latin and English. After 42 years' teaching she retired in 1939. For her long and faithful service as a teacher, Miss Weir was presented with a medal by the Ontario government. Julia Weir died in 1974.

GIRLS' HOCKEY AT THE DURHAM HIGH SCHOOL

by Wilma Coutts

It was away back in the late 1920s when we had a teacher in First Form High School, as it was called then, who introduced us to girls' hockey. Florabelle Nichol had been on the Varsity team when she attended the University of Toronto and no doubt she saw that we needed some extra-curricular activities to liven things up a bit. Miss Nichol was young and enthusiastic and we loved her for her novel ideas.

We were told one morning that there would be an open skating contest at the old George Street East rink after four o'clock, when the best skaters would be chosen for a girls' hockey team. Everyone was agog with excitement, but my enthusiasm was dampened somewhat by the thought of having to wear my sister's size 2 skates, which cramped my size 3 feet.

At noon I rushed home to pry my year's savings out of a dime bank that held close to $4.00 and was off like a shot to McIlraith's Shoe Store, a mile away downtown. Ours was a small town with only one such establishment and Mr. McIlraith's entire stock of ladies' skates had been reduced to one pair of very large, black tube skates. It was no time to be picky; I gave Mr. McIlraith $3.90 and he wrapped up the tube skates, suggesting that a wad of cotton batting in the toes might be a good idea.

At 4.15 Miss Nichol gave us a short talk on the sport of hockey and announced that the speediest skaters would be picked for the first line. We lined up at the east end of the rink; she joined the group and gave the signal to go.

In the first mad rush to get off to a flying start, some of the girls tripped over one another and went sprawling. Too excited to notice the chaos behind us, a few of us were able to make it to the end of the rink. Of course we had to skate back and repeat the performance in order to give the fallen ones a chance. This second effort took most of the wind out of our sails, but we still had to practise rushing (?) up the ice while stick-handling the puck.

I had talked one of the boys, who had come to watch us play, into lending me his woollen gloves as toe-stuffers. Still my feet slid around in those big boots and soon my legs began to ache horribly. When we had chosen sides and started the game proper we were all so exhausted that our goalie, Marj. Noble, had to give us a push up the ice to get us started. Now, when I see the NHL players rush up to the far end of the ice, get knocked down, jump up and fly down to the opposite end — and back again — without their lungs bursting, I never fail to be amazed!

We soon realized that the goalkeeper's job was the prize position. Marj. had padded herself generously with Eaton's and Simpson's sale catalogues and was having nothing much to do except to laugh at our feeble manoeuvers. We didn't hold this against her because we knew how funny we looked.

We were rewarded just before the bell rang to signal our hour was up. One of the "spares" on our team, having gathered a full head of steam, sailed up the ice, overskated the puck and crashed into the net, knocking goalkeeper, net and herself into the boards. The puck, in the meantime, slowly dribbled across the line where the net had been and our side was credited with a goal!

Somehow we had enough strength left to get to the dressing room, shed our skates and limp home. We were exhausted, not a little bruised, but not discouraged, and by the next morning we could hardly wait to get back on that ice!

In time we developed into a team that could play a fair game of hockey. The Hanover girls were our first official opponents and I can't recall the score, but I rather think it was Hanover's game. I do remember well that they had the sturdiest group of players in the league. Anna Greenwood and I were Durham's skinny defence line and when Hanover's hefty duo came down the ice they bowled us over like ten-pins!

"Play up! play up! and play the game!" — that familiar saying and "It matters not if you win or lose, but how you play the game" were the two good old maxims we tried to live by. We may not have won many hockey games; we did learn to be good sports.

Thank you, Miss Nichol, thank you for everything!

HOCKEY NIGHT IN FLESHERTON

by Wilma Coutts

It may be hard to believe now, as we near the end of the 20th century, but in the 1920s, the days of our youth, when winter arrived most of our cars disappeared. They were put up on blocks in garages and barns and stayed there until the snow melted in April. A minimal amount of snowplowing was done and just about the only motorized vehicle able to roar about the town and country was Dr. Brad Jamieson's amazing snowmobile. With its caterpillar chains on double rear wheels and sturdy skiis replacing front wheels, it was able to knife through snowdrifts and transport the doctor on errands of mercy to patients on remote farms.

On our way to and from school we often hitched rides on farmers' sleighs and cutters and, unless they were hauling a big load of chop from the mill, they were good-natured about letting us have a little ride. Not many Durham residents kept horses and sleighs or cutters; in winter we relied on "shank's mare" to get us where we wanted to go.

Bob Campbell was the exception to the rule. He had a team of handsome Percherons that he used for delivering coal and wood to his customers, for driving passengers and baggage to and from the trains and for hauling ice from the river to his ice storage shed.

On one memorable winter's night a long time ago, it was Bob Campbell's horses that hauled a big sleigh full of laughing, yelling, singing teenage girls all the way from Durham to Flesherton — and back! It was an experience that none of us will ever forget.

Our coach, Miss Nichol, had received an invitation from the Flesherton Girls' Hockey Team to come and play their newly-formed team. Somehow Miss Nichol must have talked the Board into parting with a few dollars for transportation, although that seems unlikely since our excursion would have fallen into the "frills" category. I like to think that we had an unknown benefactor, someone with a generous heart who took a great interest in young people — and that "angel" might very well have been Bob Campbell! At any rate we could hardly believe our good fortune.

When the great day finally arrived we were told to meet at Campbell's house at 5 p.m. I remember well walking on air down Durham hill with my hockey gear — skates, hockey stick and heavy wool socks — with my cup of joy overflowing. But half way down the hill I could see Campbell's yard and there was no sign of life there at all. A horrible thought struck me; had I misunderstood the time we were to leave and had they gone on without me? Breaking into a run it took me about two minutes to reach the railroad tracks, run down Garafraxa Street, past George and Pearl Campbell's store beside the river, past Kress Funeral Parlour and Furniture, Bobby Saunders' Variety Store and Hastie's Pool Room. As I rounded the corner at Mac-Beth's Drug Store there was still no sign of life at the Campbell house. Then Mrs. Campbell opened the door and laughed at my fears; she assured me that I was a little early — for once in my life! The men were down at the barn harnessing the horses, putting fresh straw in the bottom of the big open sleigh and getting the blankets and buffalo robes ready to keep us warm. Mrs. Campbell was a lovely kind lady, noted for her fine cooking. She gave me a glass of milk and a warm butter tart from a box of tarts baked for us to eat on our way.

When Miss Nichol and the girls arrived, we were bundled into the sleigh on wooden benches that went around both sides of the high box. Partially protected from the wind, we still had a clear view of everything around us and the sky above. The horses were champing at the bit as we took off, sleigh bells ringing, down Garafraxa Street to Lambton Street, turning east at the main corner and away out along No. 4 highway. There were no traffic lights at that time and no stop signs, just clear sailing to Flesherton!

It's strange how one remembers some things vividly (like butter tarts) yet forgets others. What I recall most about that trip was the excitement of having an entirely new experience. We were all in high spirits singing crazy songs that were the rage then, singing some pretty ones too. We were awed by the brightness of the stars and constellations and tried to name them, with Miss Nichol's help. Our tarts were shared and every one agreed they were the best in the world, and we sang our school song over and over and over:

> "We are from Durham, Durham are we/We hang
> together, happy and free;
> We never, never, lose any games/We'd rather not
> disgrace our good names:
> You do your best, boys/We'll do the rest, boys —
> We are from Durham High School!

I don't know, now, how Bob Campbell and the horses stood the racket!

I recall that our game went well; there were no broken noses or dislocated teeth and no million dollar salaries or TV advertising contracts riding on whether we won or lost the game. We all won, I think: we made many new friends, the food was excellent, the moccasin dance on the ice was fun and there were good feelings all 'round. What more could any one ask?

The horses had been well fed and watered too and they were ready to go. We invited the Flesherton girls to come to Durham, thanked them for their hospitality and said adieu.

Now, you might think, after all this activity and excitement, that we would be hoarse and exhausted, but we had barely started for home when someone began "Row, row, row your boat gently down the stream..." and we were away again! All the way home Bob Campbell and the horses had to listen to the Ter-

rible Twelve singing "Button Up Your Overcoat," "Abie, Abie," "Daisy, Daisy" (on a bicycle built for two), "My Blue Heaven," "I'm Forever Blowing Bubbles," and other current hits.

I have often wished that a record had been kept of the time it took those prize Percherons to cover the 17 miles to Durham. Smart horses know when they are headed for home, but I think the reason that the team broke the speed record was because they were trying to get away from the awful cacophony behind them. (Mrs. Campbell told me later that Bob said he had enjoyed our concert, but had almost died laughing while watching us play hockey!)

But the more I think about it, the more it seems to me that maybe we did win that hockey game; we were in great form that night, full of vigour, grit and energy! ...Maybe it was because of the butter tarts!

SONGS AND CALLS USED AT DURHAM HIGH SCHOOL FROM THE 1920s TO ITS CLOSURE IN 1968

Fight, fight keep fighting boys
Durham will pull through again.
Keep your chins up show your spirit
True to the white and blue.
We'll give a loud cheer for the D.H.S.
We're here to do our best.
Other schools may fight to the end
But Durham will win.

D.H.S. D.H.S.
Rah, rah, rah, rah.
D.H.S.
We're not slow
No! No! No!
What's the matter with the D.H.S.?
Call, bawl, yell, cheer
Let the people know we're here.
Raz them zag them
Zip boom bah
Durham High School
Rah! Rah! Rah!

McGowan Falls.

Churches

3

The early pioneers who settled at Durham came from England, Scotland and Ireland, many of them having been active in a church in their homelands, with support being given to the Church of England and Ireland, Presbyterian, Methodist, Baptist or Roman Catholic churches. These early settlers probably spent most of their disposable assets paying for ship passage from the homelands to Durham. What little money they had left was needed to buy tools such as axes and hammers, augers, etc., as well as cooking utensils. But they were confident that an abundant Christian faith would strengthen them to overcome any future hardships.

The following story has been told about an early pioneer family in this community which illustrates this great faith. A very young son of one of the early settlers became very ill, and as there was no resident doctor or minister here at that time, the mother and family tried to nurse the young lad back to health. A neighbour of this family called to check on the boy's progress and see if he could help in any way. The father replied that the lad had died just a few minutes previously and invited his friend into the house. With his wife and the rest of his young family around him, the father then took his Bible and read aloud the first chapter of the Book of Job ending with these words "The Lord giveth and the Lord taketh away, Blessed be the name of the Lord." After leading his sorrowing family in prayer, the father and his neighbour went out into the yard, dug a grave, and buried the boy.

Itinerant ministers were the first to visit Durham and their visits were infrequent as they had to cover a large area usually on foot. In each denomination there were lay leaders who ably conducted prayer meetings and Bible study in the homes, helping to keep the flame of faith burning brightly between visits of the ministers.

The first building erected in Durham for church services was a frame building in the north end of town, on the east side of Garafraxa Street. It was built by George Jackson to be used as a meeting place for a small Disciples of Christ group of which he was an adherent. This group placed a strong emphasis on scripture but did not believe in ritual. Other denomi-nations also used this building for church services, and it was commonly called the "Synagogue." In addition, it was also used as a court room. Church services were also frequently held in St. Andrew's Hall, a stone build-ing erected by Archibald Hunter north of the British Hotel.

The 1861 Census lists four churches in Durham:

1 Free Church Presbyterian — Frame
1 Church of England — Frame
1 Wesleyan Methodist — Frame
1 Baptist — Frame

According to an 1860 issue of the Durham Standard, a Durham Bible Society was organized as an inter-denominational group with Presbyterian Reverend Mr. Park as the President, succeeding Baptist Rever-end Stewart. George Jackson was the Vice President, and A. B. McNabb was the Secretary-Treasurer.

(Co-operation and harmony has existed over the years between the churches in Durham. This news item from the August 10th, 1896, *Durham Review* is a fine illustration of such co-operation.)

"HARMONY — The picnic of the four choirs in town last Friday on the banks of the Saugeen, west of the Station was a--, (we were nearly saying "howling" success) but, under the circumstances, the word might be taken to apply to the music, so we say, grand suc-cess. The idea originated we believe with Mr. R. Parker whose musical tastes are only equalled by his sociable nature. The fine reach of the Saugeen gave good sport boating, a tent made things homelike, an organ got somehow over the road, aided the singing which was sweet and loud enough to be heard in town. As dark-ness fell, coal-oil soaked bricks made darkness look romantic and the young moon hide its head. Solos by Mrs. Dr. Carson, Recitations by Mr. Jones, part singing, choir singing and united singing, chased the hours till 10 p.m., when a torch was made, and the children of music, laden with oars, books, instruments &c. and led by "Moses" Parker and the Pillar of Fire made their way out of the desert to the land of the Electric Light and smooth streets. Miss Frazer tried to get a negative of the crowd but the darkness and the hilarity of the singers negatived the idea."

Baptist Church, Durham.

DURHAM BAPTIST CHURCH

The Durham Baptist Church was organized by Rev. Alexander Stewart, who emigrated from Scotland in 1832 at the age of eighteen. He was interested in religion, was converted, and baptized in 1845. He was persuaded by the Baptist Union to become a colporteur, and in this work — distributing Bibles — he travelled to Durham, Owen Sound and Cape Rich.

When Rev. A. Stewart came to Durham, he purchased Lot 12, south of Lambton Street, between Garafraxa and Albert Streets. Rev. Stewart organized the first Baptist congregation, consisting of 12 members, in this part of Ontario. Meetings were held in the members' homes until 1859 when the little Baptist Chapel was built on Lot 12 Albert Street. In the early years of Durham Rev. Stewart was the only minister in town and was called upon to minister to Protestants of all denominations. He was affectionately called "Father Stewart" by all.

The following is an excerpt from the book, Rev. Alexander Stewart, written by his grandson, E.H. Stewart. It tells of his life in this pioneer community.

"In June of 1900, this writer sat beside Reverend Alex Stewart in his garden in Durham, Ontario. It was then that the grandfather told the grandson that about fifty years before he had come and sat in the same spot in a huge forest and wondered whether he should bring his family to this proposed settlement now called Durham, Ontario. It was two or three years later before he was ready to move. Delay doubtless was caused by the birth of his son, Joseph William Alexander Stewart, on January 27th, 1852. Imagine a pioneer family with some young daughters, and a mother carrying a small baby boy, moving into the wilderness. At the time of moving to Durham, the Guelph-Owen Sound Highway was only an Indian trail, widened into a rough cadge road.

"Despite the fact that the Red Sandy Stewart had had less than five months of schooling in Scotland, for which he had to walk nine miles each way, he nevertheless developed qualities of leadership, persuasion

and public speaking. Exercising these with the help and blessing of his good wife, he became a Baptist missionary preacher for the raw new country in the counties of Grey and Bruce and was ordained. He founded the Baptist Church in Durham and was the first minister or clergyman of that village.... His salary, paid by interested Baptists in Toronto was $200.00 a year. His good wife supplemented this meager allowance by taking in boarders, one of whom began the education of (her son) by teaching him "his spellings." (Until that son) was earning money for himself, he always was clothed in second-hand clothes. These clothes were cast-off, and sent up by religious people in Toronto. There are (writing in 1947) remains, however, of almost century-old quilts and shawls, made from native wool, and spun by the good wife."

(Son JWAS told a little more about how the dedicated missionary's family managed to survive.)

"How did he and his family live those early years? Two summers my father went to older parts of the province and worked in the harvest fields. One year his entire income from Convention and field was one hundred and thirty-seven dollars and fifty cents. He chopped and drew his own wood. He got all out of his little bit of ground that it could be made to yield. While he labored on my mother opened the home to boarders, sold milk, vegetables, and I know not what. The edge of actual want was reached more than once. The family could not possibly have been clothed had it not been for the kindness of Christian friends in Toronto and elsewhere whose kindness my father can never forget. I see distinctly before me now the first coat that was actually bought for me out of a store! Perhaps I might have had that coat sooner were it not that in 1858-9 when the little chapel in Durham was built, my father besides his manual help, paid on that chapel out of his own pocket and out of his poverty ninety-six dollars and twenty cents. How he did this I cannot tell, but I found the bill of it lately in rummaging his papers."

Isabella Cranston McGibb, writing in *The Canadian Baptist* in 1932, summarized Alexander Stewart's ministry and added:

"Mr. Stewart was a true pioneer. He knew what it meant to see the last of the flour in the barrel made into bread for his family and have no idea where the next was coming from. He shared the plainest fare of the pioneers. His lunch of bread and cheese carried on his journey was cheerfully shared with those who had less. He hadn't a multitude of material possessions to share with his people, but he had abundance of good cheer, kind words and a message of salvation, which he gave liberally.

"In those early days a receiver of a letter had to pay the postage, which amounted to 12½ cents. The Rev. Mr. Stewart heard there were three letters in the post office for him and he had no money. But faith did not

waver. He went to the postmaster and told him the situation and some arrangement was made and the letters were handed to him. In two of them there was money from friends. How true is the promise, Before they call, I will answer."

The agricultural part of the census of 1861 gives a few details about how the family lived. They had an acre of land (probably planted mostly in potatoes, since they give the most calories per square yard of land, as well as such vegetables as cabbage and kail), and they kept a cow and a few pigs for milk and pork. The acre certainly could not have fed the cow, so probably the children took her out into the countryside to browse and graze each day. Perhaps they were able to collect and store enough grass and leaves to keep her alive over the winter, or perhaps Esther saved some of her pennies to buy hay.

By 1861 Alexander Stewart had been able to acquire a horse again to take him on his rounds. The horse, cow, and three pigs were valued at a total of only $100 and the "capital invested in real and personal estate" was listed at $900, including the house and the acre of land in the center of the thriving village. Esther and the children must have worked as hard as their dedicated and hard-working missionary husband and father.

In his work as a home missionary sent out by the Canadian Baptist Church, the Rev. Mr. Stewart was covering hundreds, even thousands, of miles a year on foot and on horseback, preaching two or three sermons a week, and making more than seven pastoral visits a week. This would be a busy schedule for a minister even today, with a car and paved roads. On the 19th century frontier, it was heroic.

A letter from him, published in *The Christian Messenger* of 20 December 1855, gives something of the flavor of the early years of his ministry:

"Dear Brother,

You will no doubt be anxious to hear how the cause prospers in this part of the Lord's vineyard. A church meeting was held in my house on the 29th of Sep. when the brethren with one exception requested me continue my labours among them. At the same meeting it was agreed, that the brethren on the Durham Line East, should have the Lord's Supper administered in their own settlement, and that the brethren in Egremont would have the same privilege. This arrangement will divide the church at Durham in four branches, each branch having the privilege of communion in a regular manner. I went to administer the Lord's supper in due course, at the house of Donald McKenzie, on the Durham Line on the second Sabbath in October and found that he had departed to his rest and was no more to be seen here. He died of a short sickness, but in the enjoyment of a good hope in Christ. He was one of the first persons baptized, in one of the Western Isles of Scotland, and lived to the age of 78 years, always maintaining an unblemished character. I attended his funeral and endeavoured to improve the solemn event

for the good of those who were left behind in the wilderness. After preaching I baptized three persons, in the name of the Triune God, two of whom are heads of families. A universal manifestation of brotherly love prevailed through the whole of the day, and it was to me, one of the happiest Sabbaths I have ever enjoyed since I came to these parts.

On the following Friday I met with a very extraordinary occurrence. Returning to my house some time after dark, I found a woman who I had never seen before, who soon made herself known to me. She had embraced a hope in the Saviour, about six months ago, and at that time had a strong desire to follow her Lord and Master, in the ordinance of Baptism, feeling that she could not enjoy peace of mind until she had obeyed her Lord's command. There was no one in the township where she resided to whom she could apply to obtain the privilege, and she had come all the way from Saugeen with the husband's consent to Durham, a distance of 45 miles leaving two small children in her husband's care, to seek an opportunity to obey the command of Baptism. I had to preach in Bentinck on the Sunday following, and asked her to stay over that day and then she might meet with the brethren; and if they received her as a believer in Christ, I would baptize her according to her wish. She made her way to the place on Saturday, was received, and in the presence of a very respectable assembly I baptized her and she returned home to her husband and dear babies with a heart full of joy and peace. Before enjoying the delights of descending into the baptismal stream she had travelled 51 miles, over very rough roads in a new country. Her name is Ann McArthur and her native country is Scotland.

I can say to you, my dear Bro. in Christ, that I have been in the school of experience since I came to this part of the country. I have left my home to fill my appointments when my house was without a loaf of bread, and not a York shilling to purchase one. But I did not leave my family to provoke providence. I trusted in the Lord and the God of the Bible to supply our wants. Often when I have returned home weary and exhausted, I have found two or three letters pressing me to visit the places they came from to preach to dying sinners "the word of life." When will the time come to favour Zion, by raising up a host of goodly ministers, to stand upon her walls to sound the trumpet of the blessed gospel of peace.

I am sorry to hear that Maclay College is not likely to go into operation soon. One of the first questions our churches ask when they want a minister is — is he an educated man? If he is a self-taught man they say he will not suit us, but he will do for the back settlements.

What is the result if he is sent there? I can tell you from experience that it will be to meet a more intelligent congregation of people, than can be found in many of the old settled parts of the country. I am not able to hold the ground that is gained without more help. We must leave all in the hands of God. The residue of the Spirit is with him, and he knows the needy state of this part of the country.

   ALEXANDER STUART (sic)"

Many years after the Baptist Chapel was built, it was moved to the corner of Lambton and Elgin Streets. It was given a coat of rough-cast at that time and the interior was renovated. In 1902 the frame church was moved to the back of the lot and a large red brick church was erected. This church, including church hall, had beautiful stained glass windows, one of which contained a portrait of Rev. Alexander Stewart. In 1928 a parsonage was built on the lot adjoining the church.

List of Ministers:

Reverends:
Alex Stewart, 1853-1867
? Hobein
? Northrup
J.C. Dunlop, 1884-1887
John E. Moyle, 1888-1889
C. S.G. Boone, 1889-1892
? Cuthbert, 1883-1894
Wm. McGregor, 1894-1901
W. L. Newton, 1901-1910
Norman McCausland, 1910-1913
W. Wyly, 1914-1917
E. J. McEwen, 1918-1922
E. Cameron, 1911-1923

James Taylor, 1924-1927
W. Spencer, 1927-1929
J. T. Priest, 1929-1941
J. M. Ward, 1941-1947
C. K. Dolby, 1948-1953
G. F. Gorman, 1953-1962
J. A. McRae, 1962-1963
B. A. Cobham, 1964-1970
Robt. Lofthouse, 1970-1973
Peter Burritt, 1976-1980
John Pepper, 1981-1986
Bob Shaughnessy, 1986-1991
Jeff Loach, 1991-1991
Edward Reid, 1993

DURHAM FOURSQUARE GOSPEL CHURCH

Foursquare Church.

In 1929 Rev. Jack Caswell held revival meetings in a tent where the SUNOCO service station is located one block south of the lights. As a result of the tent crusade hundreds of people received Jesus Christ as their Saviour. Many were healed and filled with the Holy Spirit. Mr. Caswell held outdoor water baptismal services at the river in town which drew people from miles around.

During 1930 a permanent church was built at 193 Garafraxa Street South for the congregation's needs. Reverend and Mrs. Jas. P. Lowen, the first resident ministers to pastor the congregation, held 18 services per week in November, 1931. The following is a list of the names of pastors who ministered under appointment:

Reverends:

Jas. P. Lowen	November 1931 to May 1935
P. Lockstead	June 1935 to June 1938
M. Miller	July 1938 to September 1938
R. Vickerson	July 1938 to June 1944
W. Howes	July 1944 to December 1944
B. Ellis	January 1945 to December 1947
S. Ellis	October 1947 to February 1948
P. M. Lewis	March 1948 to October 1949
D. Runyan	November 1949 to February 1952
L. Ketchum	June 1952 to October 1953
M. Hughes	November 1953 to August 1955
J. Andrew	November 1955 to July 1957
H. Ingram	August 1957 to April 1969
Rev. R. Meyers	November 1968 to April 1969
(co-pastored with Mrs. O. Ingram)	
Rev. R. Meyers	April 1969 to June 1973
K. Watson	July 1973 to September 1973
F. R. Plank Jr.	October 1973 to September 1979
C. Mullin	October 1979 to September 1981
R. Wallis	October 1981 to May 1986
L. Foster	May 1986 to present day

The Church officially became a part of the International Church of the Foursquare Gospel in 1945 when it had sufficient membership to be qualified as a Foursquare Church. The building was expanded in 1949 to include a front entrance and an auditorium at the back.

The Church officially became a member Church of the Foursquare Gospel Church of Canada in 1980. It is also a member denomination of the Evangelical Fellowship of Canada.

The name FOURSQUARE stands for the four-fold ministry of Jesus Christ. He is the Saviour, The Healer, the Baptizer with the Holy Spirit, and The Soon Coming King. In front of each Foursquare church is the banner quoting Hebrews 13:8. **"Jesus Christ the same Yesterday, and Today, and Forever."** In this verse of scripture we are reminded that Jesus does not change. People are still being saved as they receive Jesus as Lord. People are still being healed as Jesus graciously answers prayer. People are still being filled with the Holy Spirit as in the book of Acts. And we are looking for the soon coming of our Lord and Saviour, Marinatha, even so come Lord Jesus!

A Foursquare family camp, Camp McPherson, was owned and operated in the mid 1950s on the south edge of town through which Camp Creek flowed. Many of the senior Foursquare families still have fond memories of the camp telling of how they caught speckled trout during breaks in the camp meetings. The 78 acre camp was sold to New Tribes Mission of Canada on September 11, 1967. Since then N.T.M.C. has transformed the properties into a training centre for missionaries and their families to prepare them for ministry around the world.

In September of 1990 the Foursquare Church started offering fully accredited College courses through SAUGEEN VALLEY BIBLE INSTITUTE, an extension of LIFE Bible College of Canada. These courses can lead to: a one-year Certificate of Biblical Studies; a two-year Certificate of Ministry; a three-year ministerial Diploma; or a four-year Bachelor of Theology, or Bachelor of Religious Education. Each year in early April the church participates in the annual RAIN WALK to help raise funds for the Bible College in order that the tuition costs might be kept down and thereby enable the college to keep functioning. The support of the local town people has been terrific. In 1990 and 1991 the congregation raised more dollars per capita than any other sister congregations in Canada, and for the last two years has placed second in this respect.

As of September, 1994, a Pioneer Club will be started making available to the children in our community a Bible centred programme with a balance of spiritual, social, mental and physical activities.

DURHAM PRESBYTERIAN

It is a tribute to the integrity of these early pioneers that they felt one of their first obligations was to make provision for the worship of God. In the "Synagogue," erected by Mr. George Jackson, in the dining room of the British Hotel, in schools and private houses, those of every denomination met for united worship. In the early 1850s monthly services were held respectively by Archdeacon Mulholland from Owen Sound, Rev. Clarke of the Methodist Church from Hanover, and Rev. Alex Stewart of the Baptist Church in Durham. In addition, ministers from three divisions of the Presbyterians, namely Free Church, United Presbyterian and Church of Scotland, made occasional visits to the district.

An article by S.L.M. Luke in the *Durham Review*, May 9, 1901, states: "During the 1850s up until the time of Union of the Auld Kirk and Free Church (1862), the Auld Kirk had monthly service in St. Andrew's Hall conducted by Rev. John Hay, whose other mission was in Kincardine to which he used to walk through the wilds at that time. The Wesleyan Methodists also met here having at that period no place of worship of their own, and all this free from cost, even in the winter season Mr. Hunter freely supplying the necessary fuel for heating purposes, although he was an ardent Free Kirk man himself."

It is characteristic that the earliest part of religious exercise was the Sunday School. As early as 1849 Mr. Thos. Brown, Mr. James Burgess and Mr. James McGirr united in maintaining a Sunday School, first in Mr. Brown's house and then in a building not far from the river, and later in the old stone schoolhouse. In 1856 Mr. Hugh McNabb was in charge as superintendent, a position he held for some time. Mr. McNabb walked the long distance from his farm in Glenelg to and from Sunday School along an Indian trail which followed the main Saugeen River from the 4th Concession to Durham. He later became an elder in the Presbyterian Church, a position he held for 40 years.

In the year 1852 a grant of ten acres was made by the Crown to the Free Presbyterian Church for a glebe, church building and burying ground. This land was in Bentinck Township south of the Durham Road and west of Queen Street. In 1855 the Presbytery of Hamilton sent two ministers to Durham to organize a congregation and ordain elders. It is likely they fulfilled their mission because later that year Mr. Charles Watson was employed to build a frame church on the property.

According to the booklet, *Jubilee Souvenir Durham Presbyterian Church 1909*, "The fact that there was no Presbytery nearer than Hamilton is in itself a comment on the condition of the country at that time. The church was served by various ministers until in 1859 Rev. Wm. Park was called as minister, a position he held until 1885 when he retired. There were no musical instruments in the church. The only music was the singing of the psalms led by a precentor; those filling this position were Wm. Hunter, Chas. Watson, Thos. Lauder, Archibald Hunter, J. White, and Neil McKechnie. The church grew and progressed until in 1880, when instrumental music was introduced, a number of the members withdrew from the congregation."

Previous histories have reported that the split in the church at that time was caused solely by the instrumental music question. However, the minutes of Saugeen Presbytery during that period tell a different story.

"**July 15, 1880** — A petition to Saugeen Presbytery from 44 members of Durham Presbyterian Church asking for permission to organize a new congregation, setting forth that they could not longer conscientiously remain in connection with Mr. Park's congregation in consequence of the recently sanctioned use of an organ in the service of praise. Presbytery urged both parties to endeavour to find a basis of reconciliation. The Durham Presbyterian Church before the split had 160 members.

Sept. 29, 1880 — Saugeen Presbytery met in Durham Presbyterian Church to resolve the differences. The Durham Church offered to remove the offensive organ but that did not solve the problem. A commission of Moderator and two other members of Presbytery was appointed. They met with the dissenters of the Durham Church congregation and reported that there was only one member who had difficulty with instrumental music in the church. They also reported to Presbytery that there were two and possibly three families that wanted to oust Rev. Park from the Durham Church but the vast majority of members fully supported Rev. Park. The dissenters were using the music controversy to reach their goal.

October 21, 1880 — Saugeen Presbytery met with a small attendance due to a storm. The question of granting the dissenters from Durham Presbyterian Church permission to organize a new congregation was voted on. The vote ended in a tie and the Modera-

Durham Presbyterian Church Session circa 1895
W.J. Young, Geo. Turnbull, Hugh McNab, Wm. Smith., Rev. A.G. Jansen, Thos. Lauder, John Byres, Dr. James Gun.

tor Pro-tem broke the tie by voting for consent. Some of the commissioners of Presbytery appealed to the Synod of Toronto & Kingston to overturn the vote. Synod took no action. On July 12, 1881, Presbytery appointed Rev. D. McLeod of Priceville and Thomas Binnie and A. McLeod an interim session for the new congregation." The new congregation set out to build a new brick church 38′ x 65′, plans and specifications not to exceed $20. The cornerstone was laid May 24, 1882. Seating was free. This new congregation was known as Knox Presbyterian. However, in 1885 the two congregations were united and and the church became known as Durham Presbyterian Church. A few years later an organ was permitted for leading the music. In 1900 the church was enlarged and in 1908 a pipe organ was installed.

There was a cemetery beside the First Presbyterian Church where many of the early pioneers were laid to rest. It was closed for interment in 1880. Some bodies were removed to the new cemetery but the remaining stones bear witness to members of many prominent early pioneer families.

The church once again was divided in 1925 by an Act of Parliament. The Canadian government passed a bill uniting the Presbyterians, Methodists and Congregationalists to form the United Church of Canada. Many Presbyterians objected to the union on the grounds that much of their doctrine would be lost, and they won the right to vote on the union. The Methodists

and Congregationalists did not have this privilege. The result of the vote was 218 for union, 165 against. The law said that 50 per cent of the vote plus one member would get all of the church's physical assets. Thus those remaining true to Presbyterianism were without a church, a manse, or even a hymn book. The Act of Church Union also made provision for a Commission to settle any problems pertaining to the Church Union. Since the Methodists were now going to worship with the United congregation, the Presbyterians requested that this Commission place a reasonable nominal price for the Queen Street Methodist Church so that they could purchase the building for a Presbyterian Church. The Commission held a hearing in Durham in November, 1925, and Rev. W.H.Smith, as spokesman for the United Church, argued that if it took 20 inches to seat the average person comfortably, 218 members plus their families would take up all available pew space, and it would be essential to maintain two United Churches in Durham. No decision was given by the Commission. In 1926 a red brick church was erected on the corner of Lambton and Albert Streets This was the third time that Presbyterians in Durham had built a congregation in the town, and their determination was met with success. A manse was purchased in 1942, and a pipe organ in 1946. In 1966 the entire sanctuary was refurbished. At that time the front of the church was altered, the pipe organ was replaced with a Conn Electronic organ, new pews and new lighting were installed, and the floor was carpeted. Six years later (1972) a Christian Education addition was built which contained a large meeting room, minister's study, office, kitchenette, choir room, nursery and Sunday School classrooms. At the same time a new kitchen was installed; three large I beams were placed across the church basement to support the church floor, and the two rows of posts in the basement were removed. An elevator was installed in 1991, and the church was made fully accessible. Several other community groups have used these facilities from time to time.

Three sons of early pioneers became ministers: James Binnie, John Smith and Peter Nichol. Since 1925, Daniel Firth and Gordon MacInnes have been ordained from the Durham Church.

The ministers over the years were:

Reverends:
Wm. Park, 1859-1885
Wm. Forrest, 1882-1885
Robt. McNair, 1886-1891
A.G. Jansen, 1892-1899
Dr. Wm. Farquharson, 1899-1913
S.M. Whaley, 1914-1920
W.H. Smith, 1920-1925
B.D. Armstrong, 1925-1934
David Gowdy, 1934-1937
W.S. Hirtle, 1937-1941
P.W. MacInnes, 1942-1949
Gordon Hamill, 1949-1959
Wm. Mitchell, 1960-1965
Murray Laurenson, 1966-1975
Mervyn Tubb, 1976-1992
Shirley Jeffery, 1993

Durham Presbyterian Church.

By Prof. J.W.A. Stewart
Son of the late Rev. Alex. Stewart,
now Dean of Rochester Theological Seminary
(From Jubilee Souvenir Booklet,
Durham Presbyterian Church 1909)

Mr. Park was my revered teacher and one of my most honored friends. When I look back upon my life and count up the men who, next to my family relations, had the greatest influence in making me what I am, I always place Mr. Park's name first — first in point of time, and among the first in point of helpful instruction and influence.

I began the study of Latin with him at nine years of age, Messrs. John McKechnie and Thos. Kelly being my fellow students. Mr. Park was the best teacher I have ever known in his ability to ground his students in the rudiments of the Greek and Latin languages. There was something in his methods that demanded accuracy and thoroughness. It was almost like a personal grief to him when we failed to do our lessons

well. He not only taught us Latin and Greek, but he did his best to inspire in us a love of learning and to impart to us all that he could with reference to much of the best Literature in the English language. The fact is that he was doing his best to start us on a course of real learning. Besides all this he was wonderfully friendly and kind. Frequently he had us take tea with him, trying to make us talk Latin at the table, and his interest in us never failed.

DIAMOND RING
MARY QUEEN OF SCOTS

The following correspondence was received by Mr. Wallace McGowan, Clerk of Durham Presbyterian Session, on June 5, 1964, from Miss Jessie Y. Farquharson, a daughter of Reverend Dr. Wm. Farquharson, a former minister at that church.

Dear Mr. McGowan,

I am enclosing the story of the diamond ring, belonging to Mrs. Park, wife of the first minister of Durham Presbyterian Church. This is as Mrs. Park related it to my mother during my father's ministry in Durham from 1899 to 1913. I thought that the Durham Presbyterian Church should have this story linking them with the troubled times of Mary Queen of Scots in the sixteenth century.

As the story mentions the four Maries of Mary it might interest you to know that I have living in my home a relative of direct descendents of Mary Seton, one of the Maries. Mary Seton received a watch from Mary, the Scottish Queen.

Sincerely yours,
Jessie Y. Farquharson

THE RING THAT LINKED MR. PARK'S MINISTRY IN DURHAM PRESBYTERIAN CHURCH WITH MARY, QUEEN OF SCOTS

Scottish people recall with sadness the fate of Mary, Queen of Scots, executed in the 16th century after years of imprisonment by her cousin, Queen Elizabeth of England. Mary had four ladies in waiting during her captivity, her four Maries recorded in verse that leaves a feeling of sadness for the fate of the fourth Marie.

Yestre'en the Queen had four Maries,
Tonight she'll have but three.
There is Mary Beaton and Mary Seton
And Mary Carmichael and me.

The night before her execution Mary gave a piece of jewelry to each of her Maries. Mary Carmichael, an aunt of one of Mrs. Park's ancestors received a diamond ring. This was handed down to Mrs. Park by her father who was a captain at Edinburgh Castle. Mrs. Park wore the ring and her friends saw it frequently.

One night when Mr. and Mrs. Park came home after visiting members of the congregation some dis-

Knox Presbyterian Church circa 1890s.
Steps and walk in foreground lead to Mechanics Institute.

tance from the town Mrs. Park noticed with alarm that the ring was no longer on her finger. They remembered stopping at one of the beautiful clear streams that are numerous around Durham. Mrs. Park had alighted to undo the checkrein so that the horse could be driven through the water to drink and cool his feet. They took the lantern and drove back immediately to the stream and there, on the bank, gleaming in the rays of the lantern, was the diamond ring of Mary, Queen of Scots.

KNOX UNITED CHURCH

The Federal government passed a law, to take effect in 1925, uniting the Presbyterian, Methodist, and Congregational Churches into one church. However, the Presbyterians obtained the right to vote on the question and the vote in Durham was 218 in favour of union, and 165 against. The 165 opposed to the proposed union withdrew from the church without taking any physical assets with them and held church services in the Town Hall until they could erect a new church.

On June 10, 1925, the consummation of the union of the Methodist and Congregational Churches and those Presbyterian Churches who voted to join the United Church took place in the Mutual Street Arena, Toronto. This Union was known as the United Church of Canada. On the following Sunday, June 14, Durham's two United Churches, Knox and Queen Street (formerly the Methodist Church), came together for a Communion service in Knox United Church. The service was conducted by Reverends W.H. Smith, Knox, and J.E. Peters, Queen Street, assisted by Reverend M. Sellars, Dornoch, using parts of the service used in Toronto on June 10th.

The two United Churches in Durham now became part of Grey Presbytery. Reverend J.E. Peters continued as minister of Zion United Church, Glenelg Township (formerly Zion Methodist Church). Reverend W.H. Smith now served as minister of Hampden United Church (formerly Hampden Presbyterian Church, Normanby Township). These two ministers travelled by horse and cutter in winter as roads were not kept open for motor traffic.

Knox and Queen Street began holding Union picnics in 1929. Thoughts of amalgamation grew, and on July 1, 1938, Queen Street congregation united with Knox congregation. All offices in both congregations were declared vacant in June. Seven men from each congregation were chosen as Session members, and seven men from each congregation were chosen for the Committee of Stewards. The trustees and other groups had equal representatives from each congregation. The first service after this Union took place on Sunday, July 3, 1938, in Knox Church.

In 1949 the Centennial of the first recorded Sunday School was celebrated for two Sundays. On June 13 the years in the former Methodist Sunday School were reviewed by Mr. W.A. Glass, and in the former Presbyterian Sunday School by Mr. Peter Ramage. Both men also spoke well of the present Sunday School which began July 1, 1938. Mr. W.J. Ritchie told about Sunday School in the Edge Hill community, 1880-1930, and Mr. John McGirr spoke about the Sunday School in the S.S. No. 9 community, 1887-1903-1930 and 1946-1947. The latter two were Union Sunday Schools in Glenelg Township associated with the Presbyterian, Methodist and Anglican churches, and also later, United Church. The country Sunday Schools were usually held in the afternoon from May 1 to October 31. The Sunday Schools in Durham met in the afternoon until 1939, when classes were held prior to the church service. Since 1985 the children attend church with their families at 11 a.m., and after the opening worship service, and a short meeting and prayer with the minister, go to their regular classes in the Christian Education department until the church service has ended.

For some time it was quite evident that more space was needed to accommodate all the classes. In 1957 a Christian Education extension was built on the west end of the church. The winding stairway leading to the santuary and choir loft, and a wooden stairway outside the north-west door of the sanctuary, were removed. The new building provided a wide stairway along the south wall, a large meeting room, named the Friendship Room, vestry, choir room, kindergarten, and classrooms. The average weekly attendance at Sunday School increased to 145 in 1958 with 185 pupils the highest attendance. The average attendance was 162 in 1960. Twenty classes could now be accommodated.

Miss Margaret Hunter was Organist and Choir Leader, 1911-1935. Memorial chimes and a P.A. system were installed in 1950. In 1969 a larger Ebenezer Pipe

Presbyterian Board of Managers 1909.
Back Row: Charles Ramage, W.J. Adams, Jas. Ireland, Chairman, J.R. Gun, Wm. Weir.
Ends of table: W.J. Derby, Robert MacFarlane.
Front Row: Neil McCannell, Thomas McFadden, I.S. McIlraith, Thomas Turnbull, Wm. Ritchie.

organ was installed with chimes, replacing the 1908 pipe organ. Again in 1989 the organ was replaced by an Electronic Allen Digital instrument. The opening and dedication of the new Christian Education Extension took place on January 6, 1958.

To celebrate Canada's Centennial in 1967, changes were made to the east end of the church. The two curved winding stairways were replaced by stairs along the north and south sides leading into a narthex where the raised seats had been previously. A gallery was added. An entrance to a new driveway between the church and the Public Library provided much easier access, especially from a large parking lot north of the Library, which had earlier been purchased. The steeple and tower were repaired and shingled, and a golden ball placed at the top of the steeple. The Knox rededication services were held in September of that year.

Zion United Church became part of the Durham Pastoral Charge in 1961. Knox ministers have been pastors of this congregation since 1938. Owing to changes in the neighbourhood and smaller attendance, services have been held the first and third Sunday of the month since 1992. In 1994 Zion was closed for the winter months, January to April 1, when twice monthly services again began.

In 1961 the United Church of Canada made major changes in the women's organizations. The Women's Missionary Society and the Woman's Association were united to form the United Church Women, or U.C.W. For the first time, in 1962, two U.C.W. members, Mrs. Don (Grace) McQueen and Miss Barbara Ritchie were elected to the Committee of Stewards. In 1968 Mrs. Ralph (Lena) Catton became the first lady member of the Session.

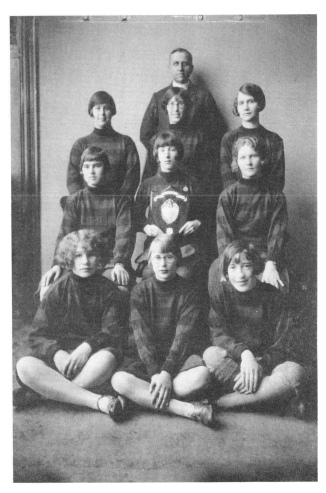

Durham United Church Girls' Ball Team 1927,
Grey Presbytery Champions, Peter Ramage, Coach.
Back Row: Grace Baird, Florence McDonald, Sarah McCulloch
Centre Row: Daisy Mather, Lizzie Hines, Violet Mervyn
Front Row: Christine McCulloch, Mary Brown, Ellen Hayes.

Early Sunday morning, August 30, 1970, lightning struck the steeple damaging the tower, P.A. system, and electrical wiring, but fortunately no fire occurred. The Presbyterian Church was made available while repairs were being made.

In 1973 Knox appointed a committee to have any remaining and fallen stones in the First Presbyterian Church cemetery erected. A cement base was poured, stones were arranged, and a plaque suitably inscribed was set in the base.

Charles R. Newton and Peter John Pace have been candidates for the Ministry, and Neil Walsam is a Candidate for the Lay Ministery, 1994. In 1972 Mr. and Mrs. Philip Pace were commissioned as Teacher-Missionaries to Japan for a term of three years.

Ministers over the years were:

Reverends:

W.H. Smith, 1920-1944	G. Howard Pace, 1969-1972
Walter A. March, 1944-1951	Theo J. Rees, 1972-1973
Fred J. Roberts, 1951-1954	Ken S. Tanner, 1973-1982
J.A.C. Kell, 1954-1961	Herb. W. Wonfor, 1982-1990
Robert F. Sherwin, 1961-1968	Donna J. Mann, 1990

(Reverend J.A.C. Kell was President of Toronto Conference of the United Church of Canada in 1959.)

In 1985 a Chair Lift was installed at the south-west entrance to the church. Ear phones were provided for the hearing impaired.

Knox Church, with its facilities, is used almost every day for meetings, or for special programmes for all ages in the community, such as Parents' Breakaway, a morning weekly programme for young parents and their children; Fun Week during March break; Vacation Bible Schools in summer holidays in co-operation with the Presbyterian congregation; Lighthouse for teens and their programmes; Fun and Fitness every week (except summer months); Adult Bible Study in Knox and weekly Bible Study in Rockwood Terrace.

Knox United Church from side entrance.

Interior of Presbyterian Church 1905.

Durham United Church S.S. Picnic, Holstein Park, July 10, 1939.

METHODIST CHURCH

In Durham's early days the Methodists were ministered to by circuit riders who travelled over a wide area on horseback visiting many remote pioneer settlements. Not surprisingly the time of services in Durham was very erratic due to the territory covered and circumstances which might be encountered along the way. However, there is record of a prayer meeting and baptismal service held in 1849 at the home of Andrew McGirr by an unknown itinerant minister.

There were two Methodist congregations in Durham at that time — The New Connexion Methodists and the Wesleyan Methodists. The New Connexion Methodists are known to have had services in 1851 conducted by Reverend James Baskerville, and in 1859 Reverend George Buggin was their minister. It is recognized that services were held in the Baptist Chapel in 1862. Two or three years later this congregation built their own church which was a frame building on Queen Street just north of George Street. The first mention of a Wesleyan Methodist service in Durham was in the mid-1850s at Joseph Allen's wagon shop, conducted by Reverend Creighton. A Wesleyan Methodist church was listed in the 1861 census report as a frame structure. It was located on the north-west corner of Queen and Lambton Streets in Durham, and Reverend Isaac Baker was the minister in the early to mid 1860s. The two Methodist congregations united in 1874 and used the Wesleyan church building. The old frame New Connexion church building was sold to the I.O.O.F. for a meeting hall. Ten years later the Wesleyan church was demolished and the congregation erected a new white brick church at the same location at a cost of $2,500.

In 1859 the New Connexion Methodists in Glenelg Township built a frame church at Zion. This new congregation became part of the Durham Pastorate and was served by the New Connexion ministers until 1874 and then by the ministers of the Durham Methodist Church until 1925, when it became part of the United Church of Canada.

The Epworth League was a Methodist Youth organization. During Reverend Wray Smith's ministry this organization became extremely active, and both senior and junior groups were formed, possibly involving over one hundred young people. Two main features of the Epworth League emphasized — bible study and worship, and recreation and sport. Over the years the league members took several day trips to points of interest in Western Ontario, leaving on the early morning train and returning on the late night train. Mr. I.B. Sharpe states that for many years the Epworth League was the focal point of the community for the young people.

The former Queen Street Methodist Church.

Group of Queen Street Epworth Leaguers 1906.

The ministers since 1874 were:

George Walker, 1874
John Hodgson, 1875-1876
Robert Godfrey, 1877-1879
D. Williams, 1880
John Smiley, 1881-1882
C. Van Dusen Lake, 1883-1885
Benjamin Hutton, 1886-1888
James Legear, 1889
Wesley Kerr, 1891-1893
Alex Birks, 1894-1896
J.C. Pomeroy, 1897-1899
James Ferguson, 1900-1903

Wray Smith 1904-1906
Thomas Colling, 1907-1908
Walter Jamieson, 1909-1911
Walter Wright, 1912-1914
W.W. Prudham, 1915-1917
Eli S. Moger, 1918-1922
Charles Cole, 1922-1926
John E. Peters, 1927-1930
Henry S. Fiddes, 1931-1933
Walter Almack, 1934
G. Holbert, 1935-1938

TRINITY ANGLICAN CHURCH

Trinity Anglican Church.

The first Anglican Church service in Durham was held at the home of John Hobson Edge near the Edge Mills in November, 1849. The minister was A. H. R. Mulholland of Owen Sound. In 1899 the Anglicans held a special 50th Anniversary service and invited Archdeacon Mulholland to participate. Because of ill health he was unable to attend but sent the following letter to the congregation:

"I do not now remember the exact date of my first visit to Durham, but it was on a Sunday in November 1849. I went to Durham on the previous Saturday on horseback, for there were no roads then for wheels, owing to the bad state of the road it took me all day to get there. The service was held in Mr. John Edge's house near the mill, it being the largest available place to be had at that time. The congregation was very large, and every apartment of the house was filled with men and women who came many miles through the bush to hear once more the grand old church service they were accustomed to in the old country. Many came from the far back concessions on sleds drawn by oxen, for there were no waggons and few horses in the country at that time, bringing children to be baptised. Among those present on that occasion were a number of families of the Edge's, the Blakes, Hopkins, Cuffs, Davises, Jones', Moody's and many other families whose names I do not now remember. The late George

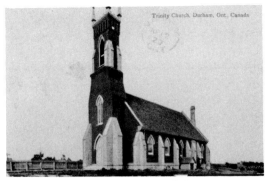

Trinity Anglican Church with high tower.

Jackson, the Crown Land Agent and old Mr. Hunter were also present. I was much pleased to see that a very large portion of the congregation had prayer books and joined most heartily in the services. Many of the young men and women came to me after the service to show me the prayer books that were given to them by their rectors in Ireland prior to their leaving for Canada.

We had no instrumental music on the occasion, but a man whose name I forget, volunteered to lead the singing. I believe he had been a parish clerk in Ireland. He commenced in too high a key, but after a number of attempts, which did not seem to disconcert him or the congregation, he succeeded in getting the key that suited the voices of the congregation, and the singing was most impressive. During the 50 years I have been in Holy Orders, I never heard that grand old hundredth psalm sung so heartily as I did at that first church service in Durham. I hope the choir will select that psalm as one of their numbers on next Sunday and sing it without any organ accompaniment, in remembrance of the first Durham congregation that assembled at Mr. John Edge's house fifty years ago.

I deeply regret that my health will not permit me to take part in the jubilee services. It would indeed have afforded me great pleasure to meet any of the members of that first congregation who are now alive and to shake hands with them, and the babies, now men and women, whom I then baptised, but now having long passed the three score years and ten and with feeble health, I am reluctantly obliged to deny myself that great pleasure. I shall ever gratefully remember the kindness and cordial greetings I ever received from the Durham congregation.

In the winter time I was able to make my Missionary tour in the counties of Grey and Bruce in a sled, or as it was called the "Parson's jumper," and the parson's jumper never left Durham without being well loaded with gifts for myself and family and I never knew who the donors were. In the mission field I then labored in alone, there are now sixteen clergymen doing the work of the church.

Thanking all old friends for kind wishes and interest, and wishing God speed to every good work.

Believe me ever, Very faithfully yours,

A. H. R. MULHOLLAND,

Archdeacon of Grey — Nov. 13 '99. Owen Sound."

Over the next ten years Rev. Mulholland visited the Durham congregation at frequent intervals. Services during these visits were held in homes, in "the Synagogue" or in St. Andrew's Hall. In the early days if a minister was present for a church service, some members of all denominations would attend.

John Edge of Clonbrook, Ireland, who had purchased a block of land East of Garafraxa Street South of Durham Road East and north of George Street and west end of Mill Street, including all water rights, donated a lot on which to build an Anglican Church. In 1860, when Rev. S. C. Haines arrived as the first resident minister, he found the congregation meeting in St. Andrew's Hall and he immediately set about to build a church on the donated lot.

A frame church was erected about the same size as the present one, and it was consecrated in 1862 and was debt free by 1863. The bell tower was built in 1864. The church bell was rung one-half hour before church service and again at the hour of service. It was also rung to sound the alarm for any fire in Durham and for many years it was the Town of Durham's only fire alarm.

In 1864 land for a cemetery was purchased from Richard Collier, Lot 56 Concession 2, E. G. R., Glenelg Township. This well kept cemetery is still in use. In 1880 the church subscribed $12 to start a Sunday School Library. 62 books were purchased and the Bishop donated 12 more.

The minister's stipend was partially raised by renting pews. The rents ranged from $20 for the two pews at the back to two dollars for the front pew. In April, 1874, the pews were made free for all and the stipend raised by collection and subscription. Apparently this did not work well and the pews were again rented in 1875 and were still being rented in 1885.

In 1876 the church burned in a fire which started in the Argyle Hotel, near the top of the hill. Following the fire, services were held in the Town Hall until November, 1877, when the present brick church was completed. The bell was cracked in the fire and was shipped back to Troy, New York, to be recast. In 1891, either lightning or wind destroyed the top of the bell tower and the bell was not used for some time. It was missed so much by townspeople that the repairs were partly paid for by other denominations. A new top for the tower was designed with wooden spires at the corners. A windstorm on Good Friday, 1913, blew part of the tower down and the remaining top was removed. In 1962 the remaining tower was replaced with a much lower one.

In 1870 the church bought two and a half acres east of Kincardine Street at Durham Road to build a rectory. Rev. W. B. Evans drew up the plans and included in them a parochial school. He left before the building was finished, and as Durham was building a new public school at that time, the part to be used for a school was torn down. The rectory was sold in 1922, and became the Durham Red Cross Memorial Hospital and was used as such until 1962. It is now St. Raphael's Nursing Home.

In 1922 the home of William Laidlaw at Mill and Albert Streets was purchased for a rectory. Extensive renovations were carried out in 1949, after which it was used as rectory and parish hall. It was sold in 1978.

In 1967 Durham Trinity Anglican Church joined with St. James in Hanover, and since that time the minister has resided in Hanover.

The highlight of the year 1985 was the installation of an illuminated glass block cross in the bell tower in memory of Mr. and Mrs. Robert Lawrence and Mrs. Dorothy Aljoe given by the Sharpe, Lawrence and Aljoe families. At this time also the Trinity window at the back of the church was uncovered and restored. When this work was being carried out, a large pattern of the window was made and each child in the Sunday School was given a piece of glass from the window to lay on the pattern — these children would always remember their involvement in this ceremony.

On March 18th, 1990, the sod was turned for the new addition which includes a new kitchen, Sunday School room, storage room, friendship room, 2 washrooms, and elevator — all wheel chair accessible.

The Anglican congregation is proud of, and grateful to, its forefathers who built the present beautiful church, and gratitude is expressed to those who through the years have maintained and improved the worship sanctuary.

Rectors ministering to the Anglican congregation were:

Reverends:

S. C. Haines, 1860-63	Ernest Hayes, 1927-30
Willian Evans, 1864-75	J. Billingsley, 1931-33
Thomas Magahy, 1876-78	J. R. Thompson, 1934-36
D. Wray, 1879-81	M. H. H. Farr, 1936-1940
? Ashbury, 1882-85	R. S. Jones, 1940-46
J. C. Farthing, 1886-88	W. K. Morrison, 1946-49
A. D. Dewdney, 1889-90	W. H. Simpson, 1949-52
F. Burt, 1891-92	J. S. Sharples, 1952-54
W. Connor, 1893-95	R. G. Jackson, 1954-56
F. Ryan, 1896-1903	Alvin Harrison, 1956-69
A. A. Bice, 1904-08	J. T. M. Swan, 1969-74
W. H. Hartley, 1909-13	J. R. Warner, 1974-78
John Morris, 1913-14	Gordon A. Reynolds, 1978-82
E. Hawkins, 1915	Paul F. Linklater, 1982-1988
E. Dymond, 1916-17	Harry A. Bryden, 1988-1992
F. G. Hardy, 1918-22	Edward Richmond, 1993
J. H. Whalen, 1923-26	

ST. PETER'S ROMAN CATHOLIC CHURCH

The first information on record of services with the Roman Catholics living in this area was in 1852 when Reverend Casper Matoga, a Jesuit missionary, visited Durham. He covered a vast area of the wilderness which was at that time being settled in this part of the Province, hence his visits were rather infrequent; but he continued to serve his people as best he could until his death in 1856. From then until 1863 Reverend Wil-

liam Blettner and Reverend George Laufhuher performed the missionary work here. After 1863 the Basilians stationed at Owen Sound provided spiritual ministration to their members in Durham until 1880.

It was during this time that the first Catholic Church was built. The History of the Catholic Church in Waterloo County, by Reverend Theobald Spetz, C.R., published in 1916, informs us that on March 1, 1857, the Diocese of Hamilton purchased Lot No. 5 on the east side of Albert Street, and that this parish was known in the early days as St. Philips. Today the homes of Norman Marshall and Ross Buchner occupy most of this lot. The *Durham Chronicle* reports that a log church was erected and opened on this location in 1867, and the same paper reports that fire consumed the church on July 4, 1870.

Nicholas Fagan.

"**Church Burned.**—The Catholic Church in this village, was consumed by fire between 1 and 2 a.m. on Monday 4th inst. It was undoubtedly the work of an incendiary as the church is entirely isolated, and there had been no service there for a week previous. We have been informed by Mr. Fagan that there was no insurance whatever on the premises. It is a great pity that such devilish deeds cannot be brought home to the guilty parties. It was the act of a cowardly, ignorant, low, miserable villain, and a man who is a living disgrace to humanity."

It appears that the Catholics in Durham worshipped in homes for many years. In 1880 a new parish was established consisting of St. Jerome's, Priceville, St. Peter's on the 8th Concession of Glenelg, Dundalk, Melancton and Durham. In 1890 Reverend Richard Maloney became pastor and many changes were made. Father Maloney moved his residence to Durham and lived in the white brick house on the south-east corner of Lambton and Countess Streets. A new church was erected in 1891 at Dundalk, and a new parish of Dundalk, Proton and Melancthon was established. Two years later St. Joseph's Church, Markdale, and St. John's Church, Glenelg, were built, and the churches at Priceville and Fardin's Corners were closed. Durham became a mission of St. Joseph's, Markdale.

Old Stone Roman Catholic Church.

In 1892 the Diocese of Hamilton purchased the old Hunter stone granary situated on ¼ acre of land just north of the British Hotel on Garafraxa Street North for $900 from Mrs. James H. Hunter. This stone building had a lower storey which was used as a granary and warehouse, and the second floor consisted of a large hall which was known for over 35 years as St. Andrew's Hall. This hall was then used as a Catholic Church, and in 1901 it underwent minor renovations. However, in 1921 the entire building received major renovations with the interior being gutted. The original building was constructed of fieldstones and during the renovations a limestone wall was built over the old exterior wall thus enhancing the beauty of the church. The October 21, 1921 *Durham Review* reports, "Clinging to the spot where for many years they have worshipped, the Roman Catholics decided to completely overhaul the building and on its strong walls and foundation erect a building in keeping with church

architecture. The side walls were lowered eight or ten feet, an entirely new much steeper roof was placed on them, and such parts of the gables left as would fit in with the roof. The front was carried up tower shape and surmounted with the emblematic stone cross. A beautiful rose window over six feet in diameter was installed over the doorway. It was the intention to erect a gallery at the west end, but this and the final seating, as well as finishing the basement, was not undertaken at that time."

In 1940 a house on the hill on the east side of Garafraxa Street, built by the late Arthur Jackson, was purchased for a rectory. St. Peter's received independent status in 1938, and St. Paul's, Dornoch, was attached to St. Peter's as a dependent mission. In 1945 a fire destroyed part of the church sanctuary. A new altar was purchased and new stations of the cross set up.

Fire again struck in 1971, and it was decided to erect a new church at the northern limits of Durham. This was a one-storey red brick edifice and it was consecrated in 1973 to St. Peter and St. Paul. The old stone church building was sold as a private residence. The parish wanted a rectory nearby, and in 1979 a rectory was built adjoining the church. As there was no basement under the church, there was need for a large meeting hall. A Parish Hall was constructed in 1984 a short distance north of the church, and this building is also used as a gymnasium by the pupils of the Roman Catholic Separate School. The Reverend Fathers who have served Durham mission and parish have been:

Reverends:

P.J. Cassin	John J. Feeney
Richard Maloney	C.O. Day
Fr. Hauck	Gordon Ryan
A. Walter	Thomas Mulhall
A.J. Savage	J.H. Higgins
T. Ferguson	A.J. Haes
J.J. Flahaven	G. Beck
J.S. McGoey	J. Van Rut
F.J. Hawkins	W.J. Hawkins
F.J. McHugh	P.J. Driscoll
Thomas Grace	Robt. C. Bulbrook
Thomas Doyle	Edward Mahony
Anthony O'Brien	John Stapleton, retired 1994

St. Peter's Roman Catholic Church.

FELLOWSHIP BAPTIST CHURCH

The first organizational meeting of Fellowship Baptist Church, Durham, was held on September 4, 1990, at the home of Mr. Percy James, R.R. 4, Durham. Eight families were present along with Dr. Timothy Starr and Reverend Thorold Marsaw from the Fellowship headquarters in Guelph. Pastor J. Swan, Lloyd Simpson and Harvey Sutton were appointed to look into finding a place to meet.

A founding meeting was held September 13 of the same year at the home of Mr. and Mrs. Harvey Sutton. Pastor Larry Bigelow, representing the Bluewater Association of Fellowship Baptist Churches, and Pastor Ted Molyneaux of Victory Fellowship Baptist Church in Hanover attended to assist the group in getting organized. Those interested in being founding members shared their personal testimonies to salvation and God's working in their lives. At this meeting Lloyd Simpson and Harvey Sutton were named as interim deacons.

The first worship service was held in the Durham Town Hall on September 16, 1990. It was led by Mr. Jim Swan, the new pastor. This was a service of praise for God's presence in the beginning of this fellowship of believers, and at this time hymn books were donated by Faith Baptist Church in Mount Forest. At a later date, an organ was donated by a Goderich church. A weekly Prayer and Bible Study Meeting started on September 26, 1990. Sunday School began September 30, and the first observance of the Lord's Supper was held on Sunday, October 7th. A weekly Ladies' Bible Study started soon after. The first Anniversary Service was held on September 22, 1991, with Reverend Jerry Vander Veen of Wingham as guest speaker.

TEMPERANCE SOCIETIES

During the 1870s very active Temperance Societies were organized in the Methodist, Baptist and Presbyterian churches. These societies may have been a result of a religious revival which took place in these churches during the late 1870s. In addition a Christian Temperance Union was formed which took in all interested residents. For a time weekly meetings were held in the old Orange Hall and at the close of these meetings entertainment was often provided by the members. There were well over 100 active members in this group and the organization was active for several years. The influence of these societies left its mark on the Town of Durham.

There were three other religious groups in Durham for short periods of time.

The **Bethel Pentecostal Church** was started in 1948, and in 1949 they purchased the old Queen Street Methodist Church. Services were held for a few years under the Reverends L. Milley, O. Wells, J.W. Morrison, R. Lyons and ? Crossman.

A **Pilgrim Holiness** congregation was organized in Durham in the 1950s, and a combined church and residence was built on Mill Street. After a few years this church closed.

The Reorganized Church of Jesus Christ of Latter Day Saints — A small group of people belonging to this faith was organized in 1956. They met in the library for twelve years, and when the Pilgrim Holiness Church became vacant in 1967, they purchased it for their meeting place. The congregation grew and prospered for a few years but then several families moved away, and the church was eventually closed in 1989. Some of the leaders were: James Jack, Elmer Jack, Ed Klein, Mr. and Mrs. Gordon Rydall and Clifford Dow.

THE REVIVAL OF 1877-1878

This account is excerpted from a diary kept by Glenelg resident, Thomas Binnie.

"The religious revival which took place in this district in the winter of 1877-78 seemed to occur spontaneously without effort or leadership. Constant prayers for many years had been that times of refreshing might come. Similar movements visited many other parts of Canada. Throughout the Protestant Christian world in the middle and latter part of the nineteenth century the great evangelistic work led by Moody and Sankey had borne far-reaching results. The revival was not limited to Durham but spread to many communities in the surrounding townships.

"In the fall of 1877 a young man from Kincardine, Mr. Grant held meetings in the Durham Baptist Church which were causing a stir in the community. I went in twice to his meetings and was well satisfied with what I saw. I believed it to be the real work of God. I felt most thankful. It seemed to be the beginning of what we had been praying for for a long time. I thought that Mr. Grant was well qualified to conduct such meetings. He seemed most deeply in earnest, pressing upon sinners to accept of a Saviour, and God was blessing his endeavours. Great numbers were going to these gatherings and souls were being saved.

"Mr. Wm. Scrimger from Galt came to assist with the meetings. He held a meeting the Sabbath afternoon in the Durham Methodist Church. I must say here how deeply obliged we were to Mr. Godfrey, the pastor of the congregation, and his people for opening his church for these meetings. Mr. Godfrey and his assistant, Mr. Baynon, had been holding meetings a few miles from Durham. After they finished at this location, they joined Mr. Scrimger in holding meetings each night in the Methodist Church which were well attended and blessed to the conversion of several persons. After the meetings were held in the church awhile, it was thought advisable to hold them in the Town Hall

as some people might come there who would not go to a church. A petition was signed by most of the ratepayers in the town asking for use of the hall and it was obtained by paying half the usual fee.

"These meetings were altogether unsectarian. They were attended by all parties, Episcopalians, Presbyterians, Methodists, and Baptists, Mr. Godfrey, Mr. Baynon, Mr. Stewart, and others helping to conduct them. Mr. Cranston and Mr. McLeish from Galt both came to Durham to take part in the meetings. Hundreds of people came to them every night some from a good distance. God's spirit was poured down upon the people.

"After awhile the meetings were again held in the Methodist Church conducted by Mr. Godfrey assisted by Mesrs. Baynon, Grier, Forman, Greig, Park and others. The blessed work still went on, several being anxious and a good number professing to have found peace in believing. I never saw such a time in my life. God's spirit seemed to be working among the people. Wherever meetings were held good was done. As to the actual results no man can tell. Eternity alone will disclose it."

CEMETERIES

In 1852 the Presbyterian Church received a ten acre grant of land for a church and cemetery site — the town's first cemetery. The parcel of land was west of Queen Street and south of the Durham Road West. There are no known burials in Durham prior to 1852, but it is quite possible there were some. Burials that took place before this date were on the private property where the deceased had lived. In some of these cases the remains of the deceased were reburied in the Presbyterian cemetery after 1852 when the cemetery was surveyed into plots and opened. The Presbyterian cemetery is the final resting place of many old pioneers, and this cemetery was used until about 1890 when it was closed.

The Presbyterian cemetery was neglected for 75 years and became overrun with weeds and brush. In 1965 this wild tangle was cut and cleaned up, the ground levelled and trees planted. A few years later all the headstones which were not too badly broken were gathered up and placed in cement as a memorial to the early pioneers. In Durham's early days a burial was a simple ceremony which laid the deceased to rest with dignity and at a very modest cost. The *Durham Chronicle* dated January 27, 1873, reported that "The Town paid for a funeral of one indigent resident: $9.00 for coffin, $1.75 for clothing, $1.00 for grave, plus an account owing by deceased of $3.50, for a total of $15.25."

A public meeting was held in 1887 at the Town Hall to ascertain if there was enough interest to organize a Cemetery Company. Mr. Gilbert McKechnie was chairman of the gathering, and a provisional board was set up consisting of eleven Durham businessmen. They decided to canvass the town to see whether

Chapel at Durham Cemetery.

enough capital could be raised to form a Cemetery Company. About a month later another meeting was called, and it was reported that the citizens of this community would give about $2,000 capital towards this project, and the first Cemetery Board was elected. The directors were: Dr. J. Gun, David Jackson, C.L. Grant, Thomas Lauder, J.H. Hunter, James Carson, John Brown and Henry Storrey. This board's first act was to purchase land north of the Durham Road immediately west of where the Saugeen River crosses it from Mr. Thomas Hutton. This property was surveyed into plots, walkways and roads and several hundred trees were planted. At this time many bodies were removed from the Presbyterian cemetery and reinterred.

At first plotholders were required to look after the maintenance of their plots. Many fulfilled this responsibility, but other graves either had no family to look after them, or the family neglected to do so. Eventually the Cemetery Board adopted a policy of perpetual care, and great improvements took place in the cemetery's appearance. In 1903 a pipeline was laid to bring water from the west hill springs to the cemetery, and at one time the Board built a house on the premises for a caretaker. This arrangement did not work out and the house was sold. Over the years the Durham cemetery has grown in area with land annexed to the west. In addition, a chapel was erected in 1948 which is used for winter burials. In February, 1971, the control of the Durham cemetery passed from the private company to the Town of Durham.

When the Edge Estate donated land in 1860 on which to build the Anglican Church, a parcel of land on the south-east corner of Kincardine Street North and the Durham Road was also donated for a cemetery. Why this property was never utilized as such is a mystery, but in 1867 the Church purchased a lot for a cemetery from Richard Collier on the Second Concession of Glenelg just north of the Durham Road. This is still in use today and is known as Trinity Anglican Cemetery. In 1844 Mr. and Mrs. Robert Edge immigrated from Ireland and took up land just north of Durham. The following year Mrs. Edge died. As there was no cemetery in the Durham area at that time, she was buried near the log house which had been erected the previous year, and after the opening of Trinity Cemetery, her remains were reinterred in the family plot there.

There is a Roman Catholic cemetery on the north side of the Durham Road just east of the Saugeen River. When this cemetery was established in 1918 on land donated by Frank Lenahan, some bodies were brought to this burying ground from the Dornoch cemetery.

All three cemeteries are well maintained in excellent condition, and are a credit to the community.

J. Hunter's House on Bruce Street
now McCulloch Funeral Home.

Scenic view looking North from
Lambton Street Bridge 1908.

Funeral Procession Main Street Durham circa 1905.

Transportation & Communication

4

Before the arrival of the railway the question of transportation was a vital one in the village of Durham. Teams travelled to Fergus with loads of grain and flour and returned with merchandise for the stores at a rate of 50 cents per 100 pounds. This high freight rate was one of the inducements which prompted Durham to support the acquisition of rail service. There was a pressing need for transportation of people and stage coaches were set up for this purpose.

An issue of the 1860 Durham Standard mentions commencement of stage coach service from Collingwood to Durham, and also that Hunter's had operated a stage coach line from Owen Sound to Hamilton starting in 1851. This may or may not be true as no other mention of this line has been found. It is known, however, that Middaugh and Cameron of Durham and J.P. Coulson of Owen Sound operated stages, giving daily service through Durham from Owen Sound to Fergus, and from Collingwood to Walkerton. Some of the drivers on these routes were: Ben Male, Charles Brown, Ben Warner and Lock Elvidge. This service ceased with the arrival of trains. In the heyday of trains there were for many years four trains in and out of Durham each day. By the mid twentieth century the train service was gone, but transportation was available by bus service — two buses a day each way. That service has now almost dried up due to the lack of passengers.

TELEGRAPH

In 1868 the Montreal Telegraph Company opened a telegraph office on the main street of Durham. This was a great asset to the town in that residents were able to have messages sent to, and received from, larger centres almost anywhere. With the arrival of the railroads, which had their own telegraph systems, competition made this enterprise unprofitable and around 1890 the Montreal Telegraph Company closed its office here.

WELLINGTON AND GEORGIAN BAY RAILWAY

In 1868 the Toronto Grey & Bruce Railway received a charter to build a railway from Toronto to Owen Sound. There were two reasons for building this rail line: Toronto wanted a line to a good harbour which would give them a direct line by ship to the Lakehead; they wanted a rail line through the good hardwood forests of Grey County so that they would have a supply of cheap fuel. The proposed rail line was to go through Orangeville, Arthur, Mount Forest, Durham, to Owen Sound. The promoters of this line approached all the municipalities along its route asking for large bonuses to assist in the building of the line. Each municipality wanted the railroad to go through its community, and there was some hesitation in approving some of the bonuses. The promoters contacted adjoining municipalities and advised them that if they came up with larger bonuses the route of the rail line could be changed. This is what happened, and the line went from Orangeville, Shelburne, Markdale, to Owen Sound, and was completed in 1873. Next the Toronto Grey & Bruce Railway built an east-west line from Orangeville, Arthur, Mount Forest, Teeswater, leaving Durham 15 miles from a rail line in two directions. All supplies and merchandise coming to Durham and all products going to other centres had to be teamed 15 miles, and this made transacting business in Durham very expensive.

An illustration of this was told over 50 years ago by Mr. W. R. Edge. He recalled how the early pioneers kept pigs for their own use or to sell for meat locally. There was no way in which they could be taken to the city markets alive (like cattle). After the railway came to Mount Forest, a new outlet for pork was developed. Farmers would have their sows farrow in very early spring. The pigs would grow in the summer and fatten in the fall and by December would dress out at 200 to 250 pounds. As soon as the weather turned very cold, the farmers would butcher all their pigs and hang the carcasses to freeze solid; the number could vary from five to 25 pigs. When they were frozen they were taken to Durham where any of four or five agents, usually storekeepers, would buy them. They would be piled on the plank sidewalk in front of the store maybe six feet high and across the width of the store. In the 1870s pork would be worth 5 to five and a half cents per pound. According to the 1883 Durham assessment roll, there were 70 male dogs and one bitch in town; in the 1870s it was probably the same. Many of these dogs would come along the street and try to tear a sliver of meat or fat off the carcass. They were usually unsuccessful because the carcasses were frozen solid. The dogs would then attempt to wash down the bottom carcasses and move on to repeat the process at the next pile. Mr. Edge recalled that it was a sickening sight but that was life in the early days.

One morning in early December 1879 a lady who lived at the south end of Durham reported that she counted 15 or 16 big sleigh loads of pork sides passing her residence on their way to the Mount Forest station where they would be shipped to Toronto.

Digging out snowbound Grand Trunk Train 1904.

Some progressive Durham businessmen realized that, if Durham was ever going to prosper and grow, a rail station would be necessary. No other railway was interested in building a branch line to Durham, so they began to investigate bringing a railway to Durham themselves. Several businessmen in Mount Forest were contacted to ascertain if they would be interested in joining the Durham group to build a rail line from Palmerston to Owen Sound. This meeting proved fruitful, and the Wellington Georgian Bay Railway Company was formed. The directors were: Messrs. Gilbert McKechnie, Geo. Jackson, H. Parker, A. C. McKenzie, Durham; James McMullen, John McLaren, Thos. Wilson, Thos. Martin, Mount Forest, and W. T. Petrie, Holstein.

This new company applied for a charter to build a rail line from Palmerston to Owen Sound and received the same in 1878, thus giving Durham and Mount Forest direct access for freight and passenger travel north to Owen Sound and south to London, Guelph, Hamilton and Toronto. It was decided to build the rail line in two parts — the first part was from Palmerston to Durham, and the second from Durham to Owen Sound. The directors immediately contacted all the local municipalities which would be benefitted by the line and all but Arthur Township responded favourably. The bonus from Durham was $25,000. The vote for the bonus was small with 93 in favour, none against.

The July 4th, 1878, *Durham Chronicle* states: "Too much praise cannot be given to Messrs. G. McKechnie and H. Parker for the ability and energy they have expended on promoting the Railroad."

In June, 1879, the annual meeting of the Wellington Georgian Bay Railway was held in Durham. The old board of directors was returned except for Thos. Martin, who wished to retire, and was replaced by Thos. Swan, Mount Forest. Mr. G. McKechnie was re-elected President; Mr. McMullen, Vice-President, and Mr. McKenzie, Secretary. At this time the contract for the section from Palmerston to Durham was let to Messrs. Frank Shanly & Co. of Toronto. In August of 1879 the men building the line to Durham went on strike. After three days off work they received an increase of twelve and one-half cents per day, which brought their total wages to one dollar and twelve and one-half cents per day.

The Wellington Georgian Bay Railway Company undertook only to build the rail line to Durham. It had made an agreement with the Grand Trunk Railway to operate trains on this line. All the company wanted was to ensure that Durham had train service, and it was not pursuing this project as a big money-making scheme.

When the surveyors finished with the first section of the track to Durham, they proceeded to survey the line to Owen Sound which they completed on December 12, 1879. This line went through the west of Durham to Concession 3 W. G. R. Bentinck, proceeding to Moore's Mill, Sullivan Township, passing close to Desboro and Keady, proceeding to the west side of Owen Sound Harbour, a total distance of 33 miles. Some grading was done north of Durham before the project was abandoned.

A bitter argument broke out about the location of the station. Lower Town wanted it west of Bruce Street and south of Lambton Street. Upper Town wanted it straight north of that location but near the Durham Road. Upper Town's glory days were beginning to wane and they lost the argument. Now that Durham was going to be a rail terminus, an engine house had to be erected and a turn-table built to turn the engine around.

On December 16th, 1880, the rails were completely laid to Durham, and in a simple ceremony J. H. Hunter, Esq., M.P.P., and W. E. McAlister, Esq., drove the last spike. Freight was shipped in and out of Durham, but it appears that passenger service did not begin until November, 1881. On November 7th, 1881, a special excursion train left Durham for a return trip to Stratford. About 800 passengers boarded the train from Durham and more got on along the way. Some ten hours later they returned to Durham where there was a grand celebration. From this time on there were two trains a day each way. Mr. George Blackburn, first engineer, James Lovelle, conductor, William Wood, conductor, and Ed. Melligan, brakeman, were all residents of Durham.

On April 1st, 1893, the Wellington Georgian Bay Railway was taken over completely by the Grand Trunk Railway and in 1923 the Grand Trunk Railway was amalgamated with the Canadian National Railway.

C.P.R. Water Tower and Station.

CANADIAN PACIFIC RAILWAY

Durham's second railway was started in 1904 when the Walkerton and Lucknow Railway Company received a Charter. It was constructed from Saugeen Junction through Durham and Hanover to Walkerton, and was built for the Canadian Pacific Railway. However, when the rail line was first surveyed in 1905, there were three serious concerns for the town: the surveyors' line ran through the corner of the Public Schoolhouse; the line would cross Garafraxa Street at the very foot of Durham Hill; and there was a row of houses on the north side of George Street which would have to be demolished or moved.

To deal with these concerns, the town contacted the Canadian Pacific Railway head office in Montreal and asked them to move the line away from the school property. Canadian Pacific officials refused, but the town officials seemed unconcerned, possibly because they thought that if the school was torn down the railway would be responsible for building a new one. In the end the railway moved the line to avoid the school building, but took part of the school yard.

A level train crossing on Garafraxa Street at the very foot of the Durham hill posed a very real safety problem. Council wanted the railway to build a tunnel through the hill just north of the present library. The railway argued that a tunnel would be too expensive as it would cost $200,000. However, Council argued that at the wages they were paying their men this amount of money would hire 200 men for 1,000 days. Nevertheless, the company offered only to install a safety gate at the crossing which would be opened and closed manually by a railroad employee. Although Council accepted this, what they finally got was an automatic bell at the crossing.

The railway moved the row of houses north of George Street and west of Garafraxa Street. Most were frame and these were moved fairly easily onto other foundations at other sites, but there were two two-storey houses — one brick veneer amd the other solid brick which had to be moved. This was accomplished without disturbing the furniture, breaking a dish, or cracking the plaster. Even the clock did not stop ticking.

C.P.R. Station circa 1930.

C.P.R. train crossing the Saugeen River bringing in ties and other building supplies 1907.

A C.P.R. train station was built north of George Street between Countess Street and Bruce Street and a water tank was erected west of Garafraxa Street to supply the steam trains with water. In 1908 this railway had two passenger trains a day each way and freight trains as required. A few years later the Canadian National Railway and the Canadian Pacific Railway ran up to six trains daily each way. With the Grand Trunk Railway this meant that Durham had four passenger trains daily each way. Indeed, when the Grand Trunk Railway first came to Durham in 1882 it was a popular outing in the summer for townspeople to stroll to the station in the evenings and wait for the train to arrive in order to check on incoming passengers and watch the freight being unloaded. Not surprisingly, the station was a popular meeting place!

For a time the National Portland Cement Company, The Durham Furniture Factory, and the thousands of carloads of sand and gravel, in addition to passengers, kept these trains busy. But with the advent of cars and trucks, the business diminished and in 1970 the Canadian Pacific Railway station building was sold and moved to Townsend Lake and in 1971 the Canadian National Railway building was moved to Mulock Road. Since then the rail tracks have been lifted and the era of the trains has passed.

TRAIN EXCURSIONS

After the arrival of the railway in Durham in 1882, there were many excursions to such places as Niagara Falls, the Experimental Farm at Guelph, and other locations of interest. For instance, a 12 day excursion to St. Anne de Beaupre, Quebec, with stopovers in Montreal and Toronto, was $10.50. On excursions a dining car was attached serving sandwiches, tea and coffee, and other refreshments at a very modest charge.

Railroad workers — Jack Gibson, Jack Teeter, Ray Eastman (Station Agent) 1943.

Building C.P.R. line at Durham Public School.

For many years (possibly 50 or 60) the railways ran excursions to western Canada in the autumn for farm labourers to assist in harvesting the western grain crop. Several men went from this area every year; the return fare was $10. The coaches were the oldest ones in service and very uncomfortable; the seats were slatted wood and sleeping in the crowded seats was impossible. Travellers were told to take their lunches with them as the only food available en route was at divisional stopping points where the train halted for twenty minutes. Those travelling on excursions from the town of Durham in 1899 were: Ewing Buchan, Wm. Willis, Jas. Willis, Chas. Scotland, Thos. Storrey, plus several times this number from the surrounding townships.

Train crossing Garafraxa Street 1908.

The Velocipede (three-wheeled hand car).

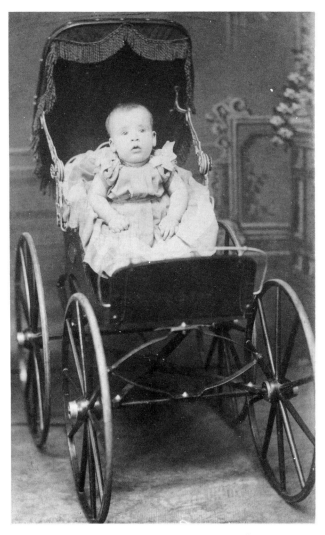

Lewis Saunders, uncle of Mrs. Iva Hutchinson,
in baby buggy circa 1880.

Baby Sleigh 1935.

Dr. Ed. Lauder and father, Thos. Lauder.

The Go-Devil (motorized bike).

DURHAM'S FIRST TELEPHONE SYSTEM

Preserved in the Bell Telephone museum in Montreal is the listing of every subscriber in Ontario. Here from December 1891 in a small pocket-size book is Durham's listing of 26 subscribers.

When in 1890 news broke about the installation of a telephone exchange in Laidlaw's store, excited people came from all over to glimpse this controversial contraption that, many people felt, would never be sufficiently improved to be of any use whatsoever. To many people it was nothing more than a fad and the butt of many jokes.

However, merchants and professional people of that day were willing to take a chance in the sincere hope that their faith in Alexander Graham Bell's invention in 1875 would one day become an indispensable instrument in bridging the distances between villages and towns and improving business and social life within the community of Durham.

Initially, Mr. Laidlaw combined the duties of his general store with operating the small switchboard. Visions of his helpers seated on a high stool, dressed in gored skirts and leg-of-mutton sleeves come to mind as the office hours were extended and the subscribers' lists grew. Perhaps the reader may recognize his or her relatives' names in this Directory of 1891:

Telephone Directory
Central Office — Garafraxa Street
Open 8 a.m. to 8 p.m. week days; 1 to 4 p.m.
Sundays; 10 to 12 a.m. and 2 to 4 p.m. holidays
Wm. Laidlaw, Manager.

Burnett, William, Merchant
Calder, William,
    Implement Agent
Caldwell, William, Liveryman
Crawford, W.J., Millman
Grand Trunk Railway Station
Gun, Dr. J., Medical Doctor
Halley, Nicholas, Bakery
Holmwood, Walter,
    Hotelkeeper
Holt, T.G., Dentist
Hunter, James A., Merchant
Jackson, David, Conveyancer
Jamieson, Dr. David Sparling,
Kelly, John, Agent,
    Standard Bank
Knapp, Conrad, McAlister House

Kress, Edward, Liveryman
Laidlaw, William, General Store
Mitchell, W.J., Editor
    "Chronicle"
McArthur, Charles, Editor
    "The Review"
McFarlane & Co., Druggists
McKechnie Bros.,
    General Merchants
McKechnie, John, Miller
McClocklin, Ed, Butcher
Parker, Henry, Druggist
Sparling, George, Grain Buyer
Stewart, W.F., Miller
Telford, J.P., Lawyer

In 1891 the Durham council passed a by-law to spend $100 for poles to carry the Bell telephone long distance wires through town. At that time the line ran from Mount Forest to Flesherton. As early as 1893 long distance lines extended from Flesherton to Stratford via Priceville, Durham, Holstein, Mount Forest, Harriston, Palmerston, Gowanstown, Listowel, Newton, Poole and Gads Hill. Over the years the Bell telephone office was located at four different sites. In 1912 it was installed next to Whitmore's Barber Shop, then it moved to Lambton Street West at two different locations. The final location was Lambton Street East in part of the Hunter Building behind the Royal Bank, which is now the Triangle Discount Store. The entrance was at the doors facing Lambton Street East. Here it remained until 1963 when the manual switchboards were replaced by automatic switching.

In 1929 a destructive fire swept through the McIntyre block in which the exchange was then located and made necessary the final move. Ten business establishments, three apartments, plus the Canadian Bank of Commerce, lay in smouldering ruins. On that night of October 24th, Thomas Saunders, a longtime manager and night operator, became a hero. Refusing to leave his switchboard, he remained in the smoke-filled office sending and receiving messages from nearby fire departments who quickly came to Durham's aid from Hanover, Mount Forest and Owen Sound. Mr. Saunders, a partial invalid, arrived by horse and buggy driven by local young men of the town each night and returned to his home in the early morning in the same way. Although not at the switchboard he remained paymaster until 1937 when Miss Barbara Ritchie took over the position of manager and chief operator.

Switchboard — Phyllis Dickson, Beatrice Aljoe, 1963.

First Telephones — The first telephones consisted of three boxes mounted on a backboard which was then hung on a wall. The *upper box* held the receiver and the magneto generator. The *middle box* had a hole in it for the mouthpiece. Here the subscriber shouted the message in the hope that he or she might be heard over the constant buzzing and crackling sounds as the current travelled along the galvanized iron lines. This instrument was called the old "Blake" telephone. The *bottom box* contained a battery for the talking current.

Mayor Frank Irwin making the first long distance telephone call from Durham on the dial system.

The next model of telephone was more compact, although the operator at the switchboard was still signalled by a hefty turn on the crank at the right side of the box. This activated a metal disk that fell near the entrance of the subscriber's number on the magneto switchboard multiple.

An operator was kept very busy in those days and a visit to the office to pay one's telephone bill proved that point. While operating the board with the left hand, the bills were stamped and the proper change given with the right hand — all with a smile and a nod.

On November 6, 1947 the Common Battery System was installed. With this system a caller had only to lift the receiver to notify the operator. By this time there were 1,300 Durham customers and the directory listings were growing by leaps and bounds. Two operators worked the switchboard and at times they stood at their work while their arms and fingers flew to ensure that people did not long remain on hold waiting for the operator's response. It was at these moments that the operators wished for the numerous arms of an octopus! The office was closed to the public and the accounts were no longer payable at the counter. Pay phones were also installed at various locations in and on the outskirts of town.

Fire Calls — All emergency fire alarm calls were also handled by the operators on duty, who then alerted the fire department. The switchboard operators could be relied upon to assist in any emergency or time of trouble, day and night. Over the years the fire signals were activated by the operators.

Remembering — In winter it was the operators' responsibility to keep the fire in the stove in the corner of the room from going out. The linemen of the day welcomed the chance to sit close to that old stove and warm their cold feet when they came in from repairing rural lines. These men somehow managed to get the work done through all kinds of weather, but sometimes when the Bell Telephone truck could not make it through the drifts for the complete journey, a farmer came to their rescue with horse and sleigh.

Night Duty — (9 p.m. - 8 a.m.)

Phyllis Dickson tells of a night to be remembered when a blizzard was raging and the old Bell Telephone sign was nearly blowing off its hinges: "Seated at the board at 3.30 a.m., a definite thumping of approaching footsteps came from the anteroom. Fear rose up from my toes — the door squeaked open, and in walked a bearded man with a cane. His coat was all covered with snow, and as he shook the snow from his fur hat he exclaimed "You should have a light on out there, young lady." Normally the entrance was used only by the linemen and rarely lit at night. Some busy lineman had forgotten to check the lock when he had left that day. On that occasion a quick call to the police gave this stranded motorist a cosy temporary bed for the night and this writer a reduced pulse rate. Another incident was the night a bat kept flying over my head and insisted on a perch on the top of the board. When morning came, we still had not made friends!

Bell Telephone service truck.

End of an Era — In September, 1963, Miss Barbara Ritchie officially retired from the Durham Telephone office. Presentation of recognition was made to her, and to Mrs. Mae Lawrence who, after 21 years' service, also retired.

Mrs. Ruby Sheach had previously transferred to Guelph and Miss Beatrice Aljoe, at the closure of the Durham office, transferred to Walkerton. Through the years and, during the war years, other operators found it necessary to relocate so they too gained additional experience in larger centres. While the change to the dial system was a positive one, it is hoped that the readers will fondly recollect the days of the reliable servant known as the voice with a smile.

The November day in 1963 on which President Kennedy of the United States was assassinated will be long remembered by the three operators on duty. On that day the operators handled over 8,900 calls.

Some of the linemen over the years have been: Art Forbes, Mac Graham, George Tomlin, John Baxter, ? Wellwood, Curley Wade, Don Corbett and Ross Taylor.

"The Operators" Bell Telephone Staff 1963.
Phyllis Dickson, Catherine Brown, Ruby Sheach, Betty Clark,
Barbara Ritchie, Margaret Baker, Beatrice Aljoe,
Evelyn Patterson, Mae Lawrence.

In 1892 N.G. and J. McKechnie, assisted by Dr. Campbell Park, built a telephone line from Durham up the Second Concession of Glenelg to the Glenroadin Mills owned by McKechnies. They installed a telephone in Dan Greenwood's home, Lot 45, Concession 3 E.G.R., as a convenience to the community in order that people could call a doctor without going all the way to Durham. Soon after this Dr. David Jamieson and W.J. Crawford erected a telephone line north of Durham on the Garafraxa road to Morden's Corner. The line ran west to Crawford's mill on Concession 2, W.G.R. at Aberdeen, and east to James Edge's house, Lot 44, Concession 2 E.G.R., in order that Dr. Jamieson would not lose patients to Dr. Park. These lines lasted about ten years, then fell into disrepair.

NEWSPAPERS

The earliest newspaper in Durham was the *Durham Standard* and *County of Grey General Advertiser*. The first issue was February 19, 1857, and the editor was S.L.M. Luke. One curious feature of this newspaper was the willingness of Luke to accept payment in produce. The following advertisements appeared in the January 18, 1861, issue:

CORDWOOD
"Parties intending to pay their subscription to the Standard in Wood, will require to deliver the same before the 18th of next January. All kinds of Merchantable farm produce taken in payment of accounts. P.S. Don't bring in such knotty logs that the devil himself can't split them."

VALENTINES
A choice selection of Valentines for Sale at this office. Apply early."

As an editor Luke was capable of ruffling town feathers. *The Durham Chronicle*, June 12, 1942, reports:

"During the early days of the Durham Standard, the editor, S.L.M. Luke, published something that infuriated some of his readers to such an extent that they over-ran the printing plant, grabbed the press and threw it in the Saugeen River. Fortunately Luke himself was unharmed — and even more important, undaunted — and soon resumed publication."

Ramage Review Office circa 1890.

The paper was Conservative and Orangeist in outlook. In 1866 Messrs. White and Johnson took over the *Standard*, and the following year changed the name to the *Durham Chronicle* and *County of Grey Advertiser*. The paper continued, as had its predecessor, to publish weekly as it still does today. Throughout this paper's history it underwent various changes in editorship, but by 1870 Johnson was running the publication by himself. Shortly afterwards A.H.N. Jenkins became editor until 1887 when he sold the paper to W.J. Mitchell. The character of the paper had followed that of the *Standard*; it was Moderate Conservative but quite anti-George Brown.

In 1896 William Irwin purchased the paper and became its editor and proprietor. When Mr. Irwin died in 1925 his son, Frank Irwin, took over the business until 1950. During these years the *Chronicle* had expressed very strong Conservative views. George Cadogan became owner-editor in 1950 and remained in this position until 1960.

In the January 7, 1954, *Durham Chronicle*, George Cadogan writes, "newspapers are like women. They have forms, back numbers are on the shelf. They have the last word, a good one is worth looking at, you can't

Setting linotype at the Durham Chronicle 1923.
Frank Irwin, Essie (Firth) Hamilton, John Stedman.

believe everything they say, few like the bold type, they're thinner than they were, and every man should have one and not borrow his neighbour's."

George Cadogan sold the newspaper in 1960 to William J. Kennedy, who in turn became editor and publisher until 1987 when he sold the business to Southam News Inc.

Over the years the method of producing newspapers changed substantially from selecting individual letters set in a bed to form a line and when the bed was full the type could be inked and a sheet of paper pressed on top of it. Later came the linotype machine, which was somewhat like a typewriter as it pressed the letters into hot lead one line at a time. They were placed in a bed and underwent the same basic method of printing as before. Today newspapers are printed automatically by an electronic process.

Another paper established in Durham was the *Grey Review*, appearing in 1878 under the ownership of Joseph Townsend. Townsend was obsessed with hunting fossils and his obsession interfered with his business to such an extent that he found it necessary to sell the paper. His brother Benjamin took it over, and around 1885 sold it to Charles McArthur, who in turn sold it to Charles Ramage in 1894. Two years later

Charles Ramage changed the name of the paper to the *Durham Review* and he took his son Peter into partnership with him. The newspaper remained in the Ramage family until it was liquidated in 1942. The *Durham Review* was Liberal in its political views and supportive of community endeavours.

THE CITIZEN NEWSPAPERS

In 1990 Durham resident, Geo. Benninger, began a local tongue in cheek newspaper called the *Durham Crocodile*. It was meant to be an alternative to the local *Durham Chronicle* which had recently been purchased by media giant Southam News.

However, it soon became apparent that people did want a serious alternative as the monopoly enjoyed by the *Chronicle* was felt to be gouging in price and lacked news concerning local businesses.

Thus the *Citizen* was born. In two years the paper grew to four local newspapers covering four areas of Grey-Bruce and these papers were soon actually competing for both readership and revenue.

In August, 1993, the newspapers were sold to a local business. However, with change of management and

Chronicle Office.
Essie (Firth) Hamilton, John Stedman, Frank Irwin, 1923.

the recession, the newspapers were closed in January, 1993. The former owner, with three other local investors, tried to resurrect the *Citizen*, but with the recession still on, and what is believed to be unfair business practices of the local Southam chain, the *Citizen* newspapers were closed permanently in January, 1994, laying off 26 people.

To this day comments are still heard that it's too bad the *Citizen* is not still being published as it had surpassed other papers in advertising benefits, value, and readership.

★ ★ ★ ★ ★ ★

In 1934 when the *Owen Sound Sun Times* was planning the 80th anniversary of the newspaper, an historical edition of *Grey County* was included, and Mr. Joseph T. Clarke, Editor-in-Chief of the *Toronto Daily Star*, was asked to write about some of his experiences when he was learning his trade at the *Grey Review*. The following article appeared in that historical edition dated June 14, 1934:

"On the 12th of May, 1880 — that is to say 54 years ago — I left Flesherton and went over to Durham to learn the art of printing in the office of the Grey Review of which Joseph Townsend was editor and publisher. It was agreed that I should spend four years there as an apprentice learning the art of printing, getting my board and lodgings with the Townsend family and drawing $20 the first year, $30 the second, $40 the third and $60 the fourth. In the middle of the third year, Mr. Townsend went to Toronto and got me a job as a typesetter with C. Blankett Robinson on Jordan Street. So in the autumn of 1882 I left the county.

"Anyone who knew Durham in the early eighties will recall the mob fights that occurred between the boys of the upper town and lower town. As carrier boy

for the upper town paper I had to go through all parts of the lower town once a week and my progress was often contested. They say that Primo Carnera, the heavy-weight champion, steps on the feet of his opponent in a fight. He learned this from me. In a fight down town with Stoughton-bottle Vollett in 1880, he being much larger, but I having boots on and he being in his bare feet, I was so awkward that every time we clashed I was standing on one of his feet. He complained of this and I suggested that he go home and get his boots on and I would wait until he got back. I saw the house he went into and decided that if I rushed away he would see me out of the window, would hurry on his boots and get after me. So I sat down, read the Grey Review, and Vollett, if he was looking out the window which he probably was, was saying: "Golly, he is waiting for me." So after waiting a reasonable length of time, I, apparently with reluctance, went on delivering papers. But once around the corner, didn't I hurry! Vollett and I were good friends after that.

"It is a curious fact that in looking back over my life I get more pleasure in thinking of the things I should not have done than in contemplating such worthy deeds as I may have had a hand in. This must be due to some flaw in my nature and when I grow old and feeble I hope to repent of it. One morning, for instance, in the summer of 1881, I came out from breakfast in the kitchen behind the Grey Review office and found I had five minutes before starting work at seven o'clock. What a morning! And yet within a few minutes I would have to go back in and begin ten hours work. Across the road was Thomas Donaghy's photograph gallery, and incongruously, a board was nailed against one door post announcing "Cash paid for Butter and Eggs." This did not seem right to me.

"South of our printing office was McFarlane's blacksmith shop and at the moment Archie McFarlane came along burling a hoop. I called him. "Archie," said I "you see that sign over there. I was going to take it off and hand it in to Mrs. Donaghy — it's a nuisance, people coming in with butter and eggs. You take it off and hand it in to her — tell her I've got to go to work because it's seven o'clock." "Sure," said Archie. So I went in and watched developments through the big window. Archie went at the sign for all he was worth but pull and haul as he best could, he could not wrench it free, but with that resolution which in after life made him a successful banker, he would not give in. He got a big stick from the roadside and pried it off, but at that very moment Mr. Donaghy, red whiskers bristling, came tearing out. Archie perceiving that something had gone wrong ran towards where I had been with the indignant photographer after him, and at every jump making a kick at him. Dave McFarlane, the big brother of Archie, had just finished breakfast and strolling to the door of his blacksmith shop looked up street a hundred yards and saw a red-whiskered photographer chasing his little brother and trying to

Ramage Family
? , Mrs. Charles Ramage, ? , Peter Ramage, Charles Ramage
holding Arthur on knee, ? , Alice standing beside mother.

kick the child. Dave gave no sound but he ran. Mr. Donaghy saw a streak coming for him and sensed the rest. He headed for home, but at every jump Dave was trying to land a kick on him. The photographer safely reached his own door, and once inside slammed it shut. Dave yelled to him that if he wanted to kick a McFarlane to come on out. Here was a full-sized McFarlane to kick at. Mr. Donaghy opened the door wide enough to tell him that Archie had come over and with a big stick had pried the sign off his shop right in front of his own eyes. When the explanations started I began setting type for all I was worth. Dave called Archie who said he was only doing it to oblige Mrs. Donaghy, that Joe Clark was going to take off the sign and hand it in but he had to go to work at seven and had asked him to do it. "Oh, he did, did he?" said Dave and he came over, entered the office, caught me by the collar and said things to me. But after all, somehow, although I admit it was most reprehensible on my part and all that sort of thing, I cannot recall any success in my career which topped the excitement of those few moments. Far better, it was, than a cycle of Cathay.

"For fifty years I have meant to say something about one of the kindliest, one of the most notable men of Grey County — Joseph Townsend. He was editor of the Grey Review. He was a small, humble sort of man. He was an editor but not really a writer. Yet he was an extraordinary man, a born geologist. He hunted fossils. In the little printing office in Durham he had fossils by the thousands and Sir William Dawson sent a man up from Montreal to look the collection over and I was present at the interview. There was a fossil there which nobody had ever found in our rock formation except this country editor, and Dawson considered the finding of it of great significance, had named it the Townsendi and it is so named and ever will be. Some of the Townsend fossils are in the geological survey at Ottawa, many of them at the University of Toronto. In later years when his devotion to fossils had cost him his newspaper and he was again a printer in the Methodist Book Room in Toronto, somebody in the federal government offered him a chance at his own request to go on foot at an allowance of $30 a month across the prairie provinces and report upon such rock formations as he should encounter. He spent two summers with hammer and chisel, happy as a child, sleeping where night found him, seeking the testimony of the rocks and making reports to some central bureau. Mr. Townsend was no hero to me when I was an apprentice in his office. Fifty years later I would like to pay tribute to this kind, childish, simple genius of a man and to say of him that I count him among the great men I have known.

"In the early eighties Mr. Townsend used to steal off to hunt fossils the way some men nowadays steal off for a game of golf — to see a ball game or to catch trout. He would decide to go to the post office downtown for the mail. His brother Ben was foreman and he would tell him not to stay anywhere as it was going to be a busy day. He would fairly rush away to show how fast he could be about it. An hour would go by and then a half hour. Ben would come to me. "Go down to the stone quarry and get the mail off him. Tell him to come at once. If you can get hold of his hammer or chisel, grab it and run." At the quarry I would find him, with hammer and chisel trying to liberate a trilobite without losing a particle of it. "I've been sent for you," I would tell him. "What!" he would demand. "Ben says for me to get the mail from you." "There it is." he would say. "But, "I would add, "he says I am to bring you back with me." What's this," he would demand. "Return to the office at once," he would say. "Ben said," I would add, "that I was to steal your hammer or chisel so that you could not go on." "That settles it," he would say, picking up his tools, "I've got to go up and give Ben a piece of my mind — turning the staff against me." And he would hustle back up the hill to the office so fast that I could not keep up to him without running. I did not want to miss his furious impact against Ben. But when he got there he never said a word, but rolled up his sleeves and pitched in.

"Do you remember that day in 1881 when midnight fell upon the County of Grey shortly after the noon hour? About noon the air took on an unholy color — a brown air filled land and sky. By 2 o'clock all was dark, by 3 a darkness exceeding the blackest midnight prevailed. A coal oil lamp in a window shed no ray. At 3 in the afternoon every lamp we had in the Grey Review office was alight and I found my way across the street to the sidewalk opposite and could not see a light to guide my return. Men said afterwards when the astonishing affair was ascribed to bush fires in Michigan, that they smelt smoke and noticed ashes in the air, but I have to testify that when Durham lay down that night, fearing the worst, nobody had to my knowledge mentioned either smoke or ashes. In every mind was one thought. Mother Shipton had made her prophecy "In 1881 the world unto an end shall come." Here we were looking at it, waiting for it. As for myself, I know my feeling was that the whole thing was rotten — the world coming to an end and me not yet fifteen! I fell asleep with my clothes on. I do not know how late it was and woke up in broad daylight to see Mr. Ander-

son's chickens scratching the good old earth for worms and getting them.

"In my two and a half years in Durham I seem to have learned something every day. One night I got into a fight with a boy without knowing who he was. It turned out to be Paddy Burns, and he made the assertion after the affair was over that his brother Henry could lick me. In that moment of elation I declared that no Burns could do it. On the following Sunday I learned that no matter how many Burns you conquer there is always another Burns yet who can do you in. Another thing I learned that Sunday is that the idea that you can cure a black eye by lying at a running spring for two hours with your eye under water is all wrong. There is nothing in it. It only makes the black eye shine brighter in the Sunday sun, and in the Monday and Tuesday sun, I learned a whole lot that day which was eventually useful to me in life.

"One night Mr. Townsend was looking at his fossils and when so engaged he was oblivious to time. On coming upstairs at 2 a.m., he entered the room where I slept. He was carrying a lamp in his hand and for some reason walked over to my lamp and felt the glass. He burnt his hand, and the chimney fell off his lamp and broke. By this time I had to admit I was awake although I had been putting on what I thought was a really good slumber scene. Two books of fiction from the Durham library I had been reading each week —Charles Lever, Samuel Lover, Dickens, G. P. R. Grant — but one evening Dr. Gunn was in the library when I called and he took me in hand. He told me to read only one book of fiction each week and one book of poetry or biography. He examined the shelves the better to prescribe for me. "Paradise Lost," he said, "No, too profound, too profound." Shakespeare he decided against. "Too soon, not yet. Mrs. Hemand, the very thing." And it was. I revelled in it. A week later I was bathing in Tom Moore. I became a sort of sun worshipper on reading Lalla Rookh. I could ramble on and on but who wants to read this kind of stuff? As the small boy said of pudding: "It is all right such as it is, and such as it is, there's plenty of it.""

The following is part of a letter written by John D. Bonner of Hobart, Indiana, in reply to the invitation he received to attend the 1935 Durham Old Home Week.

"It was at least forty-five years ago or more one bright May day that I entered the old Durham Chronicle as an apprentice under Mr. Jenkins, one of the finest writers in all Canada, and who was familiarly known as Arthur Henry Newton (gasbag) Jenkins by his enemies who seem to have been many. But it was a great joy to us all to read the comeback editorials he would write in answer to their jibes, and after a few weeks they were quite willing to give up the argument.

Frances (Black) Lauder and mother circa 1890.

Early car in Durham.

Means of Travel, Team and Democrat.

But tiring of this he sold the plant — consisting of one old Washington press, one 10 x 15 without throwoff and a slew of cases of type and other equipment more or less good bad and indifferent.

"We worked long hours each day and it was my job to get in and pile the wood in a neat pile near the two stoves, and it took plenty as the old frame building stood on stilts in the low land near the creek [east side of Garafraxa Street south of Brown's rink]. One year in particular I remember I piled up and carried in over 65 cords besides lighting fires early in the morning, sweeping and dusting, running errands, taking the papers over the river to the post office and delivering the downtown district. On New Year's we delivered a New Year's greeting to our subscribers and got several dollars as a present for work well done or the simple generosity of the public.

"We put in three years in the Chronicle and six months on the Grey Review. Many funny incidents occurred in these offices. One in particular stands out. The office bought ink in large barrels and when empty they were rolled out by the back door of the Review, where in the course of time, they filled with water from the eavestrough and caused a scum of ink to rise to the top of the water. One of the young girls working in the office was an awful tease and one day was particularly devilish and had been told to cut out the fun or she would be stood in the old water barrel just at the back door. She didn't think any one would do it, but she was mistaken for Mr. Townsend grabbed her up, carried her outside setting her down in the ink barrel, shut the door and went back to his work. She stood there screaming and we finally had to overturn the barrel — when she finally crawled out she was one sight, believe me. She went home and in a few days the editor bought her a new outfit.

"During the summer it was my job to go down to the butter factory and get a nickle's worth (5 cent silver) of buttermilk, 10 quarts or more twice a day, and, oh boy, it was good.

"I was at the Chronicle when the great ice rink was built next door and it was one of the most wonderful places I had seen up to that time. The opening night was glorious. The place was decorated, the band playing and the whole town practically in holiday attire. Old Mr. Rombough, I remember, came down and looked it over remarking that he thought he would go home and get his skates and try it out. Some of the boys gave him the laugh, but when he came back and put on his old fashioned skates, a few minutes after he got his stride he put us all to shame for he was a star; he did all the fancy stunts and a few others we had never thought of. He was the hero that night.

"It was about the same year that the new gristmill was built up near the old woollen mill and Falls on the river east of town, and they put in a dynamo and wired the town for electric lights. Arc lights were the only kind of lights at that time. The town went wild that night when the juice was turned on, with crowds passing up and down the street looking into the store windows in wonder and awe.

"We played cricket, football, and some baseball in those days but lacrosse seemed to be the favourite game and was played on the old fair grounds. Across from the fair grounds the chief of police had a ten-acre field in which he kept his horse. We would open the gate, go and lead the horse out and close the gate. Next morning he would have a long hunt for Mr. Horse, and I heard him tell Mr. Todd he couldn't figure out how his horse could jump out of the field. He blamed Steve and I for nearly everything that happened in that part of town but was about half wrong most of the time.

"I worked for a short time in Upper Town at Sparling's packing plant and it was my job to pick out the rotten eggs from the crates as they were laid out on the benches in the yard to dry where they had been brought from the big vats of brine in the basement. This yard had a high board fence around it and a big gate. It was our delight to coax dogs in and close the gate and then pepper them with rotten eggs. One day we coaxed the druggist's little dog in and gave him the works. We opened the gate and he went across the street pell mell into the drugstore where the proprietor was busy waiting on one of the high brow ladies of the community. Talk about a madman! But in a few days he got so that he could laugh over the incident.

"The merhants used to make a fashion of dumping refuse in the sawdust piles along the tail race of the sawmill, and one merchant who had put up a few barrels of eggs in the fall before, in order to cash in on the high spring prices, found that a couple of these barrels had gone bad on him. So he dumped them out on the sawdust where very few were broken. The gang coming back from down river swimming spied the eggs, sent the smallest boys home for baskets, picked out the best looking eggs and took them to town, selling them to this same dealer. Suffice to say, we had all the candy and other luxuries imaginable for the next few weeks. The next time that dealer had reason to dump eggs he made sure they were all broken."

FRANK IRWIN

Frank Irwin was born in Bath, Frontenac County, in 1881, a son of Mr. and Mrs. William Irwin. His father was a schoolteacher and later he moved to Flesherton where he taught for 11 years before buying the *Durham Chronicle* from W.J. Mitchell. At the age of 16 Frank went to the United States and joined the Buffalo Bill Show, travelling across the U.S. with the show. In 1898 he joined the Walter L. Mains circus. The next year, with the outbreak of the Spanish-American War, Frank enlisted in the 19th U.S. Infantry and went through the campaign in the Philippines that year and then went into the 29th Infantry. After spending over two and a half years in the U.S. Army in the Philippines, he was sent to the Quartermaster's Department to drive mules on Cebu Island. He returned to the United States in 1903.

In the United States, Frank worked at a number of occupations. He worked in road construction, helping build the first dirt road to Hollywood, a village about the size of Holstein at that time. He also spent six years as a publicist for the Ringling Brothers circus. He was a deep sea sailor, worked in the coal mines in West Virginia and in the oil industry before returning to Durham and joining his father at the *Chronicle*.

(Above information was taken from August 3, 1946, *Owen Sound Daily Sun Times*.)

At his father's death in 1924 Frank took over as owner and editor of the *Chronicle*. He was a staunch Conservative and usually expressed strong opinions on public issues in his newspaper. In 1950 he sold the Chronicle to George Cadogan. During his retirement years he became Mayor of Durham for three years and in 1967 he received the Centennial Medal for over fifty years of service to the community in the weekly newspaper business. In his retirement years he remained interested in, and supportive of, many community activities. He was married in 1911 to Katharine McDonald of Durham. Frank Irwin died in 1973.

CHARLES RAMAGE

Charles Ramage was Editor of the *Durham Review* for over 35 years. He was born in Scotland, and at the age of 13 he entered the printing business as an apprentice. In 1867 his family emigrated to Canada and settled on a farm in Egremont Township where he worked with them for a few years. He was anxious to improve his schooling and began studying for his Third Class Certificate which he obtained in Owen Sound in 1876. He then attended the Durham Model School and received his certificate as a public school teacher, which is good for three years. He completed his secondary education at Collingwood Collegiate and the next year entered the Toronto Normal School. He taught school for ten years, the last two of those years in Durham and taught commercial work and drawing to large night classes in Durham.

In 1894 Mr. Ramage bought the *Grey Review* and changed the name to *Durham Review*. He was a quiet, public-spirited man. On perusal of the Durham papers during Mr. Ramage's years here, one rarely finds him to be Chairman of any group trying to improve the town. If you read about the activities of such a group, you would usually find him working hard doing the ground work which is so essential to the success of any project. His philosophy seemed to be "it is more important to achieve something than to get credit for achieving it." Some organizations in which he was very active were: member of Public and High School Boards for over 30 years; Secretary of Public Library for 36 years; Secretary of Ben Nevis Camp, Sons of Scotland for 40 years; Clerk of 2nd Division Court for 15 years; but it was in the Presbyterian and Knox United Churches that he was best known. In 1914 he contested South Grey as a Temperance and Liberal candidate. He died in 1936 at the age of 87.

JOHN BAYNE MacLEAN

Sometime around 1870 Mrs. Catherine MacLean, a widow, came to Durham from Crieff with her young son, John. John attended school in Durham and in 1879 he graduated from the Durham Model School. The following year he taught at S.S. No. 9, Glenelg, two miles east of Durham. After teaching one year he left to enter the Royal Military College, Kingston, from which he graduated With Distinction. While attending the Paris Exposition of 1893, he became involved in the printing of illustrated numbers of the Exposition, and he decided to pursue a literary life.

At the time of his 70th birthday in 1932, the Durham Review stated that Colonel MacLean was head of one of the largest publishing houses in the world — publishing 28 magazines with a staff of 500, with 600,000 subscribers, and over one million readers. The local papers occasionally reported that John B. MacLean had been in Durham for a few days visiting his mother who lived in the house on the south-east corner of Durham Road West and Queen Street. In 1945 the company he founded became MacLean Hunter and diversified into a multi-media conglomerate. Colonel MacLean died in 1950.

POSTAL SERVICE

For some time after the first settlers arrived in Durham there was no postal service north of Fergus. If any one wanted to send a letter to family or friends in the older settled parts of the province, or overseas, he or she would have to find someone going to an area where there was a post office to mail the missive. In order to receive a letter the writer would be required to find someone coming to Durham who would carry and deliver the letter personally. The British government ran the postal system in Canada and it was extremely costly. The recipient of a letter was required to pay the postal fee.

In 1846 Owen Sound received postal service. Milton C. Schofield, a public land surveyor, built a log house four miles north of Durham at the Rocky in Bentinck Township on the west side of the Garafraxa Road. He opened a small store there and on October 6, 1847, he received a commission to open a post office called Bentinck Post Office. On the same day a post office was also opened in Arthur. Bentinck and Arthur were the only post offices between Fergus and Owen Sound. It is not known how the mail was delivered to the post offices in the first years, but it is known that in 1851 the mail was brought to Arthur, Bentinck and Owen Sound post offices on horseback on a weekly basis.

Archibald McKenzie's House at the corner of Countess and Lambton Streets — Durham's Post Office from 1868 to 1899.

Possibly this service was inaugurated in 1847. History also tells us that it was necessary for pioneers living at Hanover or beyond to come to Bentinck Post Office for their mail. In 1852 the first mail route west of Durham was inaugurated and a contract was let to Cowan Keyes who made the trip from Bentinck Post Office to Kincardine on foot once a week carrying the mail on his back.

In 1851 the Government of Canada took over the postal service and pre-payment of postal rates was initiated. The first Canada postage stamp, a three pence red beaver, was issued that year.

In 1853 Mr. A. B. McNab was named postmaster and he opened the post office in his small store on the north-east corner of Garafraxa and Lambton Streets. Although it was now in Glenelg, the name remained Bentinck and did so until September, 1865.

The early pioneers received so few letters that they did not often call at the post office to look for mail. Each month the postmaster published in the local paper a list of the owners' names for unclaimed letters.

This plan worked very well — if the owners of the letters did not see the paper, some of their friends would tell them mail was awaiting them at the post office.

In 1866 A. B. McNab sold his store property to J. H. Middaugh who took down the store and built a frame hotel on the corner of Lambton and Garafraxa Streets. At this time the post office was moved to the south side of Mill Street near Garafraxa Street.

Mr. McNab was a well-known business man in Durham. He was an entrepreneur, insurance agent, and the first reeve of Glenelg Township. In 1868 he absconded, and Archibald MacKenzie was appointed postmaster. Mr. MacKenzie moved the post office to his residence on the north-west corner of Lambton and Countess Steets.

Prior to the arrival of the railway in 1881 all mail was carried by stage coach, but after that date the mail arrived by rail and for many years a mail car was included in its passenger service with mail being sorted during transit. This procedure gave extremely fast mail service.

73

LETTER OF APPOINTMENT TO POSTMASTERSHIP.

POST OFFICE DEPARTMENT,

Ottawa, *3 October* 1868.

Sir,

I have the honor to inform you that His Excellency the Governor General has been pleased to appoint you to be Postmaster of *Durham* in the Electoral County of *Grey S.R.* in the Province of *Ontario* and Dominion of Canada.

You are therefore hereby authorized to exercise all the functions and discharge all the duties appertaining to the said Office, according to law.

I am, Sir,
Your very obedient servant,

Deputy Postmaster General.

Mr Archd McKenzie
Durham
Co. Grey
Ont.

½ rm. 7-68.C.

Postmaster's letter of appointment 1868.

Post Office Staff 1972 Centennial.
Jan Birr, Mrs. Velma McKechnie, Bob Braithwaite,
Mrs. Anna Koehler, Mrs. Jean Taylor.

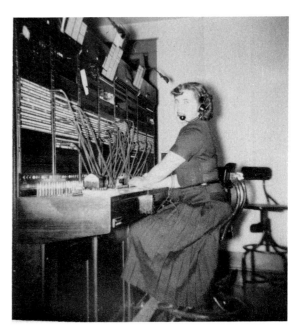

Catherine Breen at the Bell Telephone Switchboard 1954.

Durham Post Office.

LIST OF LETTERS.

LIST of unclaimed letters remaining in Durham Post Office; on the 10th of July, 1866.

Barrows Eliza Mrs	Lindsay Andrew
Ball William	Lindsay Joseph
Bell James	Morten Wm
Boyce Wm Mrs	Mack Joseph
Connor Richard	McGrade Patrick
Connor Edward 2	McGrade Thomas
Cowan Alex	M'Millan Donald
Cameron Caroline	M'Kelvey John
Colridge Daniel	M'Fadyen Martha Mrs.
Clark Donald	M Nemara Mary Mrs.
Chislett S	M'Phail Lachlin
Craig James	M'Donald Hugh
Everson Urias	M'Dermid Samuel
Ferguson Alex	M'Kechnie Allan
Gretly Peter	Oliver Thomas
Graham Wm	Odonell Mary
Grant Wm Mrs	Read James
Johnston Wm Jr.	Richardson John
Johnston Geo.	Stonehouse Sarah
James John	Taylor Mary Mrs
Ketch Wm	Watt James
Lafrinien Amable Mons	Watters Matthew

ALEX. B. McNAB,
Postmaster.

A list of all letters in the Post Office that were not picked up were published in the paper each month.

Archibald McKenzie Postmaster 31 years.

According to the 1880 Belden Atlas of Grey County, the Durham Post Office was designated as a Savings Bank Office. Only a small percentage of post offices was so designated. The idea behind this plan was to get low to moderate income earners in the habit of saving money. Any person might have a deposit account and could deposit yearly any amount from one dollar to $300. Deposits could be made by married women and deposits so made, or made by women who should later marry, would be repaid to any such woman. Each depositor would receive a Pass Book. The postmaster would mark each deposit or withdrawal and the depositor would receive a statement by letter from the Postmaster General's office in Ottawa within ten days of any change in the account. Four per cent interest per annum was paid.

In 1899, for the first time in its history, the Post Office imposed a postal fee on newspapers circulating over 10 miles from place of publication. The rate of postage set was one half cent per pound. Previously the newspapers had been handled free of charge.

Mr. MacKenzie died in 1899 and James Johnston Smith was appointed postmaster, a position he held for 41 years. The post office was moved to the Calder Block on Garafraxa Street between Mill Street and the river.

On March 5th, 1908, the following notice was published in the Durham papers: "Of late the public has been disappointed in not receiving the late evening mail on Saturdays owing to the irregular train arrivals. In future postmaster Smith will open the post office that evening only when the mail is received at the post office before 9.30 P.M."

Five or six letter boxes were placed on poles around the town for the convenience of the residents in 1917.

These were in use until the middle of the twentieth century. In 1927 the government built a post office on Garafraxa Street just north of the Hahn House, and today this building is the town clerk's office.

Mr. J. J. Smith retired in 1940, and from 1941 to 1952 Mr. Hector H. MacDonald was the postmaster. In 1953 Mr. Robert Braithwaite was appointed postmaster and he retired in 1986. The present postmistress is Mrs. Barbara Westgarth.

In 1968 the Federal Government purchased the old white brick Hahn House stables and the land to the east between the stables and the Registry office on Lambton Street and erected a fine new modern post office which is still in use.

Post Office before road was paved in 1929.

Winter method of travel 1915.

Men drinking and driving.

Dr. Gun's first car.

Flood 1929 Main Street South.

Chas. Lavelle and Wm. Laidlaw.

5

Town Services

JUSTICE AND POLICE

Prior to 1847 the townships of Glenelg and Bentinck had been attached to Wellington County in the District of Waterloo, but they had no representative on the District Council. From 1847 to 1852, when Grey County was set up as a provisional county, Glenelg and Bentinck did send delegates to the Waterloo District Council at Guelph. In 1854 Grey County became autonomous. It is not known when the first Justices of the Peace were appointed, but this was possibly in 1848. The first judge appointed for Grey County was Judge Wilkes in 1854. The following three incidents show how policing and justice were handled in the early years in Durham:

In 1863 the publisher of the *Durham Standard*, S. L. M. Luke, took action when he suspected a fellow citizen of paying too arduous attentions to his wife. Mr. Luke met the supposed culprit on the Saugeen River bridge where a shot gun blast was fired and Mr. Barnes was fatally wounded. Mr. Luke was arrested and charged with murder. At the trial in Owen Sound, almost solely on the testimony of the only eye witness to this incident, Mr. James Burt, Mr. Luke was found not guilty and acquitted. A footnote appeared in the Durham papers some 35 years later. Mr. Burt and Mr. Luke were at a public meeting and they got into a bitter argument. Mr. Luke called Mr. Burt a so and so. Mr. Burt replied, I may be a so and so, but I am NOT a MURDERER. Mr. Luke shot back, I may be a murderer but I am NOT a PERJURER.

From 1854 to 1872 the townships of Glenelg and Bentinck appointed constables who had jurisdiction over the residents of Durham, east of Garafraxa Street, Glenelg, and west of Garafraxa Street, Bentinck. These were part time jobs and the chief would possibly get $10 or $15 per year. The following is the list of Police Chiefs in Durham commencing in 1872:

Name	Chief Constable plus other duties	Year	Salary
John Rowland	Messenger of Council	1872-73-75	$ 20.00
Donald McDonald		1872-	25.00
Hugh Stoddart	Caretaker of the Town Hall Street Inspector	1877	25.00
William Johnston	Caretaker of the Town Hall Street Inspector	1878	25.00
Hugh McKay	Caretaker of the Town Hall	1879-1884	25.00
Henry Young	Caretaker of the Town Hall	1880-81-82	55.00
A. MacKenzie		1883-84	50.00
James Carson	Health Inspector Dog Tax Collector	1885- 1889-1905 1908-1911	100.00
Donald McDonald	Caretaker of the Town Hall Lighter of the Street Lamps	1886-88	50.00
George McKay	Health Inspector Dog Tax Collector	1911-19-20	
Thomas Whalen	Health Inspector	1912-13-14	
H. Pettigrew		1914	
G. Arrowsmith	Caretaker of the Town Hall Sanitation Inspector	1915-18	50.00/mo.
J. C. Adams	Caretaker of the Town Hall	1919	
Thomas Daniels	Caretaker of the Town Hall	1920	60.00/mo.
D. McLean		1920-22	25.00/mo.
H. Falkiner		1922-26	25.00/mo.
Hamilton Allen	Caretaker of the Town Hall	1926-30	60.00/mo.
Harry Scott	Caretaker of the Town Hall Sanitary Inspector Weed Inspector	1930-45	60.00/mo.
R. W. Rands	Caretaker of the Town Hall	1945-46	
Francis Illingworth		1946-51	1800.00 yr. 500.00 C/A
Major Dickens		1952	2400.00 yr.
Ted Zimmer		1952	
Neil McNabb		1953	
Frank Forbes		1953-54	2400.00 yr. 500.00 C/A
Elmer Hutchinson		1954-56	
Louis Berger		1956	2800.00 yr. 600.00 C/A
John Ward		1956-57	2600.00
Elmer Hutchinson		1957-58	
Paul Wight		1958-87	
Paul Metcalfe		1987-present	

Mrs. Ottilie McGowan tells a story of sleigh riding down Durham Hill. She said it was the best hill for this recreation for miles around, but the council had deemed it dangerous to use the hill for this purpose and had passed a by-law prohibiting it. One night a bunch of kids went up the hill with a toboggan; the road seemed all clear so they got on and started down the hill. "We looked up and saw the policeman Porky Carson standing in the middle of the road in front of us. His legs were spread apart and he was waving his arms yelling Stop, Stop. There was no earthly way we could stop; we tried to miss him but ended up going between his legs, and in so doing lifted his feet off the road and sent him flying through the air. The impact slowed the toboggan down considerably, and we all rolled off and ran for home as fast as our legs could carry us."

The August 26, 1860 edition of the *Durham Standard* reports a mysterious death at the British Hotel. A man named Lawrence Dunn was killed by falling from the veranda roof on the south end of the British Hotel. He fell about 25 feet to the ground. The deceased had been in the employ of Herbert Rowswell as a pearl ash maker at Rowswell's ashery, Glenelg Falls. He had gone to Montreal to visit his family and was returning to his job at the ashery. Between nine and ten o'clock the deceased, in company with another man who was travelling, retired for the night to a room in the third storey. From the evidence of the latter person, it appears the deceased spent some moments in devotional exercises prior to retirement, during which he seemed to be somewhat excited saying to himself no, no, no, I won't.

About an hour afterwards the landlord conducted a third man to the same room where the two former occupants appeared to be asleep. They left, and the third man disappeared into the night. A short time later Mr. Dunn's room-mate was awakened with a start by a loud crash. He looked around and everything seemed normal so he went back to sleep. At the same time the landlord was conversing with a gentleman in the bar-room on the ground floor at the south end of the hotel, when they heard a tremendous crash outside. When they went to examine the cause they saw nothing. About an hour later the body was discovered by some persons on their way home from a concert. An inquest was held the following day by Dr. Crawford, Coroner.

Mr. Dunn's roommate testified that Dunn must have gotten up and partially dressed, put up the window and crawled onto the veranda roof, and the noise that awakened him was the window falling. Almost solely on the evidence given by Mr. Dunn's bedmate, the jury returned a verdict of accidental death. But the inquest left more questions unanswered than it answered.

This story was told to the writer more than 50 years ago by two older unrelated gentlemen from different pioneer families. Their accounts were almost identical to the above with the exception that most of the early pioneers in Durham at that time felt that justice had not been done by the decision of the coroner. The verdict had been reached solely on the evidence of one stranger. Many believed this accident may have been a homicide.

The June 1, 1922 *Durham Chronicle* reports the following news story:

"Town Council met in special meeting May 25, 1922, and discharged Constable Falkiner with little ceremony when a resolution was passed ordering him to quit the job at once and turn in his uniform. It was not because of inefficiency that this action was taken by council, but because of over efficiency. When appointed a few months ago, he was warned not to be too exacting against automobile owners for slight infractions of the law. When cars were parked on the street at night, their tail-lights must be left on, or a lantern could be lit and hung on the back of the car. This was a provincial law but it only applied to rural areas, as city drivers did not have to comply despite the fact that Durham had possessed electric street lighting for years. The council said that this law was discriminatory and to ignore it. Mr. Falkiner, it is alleged, made his rounds and secured the numbers of cars showing no tail-lights. The names of the car owners were ascertained, and we are told, the information laid before Police Magistrate Laidlaw who imposed fines and costs in every case, or nearly every case, which came before him. We understand that thirty or forty automobile owners were implicated.

"The Council also decided to pass a resolution against the Police Magistrate and prepare a petition for his removal from office."

The June 1, 1922 *Durham Chronicle* reports:

"Police Magistrate Laidlaw had an information laid against him last Friday for a violation of the traffic regulations. The crime was not a serious one, but violated "the letter of the law" so carefully followed by Mr. Laidlaw in order to secure convictions. The time was opportune, and the town being indignant over the way he fined others for slight violations, there is no doubt that some thought he should be treated to a dose of his own medicine.

"He was seen driving on the wrong side of the street, and headed in the wrong direction, stopped at a supply tank for gasoline. We presume it was a violation of the law and accordingly an information was laid before Reeve Calder who fixed Tuesday as the date of hearing the evidence. The case was settled out of court, a fine of $5 being imposed."

June 8, 1922

"The Council passed a motion to ask the Provincial Government for the dismissal of Magistrate Laidlaw."

The first year in which Durham had a full time two man police force was 1957. At the present time the force consists of four full time officers, two auxiliary officers and one parttime officer.

JUSTICE IN THE COURTS BEFORE 1872

This court case took place between 1855-1865 and was reported in the *Durham Chronicle*, May 9, 1901:

An Old Landmark
(by S.L.M. Luke)

We see that the hotel stables of the Knapp House are being removed, and with Mr. Knapp's usual spirit, a more commodious stabling erection will take its place.

This revered old structure was erected in the year 1855 by the late A.B. McNabb, once a somewhat prominent business man of this town, the lower storey being used as a warehouse, and the upper part as a public hall, with an outside stairway from Lambton Street. Courts, concerts, public meetings and an occasional Terpsicorean festival were held within the walls of this ancient structure.

Of courts one may be mentioned. Lady Lewis, a gay brunette Courtezan, whose domicile was on the commons opposite the old Vollett hotel. The mothers in that locality were giving their liege lords mental annoyance (unjustifiable, of course) in this regard, so one moonlight night a select band unroofed the building. Next day her ladyship applied for law, which was refused. Hence, taking an apronful of goodly-sized pebbles, she smashed the windows of such offenders as she could recognize. A warrant was then issued for her apprehension by Beak McNab, and as none of the constables in town would serve, he employed a stalwart African, who got a dose of unmentionable between the eyes. Her ladyship gave herself into custody, and a bench of Justices convened, consisting of Geo. Jackson, S.E. Legate, James Edge, David Jackson, Sen., and A.B. McNab. The decision was that her ladyship should be sent to the county gaol for a period of two months. The culprit retorted on Geo. Jackson in language unfit for pen, type or paper, and with a cordwood bludgeon which lay conveniently at hand, she was about to give George a taste of it, when Constable Rowland clinched the little fury, and the liveliest tussel ever witnessed in Durham ensued. The constable fell to the floor, Jezebel uppermost, when Mr. Jackson named three spectators to give assistance, and one of them, in his zeal for law and order, lit with both knees in the constable's stomach, the Bench in the meantime having left on the double quick. Her ladyship, relieved of the constable's grasp, took refuge behind the stairway door, and a dozen young fellows stood with their backs thereto, so that when Rowland, panting for breath on account of the assistance he had received in the tussel, asked where she had gone, was informed that the bird had flown down the street. — The unfortunate was next day sent to her parents in the Niagara District. — Squire Edge is the only surviving member of the Magisterial Bench above mentioned, and no doubt his longevity is due to his moral integrity of character.

Durham Water System 1923.

WATER WORKS

When the first settlers went into the bush to take up land and build a house, the very first thing they looked for was a source of good water for drinking and cooking. They located their buildings as closely as possible to the supply-spring, spring-fed creek or river. This was no problem for the early settlers in Durham as there were numerous springs on the top and around the sides of Durham Hill. In fact there are reports that, for at least the first two or three decades of the town's existence, the gully north of the Durham Road had springs on both sides of it, and they extended beyond the gully to the flat land on the north. The springs formed a little creek which ran all year round, and a bridge was built on the Durham Road East over the creek as it made its way to the Saugeen River.

As the trees on the town site were cut and thousands of acres surrounding the village were denuded of their forest, the ground water level dropped, many springs dried up, and it became necessary to dig shallow wells. A pump maker, Joseph Teasdale, who operated a shop in the 1860s near the Edge Mills, made wooden pumps on a very simple turning lathe. The pipes were five inches in diameter with a two inch hole bored through the centre in lengths from four feet to eight feet. One end of the pipe had a male bevel, the other end a female bevel. These bevels were turned to precise measurements so that when they were tightened together they would not leak. (The current

Superintendent of the Durham Water Works Department, Ralph Darroch, said that in very recent years, when the Town was doing some street improvements, they dug up some of these pipes made from tamarack, and they were almost as sound and in as good condition as when they were laid in the ground 100 years ago). The pump was usually about six inches by six inches square and four feet long. The hole in the pump was a three and a half inch bore, the sides of which were finished very smoothly. A piston smaller than the bore was turned, and the bottom and sides were covered with a soft heavy leather so that it fit tightly against the wall of the bore. A handle moved the piston up and down the bore. A heavy sole leather valve at the bottom of the pump completed it. The water lubricated the leather, but from time to time it had to be replaced. Gradually these pumps appeared on most lots in Durham, although sometimes a citizen who did not have a well and pump would pay to use a neighbour's. There was also a public pump and a watering trough on Garafraxa Street just south of Highbrow, where Bruce Mighton's barber shop is now situated. Here, citizens driving along Garafraxa Street could turn off the road and water their horses before proceeding further.

In every house was a wooden bucket known as the Water Pail which was used to carry water from the spring or well into the house. Hanging beside the water pail or, more often left in it, was a tin dipper. Everyone in the household drank from this dipper.

A water trough on the edge of the road.

For washing clothes the pioneer women preferred to use rain water because it was soft. Two boards nailed together in a V would catch rain water at the eaves and run it into a barrel at the end of the house. Less home made soap was needed when soft water was used.

In 1894 there was a move to improve the water available in Durham. On June 4th James Brown was given permission to lay wooden waterpipes underground across Kincardine, Elgin, and Albert Streets. On October 1st of the same year James Crawford and others obtained permission to lay waterpipes underground to supply water to Jackson, Victoria, Durham Road, Chester, Bruce, George, Countess, Queen, and Lambton Streets. The water for Crawford's system came from Parker's springs. On October 25th, 1894, the Durham Review reported that Dr. David Jamieson and Conrad Knapp had installed a ram to supply their water tanks. Father Maloney, Messrs. Campbell, Calder, and McKenzie had windmill structures to fill their tanks. There was a windmill on Countess Street South which supplied water from the river to some homes for use in toilets only. James Gun on Durham Road East had a ram installed on a spring below his property and supplied water to a dozen or more homes in Upper Town East.

A pipe was laid underground from the spring on the west side of the hill to the Durham Cemetery for the convenience of friends wishing to water flowers, etc. It was fastened to the side of the bridge over the Saugeen River and each fall had to be taken apart at the bridge and drained. After many years water on tap at the cemetery was discontinued. One year a skunk became caught in the west hill spring which gave the owners of that water system a big headache!

In 1902 a group of Durham businessmen formed a company to drill for oil. They procured a charter, The Durham Natural Gas and Oil Company Limited, and began to sell shares. Mr. John McKechnie was President, Mr. John Kelly, Vice-President, and Mr. W.S. Davidson was Secretary. The November 13, 1902, Durham Review states "that the stock of the Durham Natural Gas & Oil Co. Ltd. is rapidly being subscribed and the Directors expect to have sufficient sold in a short time to enable them to commence operations." The next week the same paper reported "that shares were selling at $10.00 and if oil turns out as expected they could be worth $2,000.00." During the summer of 1903 the D.N.G. & O. Co. commmenced drilling for oil near Camp Creek at the south end of Durham on the west side of Garafraxa Street. At nearly 200 feet they struck a flowing (artesian) well of pure sparkling water. The stream flowing from it was almost as thick as a man's body, and if piped, it was thought would rise 40 or 50 feet in the air. The town Council held a special meeting to consider the possibility of water works. The August 6th, 1903, Chronicle reported "that a petition from Durham citizens to the Mayor resulted in a public meeting that decided the Town Council should

Durham Waterworks pump house built in 1931. This building sat on top of an underground concrete reservoir with a 200,000 gallon capacity and was kept full of water free of charge to the town by an artesian well on the property of The Durham Stone and Paving Company. The water was pumped from here to the water tower at the north end of Durham until about 1950.

meet with the Durham Gas and Oil Company to ascertain the cost of securing the rights of the well for the town. The Company agreed to sell the well for $2,700 the amount of money they had invested in it." The Council passed a by-law to purchase the well subject to a vote by the ratepayers. The vote was held the end of October, 1903; 64 people voted to buy the well, 83 were against buying it; only 147 people voted out of a possible 500. That ended the town water works plans.

In 1923 the Town Council once again brought up the matter of water works; an engineer was hired to study the town and make recommendations for establishing a municipal water works. The engineer recommended McKechnie's springs, Saugeen River, or Wilder Lake, as the source of a water system. The Council offered to purchase two acres of land, including the springs, from Gilbert McKechnie. He wanted $3,000 but Council thought this was too expensive. John Snell, who supplied about one-third of the town with water, and owned all the other large springs, offered his springs and water installation complete for $6,000. The Saugeen River had a constant risk of pollution. Wilder Lake was 170 feet higher than Upper Town, and laying a ten inch main from Wilder Lake would provide a gravity system but cost would be exorbitant.

No action was taken on any of these plans.

Acting on instructions from the Chief Officer of Health, a sanitary survey of the town was made in 1923. During the investigation 435 premises were inspected. Less than half (206) of the premises were supplied with water from Mr. Snell's water system. One hundred and twenty-five wells were sampled. Only seven of these wells were free or comparatively free from pollution, and 99 of them showed **gross** pollution, contaminated by wastes (fecal bacteria). Seven premises had private sewers to the river, and 127 had septic tanks or cesspits. There were 313 privies and there were no local by-laws governing privies. The town dump was located north of the Durham Road at the end of Bruce Street in a marshy area south of the west springs. There was one dairy retailing milk but the milk was not pasteurized. Mr. Snell's spring system showed some pollution and the Saugeen River was seriously contaminated. Wilder Lake would be expensive. Deep wells would be the best solution but the town objected to the hard water from the wells. The survey recommended: that Durham install a municipally-owned water system with all possible speed. The choice of supply should only be made after very careful investigation into the possibilities of the various sources available; that Durham instruct their engineer to make plans for a complete sewage system. This need not be installed immediately but parts could be built as the need was felt.

The names of the owners of all the wells tested, as well as the result of each test, were printed in the December 27, 1923, *Durham Chronicle*. On January 7th, 1924, at the Durham Municipal election the ratepayers voted on a by-law to establish a public water system. The by-law was 91 for, 212 against. Reeve Wm. Calder worked hard to have the by-law defeated because he said the town could not afford a water system.

The disastrous fire in the McIntyre Block on October 25, 1929, demonstrated the absolute need for a high volume high pressure water system with adequate fire hydrants. Owen Sound Fire Department responded to a call for help and with their assistance the fire was contained. Hanover and Mount Forest both responded, but they only brought their fire hoses and no fire hydrants for attachment existed. All the following year the talk was for a new water system, and in early autumn, 1930, the Ontario Government established an Unemployment Fund from which grants would be paid to municipalities which sponsored new work projects during the winter of 1931. The Town applied for a grant of $25,000, but was promised only $12,500. The council decided to go ahead with the full project and let contracts to five different companies for mains, hydrants, and a water tower, all installed for $28,000; total cost to be about $50,000. There were about 120 unemployed men in Durham. Men with dependents were given preference for the jobs, but all received a share in the labour.

While Durham had let all the contracts for the water system, the town had not yet secured a source of water for the system. The Consolidated Sand and Gravel Company offered to supply the town with 200,000 gallons of water daily from their overflowing well which was producing 900,000 gallons daily. In case of fire the town would have full use of the well. The Company already had a main laid to South Street which originally may have been the source of water for the National Portland Cement Company plant, and the town could connect with this. If so, it would have been laid thirty years earlier. The N.P.C.C. used a large amount of water mainly because all its hydro requirements were supplied by coal burning steam generators. In return, the town agreed to close several unused public streets which ran through the Sand and Gravel property. In addition the town bought John Snell's water system, which now included all the systems from the springs, for $7,000.

The mains and water tower, with storage for 200,000 gallons, were installed by the end of April. The pumphouse was built and pumps installed, and the system was in operation by the end of the summer. Initially not everyone had access to the town water, but in the following years the system was completed.

This system worked well for a number of years, but eventually a leak occurred in the main between the

Windmill on Countess Street South pumped water from the river used only to flush toilets in several neighbouring houses.

well and the town pumphouse. The Durham Stone and Paving Company offered to dig up the old main and do all the back filling free of charge if the town would buy and install a new main. The Council opted to drill its own well and pump the water. Word had spread that the water from the artesian well had deteriorated and had a bad taste. However, some time later a sample of water taken from that well was sent to the Ministry of Natural Resources for testing. The labratory which tested the water telephoned the Durham Stone and Paving Company to ask where the sample had come from becauase it was one of the purest samples of water ever tested. The town drilled a well behind the pumphouse on Albert Street which was capped in 1949. In 1966 a second well was drilled just off George Street at Rock Street and in 1989 the town drilled another well one block west of the old pumphouse. This system can produce 525 gallons of water per minute. In the mid 1970s a new storage tank was erected beside the high one in Upper Town. The new tank has a capacity of 500,000 gallons, providing a total reserve of 700,000 gallons of water.

Durham is very fortunate in that, although the water is hard, it is completely pollution free and has a most excellent taste without any chlorine whatsoever.

SEWER SYSTEM

In 1883 the Durham Council set up a Board of Health. This committee established regulations governing the maintenance, sanitation, and inspection of all wells and cisterns, privy vaults, and dry earth water closets within the town. Over the years many notices appeared in the local papers, in the spring and fall, that inspection for sanitation would be made for the Board of Health, and any unsatisfactory condition would be rectified by the same Board of Health. All persons building stables or privy vaults had to first get permission from the Board of Health about the site of the buildings.

As privy vaults were always constructed behind, and some distance from the residence, they were commonly called backhouses. The Board of Health also ruled that no offal, refuse, or matter of any kind, be dropped into the river, or placed upon a vacant lot, but that all such should be burned on the premises.

Prior to this on September 11, 1872, a complaint was made to Council regarding the terrible condition of two privies near the Durham Road on the British Hotel property. The constable was ordered to give notice to the hotel to have them removed the following day.

After the water tests in 1923 were published, the disposal of sewage became an important issue in Durham. The first step was to establish a waterworks, and then a sewage disposal plant. However, many years passed before this was to take place.

The October 1st, 1964, Durham Chronicle gives the first look at a proposed sewage system in the town. The first phase of the sewage collection and treatment programme provided sanitary sewer service to 70 per cent of the residents, as well as processing plants, and the high school. A sewer line was laid on Garafraxa Street from the bridge to its effluence into the Saugeen River at Saddler Street during the paving of 1929-1930. Raw sewage being discharged into the Saugeen raised the bacteria count to an intolerable level.

In the central developed area of the town 17,000 linear feet of 8" and 12" diameter sewer pipe was laid, and use was made of existing sewers on Garafraxa Street. Sewage was drained to a prefabricated pumping station in the south-western section of the town where pumps moved the sewage to an aerated lagoon located near the community centre. The design of this type of lagoon was the first of its kind adopted for municipal waste treatment in Ontario. The pond was lined with asphalt and polyvinal plastic membrane and had four mechanical turbine aerators. The water, from which the solids and most of the impurities have been removed, is returned to the Saugeen River, and the solid waste is disposed of in the sanitary land fill on West Park Street.

The original cost of the system was estimated at $255,000, but when tenders were called the price was

$425,000. When council approved the larger figure, the Ontario Water Resources Commission went to the Municipal Board for approval, and the project moved ahead. Over the next ten years or so additions were made to the system and it covered almost all of the town.

NATURAL GAS

In 1963 the Union Gas Company expanded its service area to include Durham and towns south of Durham. At that time over 63,000 feet of gas line were laid in Durham, and since then a large number of the residents here have taken advantage of natural gas availability as an excellent source of heat.

FIRES AND FIRE PROTECTION

After Archibald Hunter and his party took up land on May 1, 1842, in what later became known as Durham, other settlers soon followed.

The first buildings were of log construction, and after the Edge Sawmill was built in 1846 there was a gradual conversion over the next decade or two to build frame homes. There were also some stone buildings erected. Many of the houses also had a small barn at the back of the lot to house a horse (for transportation), a cow, possibly a pig or two, and some hens. The first source of heat was a fireplace which also was the source of heat for cooking. For approximately the first 40 years the only fuel used was wood, and artificial lighting was at first by candle and later by coal-oil lamps. Thus the risk of fire was very real.

The following advertisement appeared in the September 23, 1859, issue of the *Durham Standard*: "The Officers and Members of the Durham Protection FIRE COMPANY will meet at the SCHOOL HOUSE on MONDAY evening 6th inst." Due to missing papers we have no other information regarding this organization other than it was formed on June 2nd, 1859.

In 1864 the Trinity Anglican Church installed a bell in the tower and for many years the ringing of that bell was Durham's only fire alarm. There was no organized fire protection and when the fire bell rang any one able to help would hasten to the scene, bringing pails or buckets to carry water from neighbouring wells to throw on the blaze.

There were several fires over the years in industrial and commercial buildings in Durham. On September 14, 1860, R. Crawford's tannery was completely destroyed by fire.

June 9, 1870, Durham Chronicle:

"Last night the Tannery & Harness Shop of Messrs. T. and J. R. Smith of this village was burnt. There was a strong wind blowing and in a very short time the building and all its contents were lost. For a time it was thought that the Lower Village was in danger too but a heavy rain that accompanied the wind saved the surrounding buildings." Total loss set at $12,000 — no insurance.

July 7, 1870, Durham Chronicle:

"Church Burned. The Catholic Church in this village was consumed by fire between 1 and 2 a.m., on Monday 4th inst. It was undoubtedly the work of an incendiary, as the church is entirely isolated, and there had been no service there for a week previous. We have been informed by Mr. Fagan that there was no insurance whatever on the premises."

On the same date the following news item also appeared:

"Fire Engine — Another meeting will be held at Spence's Hotel this evening at 8 o'clock for the purpose of devising means for procuring that much needed institution, a Fire Engine. Full particulars regarding prices, styles, etc., have been ascertained and will be laid before the meeting. Let there be a large attendance."

Durham's First Fire Engine beside the Boathouse at the Rob Roy Mill pumping water from the river. Carl Fry, Howard McDonald, Harry Holmes, engineer, Jack Lloyd.

In September, 1876, the Argyle Hotel at Chester and Garafraxa Streets burned down. The fire spread to the Anglican Church which was also consumed by the flames. The August 26, 1880, issue of the *Grey Review* reports a small barn at the back of the Trinity Anglican Rectory (now St. Raphael's Nursing Home) was burned. The rectory was in danger of burning too, due to sparks falling on the cedar shingle roof. A ladder was put up to the roof and rain water from a cistern was dipped out in buckets and passed up the ladder and

poured over the shingles. Any water which ran off the roof ran into the eavestrough and back into the cistern for reuse. The building was saved. Again there was a cry for the council to form a hook and ladder brigade. No action taken. A hook and ladder brigade was basically a volunteer fire department. The town would buy several pails to carry water for dousing the flames, ladders, two or three shovels and axes. When the volunteers heard the bell at the Anglican Church ring, warning that a fire had broken out, they would run to a central station where these articles were stored, carry them to the fire location and endeavour to save the burning property.

In 1884 Cochrane's Foundry, a two-storey stone building 50 feet x 90 feet, was burned and again in 1894 it fell victim to fire. Also, the August 4, 1884, *Grey Review* reports: "The Town Council set up a committee of the Mayor, Reeve and two councillors to furnish at its next meeting as much information as possible regarding the cost of a hand operated fire engine and hook & ladder fire apparatus." No action was ever reported by this committee.

In 1888 Council was urged to consider buying a second-hand steam fire engine. No action taken.

August 27, 1894, the *Grey Review*:

"A disastrous fire late at night completely destroyed N. G. & J. McKechnie's sawmill on the south-west side of Durham. Also lost in the fire were over a million board feet of lumber piled in the yard. Some piles along the new railway track were saved. A request was made to Palmerston to send up their steam fire engine. It was loaded on a box car and brought to Durham by a special train but arrived too late to save anything. The fire could be seen for many miles from Durham as the huge piles of lumber burned. Every neighbouring roof was covered with blankets and other materials that would hold water. Men carried buckets of water from the river to keep the protectors soaked. No other buildings burned. The fire was believed to have been set by an arsonist."

September 3, 1894. Council decided to procure suitable fire protection by means of a steam fire engine. Carried, but not unanimously. Council could not decide which of two makes of fire engine to buy — Ronald or Watrous.

October 4, 1894. A delegation waited on the town council with a petition of 140 signatures praying the council to take steps towards fire protection and urging claims of the Ronald fire engine.

On Thursday last another exhibition of the Ronald engine, arranged by interested citizens in Durham, took place and to the satisfaction of all in town. With the engine on the brink of the river near the foundry, water was sent through 500 feet of hose easily over the ball of the Middaugh House and surrounding buildings. A lateral stream through 1¼" nozzle was thrown nearly 200 feet. The engine was then placed on the Garafraxa bridge, suction hose dropped into the river and through 500 feet of hose streams were thrown 40 to 50 feet higher than the top of the Presbyterian Church steeple (United Church). A 1000 feet of hose was then run up the hill reaching Kress's corner and through this length of pipe and up the hill its force was little diminished.

October 11, 1894. Council decided to submit the matter of the fire engine to the voters of Durham. (basically male property owners)

Result of vote: To buy steam fire engine	134
Against buying steam fire engine	23
For Ronald steam fire engine	133
For Watrous steam fire engine	2

Council built three underground water supply tanks in Upper Town, one at corner of Bruce & Lambton Streets, and a small one in Smith's creek."

Grey Review, April 4, 1895:

"In the spring of 1895 a bitter controversy developed over where the fire hall should be built. Prior to the vote to buy a fire engine the only site proposed was at the corner of Chester and Garafraxa Streets and there was no opposition to this site. Early in 1895 Lower Town wanted it built at George St. W. & Garafraxa St. The council decided to built it half way between the two proposed sites and by a motion of seven to three voted to build it on the market site half way up Durham hill on the east side of Garafraxa St. Six of the seven votes were from Lower Town, the seventh was Mr. Gorsline (the man who ordered the expensive Fireman's helmets from New York). Mr. Gorsline paid dearly for his mistakes. He ran for Reeve of Durham in 1895 and received only 30 votes.

Fire Hall and Firemen 1895.

"A test run was made and it was found two or three men could easily and quickly take the fire engine down the hill, but it took 15 strong men 3½ minutes to take it from the proposed Fire Hall to the top of the hill, and those men were so exhausted they couldn't go any farther. Thus Lower Town had good fire protection but Upper Town was at the mercy of the availability of a team of horses to bring the Fire Engine to any fire in Upper Town. A few minutes delay of the fire engine could be devastating when fires occurred in Upper Town."

There had always been a friendly rivalry between Upper & Lower Town, but this is possibly the only time in the history of Durham that it developed into a bitter confrontation. Residents of Upper Town contacted the Canadian Fire Underwriter's Association and received the following letter which was printed in the April 22, 1895, edition of the *Grey Review*:

"Dear Sir:—

Your favor 18th inst. re Durham received. I have communicated with the Mayor of Durham in reference to location of fire hall, stating that in the event of the town at some future time applying for a better classification, the proposed location of fire hall would be an obstacle in the way, even though other appliances entitled the town to a better classification.

Yours truly,
Robert McLean, Sec'y,
Canadian Fire Underwriter's Assoc."

Council did not change its mind but went ahead to build on the Market Site.

A package of a super fancy heavy fire helmets that went half way down the fireman's back arrived at the station for the Durham Fire Department from New York. Nobody would admit ordering them. Finally the Reeve had to admit that he signed an order for them, but he thought he was getting the 80 cent helmet not the $7.50 one.

The May 7th, 1896, Grey Review reports the five underground tanks cost $175 to build, the engineer got $60, the wagon to transport the fire engine cost $45, and coal to heat the fire hall cost $25. It was the duty of the volunteer fire department to check all tanks regularly and fill them if they were not full.

A platform was built behind Robert Campbell's livery stable about 100 feet east of Garafraxa Street to provide a level surface on which to set the steam fire engine when fighting fire in that area of town. Possibly other platforms were built along the river in other locations.

The contract to build the Fire Hall was let to Robt. Bull for $940. The building included a clerk's office, jail, a weigh scales (for hay, grain, livestock, etc.). The tower to dry the hoses after use was not high enough to let the hoses drain properly and after two years they began to leak under pressure as the mould and mildew had rotted them.

Mr. Jas. Crawford was appointed first Fire Chief. Members of the Durham Fire Brigade for 1897:

Richard Parker, Chief,
Robert Torry, Lieutenant
Wm. Calder, Sec. Treas.
Alex McDonald, Engineer
Alex Dargavel, Assistant Engineer

Reel 1	Reel 2
J. Harbottle	W. Benton
Ed McClocklin	W. Falkingham
N. McIntyre	C. Scott
J. Rose	J. Kilmer
J. Barker	W. Connor
Alex Gordon	L. Livingstone

Thomas Whelan, Foreman Hook & Ladder Co.
Firemen, G. Meikle and C. Leavens
Steward, C. Elvidge

Editor's Comment, October 3, 1895, *Durham Review*:
"The town this year seems to have slipped cog somehow. Our tanks gave way, the bridge went down, a lawsuit on hand, perhaps two, hose getting moulded, engine in danger of getting rusted owing to damp building. Never was there more need of good measures and good men to carry them out."

Letter in *Grey Review*, October 7, 1895:

OUR TOWN COUNCIL

"MISTER EDITER:— Ive never ad much schoolin'in my erly life, but my father, good man, bless him, was anxhus that I shood ave common sinse — common since sez he is a good thing. But I kin reed and I do reed your exillent paper, espeshilly the noose ov how our councellors are adoin' the bisness of the town. Ime a thinkin' yu kind o hit the nale on the hed week afore last when yu sed that the town had slipped a cog some how — thems wot ime a thinkin' tew. Its ben a slippin cogs all the year and its a pity if our intellergent cittersens dont see it. Youve menshoned only a few things but youve dun enuff. This law soot yu speak ov, why its a shure proof that ther was mor'n won stoopid man in the councel an fer that matter in the town when that man Ronald was aroun'. Ime afeard that ef our cittersens dont get better men in our councel that the town will get clean busted. Many ov our cittersens are supposin' that ther votes can turn biled kebbage into brane but they cant du it. Sum ov the branes in our council ime thinkin is yet biled kebbage. So many things is happenin this year without a coz that ime imaginin' no wunder at yer helmet story. It is very suggestive ov the new way ov doin things in this town. Thim New Yorkers must be wonderfully ginerus fellus tew send them helmets here tew our boys without bein' ordered. They no weer poor and ther ginerocity is appreshiated ime shure.

In September, 1924, the Council purchased a new Bickle chemical fire engine mounted on a Ford truck chassis. As well as the chemical tanks, mounted on the truck was a hose rack capable of carrying up to 1,000 feet of 2½" standard hose. The engine complete with searchlight and bell cost $1,590. In October, 1924, the Rob Roy Mills were destroyed by fire with a loss of $100,000 to $125,000, and in December, 1924, Durham installed a fire alarm system — telephone number 100, which would be answered 24 hours a day at the furniture factory, and the factory would blow the steam whistle: 1 blast for Ward 1; 2 blasts for Ward 2; 3 blasts for Ward 3.

A disastrous fire occurred on October 25th, 1929, when the McIntyre Block was burned. Mr. Thomas Saunders, a disabled man who was manager and night operator of the telephone switchboard, saw smoke seeping into the telephone exchange office and turned in the alarm. He remained at his post calling for help, including assistance from the Owen Sound, Hanover, Mount Forest and Harriston Fire Departments. Owen Sound was the first to arrive and they were very instrumental in managing to contain the fire to the McIntyre Block. At one time it was thought that a large section of downtown would be burned out. Hanover and Mount Forest fire brigades arrived with hoses but no engine, only to find that Durham had no fire hydrants to which they could attach the hoses. Harriston fire brigade was too late arriving to be of any assistance. The Harriston fire engine arrived by special train. The fire had started in Vollett's store of unknown origin. The businesses destroyed were the Bank of Commerce, the Bell Telephone office and switchboard, Vollett's grocery store, George Fine Men's Wear, Alex Aljoe groceries, R. Burnett general store and J. H. Harding, hardware. After this fire every one in Durham was talking about municipal water-

Fire in the McIntyre Block 1929.

works and fire hydrants, which came into existence in 1931.

The first motor operated hose truck was a LaFrance purchased in 1937. A pumper was added in 1946 and a second pumper in 1962 at a cost of $75,000. A new pumper was purchased in 1978, in 1979 a 1,500 gallon tanker, and in 1989 a rescue van. The department also has the jaws of life, which has been used in many rescue calls such as automobile accidents. In April, 1955 a Fire Alarm siren was installed to replace the factory whistle, and now firemen are called by pager. The year 1976 saw the fire department move from its cramped out-dated quarters in the old fire hall halfway up the hill to modern comfortable quarters on George Street West.

Another tragic fire on February 11th, 1968, took the life of a prominent Durham citizen, Miss Margaret Hunter. On that afternoon Woodrow Cook was passing the house and noticed smoke coming from the building. He turned in the fire alarm and neighbours who were summoned entered the front of the house looking for Margaret but could not go upstairs due to the flames and smoke. The Fire Marshall and police found the body in the laundry room upstairs where she had been trapped by the fire. Miss Hunter was a talented musician and choir director and belonged to several organizations in town. She was a granddaughter of the first settler in Durham and was 84 years old.

On November 18, 1971, fire struck again. This time it was one of Durham's older landmarks — the old Middaugh House Hotel on the south-west corner of Lambton and Garafraxa Streets. The building was erected in 1881 and consisted of three floors and full basement. When it was opened in October, 1881, the local papers described it as "the most beautiful and well furnished hotel in any town in Western Ontario." The edifice was of white brick and around the top of the wall was very elaborate and fancy brick work. Over the front door on the second and third floor were balconies, and on the roof was a large turret topped by a dome. On entering the front door, one faced a large beautifully curved staircase which led to the floors above. Several people operated this building as an hotel but it was later turned into an apartment house. The fire started after midnight and the building quickly filled with dense smoke making it difficult for the occupants to make their exit. Some occupants on the top floor were brought to safety by the Public Utilities Commission bucket. One young couple held their small baby out the window in order that the child might breathe. All 30 residents were evacuated safely but lost all their personal possessions. Destroyed on the ground floor were William Ritchie's Barber Shop, Credit Union office, Glen Budd's Appliance store, Simpson's order office, the Bluebird Restaurant, and Glen Reay's Barber Shop. Fire brigades from surrounding towns came to the assistance of the Durham Brigade, and the fire was contained to the old hotel. The walls were unsafe and so were demolished. To-day the property contains a Royal Bank, Becker Convenience store, and a Liquor store.

On January 19th, 1979, fire raised its ugly head again, this time claiming the life of a young Durham man. The fire broke out about 3 A.M. in William Price's apartment at the back of Price's Carpet Sales Store. Raymond Price had come home late and decided to cook some fries and the fire started in this area. Raymond yelled at his father and brother, who were asleep upstairs, that the place was on fire. Ronald awakened his father and they ran to waken Dr. Marcuzzi and his wife who lived in an apartment over the store. Ronald evidently became disorientated in the dense black smoke and didn't make it out of the burning building. The fire departments of Hanover, Dundalk and Mount Forest responded to a request for help and the fire was contained to the Price's Carpet Store and the Durham Florist Shop, which were both completely consumed. At one time it was feared that Yirr's Jewellery, McTavish Funeral Home and the Royal Bank were also doomed, but the joint effort of the four fire departments saved them.

The Durham Fire Department has a fire agreement with Glenelg, Bentinck and Egremont Townships. Area coverage for the Durham Fire Department is quite extensive. In addition to the town itself, the area extends West to Allan Park, north to Dornoch, east to Priceville, and south to the Dundalk Road (County Road 89). The furthest run in the territory is two concessions east of Dromore. The department is also a member of the province-wide Mutual Aid programme and it covers all of Grey County.

There are about 18 volunteer fire fighters, and it is interesting to note that many of the present volunteer firemen are sons of former members of the Durham Fire Brigade. History tells us that many of these volunteers have given long years of service to the town. The present Durham Fire Chief, Donald Pust, has held that position for 26 years, and William Kennedy has been Deputy Fire Chief for 9 years.

The Fire Brigade practices every two weeks. The department, as well as fire protection, is also respons-

ible for cleanup after spills of dangerous chemicals, fire prevention and rescue operations. 1994 is the 100th anniversary of Durham's acquiring its first fire engine and the organization of its first Volunteer Fire Department. The citizens of Durham owe a great debt of gratitude to the Volunteer Fire Department for the service they have rendered over the past century, and are still rendering, to the Town.

ELECTRICITY

Electricity first came to Durham in 1890. That year Robert McGowan installed a 500 candle power generator in his mill on the eastern end of town and the Ball Electric Light Company secured the right of way through the town to install a lighting system. The streets were to be lit by five lights at a cost of $215 for 300 nights. The *Grey Review* of April 24, 1890, states that on April 18th of that year there were five street lights, as well as 50 lights in places of business.

The lights were switched on at sunset and were turned off at midnight. The operator of the generator would blink the lights two or three times a couple of minutes before midnight as a warning that the lights were soon going out. The street lights were 16 and 32 candle power carbon rod lamps and had to be lowered each day to adjust the carbons. In 1891 Mr. McGowan transferred the electric service to Mr. W.J. Stewart, who, in 1893, turned it over to Hewitson Brothers, who ran it until 1897.

In 1897 Mr. McGowan sold all the poles and lines, etc. on the streets in Durham to Kilmer, Crawford and McIntyre. The energy now came from Mr. Crawford's generator at Aberdeen. Mr. McIntyre gained control of the system and ran it until 1915 at which time Durham voted to obtain its power from the newly formed Ontario Hydro Electric Power Commission. Then Mr. McIntyre sold his poles and lines, etc., in town to the Town of Durham for $3,800. For a few months before Ontario Hydro was hooked up to the Durham distribution lines, Durham received its power from the Durham Furniture Factory generator at the Rocky Saugeen. After hooking up with the Ontario Hydro, Durham at first acquired its power from Eugenia, but is now connected to a province-wide grid.

Dedication of Durham Road Plaque at Conservation Park.

Mrs. Ottilie McGowan, Durham's Grand Lady who supplied a great deal of information for this book.

Cecil and Ethel Barber.
Durham's popular Grand Old Couple — both 96 years of age.

Dr. David Jamieson's residence built by A. Cochrane.

Dr. Gun's House on Durham Road East.

J.W. Crawford House, George Street West.

A.W.H. Lauder Home corner of Mill and Albert Streets.

Jim, Isabelle and Betty Henderson at river with
Durham Mills in the background.

Swimmers in the Saugeen.

The Military

6

On November 4, 1867, Archibald Hunter donated one-fifth of an acre of land to Queen Victoria in order that a drill shed might be erected for militia training; a militia known as the Durham Light Infantry had been formed on January 10, 1861. The militia drilled every Tuesday and Friday. The Provincial Government contributed $250 towards the building's construction and Glenelg and Bentinck Townships each contributed the same amount. This

building was constructed east of Archibald Hunter's home on the Durham Road. The drill hall collapsed early in the 1900s and the land and timber were sold.

As early as the 1860s similar militia groups were springing up over the area. These groups went on to become part of the famous Grey and Simcoe Foresters.

In 1866, during the Fenian Raids, the Durham Light Infantry was ordered to Owen Sound as fear of an attack on the County Capital seemed imminent. Under

Celebration on Garafraxa Street, Durham, when the relief of Ladysmith was announced March 1st, 1900.

Durham Militia responding to call went to Owen Sound to
protect the city from the Fenian Raids 1866.

the command of Lieutenant Wm. A. Anderson the Durham Light Infantry proceeded to Owen Sound.

In 1900 the Government issued medals to all Fenian Raid veterans on the 12th of February. The medals were presented to the survivors by Mrs. E. Davidson, the oldest resident of Durham and the eldest daughter of the founder. The intervening years had thinned the ranks; many were dead, others had moved away and only eight of the 48 were present. They were Robert Allan, C.L. Grant, George Ryan, Samuel McCracken, Thomas McGirr, James McGirr, Samuel Scott and M. Scott.

In 1885 when the North-West Rebellion broke out a goodly number of the Grey Regiment responded to the call. The records of this event are scanty, but there is no doubt that a number of the militia from Durham braved the long trip by train and sleigh to cross the 500 miles of Northern Ontario wilderness in order to assist in putting down Riel's rebellion. A list of released prisoners show names of four Durham men — William Davis, G.H. Ashdown, James Devlin and Matthew Davis.

The Boer War began October 1, 1899. In February, 1900, Dr. Gun received a letter from his son Cecil to the effect that he was off to South Africa to engage in the war. This is the only record to be found of any one from Durham going to South Africa. In March Mr. George Ledingham of Dornoch, and a member of the Strathcona Contingent, visited his mother prior to leaving for South Africa. On the day he left via C.P.R. from Durham, Mayor Laidlaw, hearing about his departure, took up a collection and presented Ledingham with a purse of $50. A brother of Ledingham and a Caldwell boy from this area also served in South Africa. Mr. Sid Standen, father of David and Douglas, who was born in England, also served in South Africa as a member of the Territorials. Mr. Standen immigrated to Canada and in 1924 moved to Durham. Mr. R. Player's father, born in Coventry, England, also served in South Africa. No doubt there are many distant relatives of Durham citizens who took part in the Boer War.

The year 1910 saw the construction of the Durham Armoury which was used to store uniforms, rifles and equipment during WWI. Shortly after the war it was closed down, but in the late 1930s it was opened again and used as headquarters for the local detachment of the Grey Simcoe Foresters. It was finally closed in 1969 and sold.

In 1906 a rifle range was built north of McGowan's Mill where local members of the Grey 147th Battalion drilled.

Durham Cenotaph.

Unveiling and dedication of the Cenotaph 1922.

Marker for rifle range north of McGowan Falls.

On August 4, 1914, Great Britain declared war on Germany and Canada did likewise on the following day.

Although the town of Durham had a small population, it contributed a large number of volunteers. By January 16, 1916, the 147th Battalion was fully recruited and in February a special train brought the Battalion from Owen Sound for a parade in Durham. On December 14th, the 147th Battalion sailed Overseas for duty and became part of Canada's Expeditionary Force. Early in 1917 one of the first notices of a war casualty was received in the death of Alex Wells. By 1918 the casualty list was to grow in length.

The Canadian Expeditionary Force in France and Flanders made a contribution to victory all out of proportion to its population. It was at Vimy Ridge in April, 1917, that Canada captured the world's attention. For two and a half years the enemy defied all Allied attempts to take the Ridge, then the Canadians, fighting for the first time as a unified body, arrived and pushing through muddy fields disloged the German forces from Vimy Ridge earning the gratitude and respect of the Allied troops. This is an example of what the Canadian Expeditionary Forces accomplished on the battlefield. The casualties were heavy and 38 Durham boys lie buried in Flander's Field. Their names are:

Lieutenant Thomas A. Allan	Thomas McDonald
William Robert Armstrong	Percy McKechnie
Percy Roy Bryan	Robert W. McMeekin
Robert William Burgess	Stanley McNally
Roy Graham Calder	Robert Putherbough
Campbell Clark	James Foster Saunders
James Gordon Coutts	Earle Vollett
William Gadd	Harry Vollett
George Halliday	James W. Wallace
William John Hopkins	James Warmington

Jesse Hughes	George Webber
Reginald A. Kelly	John Weir
Major E.L. Knight	Alex. Wells
William Allister Lauder	William George P. Willis
John M. Ledingham	Harry Stanley Willis
Sergeant Caldwell Marshall	Esdon M. Wolfe
William T. McAllister	

On November 11, 1918, the war came to an end with the signing of the Armistice at 11 a.m. Church bells rang, the factory whistle blew, rejoicing was everywhere. A monster parade was organized and the Kaiser burned in effigy over a huge bonfire on the main corner. During the late 1918s and early 1919s the men and women who had fought for the cause of liberty returned, some badly wounded and some with war brides. After the end of WWI men from Durham continued military training in the Second Battalion Reserve of the Grey and Simcoe Foresters.

WW I Soldiers: **Robt. Lindsay, Frank McKay, Fox Barber, Tommy Lauder, Gordon Gun, Jack Stedman, 1916.**

On September 3, 1939, Great Britain declared war on Germany once more, followed by Canada's declaration on September 10th. Records of W.W.II are sparse, but thanks are due to Durham Legion Branch 308 who, to commemorate their 50th Anniversary, published a book, Lest We Forget, which contains a marvelous record of all the men and women from Durham who served in WWII. The town of Durham can be very proud of their sons and daughters who rushed to join one of the three services. Very few families in Durham did not have some member join the forces. The Greenwood family had eight members; the Aljoe family four, the Jamieson family four, the Lloyd family four, the Miller family four, and many families three and two members. Thus these gallant men and women, scantily equipped and poorly trained, were going off to war — the hour of their pride and of their need.

Ross and Grant Greenwood in front of a tank in France during WW II. A week later this tank was blown up.

Flight Lieutenant (later Wing Commander) Joe Noble received the Distinguished Flying Cross. He was made a member of the Most Excellent Order of the British Empire and holder of the Canadian Forces Decoration with 1st Clasp. Flt. Lt. Noble was a veteran of 57 sorties and for three years a prisoner of war.

Norman Thompson was awarded the Military Medal. When at the height of battle the First Division became separated, the enemy having forced its way between the lines and the Allied forces had run completely out of water and needed it badly, Norman took a water truck through enemy lines — an act of extreme bravery.

F/O Joe Noble, Prisoner of War for 3-½ years in WW II.

For the first time women were called to serve and were known as the Wrens (Navy), W.A.C.S. (Army) and W.D.'s (R.C.A.F.). Again Durham was well represented in the three services. Durham men serving in the Navy guarded convoys of troops and supplies to Great Britain. They served in the North Atlantic, South Atlantic, the Mediterranian and in the Arctic Ocean guarding convoys to Russia. They served in the Army in Belgium, Holland, Germany, Italy and North Africa. The R.C.A.F. flew bombing missions over Europe and North Africa. Bobbie McGowan's aircraft was shot down over Europe and he was taken prisoner of war. Cliff Gunny's aircraft was shot down and he was taken prisoner; Joe Noble's aircraft also was shot down and he was taken prisoner. Joe was a member of the Escape Committee and was active in tunnel digging where the Great Escape took place. Only three made their escape, 50 were caught and, on Hitler's order, lined up and shot.

Durham should be very proud of the following: Mary Bell (Nursing Sister), Mentioned in Despatches, Sgt. R.R. (Dick) Davey received the Distinguished Flying Medal — a rear gunner who, when attacked by a German aircraft, cooly held his fire and shot down the enemy plane, thus allowing the aircraft to fly safely back to England.

Private Robt. Meads, as part of a medical group, drove a scout vehicle to the front. This vehicle had two stretchers for picking up wounded soldiers. He successfully picked up wounded soldiers while shellfire raged overhead. For this Private Meads was awarded the Military Medal.

Flight Sergeant Delbert (Dinty) Moore received the George Medal when he rescued a trapped gunner from a flaming bomber which had crashed on landing. He received severe burns during the successful rescue. Dinty received his Medal personally from King George VI at Buckingham Palace.

Robert McGowan returned from Prisoner of War Camp 1945.

Legion Hall over Cafe 1946-1966.

Japan surrendered on August 14, 1945. The only person from Durham involved with the war against Japan was Dr. Arthur Backus. When the prisoners of war were freed after three years and eight months of indescribable torture and starvation, those who survived were walking skeletons. The boats bringing them back to Canada were anchored off Vancouver Island for six weeks while the survivors received medical and dental treatment and nutritious food. Dr. Backus, a Major of the Canadian Dental Comp., was taken aboard one of the ships to give dental assistance to these men.

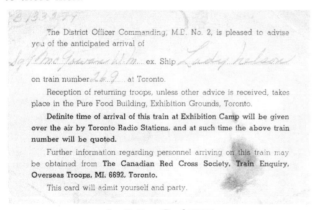

Invitation Card 1945
(to meet train bringing family member home from the war).

In 1950 the Korean War broke out and lasted until 1953. Again Durham boys enlisted and served with the United Nations Canada forces in Korea. They were Donald Arnold, Kenneth Caswell, James Hopkins, George Patton, Jim Patton, Orville Thompson and Warden Thompson.

Fifteen Durham men and women joined the Post War Forces.

In 1992, during the Gulf War, a young lad from Durham, Steve MacMillan, as a member of the Cana-

Ina Milne's Invitation to attend the first opening of Parliament after WW II.

dian Forces, was stationed in the Persian Gulf aboard a Canadian cruiser.

Durham may well be proud of its military record. As early as the 1860s men were active in the militia up until the WWI. After the war they were again active in the militia. Before WWII a group of young men and boys were members of the Second Battalion of the Reserve of the Grey and Simcoe Foresters under the command of Lieutenant I.B. Sharpe.

After WWII Durham again played an active part in the Grey and Simcoe Foresters under Lieutenant Keith Hunter. Norman Lawrence brought honour to the town when he was made Lieutenant-Colonel of this famous reserve army. Gordon Reaburn became a Staff Sergeant.

Any one interested in the names of all the veterans who enlisted from the Durham area may secure this information from the excellent book Lest We Forget, commemorating 50 years of Branch 308 Royal Canadian Legion, Durham, Ontario, 1940-1990. This book may be purchased from any Legion member.

THE ROYAL CANADIAN LEGION, BRANCH 308

At the end of World War I, soldiers returning home after months of unspeakable conditions in the trenches encountered a changed country from the one they had left; they felt that the country they had fought for was shutting them out, and, missing the comradeship of the trenches, turned to Soldier Clubs springing up all over the country. Thus, the Great War Veterans' Association came into being. The object of this organization was to help returning soldiers find jobs, rehabilitate themselves, and to press the government for pensions and care of disabled veterans. Shortly after this organization came into being, a Branch was formed in Durham. However, due to lack of co-operation among the members, the Branch phased out around 1926.

In the fall of 1927 a dinner meeting of veterans was held at the Hahn House during which it was decided to form a Veterans' Committee to assist all veterans. The first President of the Durham Veterans' Committee was Dr. Alex Bell, who served in WWII in England and Europe. Some of the executive were: Harold McKechnie, Rhys Padfield, Dan McCallum, J.B. Duffield, C.H. (Dooley) Darling and Jack Stedman.

The executive undertook to hold a Memorial Service on Armistice Day, followed by a banquet to which all veterans were invited. The I.O.D.E. and the local Red Cross donated and prepared all the food.

Dr. Bell continued as president until he left Durham at which time the Reverend B.D. Armstrong was elected president. Mr. Armstrong, who served as a Padre in WWII with the rank of Major, was highly regarded by many residents and under his presidency the organization received a degree of respectability among the town people. When he left Durham for another pastoral charge, J.B. Duffield was elected president and served in that capacity until 1940 when the Durham Legion was formed.

In 1926 the G.W.V.A. and other veterans' groups came together and formed the Canadian Legion. Due to lack of funds the veterans of Durham did not join this group until 1940 when a Charter was received and Durham Branch 308 of the Canadian Legion was formed. The first president was Art McGowan.

The Legion purchased the McIntyre Building on Main Street in 1946 and in 1947 the Ladies' Auxiliary was organized with Mrs. Adeline Morrison as president.

Her Majesty, Queen Elizabeth is shown with Prince Philip greeting Fred O'Brecht who was Dominion President of the Royal Canadian Legion at that time.

Fred O'Brecht became president of the Durham Legion in 1962; backed by a number of active veterans he worked his way through Provincial and Dominion Commands, and in 1964 he was elected Dominion President, bringing honour to the local Branch and the town. During a visit of Queen Elizabeth and Prince Philip to Canada, Fred O'Brecht, as Dominion President, was introduced to the Queen at the National War Memorial in Ottawa. Also, he had the honour of being an invited guest at Sir Winston Churchill's funeral.

A tragedy occurred during a wedding reception at the legion in 1971 when an uninvited guest shot and killed two legion members, Carmen Allan and Murray Morice.

1987 was a memorable year for the Durham Legion when Ina Milne was elected President of the Durham Legion, the first woman ever to hold that position, and the McGowan Falls project was undertaken. The Legion installed floodlights at the Upper Dam in an area set aside as a park; and on Friday night, August 19th, at a Legion ceremony the lights were turned on, Mrs. Art McGowan and Wallace McGowan participating. This project was a memorial to Art McGowan, the Legion's first President and one of its founding members, and to the McGowan family who helped to develop the Falls. A sign was erected by the Legion naming the area The McGowan Falls. Art McGowan and his brother Bill served in WWI, and his brother Wallace and three nephews in WWII.

In 1987 the Legion donated $1,000 towards the Navy's Memorial, the H.M.C.S Sackville, and $1,000 towards restoration of the Lancaster aircraft as an R.C.A.F. Memorial of WWII.

An addition was constructed to the north-west of the Legion building as a Memorabilia room; this addition was made possible by the financial assistance of Mr. Charles Watson, and was completed for the celebration of the Legion's 50th Anniversary. This building contains artifacts of WWI, WWII and the Korean War, and is open to the public. It was offically opened on Sunday, June 25th, 1990, during the Anniversary festivities with Mr. Watson cutting the ribbon.

Prior to the dedication of the memorabilia, the Legion presented the Town of Durham with a clock which was installed at the town's Municipal building. In 1990 a Legion History book Lest We Forget was published.

In 1992, under the leadership of Elmer Clark, a pipe band was formed and made its first public appearance at the official opening of a Memorial Park at the east end of town.

Over the years the Durham Legion has been responsible for the November 11th Remembrance Day service at the Monument. The Branch has also been a long time supporter of local charities, youth programmes, the local hospital and fire department, and provided scholarships to sons and daughters of Legion and Auxiliary members, Boy Scouts, Girl Guides and sports organizations.

The Queen gave consent to the addition of the word Royal to the Canadian Legion #308 in 1960.

BRANCH 308 ROYAL CANADIAN LEGION MEETING HALLS

The first recorded meeting was held by a group of WWI veterans in The Armoury Building on Elgin Street North on July 4, 1940. Branch 308 received its Charter on July 20, 1940, much to the delight of WWI veterans. The branch continued to hold regular meetings in The Armoury for the next five to six years. When The Armoury was busy the legion members met in the basement of the Durham library. For a time rooms were rented over the Royal Bank (now Triangle Discount Store) from W.S. Hunter. At many of these meetings the idea was expressed about legion members owning their own hall. The old veterans had one thing in mind — to have a meeting place for the men and women returning from WWII. They certainly had a big heart and it was in the right place.

With the ending of WW II and the return of the veterans, the need for a home of their own became even greater. Larger money raising projects were undertaken with the one objective in mind — a new hall.

At a meeting on April 2, 1946, it was voted 34 to 9 that the purchase of the Norman P. McIntyre and Jessie McIntyre building be made at a price of $5,600. The sale was completed on June 14, 1946.

The first meeting in the new hall was held on July 2, 1946. All members pitched in and most of the renovations were completed by them. Members also realized that the rent from the restaurant below would help pay the upkeep if hard times struck. The Ladies Auxiliary has always been a very important financial contributor. The back room became a games room. A new radio-record player and television were purchased. The members were very proud of this hall.

After ten years in the main street hall, the members began to think about a new building. At a meeting on July 6, 1966, it was agreed that an offer of $45,000 be made on the Kon Tiki Club. This was the former bowling alley on Bruce Street North, now owned by Macton Investments. It was reported at the executive meeting of September 28, 1966, that the offer had been accepted. For some time Branch 308 operated out of both these buildings, holding general and executive meetings in the old hall and regular dances in the new one.

With the sale of the old building known as The Hall to Morley Lum went many happy memories such as Mickey Saunders reciting Dangerous Dan McGrew, the cheery whistle of Billy Moore and the rattling and hammering of Jack Lamerson.

The first project was to build an addition on the north side to provide a private bar and a Ladies Lounge. This was completed in the first year after the purchase. The debt load did not dampen the efforts of the members. Dances, dinners, bingos and teas were among the many projects undertaken by the members and the Ladies Auxiliary. Soon the debt was paid in full.

Royal Canadian Legion Hall.

In 1990, the 50th year of Branch 308, a Memorabilia Room was opened. This was made possible by the generous donation of Charles F. Watson and family, and members of the Legion.

THE LADIES AUXILIARY OF DURHAM LEGION BRANCH 308

Early in 1947 a group of ladies met to discuss the forming of a Ladies Auxiliary to the Durham Legion. Several meetings were held, and on the advice of Mrs. Cameron, Provincial President of the Ladies Auxiliary, an election took place, at which time Mrs. Morrison was elected President.

On May 13th when Mrs. Cameron came to Durham to present the newly formed Auxiliary with its Charter, 42 ladies were present. The Charter members were: Adeline Morrison, Kathleen Welch, Velma Grant, Ina Milne, Madeline Blythe, Greta Armstrong, Eleanor Connolly, Violet Steinacher and Florence Bolger. Those eligible to join the Auxiliary were wives, daughters, granddaughters and nieces of Veterans. Meetings were held on the last Thursday of each month; dues were ten cents per meeting.

On November 8, 1947, the first Poppy Tea was inaugurated, and on November 11th the first wreath from the newly formed Auxiliary was placed at the Cenotaph by Mrs. Rose Bolger, a Silver Cross Mother, and an Auxiliary member. Later Mrs. Sadie Goldsmith, also an Auxiliary member and a Silver Cross Mother, placed the Auxiliary wreath at the Cenotaph on November 11th for many years until failing health prevented her from doing so.

Bake sales, raffles, euchres and serving of dinners in the old arena enables the Durham group to raise funds for various endeavours. In 1966 when the Legion purchased the present building on Bruce Street North, the Ladies bought chairs and tables, equipped the kitchen and paid for the renovation of a ladies' lounge. On the 25th Anniversary of the Auxiliary in 1972 at a dinner prepared by the Legion men, the Ladies Auxiliary presented the Legion with a cheque for $3,000. the first of many cheques. In addition the Auxiliary pay the Legion's town taxes every year. In October, 1970, the first Auxiliary sponsored Bingo was held.

The Ladies Auxiliary donates each year to various charities. A room was furnished at the Durham Memorial Hospital and this is maintained and updated as required. Today many Legion Branches could simply not survive without the vital services of the Ladies Auxiliary.

THE ARMOURIES

Talk of an armoury building began as far back as April 1904 when the drill shed used by the 31st Grey Battalion collapsed under the pressure of a heavy build-up of snow on the roof.

In January 1908 the town council learned that a government grant of between $2,500 and $3,000 would be provided if the town could provide the proper site for the building. Sites discussed were: the McKechnie property on Queen Street, the Vollett property on Garafraxa Street, and the Edge property on Albert Street. Council could not come to an agreement on any of these properties. During this time, Mr. Brown was building an arena on George Street East and offered the west end of the property for an armoury at a price of $100. This offer was accepted.

The Armoury was built between 1909 and 1910 at a cost of approximately $7,000. The building's main function was to store the uniforms, rifles and equipment needed in time of conflict. In May, 1910, all work on the building was complete. The following is a description of the Armoury interior as described in the *Durham Chronicle*:

"We had a look through the new Armoury on Tuesday evening last and must express ourselves as well pleased with Durham's military building. Besides being strongly constructed it is as well neatly furnished and finished throughout and now ready for occupancy. The band-room, captain's office, quarter master's office and the room reserved for the Rifle Association, and in fact the whole place, is well fitted up, with a view to answering the purpose for which it was built and is a credit to the town and the men who had the building of it. The inside finish is especially good, brass locks and hinges being used throughout, and nothing but the best of material going into any part of the building. The workmanship, too, is good. The credit for which belongs to Mr. George Kress, who had this part of the

contract and executed it with his usual ability. It was through the courtesy of Mr. James Lenahan, the inspector, that we were allowed to ramble through our military headquarters and the pains he took in showing us around the place were much appreciated."

The Armouries

On May 19, 1910 Mr. T. W. Fuller, government architect, and Mr. Perrins, representing the militia department, inspected and approved the building.

At this period of time the building did not serve in a military capacity. The town band was using it every Tuesday night to practice in, the Rifle Association held regular meetings, and when the junior form of the public school became over-crowded, the class was divided and the teacher, Miss Edith Allan, taught the children in the Armoury.

Soon war in Europe broke out and it became evident that our country would be involved and the 147th Grey Battalion was formed. During World War I the Armouries played a part on behalf of the Red Cross. Women in town working on behalf of the Society began to meet there every day to make comforts for the soldiers.

When World War I ended the Armouries became a gathering point for veterans as they arrived back home and also served as a meeting area when home-coming events for the troops were taking place.

By the late 1920s, when all things relating to the military were slowly fading to memory, the building began to go into a state of disrepair. Windows were shattered, paint was peeling off the walls and the roof was beginning to leak. The building remained in this state for quite a number of years.

Due to the unsettled nature of Europe during the early 1930s, recruiting and regular training began in December of 1936. The 147th Grey Battalion regiment amalgamated with the Simcoe Foresters to form a new unit called the Grey and Simcoe Foresters. With the outbreak of war in 1939, there was an immediate revival in the Armoury building bringing about extensive repairs. New heating, new wiring and complete redecoration was done and the building was then placed under permanent armed guard.

Remembrance Day parade to the cenotaph 1951.

By the spring of 1940 it became clear that Canada would be involved in World War II and recruitment continued. I. B. Sharpe was part of the reserve army. He was responsible for the military training of many young Durham men and he also had custody of the Armouries, as well as the rifles, equipment and uniforms contained within. Twice weekly training took place for the reserves at the Armoury for the duration of the war. Training officers came regularly every week to assist in training in weapons, map reading, tactics and wireless communication. Many officers were recruited from this reserve and served our country in many facets of the war effort.

At a July 4, 1940 meeting at the Armouries held by World War I veterans, it was decided that they should join the Canadian Legion of the British Empire. Regular meetings of the Legion continued at the Armouries for the duration of the war.

Training exercises continued, as did the war. Tactical exercises were simulated on the sand table in the weapons' room but some exercises were actually carried out in the open to give the men experience and insight into what lay ahead.

After the war had come to an end there was a large welcome home party in March of 1946 for members of the armed forces who had enlisted for active service from the Durham platoon of the Grey and Simcoe Foresters reserve battalion. During the evening a roll of honour bearing the names of nearly 90 men, who received their preliminary training here before joining the active forces for duty overseas, was unveiled. Among those listed, eight men paid the supreme sacrifice.

From the resurrection in 1939 of the Armoury until after the war, W. R. McGowan was the caretaker of the Armoury and kept the building in excellent shape. He was said to be the friend of all who entered its doors.

Through the 1950s and 1960s the Grey and Simcoe Foresters continued to drill and hold meetings in the Armoury. Keith Hunter took over the command of the Durham platoon and Armoury in 1956 when Mr. Sharpe retired.

In time, military spending cutbacks brought about the closing of many armouries in this area — Durham among them. Eventually a large armoury was built in Owen Sound and it became the site of all area military activities.

Mr. Don Pust bought the Durham Armoury building from the Crown in 1960 and it was used as an apartment building for a number of years. In 1986 Leslie Detzler bought the building for her chiropractic clinic and home. Dr. Detzler had extensive renovations done on the inside, but aside from new doors and windows and a balcony, the outside remains the same as when built.

Dr. Woods bought the armouries building from Dr. Detzler in 1994 and he and his family live upstairs, while the first floor continues as a chiropractic clinic.

COLONEL FRASER HUNTER

Colonel Fraser Hunter, one of the children of James and Kate Hunter, was the last member of the Hunter family to reside at the Hedges. He had a very illustrious career. After graduating from Upper Canada College and The Royal Military College, Kingston, Colonel Hunter made his way to England to enlist in the Royal Indian Army. He was required to outfit himself with uniforms and accoutrements at his own expense, and he served as a Bengal Lancer for over thirty years.

Colonel Hunter eventually became Deputy Surveyor General for India. During his military career he saw action on several fronts. In addition to several battles in India, he fought in the Boxer rebellion in China and was present at the relief of Peking. In 1914 Fraser Hunter was Squadron Commander in Northwest Frontier operations. He fought with the First and Fourth Armies and joined the Air Force. He spent two years as Chief of Staff to British forces in Persia. In 1917 he served in Russia and witnessed the start of the Bolshevik Revolution, was present at the evacuation of Petrograd, and helped carry the Czarist cyphers to Washington via Trans-Siberian Railroad and Vladivostok. Colonel Hunter was fluent in Hindustani, Persian, Afghan, Chinese and Japanese; and he had a working knowledge of four other languages. The Colonel had a host of decorations bestowed on him, including the D. S. O., The Military Order of the Dragon, The Persian Nishan-i-Shiyahi-l Talla's, The Croix de Guerre, and war medals from China, Canada and India.

On returning to Canada he became the Liberal member of the Legislature for St. Patrick's Riding, Toronto. On retiring, he returned to The Hedges in Durham, where he died in 1959.

In 1960 The Hedges was purchased by Dr. and Mrs. Duncan Jamieson, who sold the property to Mr. and Mrs. Ben Sieling in 1969.

Colonel Fraser Hunter's Medals
As the medals indicate the service was varied with many British Empire medals and also many foreign medals. The list of medals and decorations is as follows: The Distinguished Service Order; China Medal 1900, with the 'Relief of Peking' bar; 1914-20 War Medal; 1914-15 Star; Victory Medal, with 'Mentioned in Dispatches' oakleaf; General Service Medal, with 'Iraq' and N.W. Persia bars; King Edward VII's Coronation Medal 1902; King George V's Delhi Durbar Medal 1911; King George V's Silver Jubilee Medal 1935; King George VI's Coronation Medal 1937; Military Order of the Dragon-China 1900; Croix de Guerre 1914-18, with Silver Palm and Silver Unit Dispatch Star; and Gold Medal of Persia (1932).

After nearly five years of war the end finally came on May 6, 1945, but not before claiming the lives of twenty-seven young Durham boys. They are as follows:

Arthur Allan
Gerald Belleau
Emmerson G. Bennett
Denis Collins
William Davey
Gordon Falkingham
Victor Goodchild
Alwyn Goldsmith
R.J. Gray
Harold Greenwood
Orval Harrison
Robert Hunter
Star Jamieson
Ross Keller

Lorne MacArthur
Kenneth MacDonald
Harry McCaslin
Gordon McGillivray
Fred Moses
Reginald Ostranger
Norman Steeds
James Tilt
Howard Watson
Robert Webster
William Webb
James R. Wilson
Carson Whitmore

"Their Name Liveth for Evermore"

Flt. Sgt. (Air Gnr.)
William Harold Davey,
RCAF 102 Sqdn.
Killed August 10th, 1943.

Tpr. Gordon D. Falkingham,
21st Armoured Regiment, RCAF.
Killed October 8th, 1944.

Pte. Alwyn Garnet Goldsmith,
Lincoln and Welland Regt. RCIC.
Killed December 29th, 1944.

Victor Haig Goodchild,
Lake Superior Regt. RCIC.
Killed September 17th, 1944.

Pilot Officer Robert J. Gray.

Cpl. John Harold Greenwood,
Royal Canadian Corps of Signals,
2nd Canadian Armoured Brigade.
Killed June 7, 1944.

Orvel Harrison.

Sgt. Pilot
Robert Wight Hunter,
RCAF.
Killed April 8th, 1942.

Flying Officer
Ross Whaley Keller,
RCAF 438 Sqdn.
Killed January 1st, 1945.

Wt. Officer I Fred Starr Jamieson,
RCAF 8 Sqdn.
Killed July 10th, 1943.

Pte. Lorne MacArthur,
48th Highlanders of Canada.
Killed October 19th, 1943.

Pte.
Kenneth Hugh MacDonald,
Nova Scotia Highlanders.
Killed October 18th, 1944.

Spr. William Henry McCaslin,
1 Field Park Coy.,
Royal Canadian Engineers.
Killed August 19th, 1942.

L. Cpl. Donald Gordon McGillivray,
Stormont, Dundas and Glengarry
Highlanders RCIC.
Killed July 8th, 1944.

L. Cpl. Frederick John Moses,
48th Highlanders of Canada.
Killed October 3rd, 1943.

Reginald Ostranger.

L. Cpl.
William Norman Steeds,
RCEME.
Killed August 8th, 1943.

Cpl. James Patrick Tilt,
Armoured Regiment RCAC.
Killed August 11th, 1944.

Flt. Sgt. Howard Cameron Watson,
RCAF 103 Sqdn.
Killed May 19th, 1942.

Lt. William Spencer Webb,
12th Armoured Regiment
CAC.
Killed June 28, 1944.

Flying Officer
Robert James Webster,
RCAF 429 Sqdn.
Killed May 2nd, 1944.

Flying Officer
George Carson Whitmore,
RCAF 1 Sqdn.
Killed March 6th, 1943.

Pte. James Richardson Wilson,
Perth Regiment RCIC.
Killed April 24, 1945.

Pte. Gerald Thomas Belleau,
Royal Hamilton Light Infantry,
RCIC.
Killed July 26th, 1944.

L.A.C. William Arthur Allen,
RCAF 422 Sqdn.
Killed Dec. 19th, 1942.

Gnr. Emerson Johnson Bennett,
Royal Canadian Artillery.
Died April 26th, 1943.

Sgt. Denis Michael Collins,
RCAF.
Killed December 19th, 1943.

KOESLAG RECOGNITION

In 1948 Mr. and Mrs. Albert J. Koeslag and nine of their thirteen children emigrated from the Netherlands to the Durham area. The next spring Mr. Koeslag received a letter from His Excellency, the Governor General of Canada, stating that he had been awarded the King's Medal for courage — by concealing Allied servicemen and enabling them to escape or evade capture during the Second World War.

On May 8, 1949, Lieutenant Colonel, the Honourable Ray Lawson, OBE, the Lieutenant Governor of Ontario, came to Durham to present the King's Medal awarded by King George VI to Mr. Albert Jan Koeslag. A large crowd gathered in the Town Park to witness the investiture, including: the Durham Branch of the Canadian Legion, BESL, the Ladies Auxiliary of the Durham Legion, members of the Reserve Army, the Girl Guides and Brownies.

Mr. Koeslag had previously been the recipient of a Certificate of Appreciation from the British Commonwealth of Nations and a Medal from General Eisenhower at the command of the President of the United States. His son, Albert, received similar awards and his daughter, Gerda, received a Certificate from General Eisenhower for her work in the underground. Seven sons worked in the underground as well — Hendrick, Jan, John, Albert, William, Henk, Jerry and Herman.

Societies, Lodges & Clubs

7

THE AGRICULTURAL SOCIETY

The South Grey Agricultural Society was probably founded in 1858. No records exist of its inauguration, but the January 16th, 1861, edition of the *Durham Standard* carries a report of the annual meeting. (The secretary gives the name the Durham Agricultural Society but this is an error because it was known for 75 years as the South Grey Agricultural Society.)

"The annual meeting of the Durham Agricultural Society took place at the Old School House on Saturday, the 12th instant, when the following officers were elected for the current year:

John Miller — President
James Edge — Vice-President
S. E. Legate — Sec. & Treasurer

Directors

William McGirr	Ezekiel Aldrich
Archibald Park	Alex J. Smith
John Dickie	Thos. Davis
Chas. Gray	James Hopkins
Herbert Rowswell	

It was moved, seconded and resolved that members failing to pay up their subscription of one dollar on or before the fifteenth of April next, shall pay one dollar and 50 cents to entitle them to membership thereafter. All friends of the Agricultural interests and particularly of the success of the society, will please govern themselves accordingly." The reason for this was that the government paid a grant of about three dollars for each membership paid up at that date.

When the early pioneers had a small plot of land cleared, they would plant some wheat, and when they could store enough grass to winter a cow or a yoke of oxen, they would buy these locally as cheaply as possible. Much of the breeding stock was genetically inferior. The government responded to this situation by sponsoring agricultural fairs. It was thought that by competing against one another for prizes, and by attending fairs to witness their neighbour's competitive efforts, local pioneers would be inspired to improve their farming practices and so produce better livestock and grain harvests. That is exactly what happened. The agricultural fairs contributed immensely to the improvement of farm produce, and this was reflected in the economic improvement to every city, town, and village in the province as well as the farming community. These fairs were called an agricultural showcase or a window on agriculture.

Durham Standard, September 23, 1859:

"Messrs. Dickson have authorized the Directors of the Durham Agricultural Society to offer in addition to the prizes awarded by the County Society, $4½ for the best sample of 2 bushels of Fall Wheat, and $4½ for the best sample of 2 bushels of Spring Wheat, to be competed for by members of the Durham Society."

4 classes of Neat Cattle	—	11 prizes
9 classes of cattle	—	26 prizes
5 classes of oxen, including yoke of oxen	—	15 prizes
4 classes of Leicester sheep	—	8 prizes
7 classes common sheep	—	15 prizes
3 classes pigs	—	6 prizes
1 class fowls	—	2 prizes
6 classes grain	—	14 prizes
Best 50 lbs. Flour	—	3 prizes
Best ½ dozen ears Indian corn	—	2 prizes
Best 4 lbs. butter	—	4 prizes
Best 8 lbs. cheese	—	3 prizes
Best 10 lbs. Maple Sugar	—	3 prizes
Best Iron Plough	—	2 prizes
Best Wooden Plough	—	2 prizes
Best sett Harrows	—	2 prizes
Best Fanning Mill (local)	—	2 prizes
Best Wagon (local)	—	2 prizes
Best Lumber Sleigh	—	2 prizes
Best pair Men's Fine Pegged Boots	—	2 prizes

Crowd on the hill at the Fall Fair.

Best pair Men's Coarse Pegged Boots	—	3 prizes
Best 10 yards Satinett	—	2 prizes
Best Women's Pegged Boots	—	3 prizes
Best 10 yards Fulled Cloth	—	2 prizes
Best 10 yards White Flannel	—	2 prizes
Best 5 lbs. Carded Rolls	—	2 prizes
Best two pair Woolen Socks	—	2 prizes
Best two pair Woolen Mitts	—	2 prizes
Best pound Stocking yarn	—	2 prizes
Best sett Horse-shoes	—	2 prizes
Best two Canadian Straw Hats	—	2 prizes
Best ox yoke and Bows	—	2 prizes
Best Thousand Shingles, 40 inch 50 courses	—	2 prizes
Best two sides Upper Leather	—	2 prizes
Best one side Sole Leather	—	2 prizes
Best sett Double Harness	—	2 prizes
Best Saddle and Bridle	—	2 prizes
Best Tin Stove furniture copper Bottomed	—	2 prizes

Total prize money $240.00

At this time there were no prizes for baking, preserving, sewing, fancy work or flowers. These competition categories were added years later. By 1870 there were 15 classes of sewing, knitting and fancy work, one for flowers, and one for cooking (one loaf of bread).

No admission to the grounds was charged until 1879 when a fee of 10 cents was charged. The Grey Review reported that in that year there were well over 3,000 people at the fair.

The first fall fairs were held north of Lambton Street in a field behind A. B. McNab's store on Albert Street. The next location of the fair (about 1868) was in a field at Moody's barn at the foot of Durham Hill. Next the fair was located on the east side of Bruce Street between George Street and Lambton Street. Here in the early 1870s a framed show house was built, and when, in 1879, the Agricultural Society bought a new site south of Saddler Street West, where the Community Centre is now, this showhouse was moved to the new location. This building was used by the Society for over 100 years. It was razed in 1976.

In 1887 additional land was purchased from James Falkingham extending the grounds farther south and west. In 1890 the Town Council officially closed South Street west of the Wellington Georgian Bay Railway tracks providing the fair grounds with a full half-mile race track.

The poultry house and cattle sheds were built in 1895. It was said that from 1890 to 1925 Durham had one of the best poultry shows in this part of Ontario. Some of the local poultry exhibitors showed at the Royal Winter Fair and occasionally took top honours. In 1910 poultry fanciers in Durham decided to hold a Regional Poultry Show on January 18th and 19th, 1911. The Durham Chronicle of January 26th, 1911, reported that, although the show had begun quite modestly, the directors were surprised when they received about 400 entries, including ducks, turkeys, pigeons, pheasants, and a great many varieties of hens. Mr. Colin Blyth had the honour of exhibiting the largest bird at the fair — a bronze gobbler weighing 35 pounds. These poultry shows continued for some years and were held in the fall fair buildings. Eventually the fall fair absorbed the poultry show into their Fair.

In the early days of the Society local ploughing matches were sponsored. One of these was held at Mr. Alex Morton's, two miles north of Durham. The fee to enter the competition was 25 cents for members of the South Grey Agricultural Society and $1.25 for others. Two ploughs were awarded for 1st and 2nd prizes; 3rd prize was five dollars; 4th prize was three dollars.

At the annual meeting of the South Grey Agricultural Society in January, 1904, Mr. James Edge announced that he was retiring from active duty on the Fall Fair board. He had been working on the Fair board for 46 years and was president for 25 of those years. The Society honoured him with a recognition for his long years of service.

In 1907 field crop competitions were inaugurated. Mr. William Scarf was elected President of the Ontario Association of Agricultural Societies in 1917. To date he has been the only person from the Durham Society to have been so honoured. Ladies were first elected to office in the Society in 1917, and in 1918 Mrs. R. Burnett was elected 2nd Vice President. The year 1934 saw the name changed from South Grey Agricultural Society to Durham Agricultural Society. The 1940s saw 4H Club work being sponsored and this became an important part of the Durham Fair. In 1952 the Durham Agricultural Society gave their grounds to the Town of Durham for one dollar as a site for the new community centre. In return the Society was granted free use of the grounds and buildings for eight days each year. The Society also spear-headed a campaign to lay a concrete floor in the arena over the artificial ice pipes.

A Women's Division was formed in 1955, and it is still an important part of planning and working for a better fall fair.

Over the years there have been many special events featured by the Society: Saugeen Valley Steeplechase, Fleece Wool Show, Regional Sheep Show, Jersey Parish Show, 4H Clubs, Horse races, Saddle, Heavy and Light horses, Field Crop Competition, Cream and Butter Commercial feature, Pet Shows, Beauty Pageant, and

Queen of the Fair Competition. Past Presidents as far as the records show have been:

J. Miller	J.R. Edwards
Jas. Edge	Jas. Ferguson
D. Fletcher	Wm. Anderson
George Binnie	Robert Edwards
William Calder	E.J. Wilby
Daniel Edge	Cameron Robson
J.W. Blythe	Franklin Jackson
George Ritchie	A.J. McLean
John McGirr	Archie Turnbull
Joseph Crutchley	Neil Wilton
J.C. Hamilton	Allan Koehler
R.C. Robinson	Allie McGirr
G.S. Kearney	Harold Carmount
Geo. Bell	Thomas O'Dwyer
Thos. Firth	Art Rivest
John Baker	Jack Milligan
Geo. Cadogan	Douglas Reay
Neil MacArthur	

Presidents of the Women's Division have been:

Mesdames:	
Verna Sharpe	Velma Jackson
Glennie MacDonald	Janet MacArthur
Muriel Baker	Willie Grond
Margaret Milligan	Marie McRonald
Edna McLean	Deanna Hopkins
Margaret Ritchie	Marilyn Rivest
Irva Murdock	Doreen Hopkins
Doreen Hopkins	Pauline Reay

ST. ANDREW'S SOCIETY

The St. Andrew's Society was formed in the village that is now Durham in 1856. Its purpose was to raise funds to assist destitute people in the community. In the October 21, 1859, *Durham Standard* is a notice "that the Society had failed miserably at its purpose and that a new attempt is now started to raise funds for those in our midst in dire need."

The Society met in the large room above Mr. Archibald Hunter's granary just north of the British Hotel. Rented for use from Mr. Hunter for many years it was generally known as St. Andrew's Hall.

The following is an account of the St. Andrew's Dinner held on St. Andrew's day, November 30, 1883, at Mr. Horn's Hotel (Hahn House) as reported in the *Grey Review*, December 6, 1883:

"About eighty members of the St. Andrew's Society sat down to a delicious dinner. The haggis was declared by old Scotchmen to be one of the best they had ever tasted. Following the dinner the President, J.H. Hunter, presided and the following toasts were proposed:

To "the Queen," followed by the National Anthem;
To "Prince and Princess of Wales and the Royal Family," responded by Mr. Jas. Watson singing "Red, White and Blue";

To "The Day and a honor to it," responded by two solos by Prof. Morgan;

To "The Army Navy & Volunteers," H.W. Mockler sang Rule Britannia;

To "The Gov. General and Lieut. Gov.," Thos. Colgan replied with a few witty remarks and sang "McCarty's Mare" and encore, an Irish song;

To "Dominion Parliament and Ontario Legislature," four speeches and another solo;

To " Municipal Council," three speeches;

To "The Learned Professions," speech Dr. Jamieson, song J. P. Telford, Barrister;

To " Manufacturing Interests, two speeches;

To "Agriculture," James Lauder song;

To "Commercial Interests," four speeches and a song by J.H. Hunter;

To "Educational Interests," three or four songs;

To "Sister Societies," song "The British Lyon";

To "The Press," speech by Ben Townsend, editor of Review, song by Walter Buchan "Speak to Me";

To "The Ladies," some songs;

To "The Host and Hostess, Mr. Hunter

To "The President," some songs;

To "The Secretary," some songs;

After all the business of the evening had been disposed of a number of songs were sung until Mr. Grant got up and played several numbers on his bagpipes.

After many exchanges of congratulations the meeting broke up at "The wee sma' hours beyont the twa' amid general good feeling."

Editor's Note: Knowing that a Scotchman would not drink a toast with lemonade, the last paragraph was probably very accurately stated.

For the first 45 years the St. Andrew's Society took part in the social activities of Durham and from time to time presented concerts for the entertainment and enjoyment of the local citizens. In 1892 St. Andrew's Hall was sold to the Catholic Church and was renovated in 1901, and the Society seemed to disappear; but another Scottish organization The Sons of Scotland was formed with three Durham businessmen at its head — Wm. Black, Chief; Robert Torry, Secretary; Charles Ramage, Treasurer. An arm of this group, known as the Ben Nevis Camp, held occasional concerts in Durham. One such concert in 1908 was billed as Annual Scotch Concert featuring a brilliant trio of a young Scottish soprano who had a range of three octaves, a tenor and story teller, and their accompanist and cellist from the London Academy of Music. The concert was held in the Town Hall and was acclaimed a great success.

In 1892 Mrs. Hunter sold the property to the Roman Catholic Church, and the following article appeared in the *Durham Review*, May 9, 1901, written by S.L.M. Luke:

"Another relic of the past is now being demolished, namely the frame attachment to the British Hotel Block, long and familiarly known as St. Andrew's

Hall. The building or attachment was erected by the late Archibald Hunter, Sr., for public meetings, &c. At an earlier period the Division Court was held in a small frame building used as a church by the Disciple Brethern, who formed a small community in this town in the early 50's, and was named the "Synagogue" by an eccentric resident of Bentinck, about the year 1858, at the time the Court sittings were removed to St. Andrew's.

"Political, agricultural and other local meetings were convened here, such as church services, the Mechanics' Institute Library, Street improvements, Incorporation, &c, &."

LOYAL ORANGE LODGE

The warrant for the organization of L.O.L. #632 was issued to John Moody on September 13, 1855. According to that warrant, the officers for that year were: W.M., J. M. Hunter; D.M., John Staples; Chaplain, Christie Williams; Rec. Sec., James Staples; Fin. Sec., John Williams; Treasurer, James Edge; Marshal, George Firth; Lecturer, Thomas Stinson.

On September 3, 1857, a resolution was passed to purchase a suitable lot for a meeting hall. The lot purchased was half way up the hill east of Garafraxa Street just north of the old fire hall. The Durham Review of January 27, 1898, states: "That same year [1857] a frame building known as the Orange Hall was erected on the lot. It was in its time a very useful building, for in addition to its society use, it was utilized for public meetings of various kinds and not a few of that generation of Durhamites went to school within its walls. But the hum of the learner, the eloquence of the orator, the songs of the Salvation Army and the bleat of the Orange Goat will be heard no more. Of late years it has been falling into decay and was sold to Mr. O. Hopkins who relocated it on the Durham Road South of the Durham Cemetery. None will regret its disappearance though it severs a connecting link between the past and present."

In 1884 the Durham District L.O.L. was formed comprising officers of L.O.L. #632, 668, 689, 891 and 1192. Robert Aljoe was the first District Master and when the L.O.L. #1192 Glenelg was organized in 1865, five of the thirteen charter members were transferred from the Durham Lodge. The first officers were: P.M., T. Whitmore; W.M., Robert Aljoe; D.M., John Martin; Chaplain, A. Bell; Rec. Sec., Geo Mathews; Treasurer, T. Whitmore; Sn. Committee, A. Bell, R. McChesney, S. Lawrence, R. Bell, Wm. McFadden; Marshal, A. Bell.

In 1950 L.O.L. #1192 built a new hall on Lot 60, Concession 2 E.G.R, Glenelg Township, south of No. 9 School. In December, 1958, L.O.L. #632 of Durham and L.O.L. #1192 of Glenelg were affiliated under the warrant of L.O.L. #1192, and meetings have been held regularly in the new hall since that date.

Lady Victoria Lodge Organized 1949.
Back Row: Mrs. Tom Whitmore, Mrs. Geo. Sharp, Mrs. Jim Lunn, Mrs. F. Gerber.
Centre Row: Mrs. Bob Whitmore, Mrs. Alex Aljoe, Mrs. Art Matthews, Mrs. T. Collier, Mrs. E. Hutton, Mrs. John Sharp, Mrs. John Lunn.
Front Row: George Sharp, Mrs. A. McGirr, Mrs. Jack Picken, Mabel Sharp, Mrs. Mina Jackson, Lillian Cross, Mrs. Hopkins, Mrs. Hargrave, Mrs. Geo. Turnbull, Tom Whitmore.

LADY ORANGE BENEVOLENT ASSOCIATION

The L.O.B.A. was organized on May 22, 1949, as a ladies group to work along with the L.O.L. Right Worshipful Sister Mina Jackson and her Degree team installed the first officers: W.M. Sister Mabel Sharp; I.P.M. Sister Gertrude Sharp; W.D.M. Sister Lillian Cross; Jr. D.M. Sister Margaret Lunn; Chaplain, Sister Christine Whitmore; Rec. Sec., Sister Islay Matthews; Financial Secretary, Sister Barbara Turnbull; Treasurer, Sister Wilimine Gerber; Guardian Bro. Thomas Whitmore; Director of Ceremony, Betty Lunn; Sr. Lecturer, Esther Hargrave; I.G., Iva Hutchinson; O.G., Bro. George Sharp; second committee, Sister Dorothy Aljoe; third committee, Sister Alice Aljoe; fourth committee, Sister Ada Hutton; auditors, Sisters Violet Sharp, Nina Hopkins and Effie Collier.

DURHAM AND DISTRICT HORTICULTURAL SOCIETY

For many years the records of any early organization were not available, but recently some of these have come to light. From the first minute book of the first Horticultural society organized in Durham, it is read that a meeting for this purpose was called by several enthusiastic residents on November 19th, 1896. This was held in the Middaugh House. Dr. Jas. Gun was

elected Chairman and Wm. Gorsline, Secretary. A representative of the Ontario Department of Arts and Agriculture addressed the meeting.

On January 18, 1897, the first regular meeting was held in the public reading room to deal with the election of officers for the new society. These were: President, Christopher Firth; 1st Vice President, Gilbert McKechnie; 2nd Vice-President, R. MacFarlane. Directors for the year: D. Jackson, H. Parker, N.W. Campbell, T. Brown, Dr. J. Gun, J. Burt, C.L. Grant, George Binnie, J. Kilmer. Honorary Directors were: Mrs. A. MacKenzie, Mrs. L. Elvidge, Mrs. D. Jamieson, Mrs. N. McKechnie, Mrs. ? Mockler, and Mrs. ? McRae. John Kelly was elected Treasurer, and Wm. Gorsline, Secretary. Auditors were Thomas Allan and R. MacFarlane. On motion by Dr. Gun and John Kelly this society became associated with the Ontario Association, and each member was to receive a copy of the Horticulturalist for one year. One hundred and eight copies were distributed.

In September of that year an exhibition of plants and flowers was held, specializing in cannas and gladioli. Members received premiums — the first was twelve gladioli, costing one cent each, and two canna tubers, followed by seeds of begonias and geraniums, and later premiums were gooseberry, currant, and raspberry bushes. In 1898 a committee was appointed to canvass for members, with notices to that effect being put in both newspapers. In 1899 members were given a choice of apple trees, plum trees, and pear trees, or bulbs — no one to receive premiums of greater value than 40 cents. Later the choices were St. Lawrence, Duchess or Pewaukee apple trees, Montmorency cherries, Spiraea, Weigela shrubs, and cut leaf birch. In 1899 hyacinth and tulip bulbs were available choices. April, 1900, saw the Horticulturalist supplied to members at 80 cents each. Lecturers from the Ontario Association were invited to speak on subjects such as the cultivation of small fruits. A delegate was appointed to attend the meeting of the Provincial Fruits, Flowers, and Honey show in Toronto in November and report at a later meeting. A government grant of $52 was recorded in 1902.

In 1904 thanks were extended to the Mechanics Institute for use of the library hall for meetings. A committee of R. MacFarlane, J. McGowan, A.W.H. Lauder, and the Moores was appointed at a May, 1906, meeting to devise a fund-raising scheme to make improvements in connection with town and society. A salary was paid in 1907 to the secretary of $25 annually and five dollars to the caretaker, who also delivered the premiums. Professor Hutt gave a lecture on Beautifying Home, Public, and City Grounds at an entertainment evening in 1908. The organization held its meeting in the new rink — Brown's rink — in November, 1910.

On November 4th, 1911, the annual meeting was held in the Town Hall with President Jas. Lloyd presiding. Officers at that time were: 1st Vice President, Wm. Moffatt; 2nd Vice President, Thos. Morton; Directors: Mrs. James A. Brown, Mrs. C. Ramage, Mrs. A.H. Jackson, A.W.H. Lauder, John McGowan, P. Gagnon, John Towner, E.A. Hay, and Chris. Firth, who was delegate to Convention. Secretary-Treasurer, Chris. Firth. The annual membership fee was two dollars.

The last entry in this, the only minute book available, was for June 10th, 1912, when a lively discussion was held on how to encourage more active interest among the young people of town and neighbourhood.

A group of interested persons met in 1970 to discuss the possibility of organizing an horticultural society for the area. A Charter was presented to the new group dated March 12, 1971. Fred T. O'Brecht was the first President. Other members of the Charter Executive and Directors were:

Dr. Ian Grafton	Mrs. Gertrude Hewitt
Mrs. Billie Grafton	Mrs. Anna Koehler
Don McQueen	Arthur Derby
Mrs. Margaret McNally	Mrs. Elsie McGowan
Mrs. Tena Schut	Mrs. Iva Sharpe
Colonel C. Greenleaf	Mrs. Irva Murdock
Mrs. Blanche Snell	

Auditors: Allan Koehler, Kenneth Macdonald

Projects for the first year included assuming the responsibility of planting and maintaining flower beds at the recently constructed signs at the four entrances to Durham. This has continued as a project for the society each year with many additions.

In 1972 plans for Riverside Park got underway with much enthusiasm and as this year was Durham's centennial year, the society sponsored a Centennial Tea and Flower Show. This occasion also featured a display of Antiques.

A Tree Planting Programme for Durham and area was commenced in 1974, and has continued, with changes as required. 1977 saw the society holding a Tree Dedication Service at Riverside Park on a beautiful Sunday afternoon. This was to honour Fred T. O'Brecht, Mrs. Ida Padfield, and Mrs. Mary Wixson. These three former members had served the society well, and oak trees were planted to honour their memory. In the ensuing years many more trees have been planted to honour other members who had contributed to the work of the society.

More recently, the Horticultural Society has assumed the care of the Town Park. A foundation planting was carried out at the Community Centre, and well over 1000 bulbs were planted in various town locations.

A very generous bequest came to the society from the estate of Mrs. Clarence (Elsie) McGirr. A bronze plaque dedicated to the memory of Mr. and Mrs. Clarence McGirr was placed at the entrance to the Library where a portion of the bequest had been spent.

The Rest Awhile Parkette, where the old Fire Hall was located on Durham Hill, is also looked after by the society. It is home to a large blue spruce tree and several small pines and in front of these is a large flower bed which receives much attention from visitors. The Heritage Walkway over the old railway bridge received assistance from the society which has enabled landscaping to be completed. This has been a very worthwhile project for the town.

The Riverside Park has proven its value over the years —picnic tables and green grass provide a convenient location enjoyed by many small groups. In total, the society owns and maintains 17 park benches. These are placed throughout the town, including a parkette at the local post office. Each year bus trips are planned and have proved educational.

The society has assisted the Agricultural Society each year with the Fall Fair. Its group display, usually depicting a well-known nursery rhyme, is always of particular interest. Books and magazines of horticultural interest have been purchased and given to the local library.

Monthly meetings are held and special speakers provide much information on various aspects of horticulture. Demonstrations by local artisans are also enjoyed. The Society has now underway an Outreach programme. This will be to work with Cubs and Brownies, teach them how to garden, and instruct them with regard to conservation. The regular newsletters sent out to the members contain much information of value.

The society is appreciative of both grants and generous donations received each year. Many persons have served through the years on the executive and as members. At the present time there are over 200 members.

The 1992 Officers and Directors are:

President	Liz Cook
1st Vice President	Nancy Gold
2nd Vice President	Shirley Goldsmith
Treasurer	Nadine Saunders
Secretary	Janis Stokes
Membership Secretary	Ina Lamerson

Directors
Ken Laughlin	Marilyn Wright
Jack LaRose	Irma Clark
Elizabeth Watson	Nadine Saunders
Jake Grond	Elsie Kelly
Alex Yule	Janis Stokes

MASONIC LODGE

Durham Lodge A.F. & A. M. No. 306 was chartered in 1873 by the Grand Lodge of Canada in the Province of Ontario.

Charter members were: J. H. Hunter, 1st Worshipful Master, Abraham Gold, Archie Davidson, John Rogerson Smith, Robt. McFarlane, James Laidlaw, William Whitmore, Chas. G. Grant. First person to join Durham Lodge was W. A. Vollett in March, 1874.

There have been many members serve this District as Grand Lodge officers. Elected with the title Right Worshipful Brother were:

J. Ireland 1910	N. Greenwood 1957
J. F. Grant 1921	H. E. McNaughton 1970
W. H. Kress 1933	A. Bruce Auckland 1982
H. McKechnie 1943	Ross Clark 1993

Appointed as Grand Lodge officers with title of Very Worshipful Brother were:

Fred Arnett	Wilfred Weaver
Kenneth Hooper	Craig Vollett

Present Worshipful Master is Worshipful Brother Ian Graham 1993-1994.

The lodge meets the second Tuesday of each month except July and August. Elections are held in May and installation of new officers is in June.

Inside Dalglish Hall.
First meeting place of Masonic Lodge 306 in 1874. It was also the council chambers for the Durham Council from 1872-75.

Women's Institute Concert
Joan Patton, Olive Falkingham, Iva Hutchinson,
Verna Sharpe, Jean Breen, Lillian Cross,
Clara Adams, Jemima Tobin.

DURHAM WOMEN'S INSTITUTE

About 105 years ago a South Grey Farmers' Institute was formed. Members were farmers and the meetings were usually held in the Durham Town Hall. The purpose of this organization was to educate the farmer on all facets of agriculture, including production methods, economics, business methods, home amusements, etc. These objectives were achieved through the use of topics, discussions and lectures by well-informed people. In 1897 the first Women's Institute was organized at Stoney Creek by Mrs. Adelaide Hoodless. The South Grey Farmers' Institute was so successful that this organization decided to support the formation of a Women's Institute in the Durham area. In January, 1902, the members invited their wives, and any other interested women, to attend the Farmers' Institute meeting at which time Mrs. Colin Campbell was the speaker. After the general meeting the ladies held a meeting by themselves, and the South Grey Women's Institute was born with Mrs. Thomas McGirr as President, and Miss Kate Dixon as Secretary-Treasurer. The first Women's Institute had a membership of 79 from Durham and the surrounding district — mostly from the rural area. At the first meeting it was decided to assemble on the first Thursday afternoon of each month, a tradition that lasted over 90 years. The meet-

ings were held in the homes of the members, but because of the great distances to be travelled, branches were soon formed in other communities, and Durham had its own Women's Institute. The motto of the Institute was "For Home and Country," with the objective of improved family living conditions and the development of better citizens.

Some subjects of study have been home economics, health, education, citizenship, cultural activities, agriculture, industry, historical research, and current events. In the early years speakers could be obtained from the Department of Agriculture, but local professional people such as doctors, ministers, lawyers and teachers were also utilized. The Home Economics branch of the Department of Agriculture has over the years been a great help in providing short courses, leadership training schools and an excellent 4H programme for young girls. These programmes were supported by the Institute.

The Women's Institute is not a money-raising organization, but over the years it has assisted in many community projects such as milk for elementary school pupils and gifts for those in children's shelters and nursing homes. During the two world wars, members knitted and sewed articles for the Red Cross. They have supplied food, clothing and blankets, etc., to those in need, furnished and helped maintain a room in the local hospital, made donations towards the new hospital, made awards to secondary and elementary school students in English and Music, and supported many other organizations for the betterment of the community.

The Women's Institute's goal has been to make better homes, a better community and a better nation. This objective is expressed very eloquently in the words of the Mary Stewart Collect which are known to every Institute member, and which is quoted here in part:

"Keep us, O Lord, from Pettiness; let us be large in thought, in word and deed. Let us be done with fault finding and leave off self seeking. May we put away all pretence and meet each other face to face without self pity and without prejudice. May we strive to touch and know the great human heart common to us all."

Due to declining membership, the Durham Women's Institute ended their organization in 1991. Active members of the Durham Women's Institute joined a group which now meets in Durham.

INDEPENDENT ORDER OF ODDFELLOWS

The first meeting of Oddfellows in the town of Durham took place on June 24, 1875, in the vacant New Connexion church on Queen Street north of George Street. The moving force behind that meeting was the District Deputy Grand Master of that time, Brother John Stephen of Walkerton. The first major task of the brothers was to prepare a constitution and by-laws for presentation to the Grand Lodge of Ontario. This took over three years to complete; during that time the brothers were busy conferring degrees on new members.

In those days the Subordinate Lodge encompassed five degrees compared to four at the present time. The proposal fee was two dollars, while each degree had its own set fee with a time limit set upon the payment of the fee. The fees ranged between six and ten dollars which was a considerable sum at that time. Shortly after gaining its charter as Stephen Lodge 169, a crisis arose as a number of the members sued for a charter to be established at Flesherton which would be designated as Dufferin Lodge. Brother Stephen drew the ire of the local lodge when he processed the application and the Flesherton Lodge was instituted. The fears of the brethern were soon proven as the local lodge floundered, and Brother Stephen was blamed for the failure. A number of the Durham members set out to have his name removed from the name of the lodge, and this was done in 1878 when it became officially known as Grey Lodge 169 with approval of ten county officers.

Lodge Parade circa 1905.

By this time the Temple had been located above one of the stores south of Lambton Street on the west side of Garafraxa Street.

The lodge officers dispensed the laws with a strong hand. Restrictive laws and fines were often invoked. One brother was fined for being late, another was found not guilty by a court of inquiry after being accused of being intoxicated in the lodge and of revealing lodge secrets to the public. If a member was absent from a meeting, he was obliged to apprise the Noble Grand of the reason at the first meeting following. An officer who vacated his chair for three meetings was removed from office. The term consisted of six months with two terms in each year. These ran from January to June and July to December. Thus the officers advanced at twice the rate they do now.

At the turn of the century hard times fell on the lodge. Membership dropped, as did the lodge coffers. Records show that the brothers were forced to borrow money at the rate of one per cent! Most of the brothers took out the beneficial membership which paid sick benefits during illness. Many thousands of dollars were paid out over the years by the lodge to beneficial members.

In 1906 a great celebration took place to observe the Thirtieth Anniversary of Oddfellowship in Durham, and bands and lodges from far and wide came to mark the event. The plans to celebrate the event took nearly a year to complete, and the small fortune of $500 was spent on the preparations. Among the dignitaries present were Premier Whitney of the Province of Ontario and several of his cabinet ministers. Unfortunately, in all the plans and accounts referred to in the records, no description of the actual day survives. However, judging from the plans, it must have been one of the greatest events ever witnessed as far as Oddfellowship in Durham is concerned.

The year 1930 saw the institution of the Lady Grey Rebekah Lodge No. 310. In 1932 the lodge purchased the present building for $4,400; another $900 was spent preparing the hall for use. As the effects of the depression struck the lodge, it created a serious burden financially. One night in 1935 the lodge suspended twelve brothers for the non-payment of dues, and at the same time moved to lower dues in order to attract a larger membership. The lodge did, however, invest in bonds which were later to save the organization from financial ruin.

A popular and well-known brother of that time, Reg. McFadden, rose to the supreme office of Grand Master of Ontario in 1952. This was the highest post ever attained by a Durham brother, and the lodge still remembers with pride the word of Brother Reg. who presided over the Ontario Oddfellows Home in Barrie after his term of office as Grand Master of Ontario expired. During the lodge centennial year in 1975, the officers and brothers of Grey Lodge joined with the sisters of Lady Grey Lodge to honour his memory by placing a sound system in the Barrie Home. Grey Lodge has carried out the mandates of its Order over the years. The lodge has relieved the distressed through the combined offices of the Cancer, Poliomyelitis and Tuberculosis Committee co-jointly with the Rebekahs. The sick have been visited as the records have shown. The dead have been buried as witnessed by the Honour Role read each year at a Decoration Service, and the orphan has been educated through various unselfish and unpublished programmes in the community. During the 1970s the lodge sponsored students to the United Nations, and up to the present time has donated to the various charities in the area.

Officers for 1993-94 were:

Noble Grand — Jim Storrey
Vice Grand — Robt. Hooey
Secretary — Don Storrey
Financial Secretary — Ken Cook
Treasurer — Wm. Elvidge Jr.
P.G. — Philip Schwartz
Warden — Ron MacIntyre
Conductor — Wm. Elvidge Jr.
L.S.N.G. — Tom Wilson
R.S.N.G. — Russell McTavish
R.S.S.V.G. — Jim Peter
L.S.V.G. — Howard McRonald
R.S.S. — Bob Storrey
L.S.S. — Wayne Mighton
C.G. — Clarence Trafford
Musician — Larry Hastie

I. O. D. E.
Canadian Greys Chapter Durham

An IODE Chapter was formed in the Town of Durham on April 6th, 1918. The name, Canadian Greys, was appropriately suggested by Mrs. James Gun, the mother of a Charter member, Mrs. Gilbert McKechnie. There were ten Charter members, and at the time of writing there remains one Charter member, Mrs. Minnie (Limin) Harding of Harriston. The first Regent was Miss Eastwood, a teacher at the local High School.

The first project was the sale of poppies in aid of WWI Veterans, and the chapter catered the Remembrance Day banquet until 1938, when it was cancelled during WWII. In 1920 the first Birthday Tea was held, the Library was landscaped and the retaining wall built there.

The members attended the unveiling of the Cenotaph on September 25, 1922, and laid a wreath. The chapter contributed $800 towards this project, and to this day has maintained the grounds and planted the flowers, bulbs, trees and shrubs. Durham Legion Branch 308, the Ladies Auxiliary and the Dutch Community have been very supportive, financially and with labour, to keep these grounds beautiful.

Other projects have been the renovation of the Town Hall in the 1920s and through the years, furnishing and maintaining a room at the old Red Cross Memorial Hospital and the present Durham Memorial Hospital, and the placing of flowers in the hospital foyer, as well as cash donations for the purchase of hospital equipment. When the need was greater, the chapter kept a supply of layettes on hand at all times. Five hundred dollars was donated to the Community Centre, a memorial to WWII Veterans, and shrubs were planted at the Durham Cemetery.

During WWII the ladies were busy raising money by gathering salvage, collecting newspapers, holding Victory teas, etc., to buy knitting and sewing supplies, and sending food parcels, magazines, playing cards and cigarettes Overseas. Many of the members hosted Commonwealth Servicemen in their homes. In 1990 cookies and magazines were sent to a local serviceman during the Gulf War.

The IODE sponsored the Girl Guides and started the first Brownie Pack in town. The chapter adopted the new flag and crest and voted to retain the initials IODE when Imperial Daughters of the Empire was no longer applicable.

The flag was present at very auspicious occasions, namely: the Investiture of Albert Koeslag by Lieutenant-Governor Ray Lawson, and when Lieutenant-Governor Pauline McGibbon opened the Durham Art Gallery. On both these occasions the IODE arranged for the luncheon and reception.

As a Centennial Project, a clock was donated which was installed on the Canadian Imperial Bank of Commerce. This was replaced by Durham Legion Branch 308 when they donated the present clock in front of the Municipal Office, commemorating their 50th Anniversary.

Education has been a very important part of the chapter work. Bursaries, Scholarships and Progress Awards have been presented annually for many years. The chapter has adopted schools in Saskatchewan, Newfoundland and North-West Territories. The present adopted school is in Labrador. The Alice Ramage Fund was established to assist students in furthering their education.

Pictures of the Queen and IODE calendars were placed in the schools and public buildings. The chapter has participated in all National and Provincial projects.

The first life member was Mrs. Guy Kearney. Six members to date have received their 50 year badge. Scrapbooks have been maintained throughout the years.

The chapter presented three pageants, namely: 60th Anniversary of Confederation, Mary, Queen of Scots and George VI Coronation. The roles were played by local citizens under the very capable leadership of Mrs. Farewell and her daughter Helene of Walkerton. Other projects have been: vial of life, community parties, marathon bridge, fashion shows, bake sales and Christmas cookie sales. Members' 50th, 60th and 70th birthdays were celebrated.

In the early winter months of 1994 this organization disbanded due to the inability of securing younger members to carry on the work.

1993 OFFICERS:

Past Regent	Dianne Neff
Regent	Barbara Thompson
1st Vice Regent and Standard Bearer	Judy Hills
Secretary	Jean Masters
Treasurer	Jean Field
Education	Iris Kennedy
Services	Marjorie MacDonald
Echoes	Margaret Hills

Regents 1918 to 1992:

1918 Mrs. J. Eastwood	1954 Mrs. E. Schenk
1919-20 Mrs. D. B. Jamieson	1955 Mrs. F. Lawrence
1921-22 Mrs. G. McKechnie	1956 Mrs. D. Campbell
1923-24 Miss Julia Weir	1957 Mrs. K. Hunter
1925 Mrs. F. Grant	1958-59 Mrs. E. R. Schutz
1926-27-28 Mrs. G. Kearney	1960 Mrs. A. Backus
1929-30-31 Mrs. R. Sparling	1961-62 Mrs. A. Newell
1932-33-34 Miss M. Hunter	1963-64 Mrs. M. Fisk
1936 Mrs. C. Pickering	1965-66 Mrs. F. Lawrence
1937-38 Mrs. F. Irwin	1967-68-69 Mrs. A. Koehler
1939-40 Miss M. Calder	1970-71-72 Mrs. F. O'Brecht
1941 Mrs. V. Blythe	1973-74 Mrs. W. A. Lawson
1942 Mrs. C. Howell	1975-76 Mrs. A. Turnbull
1943-44 Mrs. J. Burgess	1977 Mrs. Al Mooney
1945-46 Mrs. C. H. Darling	1978-79-80 Mrs. Alf Sharpe
1947-48 Mrs. J. Schutz	1981-82 Mrs. A. Koehler
1949 Mrs. H. McDonald	1983-84 Mrs. E. Mansfield
1950 Mrs. C. Ritchie	1987-88 Mrs. Ron Murdock
1951 Mrs. Fred O'Brecht	1952 Mrs. K. Hunter
1985-86 Mrs. Wm. Hunter	1989-90 Mrs. Bev Neff
1953 Mrs. W. McDonnell	1991-92 Mrs. Robert Thompson

LADY GREY
REBEKAH LODGE

In 1930 ten members who had joined Lady May Lodge in Owen Sound petitioned the Grand Lodge of Ontario for a Charter. As a result, the president of the Rebekah Assembly, Sister Land, called a meeting in the I.O.O.F. hall for the purpose of instituting Rebekah Lodge No. 310, Durham, Ontario. During the same meeting 30 members were initiated by the degree team from Hanover Evergreen Lodge.

The first officers were:
Noble Grand — Mrs. Jessie Hayes
Vice Grand — Mrs. Olive Black
Recording Secretary — Miss Barbara Ritchie
Financial Secretary — Miss Jessie Ledingham
Treasurer — Mrs. Christina Falkingham
Warden — Mrs. Edna Wilson
Conductor — Mrs. Maude Bell
Chaplain — Mrs. Minnie Moorehead
Inside Guardian — Mrs. Maud Firth
Outside Guardian — Mrs. Annie Pust

Musician — Miss Winnie Blythe
R.S.N.G. — Mrs. Jessie Schenk
L.S.N.G. — Mrs. Pearl Campbell
R.S.V.G. — Mrs. Jessie Ledingham
L.S.V.G. — Mrs. Eva Lauder
Jr. P.N.G. — Brother Cameron Lauder

During the years the members of Lady Grey have not only cared for their sick and bereft members but have taken an active part for the betterment of the community.

The present Sisters serving from October 1993 to September 1994, are:

Noble Grand — Mary Wilson
Vice Grand — Anna Marie Lamb
Recording Secretary — Edna Trafford
Financial Secretary — May Watson
Treasurer — Elizabeth Cook
Warden — Shirley Wilson
Conductor — Margaret Brown
Chaplain — Lorna Griffin
Inside Guardian — Marie McRonald
Outside Guardian — Grace McVicar
Musician — Elizabeth Watson
R.S.N.G. — Eulalia Hopkins
L.S.N.G. — Margaret Sibbald
R.S.V.G. — Helen Storrey
L.S.V.G. — Rena Hastie
Jr. P.N.G. — Pat Cameron
Colour Bearer — Allison McRonald

GIRL GUIDES

In 1912, two years after the founding of the Guiding movement in Canada, Girl Guides were started in Durham. There were 50 young girls in the organization. The group met in the basement of the Town Hall.

Some of the names of these pioneers were: Mary Hutton, Florabelle Nichol, Min (Limin) Harding, Ottilie (Limin) McGowan. Their leaders included Mrs. John Graham, Mrs. David Jamieson, E. McGregor, and in 1915, under the leadership of Miss Marjorie Oldfield, they were called the Elite Society. Later they were called the 58th I.O.D.E.; and in 1940, under the leadership of Miss Marjorie Pickering, became the first Durham Guide Company. Records show the following ladies were Guide Leaders:

1944 Mrs. (Donald) Margaret Campbell
1944-1948 Madeline (Fry) Blythe, Mae (Thompson) Lawrence, Mary (McGowan) Standen
1948-1951 Mrs. Verna Morrison, Jean (McQueen) Smith
1951-1954 Ina Milne
1954-1956 Donna (Crutchley) Milne
1956-1961 Margaret (Lauder) Bell
1961 Kathryn (Cordick) Murdock
1962-1964 Margaret (Lauder) Bell
1964-1966 Valerie Vaughan

1966 Mrs. Dorla Schwartz
1967 Mrs. Thomas Thompson
1970 Mrs. O.G. (McNabb) Mead
1975-1977 Mrs. P. Morneau, Mrs. P. Majlik
1977 Mrs. P. Majlik
1978-1980 Mrs. R.French
1980 Alayna Majlik
1981 Jayne Elvidge, Eleanor Johnston
1982-1988 Jayne Elvidge, Johanna Schiebe, Tiffany Young, Lori Hargrave
1988-1989 Joanne (Truegunna) Anderson
1989 Joan Bugden
1990-1993 Lori Hargrave

To incorporate the younger girls the 42nd I.O.D.E. Brownies were formed and registered in March, 1946. Over the years the Brownie leaders have been:
1946 Dorothy Eastman
1951 Mrs. Donald (Margaret) Campbell, Jessie (Crutchley) Eccles
1954 Jean Cuyler
1959-1977 Anna (Ritchie) Greenwood
1977 Marlene Young

Tawny Owl leaders have been:
1946 Madeline (Fry) Blythe
1951 Nora Jean (Darling) Swierczynski, Jean Roseborough
1953 Jean Wood
1954 Mrs. Anna (Ritchie) Greenwood
1959 Diane (Schutz) Stewart
1961 Clara (Alexander) McFadden
1962 Shirley Greenwood, Mrs. Andrew (Patricia) Grant
1963 Diane (Campbell) Bartman, Agnes Mooney
1968 Mrs. Russell Burne
1969 Marlene Young
1972 Donna Lysohirka
1975 Mrs. P. Lysohirka, Linda Monk

District Commissioner, Betty Ritchie, Ina Milne — Betty receiving Gold Cord, one of first five girls to receive it.

Mother Daughter Girl Guide Banquet circa 1952.

The older girls' needs were met in September, 1979, with the formation of a Pathfinder Unit. Branching out to go with the times a Sparks unit has now been organized.

Under the leadership of the many Captains and Lieutenants (some names have been missed due to missing records) and their assistants, the young girls of this organization have learned many skills, made many friends and developed sound moral values.

The Girl Guide promise is undergoing changes at this time, but up until 1994 it was:

"On my honour, I promise to do my best to do my duty to God, the Queen and my country, to help other people at all times and to obey the Guide Law."

The leaders in 1993-1994 are:

Sparks — Regina Goldsmith, Stephanie H. Jort

Forty-six local Girl Guides on the lawn of the Methodist Church 1914.
Back Row, left to right: Eliza Patterson, Jessie Clark, Ruth Stewart, Rose Maidment, Chrissie McGirr, Linda Teasdale, Grace Petty, Mary McIlraith, Minnie Limin, Zell Crawford, Marguerite Hutton, Bertie Milne, Edith Hughes, Annie McGirr, Jennie McLean, Isabel Lawson, Myrtle Allen, Mary Smith, Flo. Barclay, Marion Marshall, Sadie McDonald, Evelyn Coutts, Janet Marshall.
Front Row: Kate Ritchie, Jennie Campbell, Mabel Beaton, Violet Fallaise, Vera Allan, Effie Milligan, Georgina Lawson, Edie McKenzie, Lena Ritchie, Audrey Livingstone, Ottilie Limin, Marguerite Kelsey, Meryl Livingstone, Annie Graham, Adeline Graham, Ethel Whitmore, Irene Whittaker, Belle Lauder, Mildred Vollett, Myrtle Daniel, Stella McAuliffe.
In Front: Miss McGregor, Miss Oldfield.

Brownies circa 1950
Karen O'Brecht, Pat Renwick, Gayle Wiggins, Betty Hopkins, Bonnie Rawn.
Brownies presented "Hansel and Grettel" over CFOS Radio.

Girl Guides: **Betty Campbell, Karen O'Brecht, Diane Schutz, Donna Steinacker — first girls to receive Gold Cords in Durham. Donna also attended Guide Jamboree in England. Circa 1952.**

Brownies — Marlene Young, Patricia Black Margaret
  Matthews
Girl Guides — Lori Hargrave, Claudette Redfearn,
  Christine Hauver

SILVER THREADS SENIOR CITIZENS CLUB

The Durham Silver Threads Senior Citizens Club was organized and the Charter obtained in 1952. No information can be obtained about the early years of the organization as records prior to 1966-1967 are not available. The Club is affiliated with the United Senior Citizens of Ontario Inc. (U.S.C.O.), which in turn is affiliated with the National Pensioners and Senior Citizens Federation and the International Senior Citizens Association. U.S.C.O. is non-partisan, non-sectarian and non-racial. Its object is to further the interests and promote the happiness and welfare of senior citizens in Ontario in every way possible.

The goals of the U.S.C.O. are:

To improve the quality of life for all older adults in Ontario.

To provide a means whereby seniors can work together to input on issues concerning them.

To present seniors' concerns and needs to the government to ensure their interests are well served.

To provide educational information on available resources for seniors through a network of field representatives.

To reinforce seniors' capabilities by destroying some of the old fashioned myths that exist.

During the 1970s the Club boasted a membership of 160 with some members coming from Elmwood and Hanover where there were no senior citizens organizations. Over the years there have been three active members 100 years of age, namely, Mrs. Bert (Grace) Stonehouse, Mr. William Hunter and Mr. William Atchison. Special observance is given to members celebrating 90th birthdays.

The meetings consist of both business and social programmes. The Club donates to various charities and assists with community improvements. Gratitude is extended to the Town Council for the use of the Town Hall free of charge unless for a paid event. In return, financial assistance has been given towards renovations to the Town Hall basement and hall.

Members enjoy bowling, shuffleboard and euchre. The activities of the Senior Citizens Choir have given much enjoyment to the singers and happiness to the community. The Club presently has 80 members.

Officers for 1993-1994 are:
Past President — Mrs. Irma Clark
1st Vice President — Mrs. Helen Wettlaufer
2nd Vice President — Douglas Weir
Secretary — Mrs. Vera Firth
Assistant Secretary — Mrs. Margaret Liota
Treasurer — Mrs. Elsie Woollard
Assistant Treasurer — Marius Nielsen
Pianist — Mrs. Elizabeth Watson
Assistant Pianist — Mrs. Lucille Holley
Press Reporter — Mrs. Melvina Brown

ROTARY CLUB

On Wednesday, February 16, 1938, Mr. H. H. Bowman of Owen Sound Rotary Club came to Durham to look into the formation of a Rotary Club, and met with good response from approximately 20 potential members.

The first Rotary meeting was held at the Hahn House on the following Monday night, and a club was formed with Peter Gagnon as President, Harry Kress, Vice President; Frank Irwin, Secretary; Charlie Zilliax, Treasurer; Directors: Dr. D. B. Jamieson, M.G. Calder, Sergeant at Arms, Oscar Hahn. Other members were T. F. House, A. McGowan, Rev. Farr, Vic Blythe, Nelson Clarke, C. Sarney, E.R. Schutz, Dr. Royden Burnett. This group continued to meet every Monday for lunch at the Hahn House, and usually had a special speaker for each meeting.

The move towards organization proceeded quickly, and on Wednesday, April 27, 1938, Durham Rotary Club received its Charter at a dinner meeting in the Durham Furniture Factory showroom. Twelve clubs

Irvin Sharpe and Gordon McLean. Gordon presented Irvin with his Paul Harris pin and membership.

from neighbouring towns were represented at this meeting as Geoff Wheable, District Governor, presented the Charter to the new local Club which was sponsored by the Owen Sound Rotary Club. About 100 people sat down to an unusual dinner served by the ladies of the local Red Cross Society. The menu, of furniture industry origin, was as follows: Water-Stain juice, Love Apple flavour, Dry-Kiln'd Baked Salmon with Shellac Sauce, Fumed Potatoes, Roast Antique Durham Bull with Walnut Filler Gravy, Renaissance Green Peas, Lettuce Salad, Satin Finish, Frozen Neopolitan Cream in separate crates, Compo Cakes, Mahoganized Coffee, Adam's Ale, reputed quarts, or Turpentine substitute, Walnut Veneer Cigars and Cedar Lined Cigarettes. After dinner Governor Geoff Wheable gave an address highlighting the Rotary ideals and an enjoyable evening was spent by all present.

The Durham Club has been very active over the years and celebrated its 50th Anniversary in May, 1988. A number of neighbouring Rotary Clubs attended a dinner meeting in the Durham Community Centre on this occasion to join in the celebration. Rotary Motto is as the four-way test goes:

1. Is it the truth?
2. Is it fair to all concerned?
3. Will it build good-will and better friendships?
4. Will it be beneficial to all concerned?

When these standards are followed, you have a group which shows concern for others. The Durham Club has ongoing projects: raising money for Crippled (Handicapped) Children. A special fund drive is held

Trevor Crilly, J.J. Coutts and Bill Murdock.
J.J. Coutts receiving recognition as outstanding Rotarian
from MPP Bill Murdock.

each March for this worthy cause. The Club also organizes the Christmas hamper programme, delivers Christmas food and toys to those in need at Christmas, and sponsors school breakfasts.

In 1993 Rotarians everywhere raised money for the flood victims in Mid-Western Canada and the United States. The Durham Club, with assistance from all service clubs, churches, and individuals, raised $7,500 in one week-end.

The highest honour which a Rotarian can receive is to be named a Paul Harris Fellow, after the founder of Rotary and in 1993 the Durham Club named the first two Paul Harris Fellows — Irvin Sharpe and J. J. Coutts, both of whom have been Rotarians for over 36 years. Irwin is a retired Secondary School Principal and was involved extensively in Seminar For To-Morrow's Leaders — young men 16-19 years of age to teach them good leadership qualities. J. J. Coutts has been Farmer, Timberman, Real Estate Agent, and is very active in the Real Estate world.

When Rotary was organized only men could be Rotarians; this has now been changed and women can become club members. The Durham club is privileged to have one lady Rotarian at the present time, and looks forward to more ladies joining in the future.

Rotary meets every Tuesday at 6.30 p.m. for a dinner meeting at the Cozy Corner Restaurant. During July and August the present custom is to have family night at Rotarian homes in the form of a Barbeque dinner and a social time with family. David Peach is the 1993-94 President, Albert Reay, Secretary, and Gordon MacLean, Treasurer. In 1993-94 there are 18 active members and four honorary members. J. J. Coutts is Chairman of the Easter Seal campaign. The

Club sponsors school breakfasts at Durham District Community School and Saugeen Valley Elementary School with assistance from several volunteers and other service clubs. Durham Rotary holds the Charter for Durham and District Scouts, and conducts food drives for the Hanover Branch of the Salvation Army.

Each meeting has a fun time in the form of a fine session. Charges can be anything from ignoring a fellow Rotarian, or crossing the street at a place other than the cross-walk — just a fun way of raising money. A serious side is also part of the meeting when the business of the week is conducted. Some things such as politics, religion, or personal advertising, are not allowed in Rotary.

We look forward to many years as a successful Rotary Club and are always ready to welcome new members. Just speak to any Rotarian and the exercise to accept you will be put in motion. As one Rotarian said recently: I NEED ROTARY WORSE THAN ROTARY NEEDS ME. Come and join us for enjoyable fellowship and a chance to help others.

KINSMEN CLUB

The Kinsmen Club of Durham was chartered May 30, 1950. The 26 young men who signed the charter were: Allister Aljoe, Robert Braithwaite, Leonard Chumbley, Harold Conlon, Gordon Dickson, J.D. Falkingham, Edward Goss, Gordon Greenwood, Delbert Holley, Frank Illingworth, T.G. Irwin, John Jarratt, Floyd Lawrence, George Lloyd, Orval MacDonald, Brian May, Russell McGillivray, Raymond McGirr, John McKechnie, Donald Saunders, Andrew Schenk, Patrick Smith, James Sullivan, Wilmer Vollett, Thomas Watson, Dustin Weis, W. Lewis Whitmore.

Several members of the sponsoring Listowel Club met with prospective Durham Kinsmen at least six times at the home of Gordon Greenwood on Countess Street from September, 1949, to May, 1950. In this regard Gordon Greenwood was the founder of Kinsmen in Durham.

The Kinsmen were, and still are, a very active group of young men working for the betterment of the community. Before they were officially chartered, they undertook their first project — sponsoring minor hockey. Because of their support to so many worthwhile causes, other men became interested. By June, 1951, membership was 37.

Kinsmen, only one year old, approached the Fall Fair Board about developing the fair grounds as a community centre and sports arena. An agreement was reached and Gordon McGirr chaired this campaign. The Kinsmen canvassed tirelessly and with the support of the entire community, the new arena, valued at $80,000 was completed.

The first function in the arena was probably a Civic Holiday Celebration on Monday, August 4, 1952. But that fall a unique horse show was staged for the grand opening.

Joint Meeting Kinsmen Rotary 1950.

Kinsmen, in partnership with Rotary, sponsored the first Monster Bingo in Durham during the summer of 1951 in the old arena on George Street. The Kinsmen continued with various types of Bingos throughout the years. The largest attendance was recorded in 1967 with 1,950 people. Large cash prizes, even a new car, were among the prizes offered.

In 1952 Kinsmen held open air bingos on the vacant lot between Charles Graham's store and McCarthy's Bakery on the west side of Garafraxa Street South. Cash bingos were 10 cents a game. The seating was rough cut planks and players held a square piece of cardboard on their knees on which to place the bingo card. Markers were corn kernels or heavy red papers one-half inch square. (Imagine if it was a little windy!)

Over the years Kinsmen have initiated many very beneficial projects including:

1951 First Band Tattoo with over 8 bands, including Durham Girls' Trumpet Band
1952 Kinsmen Ice Carnival
1954 Assisted in revival of Lawn Bowling
1955 Assumed responsibility for Santa Claus Parade, formerly run by the Board of Trade
1956 Sponsored first Figure Skating Club
      First Cancer campaign for Durham Kinsmen and Rotary sharing endeavour, then Kinsmen did it for 20 years

1959 Painted new arena inside and out. This was a huge undertaking — over 200 gallons of paint were used on totally wood interior. Cleared north bank of Saugeen River at the middle dam after 14 acres of land were donated by A.J. Metzger. This was the beginning of today's Conservation Park.
1961 Built two ball diamonds and installed lights at the arena grounds with continued support for the upkeep of the arena
1969 Financially supported the development of park and picnic shelter at McGowan Falls, refurbishing of arena hall, Durham Girls' Drum and Bugle Corps
1976 Again called on when the arena was condemned and a new one desperately needed. Kin Bob Braithwaite was named fundraiser
1978 Spearheaded building of new tennis courts
1980 Continual support of local fire department
1991 Durham Heritage Bridge Walkway received donations which greatly assisted them in the rebuilding of the railway bridge and its approaches as a walkway complete with lighting. This was turned over to the town just before Homecoming 1992.
1992 From 1961 to the present day Kinsmen have helped the new Durham and and District

Kinsmen Ladies' Night 1963.

Memorial Hospital, and were also responsible for the ambulance garage. By 1972 $20,000 had been raised; and in 1992 Kinsmen spearheaded a $600,000 drive for new hospital equipment with a donation of $60,000.

Since 1979 minor hockey and figure skating have received assistance with their ice time costs. From 1988 to 1993 nearly $38,000 was given to each organization.

Five presidents went on to become Zone Deputy Governors: Ed Goss, Robert Baithwaite, Don Nearingburg, Jim McMullen, and Wayne Cargoe. Life memberships have been given to Orval MacDonald, Lewis Whitmore, Robert Braithwaite, Gordon Dickson, James Duffield, Jr., Ross Taylor and Joe Detzler.

Life member Ross Taylor is still an active member and has 34 years perfect attendance out of his 38 years with the club.

Presidents were:

1950-51 Ed Goss *	1974-75 Jim McMullen
1951-52 Gordon Dickson	1975-76 Paul Hewitt
1952-53 Gordon McGirr *	1976-77 Peter Fallis
1953-54 Orval MacDonald	1977-78 Ron Murdock
1954-55 Thomas Watson *	1978-79 Douglas Schewhr
1955-56 Norman Greenwood *	1979-80 Robert Graham
1956-57 Howard Misener *	1980-81 Lloyd Love
1957-58 Keith Dickson	1981-82 Harvey Fraser
1959-60 William McDonald	1982-83 Don MacMillan
1960-61 Wilmer Vollett	1983-84 John Rydall
1961-62 Eric Cluley	1984-85 Wayne Cargoe
1962-63 Ross "Cyclone" Taylor	1985-86 Jack Greydanus
1963-64 Rhys "Pete" Padfield	1986-87 Dave Pust
1964-65 Jack Breen	1987-88 Ted McGillivray
1965-66 Glen Budd	1988-89 Gary Greenland
1966-67 Alf Corbett	1989-90 Dan Mighton
1967-68 Joe Detzler	1990-91 Brent Kaufman
1968-69 James Duffield, Jr. *	1991-92 Robert Marshall
	1992-93 Jim St. Germain

1969-70 Ross "Butch" Graham	1993-94 Bruce Armstrong
1970-71 Donald Nearingburg	1994-95 Dave Rogers
1971-72 Donald Pust	1995-96 Calvin Rydall
1972-73 Jack Lawrence	incumbent President
1973-74 Alan MacGillivray	

* deceased President

Over the 44 year existence of the Kinsmen organization in Durham, it is estimated that over $750,000 has been raised for countless community projects and over 400 young men have been Durham Kinsmen during these years.

FRONTIER DAYS

Frontier Days originated as a fund-raising event for the Durham Kinsman Club in the late 1970s. It included functions appropriate to a Frontier celebration, such as Western and English horse shows, heavy horse pulls, Western theme dances, giant parades, complete with a steam kaleidoscope and a midway. People dressed in appropriate period costumes. A mock shoot-out at the main intersection was staged with the help of radio announcers from Owen Sound and Wingham. The event was originally chaired by John Rydall, Harry Leatham and Keith Hastie. A good time was always enjoyed by everyone.

KINETTE CLUB

The first Kinette Club was started March 28, 1957. The prime objective of Kinettes was to support the Kinsmen in all their endeavours. Eighteen members were listed on the Charter. Officers were: President, Anne MacGillivray; 1st Vice President, Eileen Adams;

2nd Vice President, Jayne Misener; Secretary, Mae Lawrence; Treasurer, Marie Mooney; Registrar, Ruth (Mrs. Orville) MacDonald. Successive Presidents were:

1958-59, Jayne Misener	1959-60, Helen Whitmore
1960-61, Mae Lawrence	1961-62, Marie Mooney
1962-63, Mary Dickson	1963-64, Norah Braithwaite
1964-65, Dorla Schwartz	1965-66, Betty Pust
1966-67, Joyce Taylor	1967-68, Jan Birr
1968-69, Phyllis Dickson	1969-70, Alma Cluley
1970-71, Jeanette Lawrence	1971-72, Doreen McDonald
1972-73, Carol Lawrence	1973-74, Judith Van Geem
1974-75, Jean McMullin	1975-76, Rose Detzler
1976-77, Marion Buchner	1977-78, Irene Keating
1978-79, Kathryn Murdock	1979-80-81 Terry Fraser

Membership steadily increased until there were over 40 members.

The dinner meetings were held in Durham's first Legion Hall (above Morley Lum's restaurant). Mr. Lum provided the catering. Later, the meetings were held at the Anglican Rectory, and the Anglican Ladies Auxiliary served delicious meals for many years. In keeping with the Kinsmen motto "Serving the Community's Greatest Need," the Kinettes had many projects of their own which included: Bursary to a deserving Grade VIII elementary school pupil;Canvassing for March of Dimes; Easter Parade for Handicapped Children; Entertaining the Sr. Citizens' Club; Participating in Vanity Fair and Fall Fair; Visiting Nursing Homes; Organizing the Canadian National Banjo Competition to support the arena; Support Kin National Project — Cystic Fibrosis.

Work parties were fun parties, whether preparing for the annual Kinette Capers dance or Spring Fashion Show, assembling cookbooks, decorating floats for parades, or being up to the elbows mixing carrot puddings!

In a lighter vein, slogans were written and songs composed for Kinsmen Campaigns. Childrens' picnics and skating parties were fun-filled days. A travelling dinner, pot luck suppers, hobo teas, men's night, and dances also added to the fellowship and social life within our club.

High points in the Durham Kinette Club included winning the first Club Costume Contest, Kinettes/Kinsmen Convention, naming Rose Detzler Kinette of the year, and having Terry Fraser win the first Maple Leaf Award.

In 1969 a District 8 Kinette Interclub was held in Durham and later Durham sponsored the Flesherton Kinette Club. In 1971 the older members of Kinettes resigned to accompany the Kinsmen when the K40 Club was formed.

The 20th Anniversary of the Durham Kinette Club was recognized in 1977 by hosting an Interclub Zone, and by having an anniversary party, inviting all past presidents.

The Club disbanded in 1981.

On August 23, 1984, a reformation meeting was held and the first executive was: President, Terry Fraser; Secretary, Marie Neuman; Liason/Kinsman, Mary Cargoe; Service Chair, Chris Greydanus; Social Chair, Doreen Reay & Linda Mighton; Public Relations, Brenda Pust.

Since this reorganization presidents have been:
1985-86 — Chris Greydanus
1986-87 — Joyce MacMillan
1987-88 — Mary Cargoe
1988-89 — Doreen Reay
1989-90 — Leigh Anne Boese
1990-91 — Diane Mighton
1991-92 — Sue Salvatori
1992-93 — Nancy Greenland
1993-94 — Denise Hutchinson

BUSINESS AND PROFESSIONAL WOMEN'S CLUB OF DURHAM

This Club was formed on April 3, 1950. The President was Mrs. Ruth (Myles) Lawson and the Secretary, Miss Myrtle Mortley. The objective of the club was to improve the status of women in business and the professions locally, nationally, and internationally. The club was open to all women in the community who were either self-employed or working for others. Some of the first members were: Mrs. Mary Dinger, Miss Margaret McGirr, Mrs. Ida Padfield, Mrs. Georgia Rumble, Miss Ina Milne, Miss Mary Morton, Miss Etta Twamley, Mrs. ? Jacobi, Miss Helen Renwick, Mrs. Eunice McGirr, Miss Kay Renwick, Mrs. Irene Howell, Mrs. C. Seymour, Miss Helen Gerrie, Mrs. Wilma Coutts and Mrs. Elda Cadogan.

Antique Display in Library Basement sponsored by Business and Professional Women 1960.

In 1954 the Durham Club attended the Ninth Annual Ontario Provincial Conference held in Haliburton. Here an Ontario-wide competition among Business and Professional Clubs for the best presentation of a skit took place. The director of the Durham skit, Mrs. Wilma Coutts, was also voted the "best actress" of the evening. Other cast members were: Mrs. Esther Hamilton, Mrs. Gertrude Hewitt, Mrs. Lucy Pritchard, and Miss Janet Robb. The Durham club's winning skit, entitled The Lighthouse, was performed in pantomime, without props, and with a narrator. The Durham club was awarded a tooled leather scrapbook in which to keep its records. The prize was donated by Miss Jean Wilson, president of the Guelph Club, and it is now kept in the Durham Library's Local History Collection. The Durham club won many trophies for skit performances at other events too.

The Durham club sponsored numerous programmes for the community youth such as the improvement of the Durham Library, where children's story hours were held. And monetary awards were given by the Club to graduating Grade 8 students who achieved literary excellence.

The Club disbanded in the early 1980s due to the lack of members.

SCOUTS, CUBS, BEAVERS

No official records have been found to assist with information relating to Scouting in Durham. Since the Girl Guides were started in 1912 it is possible that the scouts would be started at about the same time. Some of the 1920 Durham Chronicles mention scout activities such as playing hockey against Mount Forest. Hiking, camping, canoeing, working for badges and helping others are aspects of the programme which encourages good character in young boys.

Some of the leaders have been:

Scouts:

H.E. "Mickey" McNaughton	Bruce Moore
John Koeslag	Jim Atkinson
George Johnston	David Atkinson
Ken Johnston	John Atkinson
Jack Atkinson	John and Janice Dillman
Dr. Ian Grafton	

Cubs:

Clive Elvidge	Paul Huellemann
Bruce Atkinson	Iris Kennedy
Marion Atkinson	Dave Wilburn

Beavers:

Ruth Ann Bartman	Debbie Wilburn
Mary Cargoe	

VENTURERS

The Durham Venturers, a programme for Scout graduates ages 14-16, was begun in 1972. Some highlights of their activities include members attending the North-West Territories Jamboree and the Can Am Jamboree in Minnesota. In 1975 Earl Wilson and Ken Cook, Jr., attended the Nor Jam (Norway Jamboree) in Norway, Sweden and Denmark. Imagine the immensity of this gathering of 12,000 boys where 3,000

The Charter for the Boy Scouts in Durham.

pounds of wieners were needed for one meal! The members have given assistance at Special Olympics and Earl Rowe Park in Alliston.

Leaders were:
1972 Ken Johnston
1973 Ken Cook, Sr., and Wm. D. Wilson
1980 Ken Cook, Jr.

ROVERS

The Rovers, a Co-Ed organization for ages 17-21 years, follow Venturers. It was begun here in 1975, the first in this area. Their activities include community work such as the Santa Claus Parade, Snow Fest and the Wood Show. Mr. and Mrs. Ken Cook, Sr., were the first advisers in 1975. Following them was their son, Ken Cook, Jr., who continues to be the adviser for both Rovers and Venturers at the time of writing.

DURHAM & DISTRICT OPTIMIST CLUB

The Durham and District Optimist Club was chartered on June 14, 1988, with 40 charter members. The Charter President was Kenneth Gardiner with William Craigie and Lynn McCallum as Vice Presidents. The Treasurer was David Wilburn and William Woollard was Secretary. The directors were Duncan Mc-Dougall, Stephanie Paylor, Ron Craft, Carol Lawrence, David Flanagan and James Routely.

Meetings are held on the second Monday of the month at 8 p.m. in the Durham Town Hall. Any one who is interested in joining a service club is welcome to come out and see what the Optimist Club is all about.

The Motto of the Optimist Club is "FRIEND OF YOUTH."

Children's winter fashions 1900 — Effie Hunter.

The purpose of the Optimist Club is to develop optimism as a philosophy of life, to promote an active interest in good government and civic affairs, to inspire a respect for law, to promote patriotism and work for international accord and friendship among all people, and to aid and encourage the development of youth in the belief that giving of one's self in the ser-

vice of others will advance the well-being of men and women, their community and the world.

On June 5, 1993, Optimist International celebrated 75 years of Optimism in North America.

The Durham and District Optimists sponsor many youth oriented activities in the community, such as bike safety rodeo, teen dances, soap box derbys, free ice skating and roller skating. This is also the first club to run a Drug and Substance Abuse Seminar from which many more have developed throughout Midwestern Ontario and the Grey Bruce area. This seminar was put together by one of the Optimist members who is a retired police officer from Toronto, and who has now gone on to form a group called GRANDPARENTS AGAINST DRUG ABUSE. (G.A.D.A.)

THE OPTIMIST CREED

PROMISE YOURSELF —

To be so strong that nothing can disturb your peace of mind.

To talk health, happiness, and prosperity to every person you meet.

To make all your friends feel that there is something in them.

To look at the sunny side of everything and make your optimism come true.

To think only of the best, to work only for the best and expect only the best.

To be just as enthusiastic about the success of others as you are about your own.

To forget the mistakes of the past and press on to the greater achievements of the future.

To wear a cheerful countenance at all times and give every living creature you meet a smile.

To give so much time to the improvement of yourself that you have no time to criticize others.

To be too large for worry, too noble for anger, too strong for fear, and too happy to permit the presence of trouble.

Industries

The Big Saugeen was the prime attraction to the pioneers who founded Durham, one of the earliest communities in the Queen's Bush. The mighty rush of water power was harnessed to run the mills which sprang up. These industries assisted materially in our subsequent development, and helped make the Town of Durham flourish in early days.

EDGE MILLS

In the mid 1840s Mr. John Edge of Clonbrook, Queens County, Ireland, purchased a mill site consisting of 22 acres on the Main Saugeen River east of the Garafraxa Road in Glenelg Township for 250 pounds. He also purchased 929 acres of land in the same township for 371 pounds, 12 shillings, 91 pence. In a letter to the Colonial Secretary of the Province of Canada, Montreal, dated September 3, 1849, he states that he has spent over 2,000 pounds on these properties, including the erection of two mills and other improvements, but has not yet received titles from the land agent for them. His letter was a request that this matter be quickly resolved.

The August 11th, 1898 issue of the *Durham Chronicle* reports that in 1846 Mr. John Edge of Ireland built a sawmill (on the north bank of the Saugeen River at a place now known as McGowan Falls), and in 1847 a flour mill was built across the river from the sawmill. The first person to operate the flour mill was John Edge, father of Elias Edge of Aberdeen. Subsequently, James Edge attended the hopper and in 1856 Mr. John Kelly came from Ireland to run the mills.

At first the road into the sawmill was a laneway almost straight north of the sawmill to what is today the Durham Road. When the flour mill was built farmers from the east of the community of Durham followed a trail across Lots 58 and 59, Concession 2 E.G.R., Glenelg, to the mill. The Mill Road was eventually purchased by the township in a tax sale and incorporated into Glenelg's road system. The road was also known as the lower road as it eliminated climbing the steep hill to get to Durham. It is now part of Highway No. 4.

In the early years sometimes there was a long line of farmers waiting to get their wheat ground, so the millers would bake wheat cakes on the mill stove to feed the men while they waited for their flour. For a number of years a general store situated just east of the sawmill on the north bank of the river was operated by the Edge Mills. This was one of the earliest stores in what is now Durham. This is now part of the Saugeen Valley Conservation Park and a pavillion is situated here.

The first sawmill had a circular saw as well as upright saws. The grist and flouring mill had three run of stones. Each mill was powered by an overshot water wheel. At a later date a woollen mill was added in the flour mill. This mill had three power looms, a spinning machine with 200 spindles and two carding machines, plus fulling and finishing machines.

McGowan's Upper Dam.

The 1861 Census valued the mills at $10,000. The flour mill bought 11,250 bushels of wheat, 3,750 bushels of oats and sold $12,000 worth of flour per year. The labour bill was $200 per month for eight men, working ten hours a day, six days a week.

Samuel Edge
Pioneer of **GLENELG T.P**
ONT.

James Edge
GLENELG T.P ONT.
Ex Warden of Grey Co.Y

Samuel and James Edge built the first saw and flour mills in Durham for their cousin, John Edge of Ireland, in 1846 and 1847.

The local paper recounts an early disaster as follows:

"Due to the melting snow in April, 1883, the Big Saugeen commenced to rise until it was higher than it had been for many years.

"Neil and John McKechnie had employed a number of men to watch the dam and bridge at Edge Mills, as they had several sawlogs in the bed of the river above Durham. On Saturday evening, Mr. Nathaniel Campbell and Mr. Hugh MacKay were watching above the bridge and putting off any log that came down. A large log was passing about nine o'clock when Mr. Campbell caught it with his pike pole. Due to the exceedingly swift current, the log was almost instantly swept under the bridge. The unfortunate man was unable to withdraw his pike and was standing between it and the water. As soon as the pole struck the edge of the bridge, Mr. Campbell was shot off it several feet, as if sent from a catapult. He was immediately swept under the bridge and down the roaring falls over the rocks. Mr. MacKay, utterly powerless, gave the alarm, but the body was never recovered (at the time of printing).

"Mr. Hugh Campbell, age 63 years, was described as a quiet, inoffensive, industrious man, working as a carder in various places, presently employed by Messrs. McKechnie. He was Scottish by birth and had also served in the Russian War.

"On Sunday morning a large stream of water ran out at McKechnie's sawmill through lower town and into Camp's Creek. The grist mill dam above the sawmill gave way, but the sawmill dam luckily withstood the pressure. Lambton Street bridge lost supports and was barricaded. The abutments of the Garafraxa Street bridge began to go about noon. Soon a large part of the approach caved in and one side of the bridge sank down considerably. A number of residents used teams and drew stone until dark and all the next day until hundreds of tons of stone were filled in to make the bridge able to withstand the pressure.

"The abutments of the railway bridge were partially washed away, and one span of the Edge Mills dam was also carried away. Considerable excitement was felt on Sunday but, like the river, this gradually subsided."

In 1887 James Colville took over management of the mill, and it was destroyed by fire shortly thereafter.

McGOWAN MILLS

Robert McGowan bought the Edge mill property and built a new mill in 1888. Robert's plans to modernize the mill included the desire to install a new roller mill for producing flour. This proved to be no easy task, as it met with opposition (from John McKechnie, operator of another mill). In October, 1887, an appeal was

Original Wooden Dam at McGowan's mill.

made to the town. Subsequently a letter was received from the office of the Registrar of the Queen's Bush Division of the High Court of Justice in the County of York, by John Moodie, Clerk, Town of Durham, describing Durham as the Plaintiff vs. John McKechnie. A petition was signed by a number of freeholders of the town. Two resolutions of the council including taxes of $50 per year to be paid on McGowan mill property, were submitted. McGowan was required to give a bond which was granted. Finally the case came before the High Court of Justice, Queen's Bush Division in the County of Bruce in the Town of Walkerton on Tuesday, October 23, 1888, at 10 a.m. Request Granted. The new roller machinery was the most up to date of its kind available. It included 5 sets of large rolls which produced flour, bran and shorts (pig feed).

In 1890 another unique facility came into operation at McGowan Mills, now called The People's Mill. Robert S. McGowan, Jr., (Robert's son) went to the Chicago World Fair and was inspired by a generator which he saw there. He returned with the idea of producing electric energy and proceeded to do so. His father Robert made application to the town, and permission was granted to erect poles on the streets for the distribution of electric lights. Soon a few homes subscribed at one dollar per light per household except where five or more lights were installed. This continued until the Aberdeen Company bought the electrical business in 1897. An article in an 1897 Durham Review newspaper stated that the question of charges

had been a lively discussion for a week. The patrons were willing to pay more than one dollar but if the price went up to three dollars, many would close down altogether and resort to lamps!

The involvement of the McGowan family continued as the ownership was passed on to Robert's son, John, in 1903. John operated the flour mill which could produce 75 barrels a day; this was 196 pounds per barrel. Grain was bought by the bushel, ground by the barrel, and sold by the bag. His son, Wallace, recalled that the mill ran fairly quietly if the rolls were set up properly. John manufactured high-grade Sovereign Manitoba flour, Eclipse blended flour, and Choice Pastry flour, shorts, bran, chop and middlings, as well as all kinds of mill stuffs. He also did custom grinding for farmers. A great amount of flour was exported abroad. During World War 1 the mill did its best to help supply good old hard wheat flour as food for the hungry nations and military personnel Overseas.

An empty flour sack was purchased at the Belgian Relief Station, Mons, for five francs shortly after the signing of the Armistice, November, 1918, by Lieutenant E. P. Whaley of the 7th C.R.T. On one side of the bag (which is now in the hands of the McGowan family as a keepsake) was printed "The People's Mills, 98 lb. Sovereign Patent Flour from No. 1 Manitoba Hard Wheat. John McGowan, Durham, Ont." On the other side was printed "Made in Canada, Gift of Flour, to the Belgians from County of Grey, Ontario, Canada, Owen Sound, County Town."

Robert and Jean McGowan purchased the Edge Mills in 1887. They produced the first hydro for Durham from power generated at the Durham Mills.

Milling involves a great deal of hard work, mostly in a dusty environment. But it also includes the satisfaction of a job well done and daily cheerful visits with customers. Slush ice (now called frazil ice) often had to be chopped to keep the water for power flowing, especially during very cold weather. This can be a dangerous undertaking as Wallace remembers his older brother Arthur having been washed over the falls while they were chopping a strip of ice. Fortunately he was washed up on a pile of ice, rather than under, and was thus saved. High water time often meant being up all night watching, removing planks and adding sandbags to prevent flooding. Floods were another hazard which went with the business. Durham has had its share of floods. In 1911 there was a severe one, and in 1912 the Lambton Street bridge was washed out. The present upper dam was built by John McGowan in 1913 following another very serious flood. The following is a flood-related story as remembered by Wallace when he was a very young boy:

"In earlier days before cars were too common, it was quite customary for families to have a horse and buggy. The stable was there and commodities like milk deliveries, etc., were not yet too well established, in the smaller towns at least. Many families kept a cow for their use and the surplus milk was sold to others who were less fortunate.

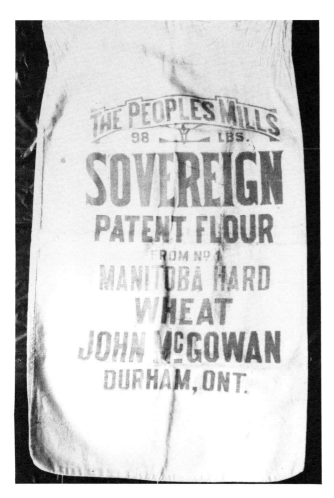

(Empty flour bag purchased at Mons, November 1918.

(Empty flour bag purchased at Mons, November 1918.

"Our family was of the former but Father, having a flour and feed mill and plenty of feed and pasture along the river, kept two cows. Two assured that at all times of the year there would be plenty of milk, cream and butter. It was the custom to keep the young cattle raised from calves to the age of two years and weighing in the neighbourhood of 1,000 lbs. There was a team of horses to do the teaming (now called trucking). The flour had to be drawn to the railroad siding or to the bakeries in town and surrounding country stores. The driver was a horse of good stature — quite fast and heavy enough to take a turn with the team if necessary.

"But the pet of the stable was a little mare that was quiet enough to entrust any of the family with, yet cute enough to drive almost all of us mad at times. Her name was Maude. By the time I became old enough to make use of her, she was old enough to know all the tricks both lovable and otherwise. When being saddled for a ride, she would blow herself up like a balloon so that the saddle girth was not quite loose enough to let your weight pull the saddle down when you tried to mount.

"This stalled off the ride until I learned to overcome it. And just try and catch her in the pasture if you had riding in mind! Any other time she would follow you around, hoping you had that lump of sugar for her sweet tooth. So help me, she could read your mind. I recall one Fall a foot of snow had covered the ground unexpectedly overnight. and of course we thought she should be brought to the comfort of the stable. But she had other ideas and even with the aid of a dozen friends we could not drive her out of that pasture gate. Father wisely came to the rescue that time, and told us just to leave the gate open and wait at the stable door; and sure enough, before long Maude came galloping down the road right down to the door to be admitted to her warm stall.

"The stable was an old mill converted to the stock when the new mill was built and was situated right beside the river, fifty yards below the falls. Behind the stable an open topped flume carrying water from the dam to the mill beyond, stood on a fairly high timber structure. This flume leaked and formed an almost solid wall of ice in the winter time.

"Up the river a log jam formed one spring and turned the water in a flood out onto the road and into the yard at the stable. As it was blocked at the back by this flume and wall of ice, the water rose to almost ceiling height in the stable. This happened in the afternoon and the word spread quickly. So did the water going through the overhead bridge and downtown across main street. Soon all available people were at the scene of the flood, either as spectators or to offer their assistance.

"Holes were chopped in the floor above so that the animals' heads could be held up enabling them to breathe. My older brother Jack and my Uncle Will went into the icy water and fastened a rope to each animal and it was then dragged up through the rushing water to safety. The two cows were first, then the driver. One of the young cattle was pretty far gone, but they tried for the other and it seemed to fare better. A large calf was also brought through to safety. While all this was going on, different ones asked: "Is the pony in there?" "How about getting Maude." I can still remember the icy pang of fear going down my back when a man said "You won't have to bother with her. No animal could stay in that cold water so long and still be alive." But a rope was fastened and out came Maude. The men on the rope pulled and a squirming body appeared at the surface of the water, hit the bank on her side, got upright and was dragged to the safety of the high bank. Then new life seemed to quiver back into her body. She scrambled to her feet, shook herself violently and whinnied a thank you to her rescuers (most of whom had ridden her as boys). The roar of applause that followed would have warmed the heart of any one.

"And Maude was with us still for many years. My brother Jack developed rheumatism when quite a young man, and I often wonder if his being in that cold water had a lot to do with it."

Upper Dam Flood 1929.

The *Durham Review* of September 29, 1938, contains a description of John McGowan's dam as follows: the cost was $2,000. Eight "John Bull" type concrete piers, 27 feet apart were built. The bed work and breast work were on top of the old dam built to a height of 19 feet. A new bridge covered the top of the dam. A spectator remarked, "That dam should last as long as the English language."

In 1925 disaster did strike. The three storey brick building burned in the middle of the night. It was never rebuilt. Grain grinding and feed sales continued, operated by John until 1935. Then, due to his illness, sons Arthur and Wallace took over under the name of McGowan Bros. A seed cleaning machine was added and alfalfa hay grinding began. This became quite a

McGowan's Alfalfa Meal Mill and Trucks.

business with markets overseas as well as in Canada. Like so many milling operations this was extremely fire hazardous. Several fires, and a diminishing demand for alfalfa, took their toll. In 1952 the milling operation ceased. Durham Crushed Stone manufactured concrete blocks for a very short time, and then, also in 1952, the land was sold to the Saugeen Valley Conservation Authority. Developed with assistance from the local Kinsmen, the land is now a beautiful park.

Through the years the property was willingly shared with neighbours who pastured a cow or two, and with young folk interested in swimming, canoeing, skating or picnics. Of course the fishermen had their spots along the river's edge! And so it seems fitting that this beautiful piece of land along the Saugeen has been set aside officially under the care of the S.V.C.A. for all people to enjoy. It is indeed a wonderful asset to the town of which we can be very proud.

DURHAM MILLS

In order to take advantage of the faithful Saugeen and the sufficient fall of water for power, Peter Patterson built a dam for water power two blocks west of Garafraxa Street on Countess Street South. Here he established a sawmill in 1853 (an old turbine from this dam was found in 1967 when a channel was made in the river to prevent flooding.)

In 1859 Mr. Patterson built a new dam just west of Queen Street South, the location of the present lower dam. Here was erected a flour and oatmeal mill with three run of stones. This building was very close to the dam and was to remain, with some alterations, until 1969. A woollen mill was added in 1865. This complex was known as the Durham Mills.

Neil G. & John McKechnie purchased this mill in 1875, and a few years later converted it to a chopping mill and feed supply.

In October, 1924, Mr. J. W. Ewen, for some time with the Rob Roy Mills, leased the McKechnie Mills.

As Mr. Ewen advertised in the Chronicle at this time, he planned to conduct an up-to-date flour and feed mill and install a modern grinding and crimping plant for the needs of the local farmers. This business operated under the name of J. W. Ewen and Son.

The very next spring, according to the *Durham Chronicle*, April 2, 1925, Mr. Ewen underwent a close disaster at the dam. The Canadian Pacific Railway had dumped brush along the river bank. They were warned, but did not move it. Due to rain and thawing the river became swollen. At midnight J. W. Ewen checked his dam and everything seemed in order, but at 5:30 a.m. on his next visit the mass of brush had been swept down the river and wedged at the dam. The west gate was gone and the entire dam was threatened. For over an hour the men who had been summoned worked, and finally managed to saw out a post to allow the water to go free. The remainder of the dam was saved. In 1929 the dam did go out and coffer dams were used with low power until 1934 when Mr. Ewen rebuilt the dam.

Keith Dickson became the owner in 1947, and his father Bert went into partnership with him after he sold his mill at Orchard. Keith recalls living before his marriage, or batching it, in John Ewen's little house in front of the mill. He also remembers the co-operation and good-will practiced among all three milling operations in town. An example involved Hurricane Hazel. At that time, in 1956, Keith and his wife Mary came out of a church meeting and realized that the rain was really coming down! Keith hurriedly alerted his men and they pulled all the planks and opened the gates at the lower dam. He went on up to alert Otto Schaus (operator of the Knechtel Mills) at his home. By this time, the box on Otto's new pick-up truck was more than half filled with water! They all hurried to the middle dam where the water was already starting over the north bank. Quick thinking saved the dam. The men worked all night and Durham was saved this time from a nasty flood. Dicksons sold to the Farmers' Co-operative late in 1956.

Lower Mill Pond and McKechnie's Mill.

In 1969 the property was sold to the Saugeen Valley Conservation Authority. The Authority has always been interested in the preservation of historic buildings but this one had become a fire hazard and the machinery obsolete. It is notable that despite the high risk of fire connected with this type of milling operation, this flour and feed mill never had the misfortune to experience a fire.

The Old Mill Senior Citizens apartment building now occupies this land and the inhabitants benefit from the scenic view of the falls, the river, and parkland.

McGOWAN MILLING CO. (ROB ROY)

This mill, built in 1909, was owned and operated by William Arthur (W.A.), son of Robert McGowan. It was situated on George Street, approximately 500 yards down river from the original family mill, and occupied a three storey brick building with basement and attic. There was also a huge elevator with a capacity of 35,000 bushels. Since the machinery was operated by water power, a dam was built — which was washed out in 1911 and rebuilt. The mill had a capacity of 200 barrels of rolled oats and oatmeal daily. Much of this breakfast food was sent to France for the soldiers during World War I. A few handfuls were also consumed by local school children who were attracted to the mill by the aroma of toasting oats on their way to or from school!

This mill was connected to the Canadian Pacific Railroad by switches and sidings for the daily delivery of a carload of oatmeal to be sold either across the Dominion, or more often exported. The brands manufactured were Rob Roy and Chieftain. W.R. McGowan was the active manager and was congratulated in the 1918 January issue of the Durham Review for his "enterprising spirit." By this time, a sister plant had been established in Yorkton, Saskatchewan, and a flour mill, cooper shop, storehouse and residence had also been purchased in Seaforth, Ontario.

Rob Roy Mills and Dam.

Older Durham residents can also recall the boathouse which housed nine rowboats and two canoes. These would be rented on a warm summer Sunday by the young dapper fellows about town.

Roy Roy Mills 1910.

Unfortunately, several fires caused havoc. After the 1924 fire, with a loss of $100,000 to $125,000, the mill was reconstructed to become a chopping mill, feed storage and blending plant. Tragedy came very close at the time of this terrible fire. J. W. Ewen and J. H. Harding were inside fighting the flames with water. Suddenly they realized that the huge east wall was toppling. They hurried out just as it came crashing down. Fortunately, they were far enough from the building for the blast of air to blow them clear.

In 1938 the mill was purchased by Knechtel Mills of Hanover and included a food depot for the distribution of New Life Feeds. Otto Schaus was hired as manager in 1940 and operated this mill for many years; Earl Paylor continued in charge of the mill until it closed. Prior to 1965 the waterwheel had no longer been needed as electric power was now more efficient. In 1965 Saugeen Valley Conservation Authority, with Government assistance, erected a larger flood control dam which created an even more substantial pond for recreational purposes.

The mill was sold to Michael Schmidt in 1984. He imported millstones from Germany and made stone ground flour for a short time. Prior to Christmas in 1985 and 1986, Michael Schmidt and a group of singers presented at the mill the Oberufserer Christmas Play which was composed and written by a Hungarian on a little island in the Danube River. This play is traditionally performed yearly in Hungary and Bavaria and other European communities. The musical accompaniment was a small electronic organ, the lighting was by candles, and the seats for the audience were bales of hay. Although the production was in the German language, the audience could understand the whole Christmas story by watching the actors and singers.

Durham from the north hill. Note Rob Roy Mills in centre of picture.

In 1989 the mill again passed into new ownership with Geoffrey Shea and Norman White as co-owners and it served as their residence and work studio. The building also housed the Durham Art Gallery for six months while the new Gallery was being built across the road from the mill.

In 1993 the mill was divided into two separate dwellings. One was for Geoffrey Shea and his wife Ilse Gassinger, the other for Norman White. The property now bears the title of United Media Arts. This is a non-profit organization with five directors, mostly local people who work in art-related projects. Geoffrey and Ilse, who are both highly skilled video artists, last summer (1993) had visiting artists from Germany and Austria as their guests and displayed their work at the mill. In November of the same year they hosted artists from Lithuania with their exhibits.

Norman White is a sculptor who deals with robotic sculpture. With a background in science, painting and electronics, he has been experimenting with electronics in his work for the past 25 years. This has included striving to bring biological thinking into his work. In his attempts to reveal the thinking process of animals, even insects, he has tried to make machines with thinking processes. He says he can start a machine, not knowing what it might do! Instead of dissecting, he synthesizes to satisfy his own curiosity. His working media, or artist's palette, includes large collections of such things as old computers — other people's junk — stored in well labelled boxes for the making of his fascinating robots.

Thus, this old mill still fills a need in the town, lending itself in a special way to the creativity of these artistic people.

FOUNDRIES

Inkerman's Foundry was established in 1854 on the south-west corner of Saddler and Garafraxa Streets. Adam and Alexander Cochrane were the proprietors. Here they manufactured agricultural implements such as plows, harrows, hay mowers, rakes and threshing machines. This writer remembers a worn out Meadow Lark mower which sat in a fence corner of a farm once worked by him. Sawmill equipment, tools, wagons and sleighs were also made, and a large business was carried on in both cooking and heating stoves. In January, 1870, there was a fire at the foundry which caused $1,000 dollars damage. The restored foundry was known as Cochrane's Foundry. The July 4, 1878 issue of the *Grey Review* reports on a mowing match spon-

Saugeen Mills Ltd.

133

sored by the St. Vincent Agricultural Society, at which nine different makes of hay mowers competed. The first prize was awarded to the Meadow Lark, made by the Cochrane Foundry at Durham, once again proving the superiority and capability of the machines made at this Foundry.

The Foundry was a two-storey stone building, 50 feet by 90 feet, plus a single storey stone moulding shop, stone blacksmith shop, and a tinsmith shop. The machine shop was on the ground floor of the main building, and the woodworking shop on the second floor. The machinery was powered by steam and lighting was by acetylene gas. Fuel was coal and shavings.

In 1884 this enterprise was destroyed by fire. The Cochranes sustained heavy financial loss and were not going to rebuild. The Foundry paid $233 taxes out of the town's total of $4,099 and employed 21 men full time, with a payroll of $7,200. Many businessmen in town agreed to buy shares in the foundry if it became a public company. The new foundry was renamed the Durham Foundry, was rebuilt, and returned to its former activities. It was again ravaged by fire in 1894 and again rebuilt. Later it was operated by Charter Smith and Sons. At the turn of the century the Durham Chronicle was published in the front part of the Foundry building. Many years later these buildings were burned again. The stone walls were razed and a one-storey cement block garage was erected on the site, where Smith Bros. operated a garage and Ford agency. This business was later operated by Jim Smith and his son Pat. It is now West End Motors operated by Don Hill.

A second foundry, the Durham Novelty Iron Works, was established in 1888 by W. A. Vollett at the corner of George Street West and Garafraxa Street. This frame building also served as a blacksmith shop. Later T. W. Moon had a machine shop there for several years and finally it was used as a garage until it burned in 1930. At present the property is in use as a children's wading pool supervised by the town.

TANNERIES

There were two tanneries in Durham at a very early stage of the town's development. The first was established at an unknown date by R. Crawford This tannery was completely destroyed by fire on September 14, 1860, and appeared to have not been rebuilt. The second was Smith's Tannery. Proprietor Thomas Smith came to Durham, opened a saddle and harness-making business, and about 1855 added a tannery. Quite a number of hands were employed at the tannery and the business created a flourishing market for hides, sheepskins and tan bark — which proved to be a marked benefit to the town. In 1870 the entire establishment was consumed by fire at a total loss of $12,000. Although Mr. Smith had no insurance on the property, it was rebuilt and operated for many years. It is also known that there was a Colgan's

Tannery in Durham because the November 8th, 1883 issue of the *Grey Review* reports that there was a fire at this business — although damage was not extensive. Little else is kown about this enterprise. Interestingly, the same paper reported the following week that the roof had been blown off Thomas Smith's tannery.

Another tannery in Durham was owned by William Wallace Gray. William Gray was born in 1841 aboard a ship bound for Canada. His father died of blood poisoning on that same voyage, and the captain of this ship, Captain Wallace, was so kind to his mother during this misfortune that she called her new son *Wallace* in his honour. William Wallace Gray eventually made his way to Durham, and in 1863 is mentioned as working upstairs in Thomas Smith's tannery. He soon opened his own tannery on the corner of Albert and Saddler Streets, and was later in partnership with Mr. Isaacs. They advertised their business as Tanners and Harness Makers Cash for Hides.

HERBERT ROWSWELL'S PEARL ASH WORKS

In 1852 a young man, Herbert Rowswell, took up Lots 1, 2 and 3, Concession 7, in Glenelg Township. Glenelg Falls was on Lot 2, and here he built a sawmill. At that time the early pioneers were clearing their land of trees — by slash and burn method. Rowswell saw an opportunity to start a profitable business with lots of cheap raw material, ashes and black salts, and so he also constructed a large ashery on the site as well. His teams gathered ashes for several miles around. The lye was leached out of the ashes and the resulting fluid was evaporated in giant castiron kettles. The remaining solids were sealed in barrels and teamed to the railway station at Collingwood for shipment to domestic and foreign markets for use in making soap.

Rowswell established a large department store and warehouse in the town of Durham on the east side of Queen Street, a short distance south of the Durham Road. He sold groceries, hardware, dry goods, ready-made clothing, shoes and fancy wares. At this warehouse he also bought ashes giving a few pennies credit per bushel of ashes. The credit was good on any purchase from his store. He paid cash for black salt. In 1863 Herbert Rowswell purchased Lots 20 and 21 Queen Street West and that summer built an ashery there.

But unfortunately this well-known and highly respected Durham business family came to an untimely and tragic ending. Herbert Rowswell died at the age of 39 in 1865, and his widow sold the Durham ashery to James Hill Hunter, who operated it for some years. The Rowswells had two daughters; the older, while swimming in the Speed River with friends from Guelph, was drowned at the age of 18 years. The second daughter also died at 18 years of age; and Mrs. Rowswell died at the age of 45.

WOOLLEN MILLS

The earliest woollen mill was at the Edge mill and was included with the flour operation in 1847. More woollen mills were established to meet the needs of the town's growing population. In 1865 The Durham Mills (Peter Patterson, proprietor) located on the west side of Garafraxa (lower dam), added a woollen mill for custom carding and fulling. In 1880 John Campbell bought Gray's Foundry and converted it to a Woollen Mill. He advertised Carding, Spinning, Weaving, Fulling and Cloth Pressing. He also sold flannels, tweeds, full cloth and stocking yarn. He accepted wool or cash as payment for goods.

Cliff's Woollen Mills, operated by steam, started operation in 1885. They were situated on Durham Road West, where there was a good supply of water from the springs in the hill. The woollen mills provided a ready market for the farmers' wool and helped the town and surrounding area. Finally, this company, also owned at one time by the Watchhorn family, like the other small mills ceased to operate.

CRAWFORD'S SAWMILL

In 1888 McCracken and Crawford's was a modern steam powered sawmill, located north of George Street and just east of College Street. It had a large log and lumber yard. There was a small stream flowing through the property which originated in a spring on the side of the hill, north of the Durham Road. This was dammed to form a log pond. It had another very important winter use. Many who read this will recall how they as youngsters enjoyed skating or playing shinny on that grand little pond.

In 1900 J. W. Crawford ran a tramway across George Street to convey lumber to the Durham Furniture Company. However, local sources of lumber were exhausted and fire destroyed the sawmill in 1904.

Again progress had taken its toll. Now the little stream and pond, and yes the redwing blackbirds, are barely visible as hundreds of truck loads of fill have converted this area into a residential zone with many fine houses constructed there.

BRICK YARDS

The June 9th, 1881 issue of the *Grey Review* reports the opening of Samuel Wright's brick yard on H. Parker's farm in Bentinck Township. This is just a short distance west of Durham across from the Durham Cemetery where the Ontario Department of Highways now has a depot. Mr. Parker, a druggist in Durham, is believed to have been behind this enterprise. These bricks were white in colour and were used almost exclusively in the early brick buildings constructed in Durham before 1900, such as the Calder Block. Three men moulded the bricks and it was expected that 300,000 would be made the first summer. This brick yard closed around 1900, and three of Mr. Wright's sons started brick yards in other locations, one of which was the Canada Pressed Brick Yard near Hamilton.

new brick company known as the Durham Brick Yard has been started in Bentinck township just west of Durham. This brick yard started largely through the enterprise of Mr. Wm. Black, a Durham merchant. The first 'burn' contained about 100,000 bricks and a second one is ready to start. Messrs. Walker were the brick makers." This brick yard operated for a few years but the date of its closing is unknown.

Crawford's Mill Pond.

Pressing bricks at Wright's brick yard.

Wright's Brick Yard.

DURHAM FURNITURE COMPANY LIMITED

In the late 1890s some of the businessmen in Durham realized that if the town was to keep its young people here a new major industry would be required to give them employment. In 1899 a meeting of interested citizens was called to see if enough capital could be raised to start a chair factory. A committee of A. McLachlan, Wm. Laidlaw, Mayor Wm. Calder, and Conrad Knapp was appointed to canvass the town to determine if sufficient stock could be raised to establish a chair factory. In about a week the committee reported that they had secured over $10,000 in firm commitments and about $3,000 in tentative commitments to purchase stock. A meeting was held of all those showing an interest in purchasing stock in the company, and a provisional Board of Directors was established consisting of Dr. D. Jamieson, Wm. Calder, Wm. Laidlaw, Conrad Knapp, Wm. Irwin, and N. McIntyre.

This temporary Board of Directors then approached the town for an interest free loan of $10,000, a free building site, and certain tax concessions. The Council decided to give the new company an interest free loan of $10,000 to be repaid in ten years, an assurance that taxes would not exceed $450 per year for ten years, and a six acre site which the town purchased for $500

and which is the present site of the Durham Furniture Company. Previously the Edge Estate had offered to donate a free site between George Street and the Saugeen River. It was necessary for the ratepayers in Durham to vote on the $10,000 interest free loan, and the result of the vote was 223 in favour and 19 against. The new company was then named The Durham Furniture Company Limited, and the directors named were: Dr. D. Jamieson, President; J.W. Crawford, Vice President; Wm. Laidlaw, Treasurer; Norman McIntyre, Secretary; and Conrad Knapp. All the directors had invested the necessary $500 in stocks. Later, J. Kelly was appointed Treasurer (non-director).

An architect was engaged, and plans were drawn for a 70,000 foot three-storey L-shaped building 150 feet long by 50 feet wide. The basement was to be 10 feet high and built of stone, and two storeys above 12 or 13 feet high built of brick. The floor space was 30,000 square feet. A later addition made it 150 feet by 100 feet. In December, 1899, a railway siding was built to the plant. There is no date available when production actually started, but the hiring of men was very gradual in order to give the new men a chance to learn how to operate the machines. The first shipment was on February 15th, 1900 — a consignment to a Mr. Brentall of Manchester, England. The goods were white (unfinished) to be finished in England. The editor of the *Durham Chronicle* had a trip through the new fac-

Furniture Factory as rebuilt after the disastrous fire in 1905.

tory on April 19th, 1900. He reported there were 32 employees and they were working hard to learn how to run the machines. All the machinery was located on the lower floor. He reported that the wages were not high — seven cents an hour for a ten-hour day. Mr. Adam Kranz was the first plant manager, then Mr. A.A. Catton took over as manager until 1919 when Mr. Peter Gagnon became manager, a position he held until 1955. Disaster struck on March 23, 1905, when fire totally destroyed the building. The dry kiln and boiler house which had been erected separately from the main structure were saved. At this time, the town gave a grant to the factory of $10,000 which was from the insurance policy which the town had on the factory to cover its $10,000 loan. The town also gave the factory another $10,000 interest free loan to be paid back in 10 years. The property destroyed by the fire was valued at $50,000, and at the time there were 60 employees.

Rebuilding after the fire began immediately. Later a sawmill was added to the factory buildings, and in 1910 the factory purchased the Dargavel Sawmill property at Dornoch and the Rockgate Mills east of Flesherton, which included 800 acres. Also that same year another three-storey addition, 120 feet by 60 feet, was added to the property at a cost of $25,000. This was for a chair and table factory.

In 1911 the company built a new dam on the Rocky Saugeen on the site of the old Dunsmoor Dam, and installed a generator to supply electricity for the factory. This plant could produce 200 horse power of electricity and was managed for 40 years by Mr. James Miller of Glenelg Township.

Around 1924 the furniture industry looked very rosy, and it appeared that it would be very profitable over the next few years. In order to take advantage of these circumstances, the Board of Directors decided to modernize the plant. These changes would be costly, and it was decided to offer a new stock issue. In order to have this done permission had to be given by the Provincial government before stock could be presented to the public. As Dr. Jamieson was president of the company, and also a cabinet member, he was instructed to procure the necessary permission. Many original investors in the Durham Furniture Company were planning on investing more money in the plant, but when the government gave its assent to sell more shares, Dr. D. Jamieson and his son's father-in-law, Mr. C.M. Bowman, who at that time was president of Mutual Life of Canada, bought the complete issue of new shares, giving them complete control of the company. That same year the company, which had been operating with a Provincial Charter, applied for and received a Dominion Charter, allowing them to do business with other provinces. A simplified explanation appeared in the *Durham Chronicle*, "Willie was getting too big a boy for short pants, so they equipped him with man's sized ones."

By 1928 the timber holdings were approximately 12,000 acres in Hastings County and 2,000 acres in Grey County and employed 75 people in the lumber operations and 180 in the plant. The factory was over 100,000 square feet and consumed over three million board feet of lumber a year. The production at that time amounted to a carload every 11 hours.

Due to the depression years in the 1930s, furniture sales dropped drastically, but rather than lay off some men, the Furniture Company instituted a share-the-work programme which worked very well in that everyone received a little money. One Durham senior citizen recounts an incident that occurred during the 1930s. He had started work in the factory prior to 1930 and had worked part time during the depression. In the late 1930s, when he went to pick up his pay envelope one day, he was given a message that the management wished to see him. He went in to see Mr. Jucksch and was told that Pete (Gagnon) had been watching him. He liked the way he worked and was going to give him a raise in pay of 50 cents a week. But in order to get the raise he had to come into the plant 15 minutes before the rest of the men to get things ready to work, and stay 15 minutes after the men left to clean up and put things away. In this way he would work 53 hours a week instead of the 50 hours the rest of the men worked, and at 10 cents an hour for labour, his raise amounted to 20 cents per week, or three and one-half cents per nine-hour day.

Dr. David Jamieson was president of the Company until his death in 1942. At that time his son, Dr. Bradshaw Jamieson, was majority owner. In 1945 Dr. D.B. Jamieson sold his interest to Mr. Peter Gagnon and Mr. James Duffield.

In December, 1951, the plant management received notice that the International Woodworkers of America were seeking union certification for Local 152. In the spring and early summer of 1952 many negotiating meetings took place, but they eventually broke off, and the workers went out on strike in July. At that time the management put through a pay increase retroactive to July 1st in order to bring the level of pay at the Durham Furniture factory up to the level of other furniture factories in Grey and Bruce Counties. But the strike continued. It was a long and bitter strike in a small town, and as a result several families left town to find work in other communities. What happeened in this strike was no credit to either management or labour. In February, 1953, the strike ended and the union local was disbanded.

Over the years the company became known across Canada as one of the best producers of fine quality furniture. A major buyer of the goods was the T. Eaton Company. In 1949 the Company had the honour of producing furniture for the newly married Princess Elizabeth and Duke of Edinburgh. The Canadian Pacific Railway wished to make a tangible contribution of Canadian goodwill.

Durham Furniture Factory 1918.

The idea was a Canadian Room in the couple's home of Canadian design, material and workmanship. The room chosen was the Duke's personal sitting room and study. The C.P.R. commissioned the T. Eaton Company to find the appropriate furniture company and the Durham Furniture Company was chosen. Dry, clear, white, flawless Canadian maple was wanted. Over 100,000 feet of lumber was sorted in the yards to find 60,000 feet of the very best. The mouldings were of special design and patterns had to be made to conform to these designs. Mr. George Jucksch, then retired, returned to do the job. His lifetime of experience and expertise qualified him to supervise the project. Special machine knives were made and the responsibility for this fell to Mr. Harry Styles, the machine room foreman for many years. The Plant employees were entitled to share the praise which came from all who saw the finished project.

In 1950 the Company celebrated its 50th Anniversary. There had been some down times during the depression and world wars, but in spite of this, the Company survived and progressed. There were about 175 employees, and the annual payroll was $500,000.

In November, 1954, the plant entered a new era when it was sold to Kroehler Manufacturing, the largest furniture manufacturing company in the world. The Durham plant became a subsidiary of Kroehler Manufacturing Company of Naperville, Illinois. At one time Kroehler had 26 plants in total — 19 in the U.S.A, five in Canada, and two in Mexico. When Kroehler officially took over in 1955, they immediately undertook major renovations and over the next 24 years added more buildings and new machinery. The 1950s brought to an end an era of employee service of over 50 years. Mr. Gagnon had arrived when the company had began operations and had sent to Winchester, Ontario, for five more young men who had experience in woodworking: Thomas Cook, Andrew Thompson, Ancil Cook, Wm. Watson, and Wm. Christie. Of these Andrew Thompson holds the record for the longest term of employment (56 years) as cabinet maker and foreman in the finishing department. His daughter, Mae (Mrs. Floyd Lawrence), still has in her possession the recipes used for mixing the stain.

Mr. Gagnon had over 55 years service and Thomas Cook, Mel Storrey, Charles Moon, and Dave Nichol, over 50 years.

The next 24 years with Kroehler were good ones. Markets for furniture fluctuated, but again the company survived and prospered. The Kroehler motto was "Kroehler People Care." The Company sponsored ball and hockey teams, curling bonspiels, etc. and frequently made donations to local charitable organizations. Employees were honoured for attendance and safety awards. In 1957 a long-standing Kroehler tradition of honouring long term employees was started in Durham. A luncheon was held for five, ten, and 15 year employees, and the 20 Year Club banquet was held in the evening.

By the late 1980s the following people had more than 40 years of service with the company: Doyle Braithwaite — 44, Muriel Snell — 49, John Alexander — 43, Royden Connor — 47, Alex Wells — 46, Herbert Trafford — 48, Stan Sewell — 43, Ralph Wilson — 46, Ivan McEachnie — 40 and Russell McVicar — 40. There may have been more from the early era but records are not available. Jim Nixon will have marked 44 years of service in December, 1994.

Five young men who came from Winchester, Ontario, to work in the Furniture Factory in 1901.
Back Row: Tom Cook, Andrew Thompson
Front Row: Ancil Cook, Bill Watson, Bill Christie.

Plant Managers since 1955 have been Wm. Wardropper, 1955-1963; Jack Dempsey, 1963-1967; O.G. Mead, 1967-1980.

By the late 1970s the fortunes of Kroehler U.S.A. had waned, and in 1979 the Canadian division was sold to the Strathhearn House Group of Toronto. The Kroehler name remained but was changed in 1981 to Kroehler Furniture Company.

Presidents
1979-1983 Wm. Singer of Strathearn House Group
1979-1983 O.G. Mead named Vice President and General Manager of Case Goods (Durham) Division
1983-1992 O.G. Mead — President of entire Kroehler Company
After 1983 Lloyd Love was Vice President of Manufacturing and Jack Lawrence was Vice President of Marketing.

Plant Managers
1980-1981 Ron Morris
1981-1987 Lloyd Love
1987-1992 Larry Reay

The 1980s were not good years for the furniture industry in Canada. The recession, the high Canadian dollar, high interest rates and free trade all worked to reduce the number of employees in the furniture industry by 50 percent. In February, 1992, the Strathearn House Group went into receivership, and in spite of having survived fires, recessions, two World Wars, and a strike, it appeared that the Durham Furniture Company had come to an end.

However, after much difficult work, the plant reopened in June, 1992, as Durham Furniture Inc. thanks to the First Echo Group of Kitchener, the Ontario Development Corporation, and many other local investors. Officers of the comany are: Orville G. Mead, President; Lloyd Love, Vice President of Manufacturing; Jack Lawrence, Vice President of Marketing; Larry Reay, Plant Manager.

While still coping with the effects of the current recession, the Company is very optimistic regarding the continued success of the plant and expects to be around for another 94 years. Perhaps an omen that the plant was to continue was the peeling of the red paint which uncovered the original Durham Furniture Company sign on the south-east wall of the plant (applied when Kroehler took over in 1955).

AWARDS AND RECORDS

In 1975 the Ontario Ministry of Trade and Tourism, jointly with the Ontario Furniture Manufacturing Association began sponsoring the Trillium Awards. These awards recognized achievement in design, production, marketing, serviceability, ingenuity and development of furniture products in Ontario. Since 1975, Kroehler/Durham Furniture has won an average of one Trillium each year, including the 1990 Grand Trillium, the Minister's Award for over-all excellence.

At the time of writing, Mill #4, the Pre-Assembly and Sample Department, has gone since March 5, 1967, with no lost day accidents.

For those of us old enough to remember, the Company had a whistle which was blown four times a day — 7:00 a.m., 12:00 noon, 1:00 p.m. and 4:30 p.m. This whistle could be heard for quite a distance in town and its meaning was to call the workers to the plant and to announce quitting time. There are plans in the offing to resurrect the blowing of the whistle, except perhaps the early morning call.

This plant has a proud history. Over the 94 years the wages have fed many families and provided the amenities of life. The workers have always taken pride in their work, and without their pride, skills, and workmanship, the success would not have been there.

John A. Graham, Bookkeeper
at the National Portland Cement Company.

NATIONAL PORTLAND CEMENT COMPANY

During the early 1890s Neil McKechnie, the senior partner of the N. G. & J. McKechnie firm, became very interested in the marl deposits in lakes near Durham and dreamed of building a cement plant here. He brought in geologists and engineers to take borings of the marl beds to determine their depth and got government analysis of the marl. Everything pointed to a successful enterprise. He wrote hundreds of letters to business investors and investment companies in an effort to secure finances and support for such a plant. The following paragraphs were taken from an editorial which appeared in the *Durham Chronicle* dated *May 18th, 1899:*

> "The cement industry which has been talked of in a quiet way for some time, is bidding fair to become a paying industry and excite public attention. Few places in Canada, from what we learn, are more bountifully supplied with raw material. The report of the government analyst is highly favourable. The prospecting

National Portland Cement Works.

> tours in the vicinity give confidence to moneyed institutions of the advisability of investing in the scheme."

> "The possibility of establishing a cement plant in Durham is now past its embryonic stage and there is a strong probability that before another year passes, preparations will be made in earnest for the manufacture of what has now become to be regarded as a necessary article. The old plank sidewalks in every progressive town are now being replaced by more permanent and ultimately cheaper granolithic. Last year nearly 7000 square feet were laid in Durham, and from a general feeling of satisfaction it is almost safe to predict that very few wooden walks will ever be constructed in the future."

> "In the event of the work going on too much credit cannot be given to Mr. Neil McKechnie who has for the past year spent his time and energies in working out the scheme. From his first discovery of the value of our marl deposits, he seems to have been thinking of nothing else, until his whole being is saturated with cement. We are almost safe in saying that bushels of correspondence has passed on the subject, until scarcely a financial concern in Canada is ignorant of the vast importance of our marl beds."

First trainload of machinery to arrive at the site of the National Portland Cement Company.

National Portland Cement Power House.

The February 14, 1900, *Durham Review* reports that a local company had been formed, a charter secured, and work of organizing the company began. The town gave the company a free 20 acre site. At this point Mr. R. H. McWilliams, Owen Sound, made a proposition from a wealthy and experienced company who wanted to be part of the cement company. This was arranged and great activity followed immediately.

A ratepayers' meeting was called to explain what was proposed. Mr. W. F. Cowham, President of the Peninsular Portland Company, Jackson, Michigan, was present. He assured the ratepayers that the raw material in the neighbourhood was in almost inexhaustible quantities, sufficient at least to furnish a possible output of 5,000 barrels of cement a day for 200 years. A new board of five directors was elected to run the company. Mr. W. F. Cowham was president, and a Durham businessman, Mr. Gilbert McKechnie, was elected director and treasurer.

The new company was capitalized at $1,000,000, in 10,000 shares of $100 each. Durham and area were asked to raise $150,000 of the capital stock; the N. G. & J. McKechnie firm took $25,000 worth. If you can think of this at today's prices, it would be equivalent to a new plant coming to town worth $100,000,000.

An examination of the water power available on our rivers was made to ascertain if it would be sufficient to produce enough hydro to supply the plant. It was deemed unsatisfactory, therefore, a huge steam-powered plant was built, fired by coal, to supply the

electricity required. The power house was 103 feet by 74 feet. The warehouse was 144 feet by 72 feet, and could hold 100,000 barrels of cement.

The following item is taken from a larger article which appeared in the *Toronto Daily Star* and was reproduced in full in the May 22nd, 1902, edition of the *Durham Chronicle*:

"WORLD'S BIGGEST CEMENT WORKS ARE LOCATED IN THIS COUNTRY

The Plant at Durham is a Mammoth Establishment with the most Modern Equipment and has made the town hum.

This is a proud boast for Canada, but it is a prouder boast for Durham. The town is already feeling the new throb of life which a large industry always brings in its wake. Houses are scarce, there is not an idle man in the place and everyone has the price in his pocket. Not only is Durham unusually prosperous but the wave of good times has touched the adjoining villages and they are singing the same chorus, lots of work and plenty of money to do it with. Those who know say that the establishment of the cement plant is largely responsible for the whole business.

On the 26th of September last, quietly, unostentatiously, the first shovelful of earth was turned for the commencement of the works. Thirty-five days after a line of railway was completed from the Grand Trunk to the grounds. From that day over 400 car loads of material have arrived for the carrying on of the construction. Some of it comes resting on two cars.

View of Durham from top of National Portland Cement Company smoke stack.

And this is the spot where cement will be made without hands, made automatically, by the magic of machinery. A marvellous thing this — a tribute to the best brains of the 20th century. The world has been hearing much of the cheapness with which Americans produce their manufactured articles, how they flood the world at will. Here the best plants in America will be surpassed, and their economy beaten. The Yankees will be met and checkmated in their own game.

The National Portland Cement Company is fortunate in that they have all the sand and gravel they need on their own property to make the cement foundations for the buildings required.

The smokestack is a huge affair; it will reach toward the blue nearly 200 feet and will be one of the tallest in Ontario. This stack is of steel and will stand alone without so much as a single guy. It will be held by anchor bolts which are fastened in 30 feet of solid concrete.

The company has purchased its material as far as it could in Canada. Some of the machinery, however, was not made in the Dominion, notably the rotaries which are used for calcinating. These terms to the uninitiated may be dark and mysterious but in plain English it simply means hugh steel affairs 70 feet long, seven feet in diameter, shaped like cannon and hollow at each end. Here the marl and the clay meet the fire for the first time and are cooked to a cinder.

These rotaries are eight in number. Great and grim they stood as if anxious to begin to whirl. Grim because they looked like immense cannons; great because they are so massive that they had to be placed on foundations first and the structures built over them. Another

massive machine is the Krupp Ball Mill which came from Essen, Germany.

The National Portland Cement Company is a Canadian Company, developing a Canadian industry from Canadian raw materials, with Canadian capital. There are 1800 shareholders in the company, almost all Canadians.

The directors are Mr. A. F. McLaren, M. P., Stratford, Ontario, President of the Imperial Cheese Company Limited; Barlou Cumberland, Vice-President Niagara Navigation Company, Toronto; P. W. Stanhope, Ontario Manager of the McCormick Harvesting Machine Co., Toronto; W. F.Cowham, Managing Director of the Peninsular Portland Cement Company, Jackson, Michigan; Gilbert McKechnie, ex M.P.P., merchant, Durham. Mr. McKechnie is also treasurer of the company.

The National Portland Cement Company own their own railroad to Wilder Lake, a distance of about five miles. They also own their own engine and rolling stock and have been incorporated under Government charter with full railroad privileges.

There are many technical terms used in the manufacture of cement and this is the way the National Portland Cement Company will produce their article. The marl is dredged by special machinery which can dig to a depth of 35 feet. It is loaded on cars by specially constructed machinery, in which compressed air plays an important part. From the marl bed to the works is a fall of 290 feet and the cars will practically land themselves at the mouth of the receiving hoppers where they are automatically emptied. These cars have a capacity of 70,000 pounds, and from the hopper the marl comes

142

into contact with machinery which granulates it, after which it is again dropped by gravity into storage bins which each contain enough to make 200 barrels of cement. These bins are again discharged by gravity into special mixing mills where the proper amount of clay is added. Provision has been made so that chemists can obtain an accurate analysis of the clay and marl so that a proper amount of each may be determined for each mix. This material goes through tube mills where the material is ground so fine that 96% of it will pass through a 100 mesh screen.

From these grinding mills the material is taken by machinery and fed by automatic feeders into gigantic rotary kilns in which the marl and clay are united in fusion at a temperature of 3000 degrees fahrenheit. From the kilns it goes to the grinding building where the clunker is ground in the machine purchased from the Essen Krupp Gun Works, Germany. From there it goes to the tube mills for finishing and then on to the warehouse. And so from the time it is marl to the moment it becomes cement, no human hand really takes part in the making."

The April 3rd, 1901, issue of the *Durham Review* states that last week they visited the Cement Plant and found there were about 150 people employed there. Soon this number may be doubled.

The large chimney at the powerhouse has been mentioned, but as well as this one there were eight more smaller chimneys, one for each of the rotary kilns. When the plant was working at full capacity, it would burn between four and five carloads of coal a day. At first the fuel was cheap soft coal containing much sulphur which created a dense black smoke and if there was a south wind, there would be a black mantle over the town. The Durham women complained loudly about this smoke; they could only do their laundry on days when there was no south wind and they had to keep an eye on any wind change during the day in order that they could rush out to their yards and take the clothes off the lines before they became smoke-blackened. Many white brick houses in Durham still show some evidence of smoke damage from the cement plant 90 years ago.

In 1905 the Cement Plant shut down before freeze-up. The manager stated that the marl at Wilder Lake was exhausted. Local shareholders could not accept this, and one of them, Mr. William Irwin, Editor of the *Durham Chronicle*, took up the fight, and for three or four months every issue of the *Chronicle* published long articles and letters from shareholders. One of the directors of the company, Mr. W. F. Cowham, Jackson,

Dredging Marl at Wilder Lake.

National Portland Cement Company.

Dinky Engine at Nationl Portland Cement Company.

Group of men who worked at the National Portland Cement Company.

Scene of Durham looking south from Garafraxa hill.
Note smoke stack from National Portland Cement prior to 1908.

Michigan, had a very large financial interest in the manufacture of cement in Michigan. He had been able to infiltrate the Durham Works with Americans, including general manager, assistant manager, head bookkeeper, and chemist. The purpose was to close the Durham Cement Works as the quality of cement produced here was unsurpassed by any other cement produced in North America and there was a keen market for National Portland cement. With the bookkeeper's knowledge about the Durham Works' customers, it could prove to be extremely profitable to the Michigan company if the Durham plant closed. Mr. Wm. Irwin was sued for libel by the chemist, a Mr. Ludwig; Irwin lost the case, and had to pay over $1,600, but individual stockholders reimbursed him over $1,100.

The annual meeting in 1906 was a stormy affair and resulted in the election of some new directors who desired to keep the plant operating. Mr. R. H. McWilliams was elected President, and he immediately began making badly needed repairs to the machinery which had been allowed to deteriorate. He brought in good Canadians for all the top positions. During 1906 the company produced 260,000 barrels of cement, 45,000 barrels more than in 1905, and in 20 days less work. The company paid off a $75,000 debt and paid the shareholders ten per cent dividend on their shares. In 1908 the marl at Wilder Lake became unsuitable for cement and the company bought the marl in the Marl Lakes at Hanover, which was shipped to Durham on the Canadian Pacific Railway.

In 1907 the cement plant started its year's operation on April 11th; this year a higher grade of coal was being used. The June 6th, 1907, *Durham Review* reports that Durham citizens still complained to council with regard to the dense black smoke, and on July 25, 1907, the cement plant agreed not to grind cement on Sunday.

The October 30th, 1913, edition of the *Durham Chronicle* reports on a banquet, given by the Board of Directors to its employees, held in the Middaugh House. Mr. William Calder, a Durham businessman, was now president of the company; he also at one time was general manager. The following information was given to those present at this gathering:

Up to October 1st, 1913, over 25,000 more barrels of cement had been shipped out than at the same time last year;
2,000 carloads of cement had been shipped and $90,000 freight paid;
5,000 carloads of marl had been brought in, $28,000 freight paid;
800 carloads of clay had been brought in, $6,000 freight paid;
1,000 carloads of coal had been brought in, $90,000 freight paid;
Rail cars end to end would reach about 70 miles;
The payroll was $45,000;
Bank indebtedness was less than $100,000. Three years ago it was $200,000

Building National Portland Cement Company Rail Line.

No history of Durham would be complete without an account of the McKechnie family whose impact on Durham was probably greater than any other family. Margaret, the oldest, was a milliner. As soon as they arrived in Durham she opened a millinery shop and also offered other articles for sale, which proved very profitable. Her brothers then formed a partnership known as N. G. and J. McKechnie; and they opened a large department store selling groceries, hardware, millinery, ready-made clothing, shoes, dry goods and fancy wares.

McKechnie's introduced a system of credit which was fairly easy for their customers to obtain. But then there would come a day of reckoning and a payment would have to be made on account. Usually payment would be a cow, or maybe a yoke of oxen or a horse, and then the credit would commence all over again. The second day of reckoning was usually for larger accounts, and the McKechnie's acquired several 50 acre farms in the surrounding townships. However, as

The future looked rosy for the cement plant, but it was not to be. All over the world cement plants were switching from marl to hard rock for the making of cement, which was a cheaper process. It is not known when the cement plant closed, but it was possibly in 1915.

The September 6th, 1917, issue of the *Durham Review* reports:

"It will be gratifying news to the shareholders of the National Portland Cement Company, and not less so to the Town, that once more our Cement Works is going to run under new auspices, new men, new methods, and new material.

"R. H. McWilliams, the new manager, has energy and experience, a great body of suitable clay has been secured at Allan Park, marl has been discarded for rock and the advent of freezing weather will not, as of old, compel sudden closing.

"A big supply of rock is on hand and the clay train service has started, so here's wishing abundant success to the enterprise that has lifted our big mill into its present gratifying position."

Ontario hydro was now available in Durham and the cement plant bought electric power from this source, rather than generating its own, which amounted to a great saving. However, the market was flooded with cheap cement and new outlets for the Durham product were difficult to find. The plant ran for a short period, then shut down permanently. The property stood idle until 1920, when the John E. Russell Company purchased it. The plant was partly dismantled and the machinery sold.

N. G. & J. McKECHNIE

The McKechnie family — Margaret, Neil, Gilbert, and John — emigrated from Scotland to Durham in 1857.

Gilbert McKechnie.

one early pioneer remarked, "the lands they received on account were almost all marginal and not worth much more than the amount of the account." Eventually when stores started advertising their products "Buy cheaper for cash," the credit system disappeared.

N. G. & J. McKechnie purchased the Patterson Mills in 1875 which consisted of sawmill, flour mill, and oatmeal and grist mills. They built a sash and door factory and a new sawmill which was burned by an arsonist in August, 1894, with a loss of over 1,000,000 board feet of lumber. They purchased the Glenroadin sawmill and cut large tracts of forest near Durham into lumber. This sawmill too fell to the arsonist's torch.

The McKechnie brothers were some of Durham's best known industrialists. Gilbert McKechnie was President of the Wellington Georgian Bay Railway

Company which brought the first railway into Durham in 1881. John McKechnie was President of the Durham Natural Gas and Oil Company which resulted in the drilling of a large artesian well. Neil McKechnie, with his research of the marl deposits in the area, and his contact with most of the large financial enterprises in Canada, was the one man responsible for establishing the National Portland Cement Company in Durham. He died in 1903. Gilbert McKechnie was the first Treasurer of the National Portland Cement Company.

In the 1890s N. G. & J. McKechnie purchased the Durham Creamery on the Durham Road at the end of Bruce Street, and greatly expanded its operation. In June, 1898, the company received a carload of butter boxes, 1,500 in all. Durham was only the second creamery in Canada to have been the recipient of so many at one time. The boxes would hold 42 tons of butter and would be filled during the season. Up until this time farmers made their own butter and sold it to the stores. But now when farmers sold their cream to the Creamery, a large volume of buttermilk was created for which the Creamery had no use. In order to utilize the buttermilk, McKechnie's established a large piggery on the north side of Douglas Street. In the spring they bought dozens and dozens of piglets and fattened them over the summer on buttermilk and grain. Some years later both the Creamery and piggery had disappeared.

From 1891 to 1894 Gilbert McKechnie was the Liberal member of the Ontario Legislature. He was a Town Councillor and Reeve of Durham for many years. He died in 1930 at the age of 88.

THE FARMERS' MANUFACTURING AND SUPPLY COMPANY LIMITED

The Farmers' Manufacturing and Supply Company Limited was formed in 1903 to build cream separators. To have the company locate the new factory in Durham the town council offered a $7,000 interest free loan to be repaid in 10 years, exemption from taxation, except school taxes, for 10 years and a free site for the factory. A plebescite was held on this offer and the ratepayers accepted it. That summer a one storey cement block factory of about 14,000 square feet was erected. The plant started production in late 1903, and employed several skilled machinists as well as local labourers. George Binnie, a Glenelg farmer, subsequently became President of this firm.

The Company sold the Oxford Cream Separator, as it was called, on a trial basis. Their certainty that the Separator was the best on the market at this time led them to encourage customers to take one home, try it, have the skim milk tested by a Babcock tester and if the customer could find a better separator the Oxford

could be returned and no questions asked. Sales were very good. But by late 1906 it was obvious that the company was in trouble because it did not have sufficient capital to provide an adequate cash flow; too much money was tied up in expensive inventory for too long a period. In August, 1907, the Company made an assignment.

In January, 1908, the Town sold the building to Siirs Bros., John and Wesley, who also purchased the patents, machinery and supplies, and intended to continue the manufacture of the Oxford Cream Separator. Less than a month later, during a severe winter storm, the factory caught fire. The fire engine arrived at the scene, but instead of stopping at the underground water tank located at Bruce and Lambton Streets, the firemen tried to go to the river and became so badly stuck in the snow and mire that they never got a drop of water on the fire. The Durham papers stated that by the time the fire engine reached the fire it was still quite small, confined to one corner, and could easily have been extinguished, but with no water everything was lost.

The property sat empty until 1916 when Zenus Clark purchased it, moved a building onto the foundation, and operated a steam-powered sawmill and planing mill. He bought logs from farmers and lumbermen to manufacture interior finish, sash, doors, frames and general house fittings. He did custom planing and sawing, as well as considerable business as a contractor and builder. During the same period a shingle and lath mill was established south of the Grand Trunk Station, operated by W.R.F. Clark.

In 1920 Zenus Clark sold the plant to Clark Metals Limited. During the 1920s Clark Metals made metal stampings such as metal buttons for overalls and work pants. They later manufactured furniture hardware, such as castors. This building was destroyed by fire and again the property was vacant for several years.

The Durham Hardware purchased the property in 1954, and constructed a large cement block building. The owner, Mr. William Hewitt, distributed all types of gases — welding, propane, hospital — both in cylinder and bulk, covering a wide area from this location, as well as selling gas-burning appliances and welding supplies. In 1972 his son Paul took over the business and since that date has discontinued handling propane and hospital gases. This Company now specializes in welding supplies and gases and is known as Durham Welding Supplies Limited.

Main Plant of Durham Crushed Stone Company Limited

The 1952 Stone Crusher Plant.

DURHAM STONE AND PAVING LIMITED

In 1920 the John E. Russell Company purchased the National Portland Cement Company and installed equipment to produce crushed stone and gravel from the gravel on the property. Mr. Russell was a wealthy aggressive businessman and a director of several large business companies in Ontario, including two shipping companies. Under his direction this plant started to ship train loads of sand and gravel in large part to Toronto. The top shipment for one day was 108 railway cars.

There are still remnants of the cement plant to be seen today — the Grey County Building, which is now a service garage for the county roads equipment, the pylon of the elevated rail delivery line and the chemical laboratory at the corner of South and Garafraxa Streets, now the Sullivan home. In 1931 the company was reorganized as the Consolidated Sand and Gravel Company.

John Schutz, Sr., and his son, Erben, bought the Consolidated Sand and Gravel Company in 1940 and the name was changed to Durham Crushed Stone

Company Limited. A portable crusher was installed and later a building was constructed around it as there was an unlimited supply of gravel on the 100 acres of land. Concrete retaining walls were built and rubber conveyor belts were set up for stockpiling. This also made for more ease in loading freight cars from shutes in the concrete wall. A washing plant was installed at the crusher.

Early in the 1950s spur lines were laid into the plant for both the C.P.R. and C.N.R. and leases with both railway companies were drawn up. At this period the plant was running 24 hours a day — from one minute past midnight on Sunday until midnight on Saturday night. Doubleheaders of both railway companies left the plant twice a day on both C.P.R. and C.N.R. carrying 12 cars each, making a total of 48 cars a day six days a week. Each freight car held from 40 to 60 tons of stone. This material went to Toronto for the building of the Toronto subway.

After the completion of the subway material was still shipped to Toronto for work done by the Harbour Commission. Gravel pits were now being opened near Toronto, and the cost of shipping by rail became prohibitive with the result shipping via rail ceased.

The original crushing plant of the
Durham Crushed Stone Company.

Soon after the business was established Jack Schutz, Jr., joined the company. He took charge of a portable crusher plant which the company had set up on Manitoulin Island. This plant operated there for many years. In the fall the crusher and equipment from the island were brought back to Durham. A building was constructed near the asphalt plant for storing this equipment during the winter months in order that repairs could be carried out during this period. In the late 1950s a fire consumed the building and contents. The loss was estimated between $250,000 and $300,000. Later a Ready Mix cement plant was built on this site which is still in operation and is leased to E.C. King of Owen Sound.

In the 1950s an asphalt plant was installed by Durham Stone and Paving and this was named the Grey Wellington Paving Limited. This plant could produce over 1,000 tons of hot mix per day for paving.

The T.G. Pounder Company, a few miles north of Brampton, had a formula called P.A.P. which was used for producing cold mix. This mix could be manufactured and stockpiled for repairing roads in the winter months. The Durham Stone and Paving company was fortunate to obtain permission to use the material and was the only company north of Guelph to obtain this formula.

Gravel in the original land was being depleted. An agreement was reached whereby gravel could be obtained from three farms east of the plant, with an option to buy if the farms were sold. Thus, in the 1960s the two McGirr farms and the Allan farm were bought by the company assuring it of an unlimited gravel supply.

The Ontario government began charging a fee for every ton of gravel taken from the land. Several years after this levy came into effect all gravel pits, when exhausted, had to be levelled off and replanted.

In 1952 the McGowan mill and property was purchased by Durham Stone and Paving. Machinery was installed in the building for making cement blocks and concrete tiles. This was never considered a money-making project but it gave work to keep employees in the winter months. Block plants with more modern machinery sprang up around the country and metal tiles replaced cement ones. Eventually the plant and land were sold to the Saugeen Valley Conservation Authority.

Early in 1962 Erben Schutz bought out his brother Jack's share of the company and operated alone until 1965 when the company was sold to A.C. Payne and his brother-in-law, Don Nearingburg. Later, Payne purchased his brother-in-law's share and continued to operate the company alone.

Prior to selling the company Erben Shutz donated land north of the Block Plant on the Saugeen River to the Saugeen Conservation Authority.

On February 1st, 1973, A.C. Payne sold the company to Seeley and Arnill of Dundalk. Prior to this a pollution plant was installed at the asphalt plant.

In the 1980s Seeley and Arnill bought Saugeen Spraying and Oiling and changed the name of Durham Stone and Paving to Saugeen Road Spraying Company Limited.

In 1992 Seeley and Arnill purchased a Cold-In-Place Asphalt Recycling Machine at the cost of one million dollars. This is an extremely efficient method of rehabilitating asphalt roadways which are in a state of deterioration. The machine reuses the existing pavement structure and this results in a stable road at a total energy saving of from 40 to 50 per cent, compared to conventional construction methods. In addition, recycling conserves the depleting non-renewable resources of aggregates and petroleum products. From a small operation in Dundalk, this company has grown to become one of the largest and most up-to-date companies in the county.

LAWRENCE'S SAWMILL

The Sawmill, located on Saddler Street East, between Albert and Elgin Streets, was purchased in 1930 by Roy Lawrence from Robert Smith who owned this property from 1914, when he purchased it from Joseph Brown. It is believed that the property prior to 1914 was operated as a sawmill and cider mill, this use having been continued by Mr. Smith. Roy Lawrence worked with Mr. Smith as a partner supplying the power from his traction steam engine. After purchase of the mill Mr. Lawrence operated it as a sawmill and a shingle mill doing custom work.

From 1920 until the 1940s and early 1950s many of the logs, timber and shingles were brought in by horse and sleigh during the winter and would be cut into lumber and shingles in the spring. Large piles of logs were in the yard when Spring came — this was a great playground for the children.

During these years the main power was steam which also caused a few problems for the neighbours with flying sparks and soot. This power was converted to diesel in the early 1950s.

Names of a few employees during Mr. Lawrence's time are: Bill Henry, Albert Pearson, Gordon Osborne, Jack Legatt, Jack Picken, and Jack Trafford. Summertime employment for students was packing shingles — Jim Storrey, ? Kalman and Homer Gerber, Delbert Moore, Reg. Reis, and Jack Cutler were a few of the students.

Roy's son, Floyd, spent his summers edging shingles and hauling wood around town to customers for one dollar per cord delivered. Another son, Norman, started to work with his father in the 1940s at the tender age of twelve. His first job was to carry a pail of water and a dipper to put out the smouldering sparks in the yard; he later cut basket bottoms and did custom sawing. Norman purchased the mill in 1955.

This mill produced many of the railroad ties used in construction of the Toronto subway. A good many homes, barns and other buildings were constructed from lumber sawn at the mill, including the Presbyterian Church, and a large barn owned by Stewart MacArthur — now the Koeslag farm. Stan Dawson and Lloyd Redford also used lumber from the mill for construction in Hanover.

The mill was sold by Norman Lawrence to William Kennedy in 1969. Since then residences have been erected on this site.

Aerial View of Durham 1919.

THE BUTTERMILK PLANT

The business was originally started in Meaford, but in 1936 Longworth Milling Co. built a plant in Durham and transferred the industry here. Mr. Albert Longworth was appointed manager.

The products manufactured were buttermilk powder, semi-solid buttermilk and Vita milk blocks. The buttermilk powder was mixed with animal feed to increase growth. The semi-solid buttermilk was put in large barrels and sold to farmers who used it to feed hogs. The Vita milk blocks were made by adding buttermilk powder to the condensed milk to make it quite thick. This cooled and hardened into blocks which were sold to poultry farmers.

The buttermilk was gathered in tank trucks from creameries within a 100 miles radius of Durham. The milk was condensed in an evaporator and then run over rollers to dry and powder. During the summer months there was enough milk to keep the plant operating 24 hours a day with four men on a shift.

In 1960 Mr. Quennell bought the buttermilk plant, and in the early 1960s following Mr. Quennell's retirement, Mr. R.A.L. "Max" Player was manager. During this period the production method was changed so that instead of condensing sour buttermilk the milk was gathered while still sweet and made into a sweet buttermilk powder. This eliminated the strong odour that used to come from drying sour buttermilk. This sweet buttermilk powder was blended with animal fat and fed to calves. Due to the high fat content the calves grew faster and so could be marketed in a shorter time.

The change to sweet buttermilk resulted in a large increase in the powder business, and 22 were required to operate a double shift.

When the plant was destroyed by fire in 1974, the business was transferred to a factory in Walkerton.

LIGHTNING ROD CO.

Mr. C.B. Lawrence started a lightning rod company in 1936. The plant was located on Queen Street South not far from the Lower Dam. After many years this business was sold to A.R. Kennedy and W.R. Kennedy. The plant was capable of producing 200,000 feet of pure copper lightning rod wire a year.

FOOTWEAR PLANT

This industrious little plant was located in the stone building on the south corner of Garafraxa Street and Durham Road. Originally it was known as C.L. Grant's store.

Owned by C.M. Elvidge and started in 1950, this business employed six people. Using sheepskin, leather, felt, plush and other materials, bedroom footwear of various styles was made.

Thousands of pairs were made yearly and sold in Ontario, Quebec, Newfoundland, Saskatchewan and British Columbia.

GEORGIAN HOSIERY

In 1945, under the direction of C.M. Elvidge and with over 30 residents as shareholders, a cement block factory was built at the north end of town on the east side of Garafraxa Street. Its purpose was hopefully to provide employment following World War II.

Initially overalls were made, then leather gloves, and it was called the Huck Glove factory. In the summer of 1950 Georgian Hosiery commenced operation at this site. Irvin Sharpe was President at that time.

The plant employed 15 men, who operated five knitting machines, and 18 women who worked on various smaller machines and did sewing by hand. During the first year of operation 216,000 pairs of nylon hosiery were produced. After several years the competition from large factories proved too much and the plant ceased operations.

DURHAM CHAIR AND STORE FIXTURES

This company was operated by J.C. Dilworth and Doug Johnson in 1956. The old public school on Elgin Street was their first factory, and produced restaurant, school, office and store fixtures. This building soon became too small and at one time, due to excess storage in the attic, the ceiling collapsed on several employees. Fortunately no serious injury occurred.

In 1961 the owners decided to use the school building only for storage and rented the Georgian Hosiery plant. They then purchased it in 1962. Thirty-four men and women were employed and five trucks were kept busy making deliveries. Some furniture was even shipped to the Bahamas. One load of furniture to be shipped by rail to Blind River arrived on the West Coast of Canada. When it was recovered five months later, the Blind River customer no longer wanted it. However, the C.P.R. did reimburse the Company.

In 1969 the Company won an award for the best display at the Furniture Show in Toronto. On Hallowe'en night in 1972 the old school was destroyed by fire and the furniture stored there was lost, as was one of Durham's historical buildings. Additional space was constructed at the main factory, including a showroom, but two unfortunate fires have occurred at this plant in recent years. The business is now operated by the family of Mr. J. Dilworth.

INTERFOREST LIMITED

Situated on Highway #4 on the westerly outskirts of Durham is the Interforest Limited veneer plant. This plant was started in 1957 when K.H. Moerhing of what was then West Germany built a veneer plant 35 feet by 200 feet known as the Maple Leaf Veneer Company Limited, and machinery to make the veneer was brought from Germany. Many additions have been made to this plant, including a C.P.R. siding. A steamer was chartered to carry African mahogany and other woods to Canada. The Toronto Harbour Commission installed unloading equipment to handle the 60 foot logs which had a diameter of more than six feet. In 1963 the Abititi Power and Paper Company purchased the Maple Leaf Veneer Company, and since that time Interforest Limited has purchased the plant. This manufacturing business is important to the town because it supplies much needed employment for Durham residents and others in the surrounding area.

Looking North from Lambton Street Bridge.

At Interforest Plant
Prime Minister John Diefenbaker, M. Boel, H. Moerhing.

Interforest Limited.

Hospital & Medical Services

THE RED CROSS SOCIETY

On September 1, 1914, thirty-five women of town met in the armoury to discuss the question of patriotic work for the soldiers and their dependents. They agreed to continue meeting daily each afternoon, from 2 to 5 p.m., knitting and sewing articles to send overseas.

In June, 1915, this organization named itself The Durham Red Cross Society. By this time there were Red Cross Societies in almost all the rural school sections in the townships surrounding Durham. These rural societies obtained their yarn and sewing materials from the Durham Red Cross Society and returned the finished articles to this Society. Money for the materials was raised through such activities as: bake sales, garden parties, picnics, raffles, auctions, concerts with various talent, box socials, serving meals at vari-

ous meetings (fall fair, etc.), donations, canvasses, collecting rags, papers, magazines, rubbers (to be sold), and teas, etc. The attendance at the society meetings was 20 to 45.

Christmas boxes were sent to the soldiers overseas. In 1917, for example, 120 boxes were sent. Each box was valued at four dollars and contained one shirt, two pairs socks, cigarettes, chocolate bar, maple sugar, Christmas pudding, taffy, lead pencil, and a cake of soap. Some soldiers who wrote back in thanks were: Mr. Owens, Ernest McGirr, A. E. Lloyd, Mr. Eastwood, Brock Grant, Fred Torry, L. McGirr, and Mr. Lanquer.

January, 1918, to pay the Red Cross Society $50 a month for supplies. Some of the items sent overseas, to name a few, were: socks 2,160 pairs, towels 15,340, pillow cases 2,560, shirts 1,150, bandages 1,800, wash cloths 600, pyjamas 460, personal bags 480; also sheets, quilts, pillows, hospital gowns, operating gowns, bedsocks, dressings, shirtwaists, thumb stalls, and caps.

DURHAM RED CROSS MEMORIAL HOSPITAL

In 1920 the Durham Red Cross wanted to create a suitable memorial to those who gave their lives in the Great War. A monument and a hospital were both proposed and both of these projects were completed.

The Durham Red Cross Society met on May 23, 1921, to decide whether a Memorial Hospital or a community nurse would be of greatest advantage to the community. The society unanimously directed all its energies to accomplishing this goal. Mrs. David Jamieson was the driving force in persuading the members to vote for the hospital and in the organization to bring it to fruition. The Red Cross Society started to work and plan for the new hospital and weekly meetings were held for the purpose of sewing, making quilts, and other fund raising activities.

Mrs. David Jamieson.

At the same May meeting, the Red Cross Society also elected the first Board of Trustees for the proposed hospital. They were: Dr. David Jamieson, Chairman, A. A. Caton, Vice Chairman, P. L. Gagnon, Ed. Kress, Michael McGrath, Wm. A. McGowan, W. S. Hunter, Dr. J. F. Grant, John Kelly, and John A. Graham, secretary-treasurer. The board's first job was to find a site on which to build a new hospital, or a suitable building. The old Anglican Rectory with its two and a half acres of land and small barn at Durham Road East and Kincardine Street was purchased from Mr. Isaacs for $2,000.

This, however, was not the first hospital in Durham. Miss Victoria Carmount, born in 1866, was a private nurse who practised in and around Durham. Seeing the very great need of a hospital to serve the community, she purchased a large frame house about 1910 on Countess Street just north of the C.P.R. tracks. This building was fitted with four beds and operating room, plus the usual equipment and supplies. The hospital was very successful, but during the war nurses and doctors went overseas and she found it very difficult to provide adequate care. In 1917 she sold the house and returned to private nursing. A year later Miss Carmount bought a house on Garafraxa Street just north of the Durham Review Office and operated a small birthing centre there. She sold the house in 1922.

Mr. A. A. Catton, a member of the Board of Trustees, drew up all the plans and supervised the work of making improvements and alterations in the building, practically giving all his time to this work. These improvements included excavating a basement under the hospital and finishing same, rewiring the whole building, a new roof, a completely new hot water heating system, moving partitions, clothes closets, etc; complete redecoration, drilling a well, and installing a new pump.

The September 21, 1922, edition of the *Durham Chronicle* lists many gifts already received without any solicitation:

David Hopkins Sr.	$100
Dr. J. L. Smith	100
John A. Graham	100
Dr. & Mrs. Jamieson	500
Jno. E. Russell Co.	200
County of Grey	500
A Friend	100
R. MacFarlane	100
John Kelly	100
A. H. Jackson	100
Dr. D. B. Jamieson	200
Dr. J. G. Hutton	50
Women's Institute	50

Many other donations were promised and there were many donations of furnishings and supplies:

Mr. John E. Russell has donated the radiators and new furnace valued at $800. The T. Eaton Co. is

Victoria Carmount, Owner-Manager First Hospital in Durham.

furnishing and equipping the operating room valued at $500.

The I.O.D.E. furnished a room.

Col. J. B. MacLean furnished a room.

The Great War Veterans Association furnished a ward — where there will always be a free bed for any needy veteran.

Belle Rutherford donated a ward in her will.

Mr. W. Vickers, a former Durham boy, now manager of the Renfrew Manufacturing Company, is giving one of their best Barnett Refrigerators.

Mr. C. M. Bowman of Southampton has sent a splendid kitchen cabinet.

Mr. J. H. Harding gave the kitchen range.

Mr. D. D. Town, a hall clock.

Mr. Oliver Hunter, knives and forks.

Cross and Sutherland, spoons.

J. & W. McLachlan, dinner set.

Saunders Variety Store, cups and saucers.

John McKechnie, groceries.

Moore McFadden, silver cup

Miss Rutherford, dishes.

John Snell, sewing machine.

The Provincial Red Cross Society, fifteen beds and a large quantity of bed supplies.

Mr. C. L. Grant, sheets.

Mr. Robert Burnett, blankets.

Mrs. Morlock, ticking.

Standard Bank, office table and roll top desk.

Mulock Women's Institute, silk quilt.

The Durham Club of Toronto, a large supply of towels, sheets, pillows, etc., plus $50 cash.

Drs. Jamieson & Jamieson, a steam sterilizer.

Original Red Cross Memorial Hospital 1922.

Mrs. Horn, a former teacher, a bed and mattress. The Cameron children, set of aluminum dishes for kitchen.

The scale of the donations, all unsolicited, attests to the fact that this was truly a community hospital and that its services were in much demand.

Miss C. Fettes was interviewed by the Board for the position of Matron or Superintendent of the hospital. She was hired for $80 a month, plus room and board and she ably filled that position for many years.

The hospital would accommodate ten patients. Almost from the beginning it was found to be too small, and in 1925 an addition was built on the east side bringing the number of beds up to 16. Again in 1928 the hospital was enlarged with a new wing on the south side. In 1929 a new X-ray machine was purchased and Dr. D. B. Jamieson proposed to the Board that there were two ways in which this machine could be operated, either the hospital could operate it, pay all the expenses, and keep all the profit, or Dr. Jamieson could operate it, pay all costs and keep all profit. It was decided that Dr. Jamieson should operate the X-ray machine for one year and report to the Board at that time on profit or loss.

During its early years, the Durham Red Cross Memorial Hospital was a training school for nurses. Four classes of nurses graduated from Durham Hospital before the government changed the rules requiring all training hospitals to have at least 50 beds. The graduates were:

1925   E. Morrison, Feversham; A. McLeod, Priceville; R. Philip, Dromore;
1926   V. Brown, Loree; E. Dodds, Mount Forest; I. Bradley, Holland Centre; M. Moulhard, Feversham.
1928   V. Marshall, Ceylon; M. Reay, Mount Forest; A. Lush, Orton; R. Gillespie, Mount Forest, M. Robinson.
1932   I. Moore, Singhampton; E. Donaldson, Caledon; E. McKenzie, Holstein; C. Milne, Elmwood.

Miss Fettes kept a day book for the first few years, and some items from it give an idea of the way in which the hospital operated.

Jan. 2   4 loads of wood slabs delivered
Jan. 6   hens started to lay
Jan. 9   2 loads of wood (donated)
Feb. 16   bought bag of wheat for hens
Feb. 22   put 330 blocks of ice in ice house
Feb. 24   bought 1 dozen bottles of liquor
Mar. 22   2 loads of hard coal
Apr. 16   2 loads of manure on garden
May 23   garden ploughed and planted
May 26   19 chickens hatched out
May 29   planted potatoes, planted out strawberries
July 14   last of hay put in barn
July 20   picking beans and pickling, canning berries, beans & beets
Aug. 15   Nurses went to pick berries
Sept.   Went to Collingwood for fruit — Bought 31 large baskets of tomatoes @ 15 cents, 3 large baskets of tomatoes @ 10 cents, 1 large basket of plums @ 90 cents, 1 large basket of pears @ 65 cents, 2 large baskets of apples @ 15 cents. 8 bags of sugar (100 lbs.) $7.00 — made jelly & jam
Oct. 1   dug 20 bags of potatoes
Nov. 4,5 Fruit gathered from community for hospital — 271 jars of preserves
Dec. 31   254-½ doz. eggs laid during year @ 22 cents a doz. — $55.99

It is noted that the nurses were sent to pick berries if they could be spared from their duties at the hospital and at least once a year some one would drive them to Collingwood for fruit and tomatoes. Mrs. Cecil Barber (nee Ethel Morrison), a member of the first graduating class, said the nurses knew that on their return to the hospital they would be preserving and canning until midnight, then up again at six a.m. If they didn't finish this work the first night, the nurses would have to work the next night until all the fruit was in jars.

The ladies in the community were also asked to put down one or two extra jars of fruit for the hospital

Miss C. Fettes, Matron of Durham Red Cross Hospital 1922.

First Nurses' Graduating Class of Durham Red Cross Memorial Hospital. A. MacLeod, E. Morrison, R. Philps.

when they were doing their own canning. These jars would then be collected by the hospital, all of which contributed to the hospital budget. The empty jars were always returned each year for refills. About 250 to 300 jars of fruit were collected each year.

Mrs. Cecil Barber relates another incident which occurred while she was in training at the hospital. Most babies were born at home, and quite frequently the doctor would telephone the hospital to see if there was a nurse available to assist him in the delivery. On one occasion Mrs. Barber was awakened very early one winter morning to accompany Dr. Smith to a home near Dornoch to render this assistance. This was in the dead of winter and the trip was made by horse and cutter. When they left the hospital there was solid darkness, and they were well beyond the The Rocky before they saw the first glimmer of light on the eastern horizon. When they arrived at their destination, they found that they were much too early. Dr. Smith left Mrs. Barber with the expectant mother and went to visit friends in the area, leaving a telephone number in the event he was needed. Mrs. Barber was still in training and did not have too much experience to cope with the position in which she found herself, and was somewhat apprehensive. However, Dr. Smith returned after supper and later a fine healthy baby was delivered, still it was after midnight before Mrs. Barber returned to the hospital and after only five hours sleep she started another day's work.

Durham Red Cross Memorial Hospital 1940.

Milk for the hospital was purchased from a neighbouring farm. Each evening one of the nurses was told to take the milk pail and walk to the neighbour's residence to pick up milk for the next day. When she returned the milk was put in a large pot on the stove and pasturized. Such was life 70 years ago!

In 1946 the name of the hospital was changed to Durham Memorial Hospital and the Ontario Hospital Services Commission began to finance the operation of all hospitals from federal and provincial grants and prepaid hospital insurance. This system relieved the local municipalities from the complete financing of major renovations and improvements to the facilities themselves and greatly improved the standard of health care in the community.

The Ontario Hospital Services Commission was contacted in 1958 with regard to renovations and extension to the old hospital. In 1959 the local Hospital Board decided to build a new hospital. Architectural drawings were made by the firm of Deacon and Arnett, tenders were let and accepted but in 1960 these plans were abandoned due to prohibitive costs. When this news reached the community the people responded with tremendous support for the new hospital and this encouraged the Board to proceed with the plans. A suitable site was purchased at the corner of Chester and College Streets for $8,000.

Kinsmen Club presenting cheque to Hospital Board in 1961. Jim Flewelling, Ross Taylor, Orval McDonald, Harry Kress, Jack Lawrence, Bob Braithwaite.

Durham Memorial Hospital.

In 1962 the Prime Minister of Canada, the Rt. Hon. John G. Diefenbaker, officially opened the new Durham Memorial Hospital. It had accommodation for 34 beds, and had an operating room, an emergency recovery room unit, laboratory and X-ray services, and auxiliary service departments. The trustees at the time were: Chairman, W. H. Kress; Vice Chairman, Wm. Hewitt; Secretary-Treasurer, Miss Norma Allen; Administrator, Miss Marie Esbaugh. The Board members were: Mrs. J. Alexander, Miss Myrtle Mortley, Messrs. E. Cluley, J. Ferguson, N. MacArthur, A. McRonald, G. Dickson, O. Lee, Wm. MacDonald, Wm. Wardroper, and Dr. Duncan Jamieson.

Up until 1966 the only ambulance service in Durham was provided privately by Russell McTavish. At this time he turned the service over to the hospital and ambulance service became available 24 hours a day and was operated by hospital staff and community volunteers. In the same year the hospital received full accreditation which it has since maintained. Under the chairmanship of I. B. Sharpe, the Hospital Board completed an expansion programme in 1972. Included in the project were: four isolation rooms, expanded office space, new outpatients reception and consultation rooms, plus storage and air conditioning. Also included was a new ambulance to replace the old one, and television sets for the rooms. Total cost was $240,000 paid by the town, government grants, and local fund raising events, one of which was a wheelathon organized by the staff. Mrs. Erma Wight was appointed acting supervisor in 1975, and later C. E. O.

On November 27th, 1975, Ontario Health Minister Frank Miller announced at a meeting in Chesley that 24 hospitals in Ontario would be closed including Durham, Walkerton and Chesley, and a new 100-bed hospital would be built in Hanover. The Hospital Board received notice that the hospital would be closed June 1, 1976, and no patients were to be admitted after May 1st, 1976. Mr. Miller came to Durham to discuss the closure of the hospital with the Board. When he arrived, he found 500 angry citizens standing in the snow on the hospital lawn waiting for him. Mr. Miller stated that by closing the Durham Hospital and moving the facility to a new hospital to be built in Hanover, the government would save $550,000. When asked to explain that statement he had no answer.

A public meeting was held in the Durham District Community School, and the auditorium was packed to the rafters with supporters rallying to keep the hospital open. Politicians Bob McKessock and John Sweeney were also there to offer their support. The Hospital Board appealed this matter to the Court for decision, and on April 29th, two days before the hospital was scheduled to close, the Court rendered its judgment. It stated that the Minister of Health had no authority to close hospitals. Thus this important health facility was saved.

Kinsman Jack Breen presents cheque to Wm. Hewitt, President of the Hospital Board 1965.

The Kinsmen donated $4,500 which built the Ambulance Garage. Ross Taylor, Dr. Duncan Jamieson, Jim Nixon, Roger Goldsmith, Arden Birr.

Peter Fallis, a local lawyer, was presented with an Award of Merit by the Hospital Board for his very active and aggressive action in fighting the hospital closure. The Award read: IN RECOGNITION OF OUTSTANDING SERVICE TO DURHAM MEMORIAL HOSPITAL. Glen Budd made a sign "NO VACANCY" and hung it on the Durham Hospital sign. The hospital which was supposed to be closed was FULL. Physiotherapy facilities were opened in 1987.

Lawrence Berge was appointed Aministrator and C.E.O. in 1989. In 1990 the Board realized a new X-ray machine would have to be purchased as the old one was obsolete and in very bad repair. With other new equipment the total cost would be $600,000, and it would be necessary for this to be raised locally. A campaign committee was set up chaired by Gordon MacLean and Larry Vollett. In February, 1991, the Kinsmen presented a pledge of $60,000 towards the project and canvasses were made of all municipalities, surrounding townships, service clubs, individuals, businesses, and door to door. During the canvass the old X-ray machine broke down completely and could not be repaired, making the urgency of the drive all that more important. At a Hospital Board meeting in

September, 1992, Gordon MacLean announced that the goal of $600,000.00 had been reached.

The Durham Memorial Hospital continues to provide an important and modern service to the community. From April to November, 1993, the Hospital facilities were used by 902 new people, as well as by many who had previously been patients.

DURHAM MEMORIAL HOSPITAL AUXILIARY

The Red Cross Society, which had spearheaded the drive for a hospital in Durham in 1921, continued to meet and raise money for hospital equipment, and to support the hospital in any way possible. In 1939 a group of young women in Durham formed a new group known as the Evening Red Cross Auxiliary. Both groups supported the hospital and also the soldiers who had enlisted from Durham and vicinity. The Red Cross Auxiliary became the Durham Memorial Hospital Auxiliary and continued its good works for many years. The Evening Red Cross Auxiliary, in 1946, decided that the organization would supply the needs of the nursery and other necessities in the hospital. The group met in the homes of the members, and the average membership over the years was 20 to 25. The officers in 1946 were: President, Ruth Myles; Vice President and Convenor of Work, Mrs. Mary Webb; Secretary, Janet Robb; Treasurer, Hilda McKechnie.

The service of this organization has been outstanding. Over the years some of the equipment which has been purchased, including items bought with Community Fair funds, has been: supplies for the nursery, large commercial refrigerator, incubator, nurses' signal system, small tractor and stove for hospital, thermal food warmer, deep heating machine, recovery stretcher, laryngoscope and opthalmoscope, obstetric table, isolette, anaesthetic machine, stretchers for emergency, gastroscope, screens for X-ray, hydraulic bath chair lift, intravenous infusion pumps, cell counter for lab, microscope for lab, tread mill, Holter monitor, hydraulic stretcher, centrifuge, Holter scanning unit, plus donations to the hospital building and extension fund and thousands of dollars to other equipment purchases. From 1975 to 1994 hospital equipment purchased by the auxiliary has amounted to over $108,000.

In 1964 the group changed its name to Junior Hospital Aid and in 1979 the name changed to Durham Memorial Hospital Evening Auxiliary. The Durham Memorial Hospital Auxiliary throughout the years had also given outstanding service to the Durham Hospital, but in 1983, due to declining membership, the group decided to disband and some of its members joined the Durham Memorial Hospital Evening Auxiliary. This group again changed its name in 1993 to the Durham Memorial Hospital Auxiliary. Three of the original members from 1939 are still active in the group; they are: Myrtle Mortley, Jennie McGirr, and Eunice McGirr.

For many years the auxiliary raised funds by hosting a Harvest Ball and a Spring Tea, but these activities have been discontinued, and the main fund-raising events are a Strawberry Tea, Easter Ham Dinner, Draws, Fashion Show, Bake Sales and tickets for a 50/50 draw sold each month. In addition, donations from a Ladies' Quilting Club in Durham are received from time to time.

The auxiliary sponsors a Community Fair which involves many church and service groups in and around Durham. They also supply tray favours to Hospital patients on special days, such as Easter, Christmas, Valentine's Day, St. Patrick's Day and operate a Tuck cupboard in the Hospital lobby that offers small gifts, toiletries, chocolate bars, etc.

The auxiliary participates in the Meals on Wheels service, and is represented on the Hospital Board of Directors.

The 1994 officers are: President, Flora Murray; Secretary, Shirley Alliston; Treasurer, Sing Chung.

ROCKWOOD TERRACE

On October 4th, 1984, the official opening of Rockwood Terrace took place. The snip of the scissors cutting ribbon was ceremonial proof that a 20-year long dream had finally come true. A 100-bed Home for the Aged was now a functioning part of the community of Durham.

This beautiful piece of modern architecture was designed by A.W. Cluff and P.T. Cluff, Architects of Toronto, and built by Ellis Don Limited for approximately 4.5 million dollars. Funding was made possible by the Ministry of Community and Social Services, the County of Grey, and the City of Owen Sound, which contributed $400,000 to the project.

Rockwood Terrace is located on 575 Saddler Street East between the corner of Rock and Kincardine Streets. This site was carefully chosen as the surrounding scenery greatly complements the home and makes the name Rockwood Terrace an apt one. The Durham Stone Quarry is situated behind the building to the far south, and a pleasant cluster of pine and other trees frames the southerly border.

The site was also selected because of its close proximity to Saugeen Valley Elementary School which sits directly west of the building. Residents have opportunity to enjoy watching the daily antics of the students at play during recesses and noon hours. As well, many rewarding activities and visiting programmes are exchanged between the older folks and the youngsters. Many precious moments are shared between the two generations.

Many of the furnishings and building materials were made and/or purchased locally. The talents of community crafts people grace several areas of the home.

There are three floors in the building with three concrete wings stretching to the east, west and north. The first floor of the east wing was designated as the Farquhar Oliver Wing in honour of the late Member of Parliament of the same name. Within this section of the building is a spa and whirlpool tub, a lounge and doctor's office intended for community outreach programmes, a chapel and administrative offices.

Other facilities on the main floor include a large front lounge, a library, a multi-purpose room for large group activities, workshops and seminars, a beauty salon and barber shop, a craft room complete with a showcase, a tea garden with a store, a dining room, a staff room, a fully-equipped kitchen, and laundry and maintenance service areas.

The second and third floors are residential areas including private and semi-private rooms. Personal belongings are encouraged within the limits of the space provided.

Each residential floor also has six leisure or common sitting rooms, a nursing station, and a small kitchenette available for residents to treat their guests with refreshments and light snacks. The second floor has a

Rockwood Terrace.

large dining room for those individuals requiring additional assistance at mealtimes. On the third floor there is an elegant, family-sized dining area known as the Kroehler Room. It was furnished by the once long established local business, and allows residents the opportunity to host small dinner parties.

Other features of the building include several balconies for outdoor access and a large outside ground area that is pleasantly landscaped with a variety of trees, shrubs, foliage and flowers. Rockwood Terrace was originally intended to be a residential facility, but it has seen a gradual transition to long term care with more frail elderly residing here. The average age of new residents is 86.4 years.

The services offered to residents include 24-hour nursing care and assistance with activities of daily living. Dietary needs are met with three full meals and light snacks prepared and served daily. All linens and other heavy duty wash are included in the daily services package. Personal laundry may be washed by individuals able to do so; and two fully equipped rooms are provided for this purpose. If unable to fulfill this responsibility, residents can purchase the service at additional cost. Independence is greatly encouraged. All indoor and outdoor housekeeping and maintenance is completed by the appropriate departmental staff.

The home also has a full calendar of recreational and social events. Residents are encouraged and motivated to contribute their talents to programme planning and to participate actively at their own level of physical and cognitive ability.

Many programmes are enhanced by community resource people and the co-ordinated efforts of caring volunteers. Family members and the general public are also invited for special gatherings on a frequent basis.

The County of Grey employs approximately 80 staff members to fulfill the various responsibilities in each of the service departments.

Rockwood Terrace is a beautifully designed, fully serviced 100 bed facility which meets the specialized needs of many elderly people within the community of Durham and surrounding areas. However, the spirit of the home rests in the unique and important individuals who take up residence here. Rockwood Terrace is truly a home of which the town can be proud.

ST. RAPHAEL'S NURSING HOME

In 1994 St. Raphael's Nursing Home celebrated 29 years of service to the Durham area. The original white stucco building was the old Anglican Manse. The property was purchased by the first Durham Hospital Board of Governors in 1922 for use as a hospital.

In 1925 an extension was added to the east and in 1928 a further addition of red brick was constructed to the south.

In 1964 when a new hospital was built in Durham, the existing hospital was sold to Pamela and Hugh MacLean. After numerous renovations the building was officially opened as a nursing home in January, 1965.

The Nursing Home is non-denominational, and the name St. Raphael's was chosen as St. Raphael is the Saint of comfort and protection. The nursing home is licensed for 48 beds and is classified as a long term care facility under the jurisdiction of the Ministry of Health and Ministry of Community and Social Services.

The home's aim is to provide the best possible care with a view to meeting, maintaining and improving the residents' physical, emotional and spiritual needs and in an environment that is caring, honest, positive and consistent.

Over the years St. Raphael's has provided not only a home for many local residents, but through satisfied residents and families we have also had applications and admissions from larger urban centres.

Because of positive attitudes toward aging, some residents have even been enabled to return to their own homes.

Residents participate actively in decision making affecting their environment and lifestyle, for example, through the Resident's Council.

Many programmes and professional services are available to the residents at St. Raphael's.

St. Raphael's currently provides employment for 48 people and is also assisted in their work by community organizations and volunteers which enhances the lives of the residents.

St. Raphael's has had accreditation status for several years, meeting the requirements of the Canadian Council on Hospital Accreditation.

St. Raphael's Nursing Home will continue to encourage the public to visit the Nursing Home and to become knowledgeable about the services provided, and are happy to answer questions and give tours of the premises.

WATSON'S NURSING HOME

In 1957 Mr. and Mrs. Ed Watson opened a 12 bed Nursing Home in Durham. Mrs. Blanche Watson, a Registered Nurse, was the administrator of the home. During the following year, due to Mrs. Watson's failing health, Mrs. Myrtle (Mighton) Stumpf was appointed Co-Administrator and Director of Nursing. The staff included R.N.'s and nursing aides providing 24 hour care. Over a period of 13 years, the number of beds increased to 20, and the facility became a licensed nursing home.

An outdoor patio was added for residents to spend pleasant days outside, where they could enjoy the home pets — two geese, a lamb, and several rabbits. One resident was Mrs. Henry, grandmother of Mrs. Joyce Goldsmith, and on cookie-baking day Mrs. Henry would be found standing at the kitchen stove with a large glass of milk as the official Cookie Judge.

Attending physicians at the nursing home were Dr. Duncan Jamieson, Dr. C. Ennis, and Dr. Mountain.

In 1971 Mr. and Mrs. Matt Dempsey, both registered nurses, purchased the nursing home. It was later sold and made into apartments. The building was partially destroyed by fire, but it has been restored and at the present time is still an apartment house.

THE MEDICAL PROFESSION

When the first doctors came to this settlement, they travelled over extensive areas. Many miles of rough unbroken trails lay between them and the clearings to which they might be called by day or night. Their only means of reaching those in need of a doctor's services was on foot, on horseback or by canoe. Dr. Moore was one of the earliest of Durham's medical practitioners. He did not remain long and was succeeded by Dr. Woods, who lost his life by drowning in the Saugeen River. Dr. J. Crawford operated a medical practice in Durham in the 1850s and 1860s and was also Coroner for the County of Grey. In February, 1861, Dr. W.C. Shaw practiced medicine, residing at Reverend A. Stewart's home. Dr. James Gun came from Scotland with his parents and settled in Durham in 1862, where he spent the remainder of his life. He had a busy medical practice, but he always found time to work for the betterment of the community. He was active in church work, municipal matters and in social circles. He was a member of the school board for many years where he worked for improvement in education. In 1873 he was the main promoter for the reorganization of the Mechanics Institute and was sometimes called the father of the Durham Public Library. There were many medical practitioners in Durham over the years, some stayed only a short time, others stayed for a longer period. Some of the early doctors were: Dr. Wood, Dr. Evans, Dr. Halstead, Dr. Luke, Dr. Pritchard

and Dr. T. Kiernan. In 1879 Dr. David Jamieson came to Durham and practiced medicine here for over 40 years.

Other medical doctors in Durham have been:

J.G. Hutton	N.T. Maclaurin
? Freel	C. Park

Bradshaw Jamieson (who bought the first x-ray machine in Durham in 1922 and had it installed in his office)

Arthur Gun	J.L. Smith
Alex Bell	Royden Burnett

(Dr. Gun, Dr. Jamieson and Dr. Burnett grew up in Durham and spent their entire lives here except for service in the Armed Forces)

D.M. Young	Claire Armstrong
T.G. Irvin	? Campbell
Duncan Jamieson	D. Bhana
Cal Ennis	Anne Lowe
Keith Mellor	Ian Grafton
Anne Doenne	M. Moharram
A.G. Denyer	Philip Zachariah
David Walley	Bruce Chung
E. Savaria	M. Pillisch

Dr. J. Gun.

DENTISTS

The earliest resident dentist in Durham was Dr. ? Campbell who came here around 1870, followed a few years later by Dr. Holt. Other dentists who practiced here for some time were Dr. C. Pickering, Dr. J.F. Grant, and Dr. Gordon Grant. Dr. J.C. Milne and Dr. David Wilde presently have practices in Durham.

VETERINARIANS

The first veterinarian to live and practice in Durham was Dr. William Rose. In 1886 Dr. A.C. Wolfe came to Durham and practiced continuously until 1934 at which time his son, Cecil Wolfe, took over his practice. He, however, only stayed a few years. In 1951 Dr. A.H. Mooney opened a practice in Durham and after serving this community for 43 years, he retired in 1994.

PHYSIOTHERAPISTS

MacGillivray Clinic, Mrs. Carolyn Austin

CHIROPRACTORS

Dr. D. Woods   Dr. L. Detzler

Dr. David Jamieson.

DR. JAMES L. SMITH

Dr. James L. Smith was born in 1861. His father came from the Orkneys and his mother from near Aberdeen, Scotland. After teaching school for six years and saving his money he entered the School of Medicine at the University of Toronto. He graduated in 1890 as a Medical Doctor.

Dr. Smith set up his practice at Dornoch, ten miles north of Durham. His practice was almost entirely rural and in those days there were no telephones, no ambulances, no motor vehicles, no miracle drugs and no hospitals. The health of sick people in those days depended to a great extent on the medical ability of the doctor. Dr. Smith was very highly respected and trusted as a doctor and as a person.

In those early days Dr. Smith's transportation was by horse and buggy in summer and horse and cutter in winter. If the roads were too badly drifted with snow he sometimes walked to the home of his patient. Although he purchased a car when automobiles became available, he always preferred the horse because on the trip home he could throw the lines over the dashboard, go to sleep, and the horse would find its own way home.

During the influenza epidemic in 1918 Dr. Smith moved his practice to Durham and he was making house calls all day and half the night. One patient, a Durham merchant, recalls that relatives did not expect him to live but late at night the doctor arrived. He was the one-hundredth patient Dr. Smith had seen since early that morning.

Dr. Smith took a keen interest in the community. He was Mayor of Durham in 1923-1924, Secretary of Latona School Board for 20 years, elder of Dornoch Presbyterian Church, and later Knox United Church, a member of the Masonic Order, and an enthusiastic lawn bowler. Dr. Smith died December 31, 1958.

DR. DAVID JAMIESON

Dr. D. Jamieson was born in Puslinch in 1855 and when he was five years old his family moved to Mount Forest where he received his early education. At age 13 he joined the Mount Forest Examiner as an apprentice typesetter. He spent five years with the paper while continuing his education. In 1878 he graduated from University with his medical doctor's degree and the following year he came to Durham and set up a medical practice. At first he walked on his rounds, then he bought a horse and saddle; later he bought a buggy, and in his later years an automobile. He married Isabelle Bradshaw and they had one son, D. Bradshaw Jamieson, who also became a medical doctor.

Dr. Jamieson was interested in municipal affairs and became a member of council in 1883. That same year a Board of Health was established in Durham. Dr. Jamieson was Reeve of Durham in 1885 and 1886. Dr. Jamieson was a staunch Conservative and ran twice for a seat in the Federal House of Commons, but was defeated both times. In 1898 he ran for the Ontario Legislature and won that seat for the riding of Grey South, a position he held from 1898 to 1926, except for the five years from 1914-1919. During the time spent in the Ontario Legislature he was Speaker of the House and a cabinet minister. When the Federal Government passed the Mother's Allowance Act, he became Chairman of the Ontario Mother's Allowance Commission. When the Old Age Pension Act was passed, he also became Chairman of the Ontario Commission for administration of that Act.

Dr. Jamieson was the first president of the Durham Furniture Company, a position he held until he died. He was the first president of the Durham Red Cross Memorial Hospital, and the last president of the Durham National Portland Cement Company. He owned 350 acres at Wilder Lake. Dr. Jamieson died in 1942.

Reminiscences

RECOLLECTIONS OF LATE '20s AND EARLY '30s

by Wilma Coutts

Back in the late 20s and early 30s, in our High School days, we enjoyed many sports; despite lack of expensive equipment that most parents buy for their children today, Durham was known as The Sporting Town.

Not surprisingly, many of our activities centred around the beautiful Saugeen River. It was in that cold, clear water that seldom reached a temperature higher than 68 degrees in summer, that we fished for speckled trout, dived and swam and went canoeing with our friends.

In winter, we cleared a sheet of ice in front of the old boat house (long gone) that sat for years on the south side of the river just a few yards east of the Middle Dam. Sitting in snow to pull on icy-cold skates over half frozen feet may not sound appealing, but we were soon warm and having a fine time skating 'round and 'round over the bumpy ice. Those of us who had hockey sticks played a strange game of shinny with our primitive equipment, but we were young, exhilarated and carefree; it was a wonderful time.

Our home was at the top of the high hill north of the river, close to the path taken by Archibald Hunter, the first settler of Durham, when he and his companions, in 1842, climbed that steep slope to survey the countryside. The High School, on the south side of the Saugeen, was only half a mile away, as the crow flies, but the route we had to take to school — west to Garafraxa Street, down the long Durham hill, then back east along Mill and George Streets — was more than twice that far. Even though we usually shortened the distance considerably by running across the railway bridge (now the beautiful Heritage Walkway) it was a foolhardy move that coincided with the imminent arrival of the 1.20 C.P.R. passenger train. It was a long haul four times a day, but our parents (wisely) wouldn't allow us to take the shortcut by crossing the rickety bridge at the mill. A few missing planks here

and there from that ancient structure gave an interesting view of white water cascading over the dam, but had we slipped or tripped — it would have been disastrous.

They were finally persuaded to let me snowshoe across the river as soon as Bob Campbell decided the ice was thick enough for his men to begin sawing the huge blocks for storage.

I often think of that experience now and wonder if Dad and Mother had any second thoughts about their decision. Had they followed my trail across the river and looked down into the black depths of open water where the men were hauling up huge slabs of ice, I think they might have had a few qualms. But I was safe; ice strong enough to support the weight of sleighs and horses and half a dozen men wasn't apt to collapse under my 90 pounds.

At that time there were few, if any, electric refrigerators in town and ice delivery was required twice a week for those lucky enough to own insulated ice boxes. Invariably the iceman was a hefty fellow who could snap his tongs around a 50 or 75 lb. block of ice and heave it, if need be, up several flights of stairs. It was a tough job, but I have never seen a cranky iceman. He was always a welcome visitor, especially popular with children.

To one who always teetered on the edge of tardiness, my little snowshoes were a godsend. There was no reforested parkland then, the hills were bare of trees and I could zip down to the river in less than five minutes. In another five minutes I was across the river and walking up George Street with my classmates. It was a fine ten minute constitutional for someone who had to sit most of the day in a classroom.

Schoolmates became interested and in time we formed a snowshoe club and went on many interesting excursions. Tom Firth has told me that his brother, Dan, and a dozen or so boys in our class had a club of their own.

Skiis and snowmobiles have taken over in later years, but remembering the quiet pleasure of a walk through silent snowy woods, I predict a snowshoeing revival.

Garafraxa Street hill circa 1895.

TO VARNEY — AND BACK

by Wilma Coutts

It was Miss Lane, one of our Grade 9 teachers in High School, who first took the class snowshoeing by moonlight. That night we tramped across the Saugeen and over fields that were bare, now covered with trees planted by the Saugeen Conservation Authority. We turned east at Dr. Gun's home, past John Graham's, Colonel Hunter's and our old home, then cut across the grounds of the old hospital and on through cedar woods to McGowan's Falls. The snowshoes came off there and we ran across the bridge and back to the High School for hot chocolate and sandwiches. I remember that the moon was full, and so were we — full of energy and fun and good food.

Some of us had older sisters and brothers who had told us about snowshoeing down to Varney and coming back to Durham on the 9 o'clock train. It was decided that this would be our next jaunt when we had another full moon to light our way. I can't recall whether it was Miss Lane, Miss Gerrie or Miss (Florabelle) Nichol who chaperoned us; they were all good sports. I do remember that there were about 20 of us who met at the C.N.R. station (now the Station Res-

taurant at Mulock) after an early dinner and took off on our three mile hike to Varney.

There was good snowshoeing along the tracks and I remember how beautiful the freshly fallen, sparkling white snow looked. We were sensitive enough to appreciate the beauty of the country landscape, with every bush, tree and fence wrapped in its fluffy white blanket. "Just like a pretty Christmas card," someone said, but one hungry lad thought it looked exactly like the big platter of sea foam candy that Homer the Greek put in the window of his candy store!

Some of us, who later lived in cities farther south, often recalled that long walk in the moonlight with our friends. When we saw heaps of grey slush in city streets we remembered our Grey County snow, as the poet put it, "inviolate, white."

A few of us took off our snowshoes and ran along the hard-packed snow between the rails. Of course we had a contest to see who could walk those rails without falling off; the boys couldn't resist having a snowball fight and we all sang silly songs. Time passed quickly.

As we approached Varney, someone with big ears announced that he could hear the train coming; we shifted into high gear and made a record run till we reached the railroad crossing at No. 6 highway and

Snowshoeing.

realized it was his idea of a joke. We had time, then, to visit Varney's General Store, where our boyfriends of the day bought us refreshments. In our time, that was not caviar and champagne, but a bag of Planter's salted peanuts and a bottle of orange crush, both tasty and nourishing, both five cents.

The lantern used to signal the train to stop for passengers was kept in a tiny station about the size of a piano box just east of where the tracks crossed the highway. Norman McIntyre and Gordon McCrae seemed to be in charge of proceedings and they managed to get the lantern lit just as we heard the first hoarse wails of the approaching train. Norman ran down the track waving the puny light above his head, but when that huge engine with its powerful headlight came thundering around the bend we doubted that the engineer would be able to spot our feeble glow; he would roar right through, we thought, just as he usually did, and we had visions of walking all the way home again.

He did stop, of course. Brakes squealing, steam flying, that big black engine pulled up well back of No. 6 and we all trooped onto the train. The conductor seemed a little surprised to see so many passengers, but proceeded up and down the aisle collecting our fares.

Wilma Coutts.

If the railway happened to be operating in the red at that time, I doubt that the revenue from those fares helped to solve the problem. The conductor, looking amused, collected fifteen cents from each of us! There probably wasn't time to issue tickets in return for our nickels and dimes before we were back in Durham.

But if you think our little trip wasn't important to us, that is a mistake. Although they wouldn't have wanted to admit it, some of those boys and girls had never been on a train before; to them this was a new and thrilling experience. You might say that we were easily pleased, and in those deep depression years that was all too true — but that isn't such a bad trait either, is it?

. . . And now all the trains are gone from Durham, but those scattered few of us who are left still remember a little trip that can never be repeated. Let's see now, that would have been about 1929 or 1930, and this is 1994 — 65 years, and we still remember!

OUR DIFFERENT YESTERYEARS

(A Durham citizen recalls life in town 50 years ago)

Life moved at a slower pace in a more carefree fashion. Children had more opportunity to wander about town to visit or investigate without fear of being kidnapped, abused or hurt in other ways. The Golden Rule was an unwritten code of ethics which was practised by most, since everyone knew everyone else, any misdemeanour by a child was soon reported to the parents and the child knew there would be consequences on arriving at home.

Organized sports for children were not yet invented, but organized chores were! There was wood to be piled, water to be carried from the pump to the house, gardens to tend, wood boxes to fill, ashes to carry out and the list went on.

Certain homes were noted as great places to visit because certain grandmas were famous for gingerbread cookies or tea biscuits. Another grandma made tasty fudge. One grandma would sometimes give her grandchild and a friend five cents each after school for ice cream from Howell's store.

Everyone walked to school and most returned home at noon for a hot dinner. Events of the morning were discussed and any problems could be eased or solved and children were better prepared for their afternoon at school.

The school bell and factory whistle were heard at least three times daily and folks set their clocks by them. The factory whistle was also used to sound the alarm for a fire. The number of blasts indicated in which district of town the fire was located.

Kearney's General Store 1930 where Midtown Boutique is today; Anne Kearney, John Rose.

During the fall I recall walking through rustling leaves, with canning and spicy pickling smells wafting out to greet me as I passed each house. Before the days of refrigerators and fresh produce in stores all year round, nearly everyone had a huge garden and made use of everything grown for winter food. Root cellars housed hundreds of jars, plus barrels and bins filled with food preserved, canned and pickled. Cabbages and other root vegetables were stored in sand or a pit in the garden which would be opened in the spring for a real treat of fresh vegetables.

Wild raspberries were picked by the pail. Two or three ladies with their children would walk, drive, or be driven to a good patch (usually where logs had been taken out) early in the morning. Picking continued until nearly suppertime with a break at noon for a picnic. No matter how much water or lemonade was taken along, it never was enough for the hot thirsty group. If a particularly prolific berry patch was discovered, a rumour of a bear sighting would be circulated in hopes of keeping others away. Despite the heat, mosquitos, scratches, grumbling and fatigue, these outings were fondly anticipated as a happy ritual

of summer. On arrival home, the berries had to be sorted by weary hands and stored in a cool place for the night. Early next morning a fire would be started in the cookstove to preserve or can the best berries, make jam from the crushed ones and, of course, a fresh pie for dinner. The stove would be allowed to burn out as soon as possible in an effort to keep the house cool.

Looking North from Lambton Street Bridge.

Coal-oil stoves, and then electric hot plates, were considered marvellous inventions by housewives prior to our electric stoves.

Washday was different too. Monday was designated as washing day so every Sunday night a copper kettle filled with water was put on the stove to heat. Soft water was almost a necessity since detergents were not yet known. Rain water, which was gathered in a cistern outdoors, was pumped by hand from there and carried indoors for use. Clothes were scrubbed on a scrubboard with home-made bar soap, or later with Sun Light Bar soap, then wrung by hand — huge sheets and all — rinsed, wrung again, and hung outdoors to dry. In winter the clothes came in frozen stiff and the long johns looked like walking ghosts. These were often hung in the kitchen or attic to complete the drying. Homemakers took great pride in their sparkling white washes, and some preferred to refrain from hanging out their wash if they couldn't be first to have clothes on the line early Monday morning!

Ironing was done with flat irons heated on the stove. Everything had to be ironed — because there were no drip dry fabrics. Later, when electric irons and radios were invented, the ironing was done while listening to the radio. Lux Theatre on Monday nights helped many loads of ironing get done with ease.

Outhouses, a vital necessity of life, and the subject of many comical stories, were gradually replaced by indoor plumbing. When my family acquired this luxurious accommodation, we children made sure the toilet was flushed whenever we had company just to let them know we were now in possesson of such a prestigious facility!

Neighbours looked after neighbours. Elderly folk, surviving frugally on minimum incomes with no supportive family members, were not forgotten. Neighbours helped by delivering mail, sharing baking and food from gardens, assisting with chores and paying visits. Invitations were received to share Christmas dinner with some family. Since there were no funeral parlours, sometimes a neighbour's living room or parlour, as it was then called, was used to accommodate visiting at the time of a death. These elderly people

contributed by knitting, mending, baby-sitting, or telling stories to welcome young visitors.

Uptown parties were very popular — picnics in summer and toboggan and snowshoe parties in winter. There was even a huge toboggan (about 12 feet long) which was bought by a group of us, stored in a barn, and shared communally. House parties were also the way to celebrate a wedding or anniversary.

During World War II before an uptown boy went overseas, family and friends would gather at his home to present him with a gift. One Durham Chronicle article mentioned a boy receiving a signet ring and a moneybelt containing a sum of money. Cards, other games and contests would be played. If there was a piano, a singalong was very popular. The size of the house didn't seem to matter. Children would be perched on the stairs and card tables would be set up, even in a bedroom, for a game, usually Euchre. Even the kitchen stove would be removed to the lawn to make room for a square dance if a fiddler and caller were present! At the close of the evening, or early morning, an address would be read, a gift presented and a reply made. Then everyone would enjoy a delicious pot luck lunch.

Methodist Church, Parsonage and Mrs. Nichol's Boarding House next door on Lambton Street West.

Upper Dam washed out 1929.

Businesses Past & Present

DAIRIES AND CREAMERIES

In the early days of Durham the settlers either had their own cow or bought milk from a neighbour who had surplus milk. As the town grew and new pioneers arrived, farmers living close to the town increased the size of their dairy herds. The milk would be put into a large milk can which in turn was placed on a light wagon and the farmer drove around town calling "milk, fresh milk"; those wishing to purchase milk went to the street with a jug or other container. The farmer carried pint and quart tin measuring cans with him and he measured out the required amount of milk, placed it in the container provided, received his pay and continued on his milk route. This was the milk delivery system for some time. The first dairy in Durham to deliver bottled milk was the Durham Dairy operated by Cameron Lauder. Around 1940 this dairy was sold to Fred Miller and after WW II it was sold to Fred O'Brecht. The dairy ceased operations in 1964.

After the McKechnie creamery closed at the end of Bruce Street, it was reported that a small creamery operated for a short time in the basement of a store between Lambton Street and the river on the west side of Garafraxa Street. The next location was in the west end of the Middaugh House and then in Hamilton Allen's old blacksmith shop where the Durham Cleaners is now located. Mr. Fred House purchased this creamery around 1930 and later bought Atkin's blacksmith shop, which was originally the Middaugh House horse stables. He moved the creamery there and added a cold storage business with 200 or more wooden boxes for rental storage of frozen meat and other foods. This was very popular with farmers who did not yet have hydro available to them. He also added a dairy to his business known as The Pride of Durham.

Mr. Eric Cluley purchased the creamery and dairy in 1957 and operated it until 1973, when the creamery was closed, but he continued the dairy business until 1979 when it ceased operation. This was the end of door to door milk delivery in Durham. The building was sold and is now the Durham Florists.

Henderson's Bakery Bread Delivery Wagon — T. Henderson.

One small business has operated in Durham in the same location for almost a century. Around 1900 Thomas Stinson started a bakery on Garafraxa Street south. Two other owners and operators have been "Happy" Harry Burnett and Thomas Henderson. When Mr. Henderson died his daughter, Isabelle (Mrs. McCarthy), operated the business until 1950 when it was sold to Willard MacDonald. Later, his son, Murray, took over the bakery and at the present time Murray's son, Willard, is the proprietor.

Henderson's Bakery Bread Delivery Sleigh.

Henderson Bakery Window decorated for Queen Elizabeth's coronation. The Crown is baked and decorated with icing and cut gumdrops for the jewels.

The *Grey Review* of January 29, 1880 reports:

"A cheese factory has been started at Durham and during the last half of last season turned out 25,000 lbs. of cheese. This year it is expected to make 300,000 lbs. of cheese."

(It evidently did not have too long a life in Durham.)

The same paper reports in the July 7, 1875 issue:

"Henry Cole asked permission from the council to build a lime kiln on his property in Durham. Permission was granted."

W.J. Lawrence Blacksmith Shop — now Fallis Law Office — Mr. Lawrence on the left.

The *Grey Review* reports on August 2, 1883:

"An important Industry — K. Greenwood, Esq., has purchased the brick building lately occupied as a blacksmith shop by Mr. R. Horn, and has been pickling eggs for some time past, and at the present time over twenty thousand dozen are "sealed up" in large tanks, each tank holding nearly one thousand dozen. Mr. Greenwood expects to preserve nearly as many more this season, by which time he will have nearly a half million eggs on hand."

These eggs would be bought at the cheap summer prices and sold from November to April when the hens did not lay and egg prices would be very high. This industry lasted for possibly 60 years.

The April 13, 1899 *Durham Review* reports:

"Three millinery shops in Durham had open house in their establishment last week to show off their spring stock of hats and bonnets. They were Samuel F. Morlock, Wm. Laidlaw and Miss Cuthbertson."

The editor states: *"Such ingenuity, such recklessness of design, such profusion of frills, flowers, feathers and fal-de-rals is seldom seen."*

In 1921 Thomas J. Jackson purchased the old McKechnie planing mill and, under the firm name of Jackson Manufacturing Company, began to make phonograph cabinets. This was a new company and it soon ran into cash flow problems and could not make the necessary bank payments The bank foreclosed and, on taking inventory at the factory, found rows of sealed cardboard boxes piled up as though ready to be shipped out. However, on closer examination it was found that the boxes were empty and all that could be moved was gone. The bank reopened the phonograph cabinet factory, which supplied work for a few men, and hired Mr. J.H. Harding as manager. The business appeared to boom for awhile but later the bank closed it and the plant was sold to Voker Bodies Ltd. who built truck bodies. This company also failed, and the plant was sold to Mr. Alfred Sharpe who operated a planing mill and sash and door factory for many years. Today the Old Factory Furniture Store is located in this building.

HOWELL'S UPTOWN GROCERY STORE

In the late 1920s Clifford and Irene (Ritchie) Howell purchased the Upper Town Grocery Store from the Mills family. This two-storey white building was situated on the east side of Garafraxa Street, a few lots south of the Durham Road. It was also their family home and surrounded by beautiful flowers, trees and lawns.

At the curb in front was a single gas tank and a stand of oil cans for sale to the passing motorists. When the glass at the top of the tank was getting empty, there would often be two or three youngsters offering to "help" Mr. Howell pump up the gas with the hand lever.

Inside, a whole cluster of bananas hung from a hook, and a huge, circular, well-aged cheddar cheese sat on the counter covered with cheesecloth. Ice cream cones were five cents each and bread was nine or ten cents a loaf for many years. For a time the Howells had the agency for Renfrew Washers and Kitchen Ranges.

The Howells were wonderful neighbours. During good times they shared the joys and were always ready to give generous assistance in times of trouble. Mrs. Howell loved a social gathering and was a great organizer. Most of the Upper Town parties were made possible because of her initiative and ability to make things fun.

Mr. Howell passed away very suddenly in the late 1950s, but Mrs. Howell continued with the business until about 1967.

FINANCIAL INSTITUTIONS

THE ROYAL BANK OF CANADA DURHAM BRANCH

Sometime between 1902 and 1906 The Sovereign Bank of Canada opened a branch office on the east side of Garafraxa Street in the Laidlaw Block one door north of what is now the Town Clerk's Office. A local newspaper described the bank to be "centrally located, and occupies handsome banking quarters, elegantly furnished in oak, Mr. J.C. Telford, manager." In 1908 the Traders Bank absorbed the Sovereign Bank and continued to operate from that location until 1912 when the Traders Bank amalgamated with the Royal Bank of Canada. The Royal Bank remained in this same office until 1932 when the business was moved to the south-east corner of Garafraxa and Lambton Streets. After fire destroyed the Middaugh House in 1971, The Royal Bank purchased the property and built a new bank which is still in use today.

The Albert Middleton Family in front of Grant's Store on left, British Hotel, centre and Woodland's Store on right, now Heritage Store, Upper Town.

Standard Bank 1917 Minnie (Limin) Harding, Maude (Kress) McDonnell.

CANADIAN IMPERIAL BANK OF COMMERCE

The first bank in Durham was the Central Bank which was located about one-third of the distance from Durham Road to Chester Street on the west side of Garafraxa Street. The date on which the Central Bank commenced business is unknown, but on December 1, 1887, the Standard Bank of Canada succeeded the Central Bank and continued business in Upper Town for ten years. At that time the bank decided to relocate in Lower Town because much of Durham's business was moving there.

Mr. Norman McIntyre was building a new commercial block at that time and the Standard Bank leased part of these premises for an office. A large vault was built into the first floor and two smaller ones were located on the second floor. The second floor also contained a small bank office and accommodation for the bank employees. In the upper hall there was an immense tank which held rain water. This was intended for use in washing, flushing three closets in the building and, if need be, fire protection.

Horse and Buggy in front of the Standard Bank.

In 1910 the Standard Bank moved to the north-west corner of Garafraxa and Lambton Streets. (The old bank premises has been a Chinese Restaurant for decades). The Bank of Commerce, as it was now known, was destroyed by fire in 1929. After the fire the bank bought the site and constructed a new building in the same location and today this is still the location of the Canadian Imperial Bank of Commerce. Mr. John Kelly was manager of the bank from 1887 to 1926.

Royal Bank of Canada First North of the Municipal Building.

CREDIT UNION

In 1952 the board of directors of the Durham Farmers Co-operative decided that a credit union would be a real asset to their members, as well as to the Co-operative, and a credit union was formalized. The directors of the Co-operative were also directors of the newly formed credit union. New members were required to buy a share in the Durham Credit Union and the Ontario Credit Union loaned the new organization money to lend out in order to get started. At first the business was conducted in the co-operative building in the Hahn House. Next it was moved into its own office in the Middaugh House and later the vacant Storrey garage near the river was taken over. At first all loans were reviewed and approved by the board. Eventually offices were opened in Holstein and

Elmwood and affiliated with the Durham Credit Union. At this time the name was changed to the Saugeen Community Credit Union Ltd. About ten years ago business started to turn around for the company. In 1990 a office building was constructed on Queen Street South. The volume of business in 1993 was over twenty-two million dollars and with the current year showing a sufficient reserve on hand, it is probable that a dividend may be paid for the first time.

PHOTOGRAPHERS

Durham has had a photographer from the very early days. In the July 26, 1860 issue of the *Durham Standard* is an advertisement for the Durham Ambrotype and Photographic Gallery. The name of the photographer is unknown, but it is known that he came to Durham in July, 1850, and left in the early 1860s. The February, 1867, issue of the *Durham Chronicle* announced "the opening of New Gallery Ambrotypes — one door north of Cameron and Ross Store, Upper Town." No name of the photographer was mentioned, but it was possibly T. Donaghy, because the *Grey Review* of June 14, 1883, has a notice, "New Gallery opened in a new studio with new cameras, scenery and furnishing. T. Donaghy."

Nelson Kelsey opened a photographic studio in Upper Town in the early 1870s. Also, in the early 1880s G.F. Chapman opened a photographic studio on the west side of Garafraxa Street south of the Saugeen river. In 1895 he moved his studio to Mount Forest.

In the spring of 1895 there was an advertisement in the *Grey Review* "Introductory Offer. Photos enlarged to life size and placed in elegant frame for $4.50. E.J. Shewell."

Robert Tory opened a photographic studio opposite the Grey Review in 1882. He was very active in the community for more than 40 years. He was a member of Durham's first fire brigade. It is known that he photographed many old buildings in town and also many social activities around town. Where, oh where are those pictures!

In 1880 Malcolm McIntyre operated a studio between Mill Street and the river, on the east side of Garafraxa Street. Another photographer in Durham before the turn of the century was a man by the name of Browne. The October 16, 1902 issue of the *Durham Chronicle* states, "Photographer Browne of the Elite Studio is offering a special line of photos, cheap." The year 1903 saw F.W. Kelsey come from Perth to enter partnership with his brother Nelson who had been a photographer in Durham for a few years. They originally purchased the Browne Studio, but some time later F.W. Kelsey moved downtown just south of the river on the east side of Garafraxa Street.

(The following information was obtained from an editorial in the 1962 *Durham Chronicle* regarding John Bergenhammer.)

Garafraxa Street Bridge and Vollett's Foundry.

John Bergenhammer was a native of Denmark and a graduate of the University of Copenhagen. He was very athletic in his youth and held the lightweight boxing championship of Europe. Before 1920 he was number one steeplechase rider of Europe and earned over $30,000 yearly as a jockey. He became a photographer and travelled throughout Europe, Canada, and the U.S.A. He had returned to Toronto and was walking to the city after visiting at a farm when he was offered a ride by a passing motorist. This just happened to be Lance Rumble, and the two men had a mutual interest in horses. The result of this chance meeting was that John was hired to look after hackney horses at Lance's farm — Lawrum Farms — at Durham. While working on the farm he began taking pictures of horses, and also of the men and women who visited Lawrum Farms. Two years later around 1950 he opened Bergenhammer's Studio in the Middaugh House and photographed hundreds of citizens from far and near. His portrait colour work was outstanding. He also taught night classes in photography at Durham District High School. Later he moved his studio to behind Calder's Drug Store — where it was owned and operated for a few years by Jim Allen, a protege of John Bergehhammer.

Apparently he found something extra in Durham as he spent nearly 15 years here, more than any other place he had been in his life. One of his most popular pictures was a frosty winter morning scene of the Durham Park and river — he sold over 100 prints of this picture. At the age of 75 he returned to his native Denmark.

The present photographer is Auki Vandevrie who opened a studio at his residence in 1976. In 1981 he moved his studio to Garafraxa Street South; his present location is on Garafraxa Street West, north of Lambton Street, where he located in 1982.

Norman McIntyre with grandson Norman.

Massey Harris picked up at the station. Picture taken at main corner 1915.

Bobbie Saunders Gift Store 1940.

Don Campbell drawing ties 1896.

KATE COCHRANE

In a house set well back from the street up on the hill in Durham lived Miss Kate Cochrane, who was probably the only Canadian woman ever to make a success in a large way of the agricultural implement business. Miss Cochrane, a quiet, kindly person was modestly loathe to talk about her career. She was a pleasant surprise to any one expecting the stage type of successful business woman. "I would not care to do it over again," she admitted, regarding her years as an implement dealer.

The work, in her opinion, was too heavy for a woman and problems arose which were made more difficult because of her gender. Yet, in spite of this she won a number of awards for salesmanship. While in business with her cousin, Merritt Cochrane, she won a gold-headed walking stick and a silk hat, two trophies which were never of much practical use.

Kate Cochrane was born in 1863 and her business experience began when she was only 15. A sewing machine company wished her to go on the road handling their goods. Her family would not hear of it — travelling saleswomen at that time were not held in high regard. The company inveigled her into starting a local agency and that was her entry into the business world. She maintained a large warehouse in which to display her goods.

One by one various companies and lines were added to her responsibilities. At first there were only plows and some of the less complicated farm machines; later binders, mowers and carriages were added.

Miss Cochrane tried one line of binders which did not prove very good; then another binder company came along and tried to have her handle their machines, but she said no. However, the company's representative took Tom Barclay, her general assistant, out to lunch and when they came back she gave in. She sold those binders for 11 years and had top sales for eastern Canada.

Carriages and stoves were also included in the list of articles handled. Sales were good. "I had lots of competition, too," said Miss Cochrane. Older established agencies with plenty of manufacturers' backing went after business aggressively. She had to find her customers and sell them. It was not easy.

When her assistant was away from the office and trouble calls came in, Miss Cochrane had to hire a livery horse and drive out to the scene of difficulties. "Some older people thought I was foolish when I first began, and maybe I was," smiled Miss Cochrane. "At any rate I finally had to give it up." Her other business interests were in sharp contrast to farm machinery. She sold fancy goods, embroidery, etc., from a shop. Kate Cochrane died in 1946.

MURDOCK FAMILY BUSINESS

In 1910 John N. Murdock bought the McKechnie coal business. The warehouse was located at the C.P.R. tracks at George and College Streets and the coal arrived via rail cars, often as many as seven carloads at a time, and was unloaded into storage bins. The hard coal ranged in size from rice to egg, soft coal lumber to stoker, coke nut to pea size. J.N. usually had hired help to make deliveries by horse and wagon. In 1929 when he bought a truck, he and his sons made the deliveries. John Murdock was a member of Town Council and Mayor of Durham for seven years. In 1947 his son Fred bought the business and he added lumber and building supplies to the product line. His wife Catherine kept the books and their sons worked part-time. By 1970 Union Gas had spelled the end of the coal business, and in 1973 Fred's son Ronald took over the operation and affiliated the hardware business with Home Care and its advertising agency. The present Murdock Hardware store on Garafraxa Street South was erected on two and a half acres of land in 1976, and has expanded since then. Ron's son Tim is now working with his father in the business which has been eighty-four years in the Murdock family.

CANDY FACTORY

During the late 1930s and early 1940s C.B. Lawrence operated a candy factory in the N.G. & J. McKechnie's old sash and door factory (now the Old Factory Furniture). In 1965 another enterprise converted the same building into a plant for the manufacture of hockey sticks. These "Huskie" hockey sticks were sold across Canada and in the United States. The plant employed up to seven people and it closed in 1972.

From the February 1, 1922 *Durham Review*:

"One of the oddest looking Fords we have ever noticed is one reconstructed for winter travel from an old chassis, which has been careening around our streets last week. It was built by Smith Bros. in their garage here. The chassis has been cut down so that the rear wheels are now only about three feet apart and will run in ruts made by the sleighs and cutters. The front wheels are replaced by runners which are moved by the same steering gear as was used to turn the wheels of the car.

"On the outside of each rear wheel a steel wheel has been fastened. This steel wheel is not as large in diameter as the ordinary car wheel and so does not touch the ground unless the car wheels sink into the snow about three inches. Then these steel tractor wheels pull the car out of the rut.

"On Monday George Smith and Sam Levine demonstrated its ability to travel over winter roads by making the 28 miles to Owen Sound in two hours and

although the roads were pretty badly drifted in places, it pulled through on its own power. In Owen Sound the driver ran foul of the local police because they had no muffler on the car and were using last year's license places but were let off with a warning."

From 1958 to 1983 Wm. Sharp operated a busy wood-working shop on Countess Street South at the lower dam. He produced sash and doors and was an excellent cabinet maker. When the more modern aluminum became popular, he sold doors and windows for various companies, mainly the Aluminum Company of Canada. He also did siding, roofing and renovations. Since his retirement he still enjoys creating novel wooden figures.

Garafraxa Street. Mark Wilson buying meat in front of his butcher shop from Ideal Pork Products 1930.

Front of Cross Hardware.

BUSINESS ESTABLISHMENTS IN DURHAM — 1994

A & M Surplus & Variety
Alf's Family Meats
Amanda' Treasures
B & B Commercial Cleaning
Becker's Milk
Beer Store
Bruce Grey Health Unit
Canadian Imperial Bank of Commerce
Century 21 Realty
Chapman, Graham Insurance
Children's Aid Society
Coldwell Banker Realty
Co-Operators Insurance
Country Skillet Restaurant
D & S Auto Sales
Detzler Plumbing & Heating
Durham Car Wash
Durham Chronicle
Durham Cleaners
Durham Denim
Durham Florists
Durham Foodtown
Durham Laundromat
Durham One-Stop Convenience
Durham Furniture Inc.
Durham Welding Supplies
E.C. King Contracting
Eckhardt's Floral Treasures
Eden Automotive
Edge Water Trophies
Fettes-Wilson Travel
G & G Automotive
G & P Furniture
Gardiner's Carpet & Vinyl
Godfather Pizza
Golden Donuts
Happiness Is
Hastie Small Engine Repair
Hastie Tobacco Shop
Heritage Corner Variety
Hewitt Therapy Services
Highland Water Well Drilling
Holliday's I.D.A. Pharmacy
Hooked on Crafts
In-Focus Studio
Jerrie's Place
Johnson's Enterprises
Ken Cluchey Ltd.
Kustom Kuts & 'Kurls
L & M Foodmart
L.C.B.O. (Liquor Store)
Macdonald's Apiaries
MacDonald's Building Supplies
MacDonald's Home Bakery
Macko Sports
Majestic Beauty Salon
Mama Rosa's Pizza

Martin Plastics
Mary's Beauty Bar
McIntee & Co. Ltd. (Real Estate)
Mid Town Fashions
Mr. T's Donuts
Murdock Building Supplies Ltd.
Neff's Esso Service & Garage
New Image Hairstyling
Northend Furniture Refinishing
North Wellington Co-op
Old Factory Furniture
Olympic Restaurant
Owen's Home Hardware
Padfield's Pro Hardware
Para Med Health Services
Phil's Taxi
Poulton Insurance Brokers Inc.
Priced Right Stores
Printing for Everyone
Re-Threads
Reta's Beauty Salon
River's Edge Bookstore
Royal Bank of Canada
Royal City Realty
Saugeen Community Credit Union
Saugeen Gift Shop
Saugeen Motors
Saugeen Water Systems
Saunders Menswear Ltd.
Seeley & Arnill Aggregates
Simon Sez Restaurant
Snack Shack
Snowmobiles Unlimited
Stedman's V & S
Steph's Hairstyling - Ultra Form
Strand's Unisex Hairstyling
Susan & David's
The Cozy Corner Restaurant
The Curtain Outlet
The D.F. Shop (Durham Fashions)
The Pizza Company
Thuro-Web Ltd.
Treasures & Pleasures
Trevor Hunter Accounting
Triangle Discount Store
Uptown Revue
Ursula Drews Real Estate
Velma's Beauty Salon
Video Movie House
Vollett Insurance Brokers
Ward Mallette Chartered Accountants
West End Motors
Wilson Carpet & Upholstery
Young's Garden Restaurant
Trail's End Coffee Shop

BARRISTERS, SOLICITORS
Fallis, Fallis & McMillan
Harris, Willis, McGarry & Ferris
Ian Johnson

Robert Lindsay's Store circa 1920.
Harper McGirr and Cecil MacLean.

Truck load of tractors delivered to Blythe Motors 1969.

Ed Limin's Butcher Shop.

Garafraxa Street looking South 1895.

Jack Breen, curling.

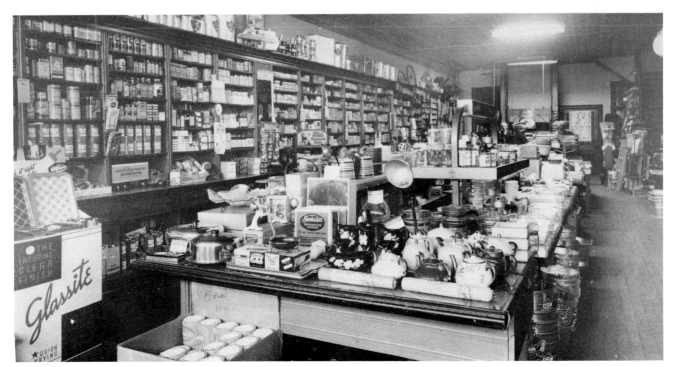

Cross Hardware Store 1950s.

Ed Hunt in Carroll's Store 1941.

Ed Hunt's Food Market 1960.

Politics & Town Affairs

POLITICS

When the pioneers began settling Durham there was only one governing body they could vote for if they qualified. That body was The Legislative Assembly of the United Canadas 1841-1867. To qualify a voter needed to be male, 21 years old, holder of a deed of property or have freehold status. In the early years few people would qualify. In the 1848 election there was activity in the Durham area. James Webster, Conservative incumbent, was running against Liberal candidate Adam Ferguson-

Land agent for Grey and Bruce County, came to Durham in 1848.

Blair. When the ballots were counted, Webster had over three times more votes than there were qualified voters. Ferguson-Blair charged Webster with fraud, the election was declared invalid, and Ferguson-Blair became the member of the Assembly. There was no secret ballot in those days and often a voter would suffer abuse if he did not vote the "right way." This was especially true if some of the observers at the polling place were under the influence of liquor. The following excerpt from *The History of the County of Grey*, by E.L. Marsh gives some insight into voting in the early years of Durham:

181

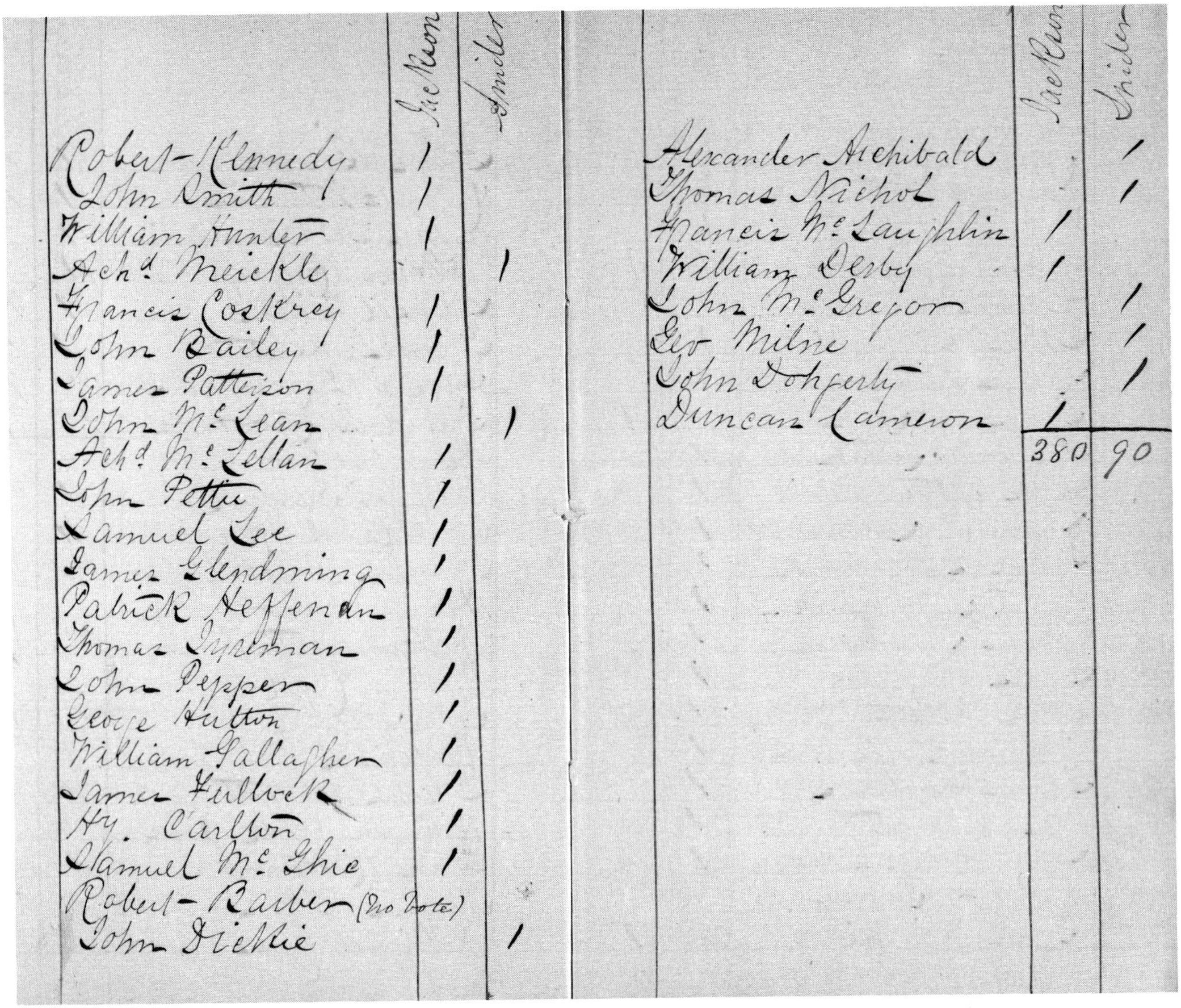

Robert Kennedy | 1
John Smith | 1
William Hunter | 1
Ach.d Meickle | 1
Francis Costtrey | 1
John Bailey | 1
James Patterson | 1
John McLean | 1
Ach.d McLellan | 1
John Pettie | 1
Samuel Lee | 1
James Glendming | 1
Patrick Heffernan | 1
Thomas Ingleman | 1
John Pepper | 1
George Hutton | 1
William Gallagher | 1
James Fullock | 1
Hy. Carlton | 1
Samuel McGhie | 1
Robert Barber (No Vote)
John Dickie | 1

Alexander Archibald | 1
Thomas Nichol | 1
Francis McLaughlin | 1
William Derby | 1
John McGregor | 1
Geo Milne | 1
John Doherty | 1
Duncan Cameron | 1

380 | 90

Poll Book 1863 Election for "The Canadas".

"But scenes in the early polling booths on election days abounded with movement and life. A pioneer who served as a poll clerk tells some incidents which occurred in the log schoolhouses where polls were held in those days of open voting. Each poll clerk made himself a voters' list from the assessment roll of his division and when the voter made up his mind for whom to vote, the clerk placed a mark under the candidate's name, being all the while under close observation of two scrutineers appointed from either party. The expression "made up his mind" is used advisedly for the bestowal of his vote was not always a matter which the voter settled with his conscience or in his own heart before he arrived at the poll, where the room would be filled with excited representatives of either party expressing their feelings in language by no means restrained.

"Another customary proceeding which enlivened election days was the record (secured by looking over the poll clerk's shoulder) kept by a volunteer scribe on the blackboard. When candidates had a little advantage, all incoming voters were urged loudly and earnestly to "Vote for So-and-So. He's ahead!" and the logic of this very frequently indeed influenced votes."

In 1854 Grey became a full fledged county and also became the riding for a member of the Assembly. Mr. George Jackson, Crown Land Agent at Durham, resigned and ran as a Liberal candidate for the 1854 election. He won the election, but due to his stand regarding the secularization of the Clergy Reserves, he displeased many of his constituents and he did not run in the 1858 election. John Hogan, a Toronto lawyer, ran as a Liberal in the 1858 election and won. In 1860 he disappeared, and was later found dead in the Don River in Toronto having been thrown off the Don Bridge by the Brooke's Bush gang. Jesse T. Purdy, Liberal, finished Hogan's term of office. In 1864 George Jackson changed his colours and ran as a Conservative. He won and filled the post until 1867.

After Canada became a Dominion in 1867, there were two Parliaments in which Durham residents were required to vote. It was not until 1920 that women obtained the right to vote in Federal and Ontario elections.

The Parliament of Canada 1867-1994
1867-1872 George Jackson, Conservative
1872-1878 George Landerkin, Liberal
1878-1882 George Jackson, Conservative
1882-1900 George Landerkin, Liberal
1900-1904 Mathew Richardson, Conservative
1904-1911 Henry H. Miller, Liberal
1911-1921 Robert J. Ball, Conservative
1921-1940 Agnes McPhail, Progressive,
           first woman member of Parliament
1940-1957 Walter E. Harris, Liberal
1957-1968 Eric Winkler, Conservative
1968-1972 Marvin Howe, Conservative
1972-1979 Perrin Beatty, Conservative
1979-1993 Gary Gurbin, Conservative
1992-   Ovid Jackson, Liberal

The Parliament of Ontario 1867-1994
1867-1875 Abraham W. Lauder, Conservative
1875-1883 James Hill Hunter, Liberal (Durham)
1883-1890 John Blythe, Conservative
1890-1891 James Hill Hunter, Liberal (died 1891)
1891-1894 Gilbert McKechnie, Liberal (Durham)
1894-1898 David McNichol, Patron
1898-1919 David Jamieson, Conservative (Durham)
1919-1923 Mansfield Leeson, United Farmers of Ontario
1923-1926 David Jamieson, Conservative
1926-1967 Farquhar Oliver, United Farmers of Ontario
           to 1941, then Liberal
1967-1974 Eric Winkler, Conservative
1975-1990 Robert McKessock, Liberal
1990-   Bill Murdock, Conservative

COUNTY COUNCIL

In the early 1840s the Owen Sound Settlement, which included all the surveyed land between Garafraxa Township and Owen Sound, was included in the District of Wellington. In 1847 Archibald Hunter was elected as the first Councillor from Glenelg Township to the Wellington District Council. He went to Guelph for the Council meetings in February, 1848, but was not allowed to attend because he had not taken the oath of office. Mr. Hunter returned to Glenelg, was re-elected, and took his seat on the council until 1850, when Mr. A.B. McNab succeeded him. That same year Mr. George Jackson became Reeve of Bentinck Township. Around 1849 Wellington District was divided, and the western part of Grey County was attached to the County of Waterloo. In 1852 the old Wellington District was divided into three counties, Grey, Wellington and Waterloo, and they formed a provisional County Council until 1854. The first and most important decision for the Council was to select a County Town. Two communities were considered, Durham and Owen Sound. A "straw" vote taken on these sites ended in a tie, and Owen Sound, realizing the situation, considered all the Reeves in the south of the county who voted for Durham and decided that the Reeve of Osprey would be the easiest for persuasion to change his vote. A lobby group from Owen Sound went to see him, and when the final vote was taken Owen Sound won the County Seat by two votes. It is difficult to imagine the impact that this decision has had on Durham, or what Durham would be like today if the vote had gone the other way. It would also be very interesting to know what argument or inducement was offered to that reeve in order for him to change his vote.

Wm. Calder, Warden of Grey County 1915.

Allan Bell, Warden of Grey County 1932.

The June 28, 1900 *Durham Chronicle* reports that, "the County Council met in Durham the past week for its June session. 16 members were present. Only once before has County Council met in Durham and that was in 1869." Reeves who lived in Durham and were elected to the office of Warden of Grey prior to 1872 were: George Jackson, 1858-59-1860, 1863 and 1875, and James Edge, 1871. Mr. Edge had lived in Durham for nine years prior to being elected Warden, as reeve of Glenelg. Durham Wardens of the County of Grey have been: George Jackson, Charles McKinnon, representing Bentinck, Glenelg and Durham, 1902, William Calder, 1915, Allan Bell, 1932, W.S. Hunter, 1941, and Harry Kress, 1965.

W.S. Hunter, Warden of Grey County 1941.

Harry Kress, Warden of Grey County 1966.

TOWN HALL

In 1874 Mr. H.J. Middaugh offered a free site for a Town Hall building just north of his hotel on the north-east corner of Garafraxa and Lambton Streets. This offer was accepted, and council ordered the building to be, "frame, boarded up and down, battened and painted, with basement and storey." This was later amended to a two-storey building 35 feet x 65 feet. Mr. Alex Webster was awarded the contract to build the hall for $1,720. The lower floor was to consist of council chambers and a meeting hall; the upper floor had a stage for concerts. Over the years there have been countless meetings held within its walls along with many varied and enjoyable entertainments. Almost every group in town has used the building for some purpose. For example, it has been utilized as a church on several occasions as well as for educational

purposes. On April 7th, 1890, the Durham Council moved that a lockup (cell) be built in the corner of the Town Hall, at a cost not to exceed $15.

However, not long after the Town Hall was erected, some townspeople began to think that this building did not do justice to Durham, and a move to construct a better and fancier brick hall was initiated. At the January municipal election in 1902 the ratepayers were asked to vote on the question of the Town buying $7,000 debentures in order to build a new Town Hall. The voters turned down this idea by a large majority; so the original Town Hall remained.

In 1913 the Town decided to move the Town Hall from its original site where the Town Clerk's office is presently situated to the corner of George and Queen Streets. Mr. Reuben Rogers acquired the job of moving it for $350. Thanks to the efforts of the I.O.D.E., the Town Hall was also remodelled and redecorated at this time. They contributed almost $2,500 towards the work, which included stuccoing the exterior and erecting a portico over the front door. It continued to be the meeting place of many groups in town.

During the Depression years of the 1930s the town made adjustments to the basement in order that transients who were unable to pay for accommodation could spend the night there.

MacDonald Building Supplies received a contract by tender in 1982 to renovate the Town Hall for $71,731 and the building continues to be well used — it houses a nursery school in the mornings, and is regularly made available to the Women's Institute, senior citizens, and numerous other organizations around town.

Town Hall, Fire Hall, Police Station 1994.

The following article appeared anonymously in a 1928 publication:

"DURHAM'S NEWLY-OPENED TOWN HALL, IN A SOLILOQUY, REVIEWS ITS PAST CAREER

Considering the vast improvement in my make-up and those nice, kind words recently uttered by Judge Sutherland, on my up-to-date appearance, in addition to many superior verbal bouquets, from friends who formerly hurled brick bats, I, the old Town Hall, wish to blossom forth and tune up my voice to record past history. For I have a history as a Durham landmark — one to be proud of — one which may outshine any report of celebration, gathering, obituary or function ever published in these columns. The only danger will be the unavoidable omission of many high spots in my career. If so, please remind me of them as my memory is failing like the melting snows of winter.

I am 53 years old — still in my prime — and the present rejuvenation, thanks to the 1927 Council, to the I.O.D.E. and other public spirited bodies, places me right back to the also-ran class. Once more I am a blushing maiden, highly rouged up —over 50, look 30 and feel kittenish as 20.

Way back in 1875, a Mr. Webster of Priceville received a contract for my erection and to the sizz-zzz of Mr. Robert Moffat's saw (who was head carpenter) my timbers were squared and erected. He still glances the friendly eye at me in passing and it does not fall to many men to say that they first helped to bring me into the world and then overhaul me 50 years later. I also look with a kindly eye on Mr. W.B. Vollett, who assisted Mr. Moffat in the work. More than that I am still proud to bask in the sunshine of Mr. Vollett's smile. He is my neighbor on the starboard side and a good one. The men employed in erecting my timbers were paid $1.25 per day and it was a kingly wage and no questions asked. The timber was purchased from Kelly's Mill, east of town and was A1 material in every inch of my framework. Upon completion, I was voted a first class job and treated with due veneration and respect. I trust my successor on the Garafraxa Street site, namely the Government Post Office will command the same respect as was accorded to me in pioneer days.

My uses were legion and still are. "The old Town Hall" name was wished on me years ago and will cling for years to come. The people of this good town and community have had me serve for church purposes and large political gatherings, then again I have staged more than one "drunk" court. It's a great life and I haven't weakened yet. I remember the "Temple of Fame" back in the 90's. It was the grandest pageant ever witnessed within my walls. Bert Mockler and Brad Jamieson were pageboys in that show. Then again, great singers like Harold Jarvis and Jessie McLachlan have appeared on my platform. But I never liked Jimmie Fax as well as the crowd did. He gave me more than one unmerciful jibe which made the folk laugh at my expense. But the entertainments which have been the best drawing cards were the School Commencement concerts. The boys and girls are sure to produce packed houses.

Among the former Canadian premiers advertised to use the Hall as an auditorium were Sir Wilfrid Laurier

185

and Sir John Thompson, but it was not to be. The crowds were too big and my walls would not stretch. I recall the day when the famous Liberal chieftain came, as the Grits came out to worship and the Tories came through curiosity of the most brilliant French Canadian of his day. The crowd which came could have filled four halls my size; so the meeting was held elsewhere.

Then there was A.G. MacKay, of Owen Sound, whose whirlwind, dynamic speeches electrified the house on many an occasion. Many readers will remember when "A.G." came to Durham one Saturday to speak at a double-header, — afternoon to catch the farmers and the evening for the benefit of the town folk. The matinee gathering was a washout the weather was too fine for the country folk to leave the soil, so only about twenty of the old guard were present. "A.G." was in great form on that pre-local option day and he lashed every Tory in Canada, finally turning to Bowser of British Columbia, remarking dramatically, "Bowser, Bowser, what a name for any man" and at that moment outside an open window a hound gave some whooping barks. The North Grey member said caustically "Even the dogs bark their disapproval of him."

Other notable speakers who have spoken include Sir George Foster, Sir Robert Borden, Mayor Sam McBride of Toronto and our own Agnes MacPhail, who popular as she is in the Riding, does not magnetize town voters to her side.

Other political high spots were "receiving the returns" on election nights. If the returns, (which came slowly in, in early days) showed the Tories leading, the number of Grits gradually thinned out and so did the Tories if the fortunes of the day went against them as in 1896 and 1901. Some will yet remember on these occasions my walls rang as Tom Harris kept announcing "Gain for the Government" or the reverse. These days are past now; the gradual use of the telephone and radio have sobered the enthusiasm.

Old boys and girls are numerous who have danced the light steps on the upper hall floor. It is hard to dance on and my pine knots were the subject of sarcastic comments, but the young people always came back for more. My new lower floor is a boon to dancers and draws larger crowds.

Many of the younger generation have at times expressed the desire to have me burn down so a new hall would be built. It nearly happened too, when I was crossing the Garafraxa street bridge, en route to my present site, several years ago, when a lighted lantern on the back end caught the timbers one night, but an unknown late traveller saw the smouldering embers in time to prevent a bad fire. Those same young people in the past who often wished for my extinction, have now grown up and with a maturer viewpoint now regard me as a sacred thing and point me out to the visitors (some do it in an apologetic tone) as one of our town landmarks and institutions. I still exist and expect to carry on in my renovated garb for many years to come. Good bye."

SOUTH GREY REGISTRY OFFICE, DURHAM

From 1842 to 1848 the Crown Land Ofice was situated in Owen Sound, and it was necessary for early settlers in the township, and in Durham, to go there to either reserve their land, for which they received a land settlement ticket, or the land could be purchased and an ownership document received. By 1848 Concessions 1 and 2 in Bentinck and Glenelg townships were completely settled, together with part of Concession 3, as well as many lots in Durham. At this time the Crown moved the Land Office to Durham and appointed Mr. George Jackson as Land Agent. He erected a frame Land Office south of the Durham Road and about 100 feet west of Garafraxa Street. This building is a residence today and is the oldest house in Durham. The location of the Land Office in Durham attracted many prospective settlers who would otherwise have located elsewhere, and thus the village received an impetus which soon raised it to the dignity of quite a centre. In 1871 Grey County was split into two divisions (north and south), and the Province of Ontario established a Land Registry Office in Durham to record all further property transfers in South Grey.

South Grey Registry Office.

Until 1978 the Registry Office functioned without incident providing a needed service to the region which saw many generations of lawyers, all of whom practiced their profession in the ambience of a pleasant rural setting. Although the office seemed casual in appearance the entire land business of the region was transacted there. The Land Registrars included Thomas Lauder, the first regular Registrar from 1871 to 1913. Next came Mr. M.K. Richard to 1918, Mr. Arthur Jackson until 1930, Mr. J.N. Perdue until 1938, Mr. Harold McKechnie until 1965, Mr. Fred O'Brecht until 1974, Mr. James Sullivan until 1978, and Lee Trevors. It was a cheery place to visit and there was an over abundance of Royal Family pictures. (They were later clandestinely taken by a senior regional person in the employ of the Ministry who removed them to his personal trophy wall in his recreation room at his home near Toronto, along with an antique desk similarly removed by him from the Arthur Registry office for a similar destination. The O.P.P. refused to prosecute this government official, although subsequently the desk made a mysterious reappearance at the Arthur Registry Office.)

It was a very black day in the spring of 1978 when the Provincial Conservative Government of William Davis announced that in a cost cutting move they would close the Durham Registry Office, effective October 27th, 1978. They, however, did not bargain for the resolve of the local lawyers and the community. Fortunately the Grey County Law Association President, Peter T. Fallis, happened to be from South Grey that year, and was able to hold the all important bar meetings in the south of the county, needless to say fully attended by the South Grey Bar, which always happened to outvote the North Grey (Owen Sound) Bar, and thereby was able to challenge the decision. They were totally successful in their task and caused the responsible minister, Larry Grossman, to be removed from his cabinet position so that the government could save face.

The Premier intervened, and the Registry Office stayed open. Registrations then were $15 an instrument.

Thomas Lauder — First Registrar of South Grey Registry.

The New Democratic Party came to be persuaded, by their top civil service officials, to computerize the entire registry system, and to privatize the service. Without a proper tender call and, as many have alleged, with political favouritism, the government awarded the privatization contact to Terranet, a company that apparently had Middle East financial backing, since discovered to be almost non-existent and since out of money and the wherewithal to carry forward the task. That company, and as a condition of doing business, effectively required the government to reduce the number of registry offices to cut down on the number of computer terminals it would have to buy. Notwithstanding the fact that the registry fees had been increased to $25 an instrument, and the further fact that the registry system, excluding Land Transfer tax revenues, generated an excess annual profit of $21,000 from fee revenues alone, the N.D.P. Government purported to again announce in the spring of 1991 the closure of the Durham Registry Office in December of the same year. They again raised the reason that the closure was being effected to save monies, but never were able to provide any figures whatsoever to substantiate their allegations. The Mandarins were successful in persuading the very green new M.P.P.'s of the N.D.P. party that it was good for the Province , and they stood by their mandarins, notwithstanding that under the new system the profits would befall the private company Terranet, and would not go to the Province, and notwithstanding that service would be cut and diminished to many citizens across Ontario, including those then currently served by the Durham Registry Office.

The research for the history of this book was greatly diminished by the closing of the Durham Registry Office. Greater use would have been made of the registry office if it had not been necessary to drive 60 miles to Owen Sound where it is now located. Also, in the South Grey Registry Office in Durham were some filing cabinets full of old area records prior to 1900 which would have been invaluable to the research work. The Durham History Committee endeavoured to ascertain where these records had been taken, but no one seemed to know. Possibly the records of our inheritance were thrown out on the ash heap by arrogant civil servants and government!

So the Registry Office closed in early December, 1991, and the unsubstantiated savings were supposedly achieved. A few months later the Government raised the fees to $27 an instrument from $25. Then later in 1992 the Government again raised the registration fees to $50 an instrument. A slight raising of fees was a suggested alternative made to the N.D.P. government as an alternative to closing the registry offices, but this was rejected out of hand by N.D.P. Government officials as entirely unacceptable to it and to the public. But principles and fiscal morals gave way to the greed and smell of the easy money. What was originally a service to those requiring their original wills and deeds to be registered for posterity for safekeeping, at the cost of custodial and registry services only, now has been turned into a cash cow, with a much diminished service to the public.

GARAFRAXA ST., DURHAM, ONT.

Garafraxa Street North. Note cement sidewalks across unpaved road early 1900s.

TOWN CLERK'S DUTIES
(Circa 1800s to 1940s)

Prior to its present location on the main street of Durham, the Town office was situated on George Street, east of the Town Hall. This office was occupied by only one person, who acted as both Town Clerk and Treasurer.

In cold weather his first duty of each day was to build a fire in the stove, or stoke up the existing coals left from the previous day. During the 1940s a pipeless furnace was installed, but it still needed tending. The clerk's job was a busy one. He sold dog tags, collected taxes, was secretary of the Board of Health, issued marriage licenses, registered births and completed death certificates. He attended all council meetings, including emergency meetings, and recorded the minutes. The regular meetings were held in the evening. When a typewriter was purchased for the town office, the policeman often asked the clerk to type his records too.

An enclosed weigh scale was attached to the side of the building for weighing cattle, coal, hay, etc. It was the duty of the clerk to do the weighing. Sometimes he was needed to help round up the frightened animals and get them into the pens behind the scales before he could weigh them!

During Depression Years (1930s) the Town school treasurer's duties were also assumed by the town clerk. He was also appointed Relief Officer and started a vegetable garden in Upper Town near the water tank. This, like the construction of the town park, was a project for those on Relief. If people were unable to pick up their vegetables, the clerk delivered them at night. Also, during the Depression, transients were given supper in exchange for chopping wood or doing other work for the Town and they were allowed to sleep in the basement of the Town Hall. Locals, who became inebriated were also, if necessary, put in there for the night by the policeman. When this occurred, the clerk would check the Town Hall basement in the morning to make sure the occupants had left. This allowed the policeman a bit of rest following a hectic night.

After hour duties also were numerous. The driver of a coal or hay truck, too late to make office hours, would stop at the clerk's home and give him a ride to the scales for the weighing of the load. In severe winter weather an evening trip to the office to tend the fire ensured a bit of warmth in the morning. During summer the beautiful flower gardens were watered on Sunday, or perhaps in the evening, if there was no rain.

It was the clerk's responsibility to prepare the tax notices for every Town property. Taxes were calculated by multiplying the mill rate times the assessed value for each property. This involved many hours of tedious work. Also, long columns of figures had to be balanced in the ledgers. These tasks were all done without the aid of any computer, calculator or adding machine. So, especially at the end of the year, overtime hours were sometimes spent ensuring accuracy.

Yep — those were the "Good Old Days."

CLERKS

1872	S.E. Legate
1872	Arch. Butter
1874-1876	John A. Munro
1877-1882	John Moodie
1883-1884	T.H. Easton
1885-1892	John Moodie
1893-1898	George Russell
1899-1902	Wm. A. Anderson (Died February, 1902)
	C.C. Elvidge pro tem until W.B. Vollett was appointed March, 1902
1902-1929	W.B. Vollett (Died in 1929)
	Hamilton Allan pro tem until appointment of H.C. Rose 1929-1931
1931-1945	B.H. Willis, Clerk and Treasurer combined in 1937 (Died in December, 1945)
	Harry Scott pro tem until appointment of
1946-1951	Gordon Greenwood
1951-1956	George Prew
1956-1958	Wm. Renwick
1958-1973	Edgar Patterson (Died in 1973)
1973-1983	Wm. McDonald (until June)
	Tammy Vaughan and Heather Webb, who were employed in clerk's office, carried out clerk's duties until appointment of Judy Gray in September, 1983.

TREASURERS

1892	Archibald Davidson
1892	John Kelly
1905	Arthur Jackson
1919	Peter Ramage
	(received $100 severance pay in 1937)

In 1937 the position was amalgamated with that of the town clerk.

TOWN PARK

At an early date in Durham's development, possibly in the 1860s, W.A. Vollett established a second foundry in Durham at the south-west corner of Garafraxa and George Streets. It was a two-storey framed building on top of a stone basement and was known as the Durham Novelty Iron Works. When the foundry closed the building became a blacksmith shop. T.W. Moon then operated a machine shop there for several years and after this it became Noble's Garage. In 1930 this building was completely consumed by fire.

Fountain Town Park.

This was at the height of the Depression (Dirty Thirties) when unfortunate men (and women) were sometimes compelled to accept Relief (now called Welfare) because of job scarcity. Members of the town council formed a Charity Committee to deal with relief. Councillor W.R. McGowan was responsible for the work programme and one of the main aims was to beautify the park.

In 1934 the town purchased the above property for $390. A major project was initiated to clean up the rubble and debris on this lot and develop a town park on a block of land including the land just purchased. This extended from Garafraxa Street to Queen Street. George Street was the northern boundary and the southern extremity was the Saugeen River. The property included the town clerk's office and Town Hall grounds. Mr. B.H. Willis, Clerk Treasurer and also Relief Officer, was in charge of designing and supervising the creation of flower gardens and the planting of trees and shrubs. Mr. Willis took a very personal interest and dedicated many extra hours of his own time to work on the grounds. Enthused citizens also generously donated many perennial flowers and shrubs from their own gardens. During the spring and summer of 1936 a beautiful water fountain was constructed in the park just west of the present kid-

Saugeen River flowing through Durham Park circa 1935.

die's pool. This circular limestone structure was at least 15 feet high with an approximate 30 foot circumference. Surrounding this was a wading pool with a six foot radius. Using automobile headlight glass two floodlights were inserted on opposite sides of the wall around the pool to illuminate the falling water. The fountain was an impressive sight both day and night and was a very popular spot for children on a hot summer day. A log cabin was erected on the bank of the river. This could be used by picnickers. The cabin had an electrical outlet (for boiling water) and also served as a shelter from a sudden rain shower. A bandshell, close to the Queen Street side, and children's play equipment were added. The park was well used by local families and groups such as Churches or Institutes for picnics, just as it is today.

The flower gardens beside the clerk's office became so attractive that council also installed a floodlight to illuminate them. A local electrician, Mr. Addie Watson, did the initial electrical work on this project, as well as on the fountain.

For a few years Amateur Hour was held every Saturday night in the park. The stage was the flat bed of a truck (belonging to Bob Campbell or McGowan Bros.). Local folks with a bit of talent would perform. Singing, dancing, playing various musical instruments, even joke telling, were all enjoyed by the crowd. As

World War II progressed these concerts disappeared.

For the past several years the park has been used for an Herb Fair which attracts over 5,000 people who come from distant parts of Ontario. The fair takes place in June and bedding plants, including almost every kind of herb, are offered for sale. Crafts, baking and musical entertainment are also part of this popular event.

In 1947 the Rotary Club sought permission from council to construct a wading pool in the park. This is located close to Garafraxa Street. It is well used for pleasure and swimming lessons are given for youngsters up to eight years of age.

During the early 1950s, when the fountain required repairs, a decision was made to demolish it. An office building was erected facing George Street and later the town office and flower garden gave way to the new Public Utilities and Police building, as well as the fire Hall.

RATION BOARD

In December, 1942, the local War-Time Prices and Trade Board Ration Committee held its first meeting in the Town Hall, Durham. The newly appointed Board consisted of Chairman, J. B. Duffield; Vice-Chairman, J.F. Irwin; Secretary Peter Ramage; Thomas Bell, Glenelg; Samuel Patterson, Egremont; Harold McKechnie, Bentinck; Charles Holm, Normanby; Louis Himmler, Neustadt; Mrs. Austin J. Ball, Hanover; Mrs. J. H. Harding, Durham.

This committee began its work by registering and issuing a card to every person living within its jurisdiction. These registration cards were necessary before ration books could be issued. This Ration Board served a population of 13,968; Canada had 500 such Ration Boards. Rationed items requiring coupons for purchase were: butter, meat, tea, coffee and sugar. Gas was also rationed, but these coupons were handled by the licence division of the Ontario Department of Transportation.

On May 17, 1943, the Ration Board Committee met to decide how to allot the 121,380 pounds of sugar allowed to this district for canning purposes. 10,700 persons applied for the extra sugar and the Committee decided to allot 10 pounds per person to residents of Durham, Hanover, Neustadt and Ayton, and 13 pounds to all others in the district. Each year the Committee prepared and mailed out all the ration coupon books for this area. These coupons continued to be issued until some time after World War II.

DURHAM ENGLAND EXCHANGE

Mr. Jim Lattimer, the Mayor of the City of Durham, England, was approached by Mr. Arthur Bonnett of Durham, Ontario, who was visiting England at that time, with regard to the exchange of Art between the Durham Art Gallery in Durham, Ontario, and a similar gallery in Durham, England. Mayor Lattimer thought that the Art exchange was not feasible, but believed that a cultural exchange between the two communities would be worthwhile. Arthur Bonnett came back with the recommendation of a yearly exchange project, and approached the Durham council, "as an official notice" from the mayor was requested by the Mayor of Durham, England. This idea was approved by council.

The first Durham, England Committee exchange consisted of the following: Mayor Bev. Wiggins, Mr. and Mrs. Allan Koehler and Mr. and Mrs. Bill Kennedy. The population of Durham, Ontario, is 2,500 and the population of Durham, England, was 95,000. In 1980 thirty British visitors including the Rt. Worshipful Mayor of Durham, England, James Lattimer and his wife Sylvia, arrived in Durham. Accompanying the Mayor were l4 guards. The tradition and uniforms of the guards were 100 years old. Durham, England is one of only two British cities with such a personal guard for the Mayor — London being the other. The agenda was a hectic one and a few of the many places visited by the English people were the Ontario Parliament Buildings in Toronto, Kleinburg and the McMichael Canadian Collection, and Kroehler Furniture Ltd. in Durham.

At the Civic Reception the presentation of a goatskin scroll to Mayor Bev. Wiggins of Durham carried the seal of the City of Durham, England. It was carried in a specially made wooden casket which was designed, made and donated by Christopher Norman Lee France of Durham, England. Four volumes on historic old Durham, England, which were given to the Town of Durham, are on display at the Durham Public Library.

In 1981 thirty-three citizens from Durham, including Mayor Gordon MacLean, journeyed to England. The gift which was brought back from Durham, England, by the Mayor was a replica of the sanctuary knocker of the historic Durham Cathedral.

In 1982 thirty-four visitors came from Durham, England, to visit in our community. One of the gifts presented to Mayor MacLean was a Spode English Bone China plate called The Durham Place, which depicted Eighth Century manuscripts originating in Durham Cathedral.

The last exchange of visitors occurred in 1983. Due to the lack of interested people who desired to participate in these exchanges, the programme was discontinued. However, it was great fun while it lasted.

McGowan's Falls and Mill.

The Wm. Laidlaw House.

THE HEDGES

This gracious home on Durham Road East was built in 1867 by James H. Hunter for his bride, the former Kate McDonald, the only granddaughter of Simon Fraser, the explorer of the Fraser River in B.C.

James H. Hunter was the youngest son of Archibald Hunter, the founder of Durham. He was born in Scotland and came to Canada as a child with his parents. He was educated in Goderich Grammar School and Upper Canada College, afterwards returning to Durham where he operated a prosperous mercantile business. In early records his name appears as a supporter of organizations to improve the community, and in municipal affairs he had been councillor and reeve of Glenelg Township. In 1875, 1883, 1890, he was elected as a Liberal to the Ontario Legislature. He died in 1891.

The house is predominantly Georgian with some Regency and Tuscan touches. This is one of the most historic houses in the area. There are three fireplaces in the house. One in the large living room has a wooden mantle and very ornate wooden mouldings around an iron firebox. Much of the house has high ceilings and large rooms which make a beautiful setting for the furnishings, antiques, prints and tapestries which complement the character of the house. Many of the rooms are finished with heavy wooden mouldings and panelling.

The Hedges

Old cars in Durham.

"THE MAPLES"

At the north end of Durham stands one of the most interesting and historical houses in the area. It is generally believed that the stone house was built in 1852-1854 by George Jackson. Records show that Mr. and Mrs. Peter Patterson sold the property to Mr. and Mrs. John Scott in 1855 for 15 pounds, and in turn Mr. and Mrs. Scott sold it in 1856 to George Jackson for 300 pounds.

George Jackson was born in Hutton, Yorkshire, England. He came to Canada in 1844 and operated mills in Collingwood and Meaford. In 1848 he was appointed Crown Lands Agent for Grey and Bruce, and he moved the Land Office from Owen Sound to Durham. He was extremely active in local community organizations as well as in politics. In 1849 he was district councillor for Bentinck and Glenelg Townships, and was the first Reeve of Bentinck in 1852 when the Municipal Act came into operation. He was Warden of Grey County from 1858-1860, and again in 1863 and 1875.

In 1852 Grey County became a independent municipality and a separate parliamentary constituency. Two years later George Jackson resigned as Crown Lands Agent to run as a Liberal candidate. He won the election, but during his years in office he lost the support of many constituents because of his stand on the secularization of Clergy Reserves, and he did not contest the election of 1857.

By 1861 he had changed his political affiliation and ran as a Conservative. He won that election, and again in 1863, the year of the last Government of the Province of Canada. In 1867 George Jackson won again and sat in the first Parliament of the House of Commons. He won a seat again in the election of 1878.

The original house had eight rooms, two halls and three fireplaces, all contained on the main floor and basement. When George Jackson and his wife died childless in 1885, the property went to a nephew, David Jackson, who built an addition on the west end of the house. The addition included the present kitchen and pantry, a storage room in the basement, two bedrooms on the ground floor and three bedrooms on the second floor. Two small rooms on the main floor were converted into a single large dining room, and a verandah was built across the back of the house. David Jackson died in 1898 and his widow remodelled the house again in 1901.

At this time the back to back marble fireplaces were removed from the centre wall to make room for a beautiful 22 step staircase to the second floor from the front entrance. The north front room and the bedroom behind it on the ground floor were made into one room called The Ballroom. The white marble fireplace was put into this room, and the black marble fireplace was put in the other front room The Library.

The house later passed to Christine Jackson (Mrs. Charles Seymour) who sold it outside the family in 1958. It changed hands many times since then, and the house and grounds gradually deteriorated until the property was purchased by Mr. Douglas Lloyd. Mr. Lloyd did an admirable job of restoring this fine house to its former elegance; he himself did much of the restoration work both inside and outside the house.

The present owner of the property is Mr. Theodore Gaitanakis.

MARION CALDER

Marion Calder was born in 1898 to William and Margaret (Graham) Calder. Her father was a substantial businessman in Town and was involved in many activities within Durham. William built the Calder Block

The Maples.
A beautiful stone house at the north end of town built in the early 1850s. George Jackson, Land Agent, lived here until his death when it was taken over by his nephew, William. Christine (Jackson) Seymour, Williams's daughter, lived there until the 1950s.

Marion Calder, First Woman Grey County Councillor 1954-1956.

on the east side of Garafraxa Street between Mill Street and the Saugeen River. He was a president of the National Portland Cement Co. He was also a member of the Durham Council for many years having served 13 years as Reeve and four as Mayor. William Calder was also Warden of Grey County in 1915. He was a staunch Liberal.

Marion followed in her father's footsteps and became Reeve of Durham in 1954. She was the first woman to sit on the Grey County Council and was Mayor of Durham from 1960-1962. One of the former councillors in referring to Marion said, "What I remember of her as a Mayor, and Reeve before that, was that she was in politics for the good of the town. That was her number one priority. Beyond that she was a friendly, gracious lady. And in politics she had an opinion — she always had an opinion. You knew exactly where you stood with her." Marion Calder died on May 9, 1988.

Garafraxa Street at North of Durham.

TOWN MATTERS

(From the *Durham Review*, December 13, 1883)

"To the Editor of the Review:—

Sir:— I was called upon the other day by the tax collector to pay the amount due by me to the Town funds. I said I did not think that I had received value for the amount demanded, but he assured me that I certainly had done so, stating that extensive local improvements had been made, sidewalks had been built and repaired, grading and gravelling of streets had been done, a market site procured, market scales purchased, a market house built, the Garafraxa St. hill cut, and the Lambton St. bridge built. I was quite overcome by the long array of improvements, and asked myself, can these things be. Having an hour to spare I concluded to walk round the Town and see in what state the thoroughfares actually were. It was raining smartly, so lowering my umbrella in front I started at a brisk

pace northward, but alas, I had only proceeded a short distance when I collided violently with a telegraph pole; Yes in this progressive Town, which the authorities say is one of the most enterprising in the Province, there is actually on the main street and in the middle of the sidewalk a row of telegraph posts, and those who built the walk were so considerate of the rights of the telegraph company, that when the post was in the way the plank was left out. Going north a little further I actually found a crossing over Garafraxa Street, and here the Town authorities have certainly done a great and good work, so that pedestrians can now walk boldly on and not fear the mud. I cross and safely reach: what? the other sidewalk, oh no! I only reach the other side of the street and am still sixty-six feet — or the width of a street — from the sidewalk, and just here the intelligence and administrative faculties of the council are fully exhibited. Had they continued the walk on the east of Garafraxa St.: sixty-six ft. north and then put in the crossing, people could have got cleanly across but as it is, travellers have to wade through the mud across one street to get to the crossing leading over the other. Truly our Council are an intelligent lot. Continuing my way north I, after sundry missteps down holes in the sidewalk, reach the corner of Lambton St. and turn west. Now, I say to myself as I approach the new bridge, here at least is something in which the town money was well and intelligently expended, but what is this I see, the filling is washing away, the sidewalk is warped and twisted and has assumed a serpentine and rickety appearance, teams are working and men are laboring and sweating putting in immense rocks, and all because the river has risen a foot, and vigorous efforts must be put forth to save this triumph of engineering skill. What will be the result should we have such a freshet next spring as we had last?

On westward I pass the Post Office and see to my left a small frame building standing on a small plot of open ground, two teams stand idly near the building one of which is attached to a waggon on which is a load of hay, and the other to a waggon in which there are a number of bags containing grain. I stop and look around wondering what this can be, when the owner of the hay waggon saluted me with, "Say you, are you the Market Clerk?" Amused at the impudence of the fellow, I am for a few moments speechless, when a small boy, who is running past, answers, "No, he is up town quarrelling with a man about a few loose planks." The truth now dawns on me — this must be the market and the board erection must be the market house. I cross the street through the mud and ask my granger acquaintance of the hay waggon why he is standing here in the rain. "Don't you know," he replies "that there is a town By-law, and that I must get my hay weighed here as they do not allow the owners of the other scales to use them, and I have to await the convenience of the official known as the Market Clerk, Town Clerk, Caretaker Public Schools, Caretaker Town Hall, St. Inspector, etc., etc., ad nauseam usque?" and with expression more forcible than polite, and one which is calculated to shock ears used only to sweet and dulcet sounds, he turned away muttering "curses not loud but deep" against the town in general and the town officials in particular. Turning now to the man with the bags I found him to be from Glenelg, driving in by the lower road he went straight to the market, only to find that the Clerk was away, the fire gone out, and not a buyer to be found. He said nothing, but any ordinary observer could plainly see that he was

> "Gathering his brows like a gathering storm
> And nursing his wrath to keep it warm."

and I inferred from the grim look on his countenance, that if he was situated so that he could reach within a reasonable distance another market (and who is not?) that it would be some time before he would be again seen standing on the Durham market where buyers are so seldom to be found. Just at this juncture a man came along from the direction of the station. He was dressed in pepper and salt tweed suit and his jovial face fairly beaming through the chill December rain, as he halted and raised his Scotch bonnet to wipe the presperation [sic] from his bald head, called out in a voice suitable for an auctioneer, "Say by Jinks" what are you waiting for, drive your hay over and they will weigh it, and you go up the hill to Burnet he will buy your grain, and never mind the Town By-law." They drove off and I turned to examine the building and contents, of which I propose to say something next week.

Yours   WANDERER"

One of a few remaining hitching posts in Durham.

Durham Review, December 20, 1883.

"To the Editor of the Review:—

Sir:— A little more than a year ago a committee of the Council was appointed to select a site for a market. After inspecting a number of sites offered, they recommended the purchase of the present one and the Council decided upon doing so, but a difficulty was encountered in that the lot selected belonged to a member of the Council. Now, the law is such that no member of the Council shall have any business transaction with the corporation, however, the difficulty was overcome by the title being made over to a third party and the deed to the corporation was executed by him, thereby complying with the letter and (yea, verily!) with the spirit of the law. The lot is one half acre in extent and cost the Town four hundred and eighty dollars. Upon this lot is erected what is simply a shed over the hay scales with a leanto attached, about eight by fifteen feet in size and for the erection of which the Town payed one hundred and ninety-seven dollars. When the house was built, scales were required, and notwithstanding that there were already two set of excellent scales — one in upper and one in lower town, — it was decided that another set should be purchased. A certain party, who had distinguished himself in ward politics, and who was prepared at all times and in all places to defend the action of the Council, no matter how partizan or how corrupt, and who notwithstanding the fact that he professes to be an advanced Liberal, yet believes most heartily that minorities are entitled to no courtesy and have no rights which should be respected, in fact one of those men of whom it can be truly said "That new Presbyter is but old Priest writ large," offered to procure the scales required. At this time another offer was made to the Council of a set of scales equally as good as those subsequently purchased, and for one hundred dollars less in price. The opportunity to reward a supporter was however too good to be lost, the new scales were ordered, the dealer pocketed his profit and the Town was one hundred dollars poorer than they would have been had the other offer been accepted. But what does that matter, did not our astute Council beat the Townships out of one thousand and nine dollars; why we are rich, and surely can afford to be a little liberal once in a while.

But what use is a market unless the buyers and sellers are compelled to attend? and in persuance of this object a red hot, cast iron By-law was passed imposing divers and dreadfull penalties on such as should have the hardihood to set it at defiance, and what is the result? Why? will it be believed that the firm of which the Reeve of the Town is a member is violating the provisions of this By-law daily. Come Mr. Reeve, if you expect others to respect your previous bantling, have some respect for it yourself. Set an example to the rest; put a buyer on the market and keep him there. And now, fellow rate payers, what value have you got for the money expended in purchasing a market?

As I approach the corner of Garafraxa and Lambton St's, on my return I am saluted with a volley of snow balls from a number of boys ranging in age from seven to fifteen years. I succeed in escaping without being hit but an elderly lady, who follows at a short distance, is not so fortunate. She is hit on the back of the head by one of the larger boys and the accomplishment is greeted by the crowd with shouts of delight and laughter. A couple of gentlemen who were witnesses of the affair advance to the Lady's assistance and one of them remarks, "Madam I should certainly have those young rascals punished, they most richly deserve it. Summons them before the Mayor." But a stop is put to further suggestion by the quiet remark, "My dear Sir you must be a stranger in Durham; we have no laws here, and when our people want law they go to Hanover." What has become of our Town Constable that the Town is given over to the government of the hoodlums and blackguards who infest our street corners and public places. Things have come to a pretty pass when a respectable woman is not safe from insult and actual personal injury at the hands of the roughs who seem to pay no attention whatever to the common decencies of life.

Surely the authorities will take rigorous measures to suppress the evil and to put a stop to the conduct that has made the name of the Town a by-word of reproach on account of the blackguardism rampant on its streets. One of the chief reasons urged for the non-interference of the authorities is that this properly belongs to family government and that every head of a family should properly train his or her own children. But when we find that this matter is entirely neglected by them and that their progeny are fast becoming a public nuisance then it is time for public interference. It is said that the shortest way to a man's heart is through his stomach, and likewise the shortest way to the conscience of the man who lets his boys run wild is through his pocket, — let him understand distinctly that all misconduct on the part of his boys will be met with the severest fines and penalties and an impulse to family government will be given such as we have not seen in a great many years, and the active demand for cow-hide will be such as to make the heart of the tanner to sing for joy. I turn the corner and face the hill. At the foot I find that the bridge is tottering to a fall, and at the sight of it the thought at once strikes me, what could our council have been thinking of to put in a bridge on Lambton St. having only fifty feet of a span when they saw the state of the other one which has forty-five feet clear? Will the ratepayers of the Town ask themselves this question? On up the hill, and where, oh, where is the sidewalk? About a year ago a job was let for the building of a sidewalk on the east side of the hill, and has nothing been done? Oh yes, here is a portion of a filling and further up you can see the cutting done, and strewn along the water course is cedar-timber, for which I believe the Town paid, and here begins and here so far ends the hill sidewalk."

Main Street Upper Town early 1900s.

Durham Review, December 27, 1883.

"As I reach the top of the hill I find that here again there are improvements going on or completed. When the Lambton St. bridge was to be built it was decided to take the filling required from the top of Garafraxa St. hill, and thereby kill two birds with one stone. Plans and specifications of the work required to be done were prepared and the contract let. Now any person of common sense would suppose that the work would have to be done according to the plans and specifications, or that in default of the contractor completing the work satisfactorily that a sufficient amount of money would be retained to complete the job. What is the result? The work has not be done according to contract; the plans and specifications have not been complied with, and yet all the money that would be due the contractor on the proper completion of the work has been paid over. Who is to blame for this? We elect a Council to do the business of the Town, and when we find that our affairs are managed in this manner it is time that we elected men who have both the desire and the ability to manage the affairs of the town in a business-like manner. When the work on the hill was in progress the sidewalks were torn up and have never been relaid. Although it is nearly five months since these walks were torn up, yet there has never been sufficient energy exhibited by the Council to succeed in getting the work of relaying it even started. I believe it is true that tenders for this work were asked for, and thereby hangs a tale. A certain official of the town was instructed to prepare the plans and specifications and an estimate of the cost of the work. This was done and tenders asked for. Some two of three tenders were received, one of which was, I am informed, found to correspond exactly with the estimate of the Council. This is very singular that two men working from extreme points — one desiring to let and the other to secure a contract, — should hit upon the same amount. I do not say that there is anything wrong. It is just possible that there was no collusion between the parties, but when we come to compare notes and find that the official who was entrusted with the preparing of the plans and estimates was the same person, who as street inspector passed the unfinished job on Garafraxa Street hill, and that the contractor who was the one favored by the passing of the hill job was also interested in the contract which tabled with the estimates, then surely we are justified in saying that it looks a little fishy. The nomination will soon be on and the strictest enquiry should be made into Town affairs, and if it is found that public interests are being made subservient to the personal agrandizement of any individual or any ring of individuals, then we will make short work of the whole lot. It gave me considerable amusement to watch the faces of the different people as they came up or down and had to encounter the mud where the sidewalk should have been. There is no avoiding it. In this respect at least the job has been well done — from fence to fence there is not sufficient firm footing for a sparrow. All is mud and most undisguised mud at that. Here comes a couple of men — apparently bound for the Post Office; they are both tall and in the prime of life, but here the similarity ends; the first one is a thin sour and dispeptic looking man who steps quickly forward. One glance has shown him that there is no way but to face it, so he goes at it with the determination to get the disagreeable tramp over as soon as possible, but he gives very free expression to his views on Town matters, mutters, grumbles and sometimes swears. His companion is a big good natured man who takes the disagreeables of this life very quietly. It is too much trouble to get mad, and his chief characteristic as he wades along is indifference. Following closely is a little sharp peppery individual who makes the passage in a series of jumps and bounds. This is of no advantage whatever but it serves to relieve his over burdened heart. He is a good and consistent church member, and of course does not swear, but as he halts by my side to stamp off a little of the adhesive clay he gives expression to language which, to say the least of it, is far from being strictly orthodox. Two ladies were the next; they looked dismayed at first, but there being no alternative they step gingerly forward. They said nothing but their silence was far more eloquent than any language which I can use. How long is this disgraceful state of affairs to continue. Surely the Durhamites are a patient and longsuffering generation. We have submitted to it all fall and have the dreary prospect of submitting to it all spring also. Durham is a Town and should have some pride and

Russell Family Home at corner of Lambton and College Streets.

self respect, but the manner in which our public affairs are managed would be a disgrace to the veriest one horse country village in the Province. A disturbance at this time arises at one of the hotels to the north, and in common with the rest of the bystanders I go up to ascertain the cause. A young man, who may have been drinking, but at the same time is in full possession of his reasoning faculties and is perfectly responsible for his actions, has raised a row in the house and has been put out. He effects a reprisal by threatening the life of the proprietor, and then taking a large stone hurls it through one of the doors. This done he picks up a large stone in either hand and ferociously attacks the other door. I turn to one of the onlookers and ask where is the Town Constable? and the reply is we have none. Then why not go to the Mayor for a warrant and have the fellow arrested? and the answer is — a warrant has been applied for, and the Mayor answered: "Come at 10 o'clock tomorrow and I will give you one." Ere 10 o'clock on the morrow had come a warrant had been secured in Hanover, and on that warrant the fellow was severely punished. Again there is a disturbance a little further north, but at a store this time. A man under the influence of liquor has been grossly abusive. He breaks some windows or glassware and after considerable trouble is finally ejected. Once on the street his abuse knows no bounds. The language used is fearfully blasphemous and exceedingly disgusting. Again the Mayor is interviewed and a summons asked for, and the reply is "Tut never mind him; let the poor devil go." Had the

Mayor done his duty in these two cases we would have got enough money out of the blackguards to have built the missing link of sidewalk. Comment is unnecessary. What more can be said. The ratepayers have matters in their own hands and if they persist in electing men to office who are incapable or worse, it is their own fault should they get little or no value for the taxes which they have to pay."

THE CATTLE FAIRS

The cattle fair is a rather misleading name as it had nothing to do with a fair. Instead it was one day in the month when any farmer in the surrounding area who had cattle to sell could bring them to a central place in Durham where buyers would be present to bid on them. The following partial account is taken from *A History of the County of Grey* by E. L. Marsh:

"The Durham cattle fair was founded in the early sixties and continued through the sixties and seventies and into the eighties of last century. These were the days before the railway came to Durham, and the buyers reached the place by stage or outfits of their own, generally on the night previous to the big day. If the markets were brisk, there might be twenty or more buyers on hand, all eager to pick up bargains. The third Tuesday of every month was the day fixed for the fair.

Horse Fair 1895.

198

Frost and Wood farm machinery pickup 1900.

The night before the fair was a busy time in hundreds of homesteads in a wide area around Durham. The cattle to go to the fair must be well fed and groomed, for early Tuesday morning preparations must be in progress to get the cattle on the move. Perhaps it was a lonely cow amenable to leading with a rope; perhaps a yoke of oxen, of a size rarely seen now, and easily under control; but perhaps it was young cattle that had to be driven, and then frequently there was trouble. Though there would be no trouble in lining them up on home grounds, they objected to travelling strange roads. In so many parts the roads passed through unfenced bush, where sometimes in spite of two or three vigilant attendants, a daring young steer would outwit its drivers and make for home, and precious time would be taken up in getting him faced toward Durham again. But before the end of the journey they were tired out and more easily driven.

Hopes of a good sale sprang up in the minds of the drivers, when perhaps a mile or more from the rendez-vous they met one or more buyers (each with the conventional cane) trying to catch a bargain before reaching the fair grounds where there would be competitive buying. They would flourish the bills as a temptation and sometimes a deal was made then and

there. Generally, however, there was a good bit of "Canny Scot" in the owners who reasoned that if buyers were so keen, there would be better prices in town. Sometimes they were right, sometimes not.

The fair grounds were in "upper town" in a small field surrounding the Drill Sheds. Part of the field opposite the well-known Dr. Gunn residence belonged to Archibald Hunter. These grounds were not altogether level, and the knolls were greatly in demand as the young farmers especially would try to get their charges on the high ground to add to their inches. The grounds proper were an enclosed area of perhaps two acres. But that would not hold the men and beasts gathered there. The roadway from the Drill Shed to the British Hotel corner was sometimes jammed with cattle, which occasionally spread even north and south on Garafraxa Street. Dickering went on everywhere but the man with a good beast generally got his price, and was told where to deliver the animal.

These were days when United States money was at about 20% discount. Both United States and Canadian silver was used; what pocketsful of silver these buyers must have had! The buying was all done in the forenoon; and in the afternoon the small boys got a job driving the cattle in scores and droves to Mount Forest. And as no trains were available in those early

199

days, they walked the weary sixteen miles home again with a hard-earned penny in their pockets.

Of course there were many who did not sell, perhaps having lots of feed, and so could afford to hold on. There were others who, for lack of feed, sold at a sacrifice. "Given away" was a common remark. Occasionally exchanges were made among farmers themselves to the advantage of both. Many buyers came so regularly that they became well known and trusted. So far as we remember, there was seldom any friction arising from dishonesty.

On the day before the Durham fair, a fair was held at Johntown (Chatsworth); and the day after, another at Mount Forest. Friction was aroused when Mount Forest and some buyers tried to announce that the Durham Fair was not on the third Tuesday, but the Tuesday before the third Wednesday, which, of course, would occasionally be the second Tuesday. Durham listened, but stoutly maintained the third Tuesday as being the day of the leading fair, and continued to keep this day till the early 80s, when new methods were introduced and interest in the fairs weakened after the arrival of the railroad.

The Durham fair became a great institution, and ran for over twenty years. In its later days, when work-oxen were not used so much, there was considerable buying and trading of horses on fair days, but the fair was doomed, and it never regained the prestige of its early days. The fair was not always on the old spot, at the Drill shed, where it saw its palmiest days, but later was held on the face of the hill where now is the Fire Hall.

There was no restriction on liquor selling at the time of those early fairs, and as a consequence many indulged too freely. Quarrelling and fighting and swearing often marred the afternoon. Fair-days were good business days, however, and merchants benefited by the ready cash."

From time to time letters critical of the behaviour of people attending these fairs appeared in the Durham papers. The following letter was published in the November 23rd, 1876 issue of the *Durham Chronicle*:

"Editor of the Chronicle.

Dear Sir,— I have no doubt but that any communication to your paper which may appear to reflect upon the character of any of the inhabitants or that might in any way injure the reputation of our Town will be received and published with regret. There are times when reticence in these matters may be observed to a fault. It is too true that the scenes of disorder and vice which were prevalent in our town to-day — the day of the Fair — were discreditable to those who profited by it, disgraceful to those who partook in it and ought to be humiliating to the townspeople, who seeing that the infamy is on the increase adopts no means to restrain it. During the greater part of the day the thoroughfare opposite the upper town hotels was obstructed with a number of persons — some of them

passing in society as respectable — in every stage of drunkenness, fighting and blaspheming the meanwhile the stuff that was maddening the crowds was being dealt out at the respective bars at five cents a drink as fast as bottles could be handed round. I am not a Dunkin Bill man, but anything that would put an end to that abominable system by which low groggeries are sustained is preferable to things as they are now. I am informed that the License Inspector intends to institute proceedings to revoke some licenses, if he does he deserves to be countenanced and supported.

Yours,

OBSERVER."

HOTELS

Mr. Archibald Hunter took up his farm property in Durham on May 1, 1842, and immediately built a log house on Garafraxa Street a short distance north of the Durham Road. The next year he brought his family here, and continued the process of clearing the land. Soon settlers began passing his door as they came into the Queen's Bush looking for land. There was no tavern between Mount Forest and Owen Sound and Mr. Hunter was constantly asked for food and overnight accommodation, which he graciously supplied. Often there was no room available, and Mrs. Hunter would collect all pipes, tobacco and matches, and allow these new pioneers to sleep in the barn or stable; and their belongings would be returned to them in the morning.

Mr. Hunter set about to erect a log tavern. It is not known whether this was an entirely new building or an addition to his log house. From information available it would appear this log tavern was about 24 feet wide and possibly 60 feet long. The north end started about the middle of the present house just north of the old Roman Catholic stone church, and continued southerly along Garafraxa Street. The hotel horse stables were across Garafraxa Street on the west side.

The Middaugh House.

The 1880 Belden Atlas of Grey County states with regard to this tavern: "The entertainment here offered was of course of a rather primitive character"; but an historical writer in the Meaford Monitor, discussing the features of this hostelry, assures us with the greatest gravity that "it was kept as comfortable as the accommodation would permit of."

In 1854 Mr. Hunter built a two and one-half storey, plus basement, stone hotel south of the log tavern commencing at the Durham Road and continuing along Garafraxa Street. The following year he extended the hotel north and constructed a two and one-half storey L, plus basement, across the north of the building which was used as a store for many years. Some years later he extended the L eastward with a two and one-half storey brick building which provided living quarters for the hotel employees. This hotel was known as the British Hotel. At the same time Mr. Hunter erected large stone arches through the basement wall of the L to allow stage coaches or other vehicles to drive through the basement around the back of the hotel, and passengers could arrive or depart, if the weather was inclement, without going outside. The hotel had a verandah on three sides on both the first and second floor levels. The barn and stabling were east of the hotel on the edge of the ravine. Mr. Hunter managed the British Hotel until 1864 when H. J. Middaugh became the proprietor. In the years following there were many owners before the building was turned into an apartment house.

In the W.W. Smith Gazateer and Directory of Grey County 1865, four hotels are mentioned in Durham:

"Middaugh's (formerly Hunter's) British Hotel situated on the corner of Garafraxa and Durham Roads in Upper Village is a large and commodious first class hotel, extensively patronized. H. J. Middaugh, Proprietor."

"Durham Hotel — Upper Village nearer top of hill on west side of street is a comfortable, well conducted house. James Koiley, Proprietor."

"Argyle Hotel on the east side of street near top of hill in Upper Village. A commodious house with extensive stabling. Hugh McKay, Proprietor."

"Royal Exchange Hotel on the main street in the Lower Village some distance south of the river. It has excellent stabling attached. Henry Cole, Proprietor."

In 1866 Mr. H. J. Middaugh purchased Lot 13, Garafraxa Street East from A. B. McNab just before he absconded. Situated on the lot were McNab's store lately occupied by Mr. J. Carson, a warehouse and hall, and a small tavern. The May 18, 1866 issue of the Durham Standard stated the raising would take place next week when the frame of the hotel was to be erected over the tavern and store utilizing as much of these buildings as possible in the new building. Mr.

The British Hotel, corner of Garafraxa Street and Durham Road,
built in 1854 by Archibald Hunter (from a photograph made in 1858).

201

John Murdock in front of the Central Hotel.

Middaugh was the owner of this hotel until 1878 when he sold it to Mr. McAllister. Thirteen years later it changed hands again, this time to Mr. Conrad Knapp.

In 1903 Mr. Knapp sold the hotel to Mr. Valentine Hahn. Mr. Hahn constructed the large brick addition to the east end of the Knapp House and otherwise improved the property. He was known as a very kind genial host with a great sense of humour. About 50 years ago the hotel ceased to exist as such and became a commercial building.

In 1881 H. J. Middaugh built a new modern three storey brick hotel on the south-west corner of Garafraxa and Lambton Streets. The October, 1881 issue of the *Grey Review* states "Middaugh's new hotel is now complete. This is one of the finest hotels in Ontario." Mr. Middaugh operated the hotel for some years and later there were several other proprietors. Eventually the top two floors became apartments, and the bottom floor housed commercial business. Fire destroyed the hotel in 1971.

After the arrival of the railways, the Knapp House and the Middaugh House each provided a carriage to meet all the passenger trains, thus hoping to encourage travellers to stay at their establishments. This was especially true of salesmen as they made their rounds usually about once a month; and if they could be enticed to a certain hotel, this meant considerable business over the year. The hotel proprietors did their utmost to obtain this repeat business and many were

the inducements offered to this end as can be illustrated by the following stories:

One new salesman came to town and stayed at the Middaugh House. On the table that night was a pot of new honey for use on his hot biscuits. The salesman told Mr. Middaugh that he had never tasted better honey. The kitchen staff was instructed to always have a little pot of honey on his table every time this salesman came to the hotel, and they were also told he would be there regularly every four weeks. On this particular trip the salesman brought his wife with him, and when they were eating supper he looked for the honey and there was none on the table; he asked the new waiter where his honey was. The waiter looked at him and said "You mean the little girl with black hair? She got fired and doesn't work here anymore."

British Hotel Card.

Henry J. Middaugh,
Mayor of
Durham, Ont.

Lambton Street looking West.

The stories of Mr. Hahn and the salesmen trying to outdo each other are many. One salesman whom Mr. Hahn wanted to best was coming back that day. Mr. Hahn had bought some new bedchambers so he washed one out, put some beer in it, and pushed it under this salesman's bed. The salesman went to his room and returned quickly to complain that the room had not been properly cleaned. Mr. Hahn said there must be some mistake and they went up to the room. Mr. Hahn removed the chamber pot, smelled it, then took a long drink and said to the salesman "that's good beer, here have a drink." The salesman rose to the occasion and replied "I would if I had only known it was beer before I peed in it."

Around 1895 the Central Hotel was built by Crawford and McCracken on the west side of Garafraxa Street North, midway between Chester Street and the Durham Road, to satisfy the additional hotel accommodation required at that time. The first proprietor was Mr. Joseph Cairns. About 1903 Messrs. McGrath and McAuliffe took possession of the hotel and ran it for six years, at which time Michael McAuliffe and his wife Elizabeth became the owners and operated this hotel until 1949.

It was a two storey, white brick building always well maintained with fresh paint, shining floors and window boxes of flowers in the summer. The back yard extended to Queen Street (as did most properties in that block), and had a huge vegetable garden, horse stabling and lawns. After the automobile became the accepted mode of travel, the stabling was removed and a parking lot was established.

Each weekday night the boulevard in front of the hotel was filled with angle parked cars of weary travellers — mostly salesmen who stopped here on a routine basis as they serviced their routes. Mrs. McAuliffe and her sister Margaret prepared delicious home-cooked meals which were served in the dining room. White linen tablecloths and linen napkins were used on the tables. This was entirely a family business and the McAuliffe children assisted their parents. At one point the hotel's name was changed to Hotel Hillcrest, but the warm McAuliffe hospitality did not change. On warm summer evenings the neighbourhood men would gather on the wooden chairs in front of the hotel (while their wives washed dishes!), smoke their pipes and exchange news with one another and the salesmen staying at the hotel. Because of gas rationing during World War II, this type of lodging was needed even after roads and automobiles were improved.

As the McAuliffe's became older, daughters Cecile and Helen and son James gradually assumed more responsibilities until they were managing the business mostly on their own. After 40 years, this hotel, the last of its kind in Durham, was sold to Goodwin's, thus marking the end of an era. It is interesting to note that five McAuliffe families lived in that one block along Garafraxa Street for many years.

The next owner of the property was Brian Keating, and the present owner is Douglas Fogal, who established the Uptown Revue, a fine family restaurant.

Two other old time hotels in Durham were Vollett's Hotel, later known as the Cattleyard Hotel, at the south end of Durham, and the Moodie Hotel on Garafraxa Street at the foot of Durham Hill.

Cross and Southerland Hardware Store.
Mr. Herb Cross and Mr. Southerland.

Main Street Durham during the 1930s.

Recreation & Sports

The dictionary defines sport as: a diversion, recreation, and fun — pleasure created by physical activity. With this in mind it would appear that Durham has been a real sports centre over the past 150 years.

At first there was little time for sport; it was necessary for even the children to contribute to the family's survival until the family became somewhat established. Possibly the first winter sport in Durham was sleigh riding on Garafraxa Street — Durham Hill on the north and Corktown Hill on the south — or on the Durham Road West or East on Watson's Hill, which in those days had a sharp S curve providing fun to navigate. Sleigh riding on these hills was popular into the first two decades of the twentieth century. Another popular winter sport was skating. When the ice on the millponds became thick enough for safety, the older boys would clean off the snow and a skating party would be held. The skates in those days consisted of flat blades fastened with small screw-nails to the thick leather soles of boots. Soon games of shinny were being played by the children. In the summer swimming was enjoyed, and children would in addition invent their own games.

During the 1850s curling was also played on the millpond ice. The January 25, 1861, *Durham Standard* reports that a curling match had been held in Mount Forest, and Durham won despite the fact they had not practiced for three years. A return match was arranged for the following week. Curling remained a very important sport in Durham for the next 50 years and a large number of Durham's citizens spent many enjoyable hours in the wintertime pursuing this activity.

Another early recreational sport in Durham was cricket. The September 7th, 1860, *Durham Standard* reports a cricket match between Durham and Mount Forest. "The match took place on the Durham Cricket grounds on September 1st and was a return match. The match began in the morning and was played until noon when both parties then repaired to the British Hotel, where a sumptuous lunch was prepared for

them, to which the morning's exercises added considerable relish. The match continued during the afternoon and ended in a tie." The Durham players on that team were J. Miller, ? Carmichael, A. Paterson, D. Jackson, W. Jackson, ? Thornbury, ? Hunter, A. Collins, P. Paterson, ? Macdonell."

No mention is made about the means of transportation to these activities — was it by stagecoach, private coach, horseback or on foot? Did the participants arrive on Friday night, or travel both ways on Saturday? By the late 1860s Durham was playing return cricket matches with Owen Sound, Chesley, Walkerton, Listowel and Mount Forest. The mode of transportation is still uncertain because there were no trains and the roads were rough. Some time after the arrival of train service in 1882, Harriston and Dundalk joined the league. Durham had an excellent cricket team and derived great delight in winning over Owen Sound, which they did frequently. For some 40 years Durham had three cricket teams — senior, junior and a school team. Cricket was played in the town into the first decade of the twentieth century.

Children playing indoors.

Durham Junior Cricket Team 1889
Back Row: W.S. Hynds, Archie Robertson, Robert Laidlaw, Arthur H. Jackson, John Robertson
Middle Row: Edward Lauder, David C. McKenzie, James McFarlane (Captain), David B. (Allen) McFarlane, Archie McFarlane
Front Row: John Cameron, James A. Hunter, James Robertson, William L. McKenzie.

Another sport which became very popular in the late 1870s and 1880s was football, or as it is called today, soccer. Not only did some Durhamites enjoy playing this game, but many of the rural communities also had football teams. Two of the better teams in this area were Varney and Holstein. This sport declined around the turn of the century and lacrosse gained more support and prominence. There is documented evidence that there were junior teams of baseball and lacrosse in Durham by 1880, as well as cricket.

The *Grey Review* of May 23, 1878, reports that, "Queen Victoria Day, May 24th, is to be celebrated in this town by a series of athletic sports. This is a step in the right direction. There is too little recreation among us. The race for fame and fortune is so eagerly pursued that the time, if any, given to recreation, is regarded as lost. This is a most mistaken notion." Some of the sports activities of that day included: foot-races, jumping, throwing the shotput, tossing the caber, cricket, football (soccer) and lacrosse. The newspaper continues, "We are glad, therefore, to be able to notice any indication of a return to a healthier state of things and a desire on the part of our young men to cultivate these sports which will make them better able to fight the battle of life. However, we cannot congratulate the committee having this year included the fairer sex in the programme. The excellent sports we have referred to are sadly marred by such degrading exhibitions as foot-races for women and baby shows. The chaste Greeks forbade women taking any part in the games and in the early days of the Athenian republic they were prohibited on pain of death being present at the festivals." This was Durham in 1878!

By 1900 there were three full days of various sports in Durham every year — May 24th, July 1st, and Labour Day. The following is an outline of activities as reported in the *Durham Review* dated May 24th, 1903:

"The day commenced with a Calithumpian parade. This motley aggregation paraded streets in the forenoon and their grotesque outfits gave no small fun to the onlookers. "A little nonsense now and then is relished by the wisest men." The stout old German with his bottle was voted among the best and a shaving outfit was the acme of ludicrousness. To the cry of "Fire," a grotesque Fire Brigade made its appearance manoeuvring the hose in such manner as to dampen the fire of a few of the spectators. The weird music rendered by the Calithumpian band was also a feature.

"A lacrosse game played between the School team and the Junior team was won by the School team 2-1. Next was a football game (soccer) between Holstein and Varney; score ended in favour of Holstein 1-0. While the football game was being played on the Agriculture (Fair) Grounds, a Rifle Match was keenly contested at Saugeen Park (north of McGowan's dam). The Shooting Match was between a team of Rifle Club members versus a team of ex-members; the ex-members won by a score of 143-125.

"The chief attraction of the day was a lacrosse game between Durham and Walkerton; Durham won handily. Durham players were C. Lavelle, Jeff Mc-Cracken, J. Baker, ? Glendillon, A. McIntyre, W.S. Hunter, P. Matheson, G. Booth, D. Munro, F. Glass, J. Lavelle, P. Gagnon. Referee A. Whitney. There were several races including relays. A game of cricket was also played — the Grits versus the Tories with the Grits winning 50-30. A Tug of War rounded out the day with Bentinck against Glenelg; Bentinck won 2 ends, Glenelg 1. Throughout the day the band played under the leadership of Mr. Peel.

"At night a concert was presented entitled "The Scout of the Philippines" — a mixture of farce, comedy and tragedy, put on by local talent. It was an excellent performance and well received."

Lacrosse Team circa 1890.

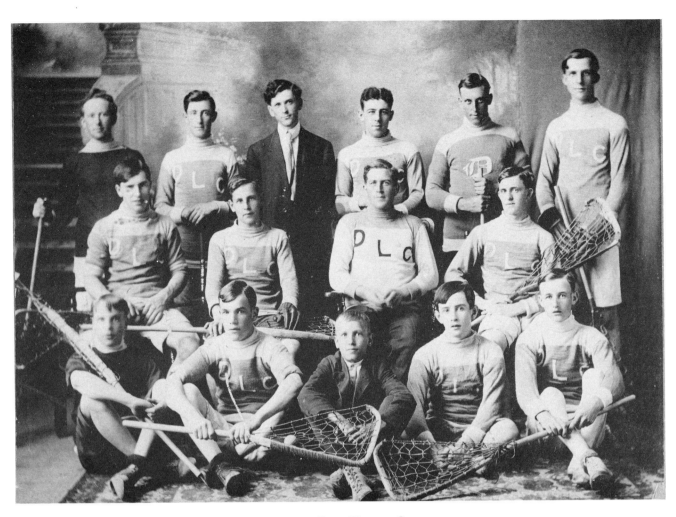

Lacrosse Team Circa 1910.
Back Row: Ted McKenna, H. McKechnie, G.S. Burnett, Fred Falkingham, J. Vollett, Roy Calder
Centre Row: Jim Allen, Vern Elvidge, Howard MacDonald, Lou Lavelle
Front Row: Fred Laidlaw, (Mac) Saunders, Fred Saunders, J.C. Lenahan, Bob Saunders

From the *Durham Review* of 1909 is an outline of Durham's Day of Sports held on July 1st. "Durham will present more attractions on the great holiday than will any place within 50 miles. Under the auspices of Ben Nevis Camp of the Sons of Scotland a gala Day of Summer Sports will be held in the Agricultural Park on the National Holiday. Included in the entertainment are:

18th Highlanders' Pipe Band
School Drill Competitions
Processions, Races, Jumping, Vaulting
Tug of War, Tossing the Caber, Throwing the Hammer
Highland Dancing, Pipe Competition
Professor Riley on the High Wire, 40 feet in mid air
Triple Trapeze Acts and Flying Performers
A Professional concert at night
Dr. Hutton, Chief; John H. Hunter, Chairman, C. Ramage, Secy."

A Labour Day of Sports in Durham — 1904 is taken from the *Durham Review*:

"The day began with a cricket match between the Grits and the Tories which was interrupted by the football game (soccer). The teams were evenly matched which resulted in a very entertaining game with fast and furious play. Varney won over Holstein by a score of 1-0. A game of Quoits was keenly contested, players from Lower Town beating those from Upper Town by only one point. The Lower Town team consisted of Archie Little, Thos. Allen, Norman McIntyre, R. Aljoe, T.G. Holt, F. Lenahan; Upper Town team were W.D. Mills, R. Cochrane, Clifton Elvidge, E. Brooker, W. Hunt, R. Scott. A short game of lacrosse between the "Hiawathas" and the "Mintos" was won by the former 2-1. A game of baseball was played, and an excellent concert featuring local talent was presented in the rink at night."

Durham Arena on George Street built 1908 by Mr. Brown.

RINKS

The first recorded open air rink was in Upper Town on Queen Street next to what was later known as the Colin McDougall Property. Another was Moody's rink, a frame building whose dirt floor was flooded for ice, at the foot of Durham Hill west of Garafraxa Street. The second covered rink was built by Thomas Brown on the east side of Garafraxa Street north of Saddler Street, where Neff's Garage is located today. This rink had a half round roof with several posts in the ice surface to support the roof; it was fine for skating or curling but was not suitable for playing hockey.

In 1908 Mr. Brown built a new rink 200 feet by 75 feet at the corner of George and Kincardine Streets. This rink had two rows of seats along the length of each side and seven seats along the east end, ladies' and men's dressing rooms, and club rooms — and a canteen made it one of the best rinks in this part of the province. The first game of hockey was played in this rink on January 1st, 1909. It was known that local boys would climb an adjacent hydro pole and gain admission through an upper window. This lasted until the manager caught on, and one evening the boys found the pole greased. The rink was by no means soundproof. The home of the researcher on this subject was situated across the corner from the rink, and if one didn't manage to attend the games, one could always tell which team was winning by the roars or moans of the crowd.

In 1918 the rink was sold to a group of local businessmen who formed The Durham Amusement Company. It was operated by this group until 1932 when it was sold to Mr. Cameron Lauder. After his death it was again taken over by local businessmen. Due to the efforts of the Rotary Club, the rink was repaired and reroofed and continued in use until the new arena and community centre was built in 1952. At this time the old rink was used for a short period by the Department of Highways, and in 1962 the building was removed and the land sold for building lots.

In 1951 it became evident that the old rink was not meeting the needs of the community and the Kinsmen Club launched a campaign for a new facility with Gordon McGirr as Chairman of the Fundraising Committee. The Kinsmen were assisted in canvassing the town by the Rotary Club and the Royal Canadian Legion. The first money raised was by selling tickets on a baby beef donated by Tom Lawrence and drawn for at a Kinsmen dance. The Kinsmen Club started the ball rolling by pledging $10,000. Many draws, dances and fundraising projects sponsored by the service clubs were held.

Land on Saddler Street West for the new arena was donated by the Agriculture Society for one dollar. The Wilson Lumber Company of Cannington was awarded the building contract for $65,000. The Agriculture Society assisted with the expense of the concrete floor and the town issued debentures for $25,000 to cover the cost of the artificial ice plant. The lobby of the building was 100 feet by 40 feet with a hall above, and dressing rooms, canteen and offices were on the main floor.

Durham Memorial Arena and Community Centre 1952.

Hap McGirr was again guardian of this arena for over 20 years until his retirement in 1974. The building was owned by the town and operated by a commission appointed by the council. The arena was officially opened in the fall of 1952 with the Saugeen Valley Horse Show. The first arena manager was Lou Fawcett followed by Bill McIntosh, Hap McGirr, Ross Taylor, Jim Stone and Brian Crozier.

In 1975 this building was considered unsafe and was condemned. Again the process of fundraising began and the Kinsmen undertook the job. Bob Braithwaite was Chairman of the Canvass Committee and, along with the other service clubs and grants, the arena was paid off in a very few years.

The new complex is 215 feet long and 186 feet wide housing an ice floor and community hall, six dressing rooms, First Aid room, washrooms, referee's room, two electrical rooms, one mechanical room, a ticket booth and canteen. A canteen, office, meeting room and washrooms are on the second floor.

When the original contract was let, it called for an expenditure of $640,000. At that price many items were omitted with the idea that they would be installed at a later date when the town's financial affairs were in better shape. The grants at this time included $150,000 from the Ministry of Culture and Recreation; Wintario matched one-third of the remaining cost, provided remaining costs were raised through donations. The town's plan included obtaining a debenture of $90,000 and this was approved by the Ontario Municipal Board.

After the contract was let a new grant became available based on the engineers' report on repairs to the old arena. Of this cost Wintario would grant $282,000. It was decided that items omitted from the original plans would be included — a sound system, plastic boards, sports timer, air conditioning for the hall and heaters in the rink. The additional cost and subsequent grant decreased the town's contribution to $64,000, most of which was raised in 1975 and 1976; hence the town did not have to take advantage of the $90,000 debenture.

The townships of Glenelg, Bentinck and Egremont contributed $38,000 and Grey County made a donation of $3,500. The painting of the completed arena was financed through a $14,450 Local Initiatives Programme Grant and the landscaping was covered by the Young Canada Works Programme Grant of $6,784.

The existence of these last two arenas would not have been possible without the time, effort and monies raised by the various organizations in Durham and district. Equally important are the people who supported the fundraising events and made donations.

When the new arena complex opened in 1977 a familiar face was missing — that of "Hap" Raymond McGirr. The *Durham Chronicle* contains an article written at this time: "When the new Durham Arena Complex opens the doors officially this weekend, there will be a familiar face missing to greet the public. Raymond McGirr, better known as "Hap," will not be around to welcome the summer's roller skaters or the new up and coming hockey super stars of the minor league. Three years ago Hap, the town's third arena manager, retired from his post as manager of the Durham arena after almost 30 years of operating arenas for the town. Hap retired just months after the town received word that the old Durham arena complex had been condemned. He was there when the old arena went into operation in 1955 and he was there to see it torn down. Today, although he won't be managing the arena, Hap says he and wife Eunice will be in the spectators' stands to cheer on the home teams.

A modest, wiry little man, Hap will long be remembered for his gruff exterior that houses a heart of gold. A believer in discipline, he said that he never had any problems with the "kids" who came to the arena. It was always the adults. Those same "kids" have since grown up and had "kids" of their own but they still remember how a look from Hap could leave them standing scared in their shoes. When they weren't playing hockey or watching hockey games, the boys of yester year were trying to get the old grumpy looking face of Hap McGirr to break into a smile.

Hap's dedication as the town's arena manager went beyond the confines of the building and extended to his home. Mornings would find a half dozen or so young minor hockey players sitting around the McGirr kitchen in over-sized hockey uniforms waiting for a ride to the arena with Hap, Eunice said.

The new Arena complex with all its modern features and comforts is a far cry from the arena Hap came to know in the 1940s. That first arena sat on George Street and housed a natural ice surface. The ice surface came with the good weather and melted away with the spring thaw. There were long nights of watering the ice surface — nights when it was so cold

Durham Community Centre built 1977.

the water hoses would freeze, Hap recalled. Public skating and hockey were the only events held in the building during the winter, and all were held at night. There were no food booths or canteens and the only heat to be found was around the pot-bellied stove in the dressing rooms. There were more public skaters then, Hap said, usually providing the only type of entertainment for the local folk in the winter months.

Playing hockey was a little rougher too. The game would go for two periods before the ice would be scraped off and when it was, with clumsy wooden scrapers. When that first arena was closed due to roof posts interfering with the spectators' view of the game, the old arena complex on Saddler Street was born.

Although Hap was not the first manager of this second arena he was there within a few short months. Conditions were a little better and a little more comfortable in the new arena and community hall but compared with the operation of an arena today, it wasn't all that comfortable in the beginning. There was an artificial ice surface requiring that it be flooded with hot water to freeze. The ice flooder consisted of a barrel of hot water being pulled over the surface by a man. A pipe at the other end of the barrel trickled the water onto the ice surface that was spread at first with a layer of terry towelling and later with flannelette. The town's first mechanical ice flooder was donated by the Kinsmen Club in 1956.

The arena and community hall required Hap to be at the structure from 14 to 18 hours each day. Whenever the building was in use, Hap was on hand. He worked alone at first until part time help was supplied. The days seemed more or less the same until the arrival of Ross Taylor and Lyle Dodd made work a little more cheerful and a little bit better.

The new arena complex was warmer to work in and more modern and seemed to have something to do with calming the savage breast of the hockey specta-

tor. Hap said he remembers games in the old natural ice arena, usually against Listowel, where there would be more excited fans on the ice than in the stands. Moving hockey games into the arena complex seemed to make the spectators more civilized, and he said he remembered very few fights breaking out in the new structure."

Street hockey with a ball. Clem Rowe, Fred Murdock, Sherwood Rowe, Yank McKechnie, Hamilton Davis.

HOCKEY IN DURHAM

Credit for the organization of hockey in Durham goes to Frank Irwin and Peter Gagnon in the early 1900s. There was some attempt to play the game in the Garafraxa Street arena but the support posts interfered and a new arena was built on George Street. Prominent players in the Durham area were Mickey Saunders, Jim and Cam McLachlan, George Catton, Bobby Saunders, Eric Elvidge, Harper and Harry Kress, Martin Lauder, Peasie Morlock, ? Buschlin, Harper McGirr, Erben Schutz and ? Moorehead.

Durham Huskies 1953-54 Ontario Int. "B" Champions.

Front Row: Jack McCreight, Ed Mitchell, George Fairchild, Bill Nixon, Joe Bell, Irvie Elvidge, Coach, Andy Schenk, Ken Jackson, Bill MacIntosh, Jim Nixon, Bob Braithwaite, Manager.

Centre Row: Hap McGirr, Treasurer, Cliff McGirr, Executive, D. Deeves, Gary Lawrence, John Bell, Art Aljoe, Scott Baines, Alt., Jack Snell, Alt., Mel Thompson, Goal, Bill Brocklebank, trainer.

Back Row: Bob Ball, President, Jim Duffield, Honorary President, Ray Adams, trainer, Don Campbell, trainer, Tom Watson, Executive, Royden Burnett, Club Doctor, Frank Irwin, Publicity, Bowman Jamieson, Executive, Gordon McGirr, Executive, Art Newell, Executive.

Inset: Don McGillivray, Club Masseur, Andy Grant, Harry Kress, Executive, Pat Smith, Treasurer.

Durham Huskies Continental Sr. A. Champions 1973-74.

Front Row: Dave Schafer, Brian Caley, Dennis Farwell, Alan Koehler, Larry Schafer, Jim Nixon, Bill Clement, Gord Becker, Jim McMullin

Centre Row: Wayne Rawn, Mike Jackson, Jim Aitken, Chuck Niesen, Glen Reid, Don Vipond, Dale Rawn, Drew Haldane, Jerry Herman, Joe Grundy, Gary Sproule, Mayo Paquette, Terry Whiteside

Back Row: Lloyd Lorenz, Ross Taylor, Orville Mead, Bob Braithwaite, Arden Birr, Walter Schafer, Ed Schwass, Don Lunn, Virgil McNabb, Bill Nixon, Jerry Peterson, John Fleishman, Hap McGirr.

O.H.A. Champions 1935-36.
Back Row: Chas. Zilliax, Executive, Larry Miller, Sec. Treas., Norm Tucker, Clarence McGirr, Duke Schutz, Dr. D.B. Jamieson, President, Len Trushinski, Hap McGirr, Punk MacDonald, Jim Duffield, Executive, Mel Calder, Executive.
Front Row: Marty Lauder, Ass. Coach, Hugh Cassidy, Joe Raybould, Hiram Dean, Jack Schutz, Fanny Moses, Gordon Reanie, Irvie Elvidge, Dr. Royden Burnett, Coach. Front: Len Vollett, Trainer.

In the 1920s there were three leagues — the Northern league, Junior and Senior league and the OHA Intermediate league. Some players were on all three teams. When Irv Elvidge was asked if he played every night of the week his answer was yes. Sometimes these teams had only nine or ten players. The season could be very short, depending on the weather. Travelling could be a problem and often they travelled to games by horse and cutter.

In the mid 1920s two local players, Erben Schutz and Martin Lauder, played professional hockey with the Boston Bruins. In 1935-36 the Durham Hockey Club won the first OHA championship for Durham. The team was coached by Dr. R. Burnett, assisted by Martin Lauder. Members were:

Jack Schutz	Erben Schutz	Cliff McGirr
L. Trushinski	J. Raybould	G. Rennie
Hugh Cassidy	Norm Dean	Irv Elvidge
Norman Tucker	Fred Moses	Raymond McGirr
Ken Wilson	E. McDonald	

While awaiting playoffs against Whitby, the team practiced in Maple Leaf Gardens. This was arranged by Eddie Allen, a former Durham boy who was then sports editor of the Mail and Empire.

Although the team name was the Durham Hockey Club, in 1935 one newspaper reporter tried to put the name Hornets on the team but it did not stand. In 1949 the same attempt was made with the name Phantoms. In March, 1952, a *Chronicle* reporter, possibly by mistake, called the team the Huskies. It was thought that this was the origin of the name and the Durham Hockey Club came to be known as the Huskies thereafter.

In 1952 and 1953 the Huskies won the WOAA Grand Championships. These were the first senior championships won since 1936. The team coach was Irv Elvidge and the manager was Bob Braithwaite. Team members were:

Jerry Strong	Doug Deeves	Wally Goodwin
Lou Fawcett	Jim Nixon	Scotty Bain

Norman Tucker	Ed Michanik	Gary Lawrence
Norman Dean	John Bell	Bill Nixon

In 1954, 1956, 1968 and 1969 the Huskies were OHA intermediate B champions.

Jim Nixon coached the 1968 and 1969 teams and Arden Birr was the manager. Members of the 1969 team were:

Gord Becker	Murray Stephens	Larry Schafer
Bob Bogden	Ross Clark	Garry Vaughn
Len Long	Jerry Herman	Bob Heatherington
Jim Aitkens	Dale Rahn	Bev Allen
Cec Cowie	John O'Flaherty	Ken Parker
? Bartram		

The 1984-85 OHA B championship was won by the Huskies. The coach was Andy Grant, Sr. and George Clarke was manager. Team members were:

John Bak	Mark Aitken	Dean Neuman
Ken Nelson	Ralph Reeves	Bruce Marshall
Brent Marshall	Paul Lahn	Andy Mueller
Doug Zetter	Andy Grant	Paul Nelson
Merv Griffin	Fred McKechnie	Kevin Eccles
Brad Law	Keith Hopkins	Brent Hopkins
Ken Nixon	Paul Love	Jim Roberts

In the 1986-87 and 1988-89 seasons the Huskies played in the Hardy Cup semi finals, but lost. The Hardy Cup is the symbol of the Canadian Senior A championship.

At the beginning of the 1992-93 season it was apparent that there were not enough players to ice a team and the decision was made to disband for one year. Unfortunately, when the 1993-94 season arrived the situation was unchanged. This team had won eight All Ontario championships and six All Ontario Finalist.

A tribute must be given to Bob Braithwaite and Allan (Kelly) Koelher who served on the Huskie executive for over 30 years.

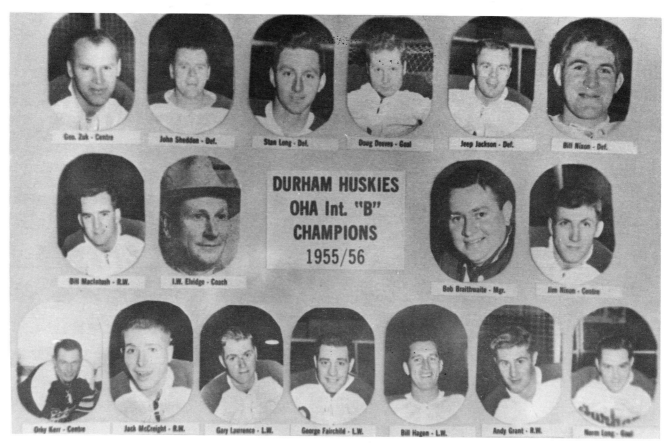

Durham Huskies 1955-56 Intermediate "B" Champions.
Back Row: George Zuk, John Sheddon, Stan Long, Doug Deeves, Jeep Jackson, Bill Nixon.
Centre Row: Bill McIntosh, I.W. Elvidge, Bob Braithwaite, Jim Nixon.
Front Row: Orky Kerr, Jack McCreight, Gary Lawrence, George Fairchild, Bill Hagen, Andy Grant, Norm Long.

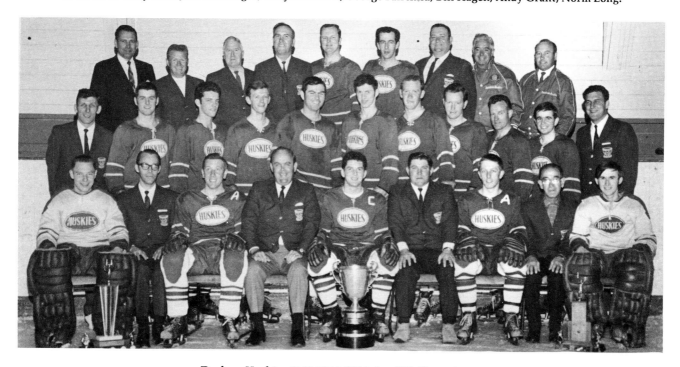

Durham Huskies 1968-1969 OHA Int. "B" Champions.
Front Row: Gord Becker, Orville Mead, Murray Stephens, Don Nearingburg, Larry Schafer, Bill Nixon, Bob Bogden, Raymond McGirr, Ross Clark.
Centre Row: Jim Nixon, Gary Vaughan, Ken Long, Jerry Herman, Bob Heatherington, Jim Aitken, Dale Rahn, Bev Allen, Cec Cowie John Flaherty, Arden Birr
Back Row: Ross Taylor, Virgil McNabb, Alan Koehler, Walter Schafer, Ken Parker, Yves Bartram, Bob Braithwaite, Don Campbell, John Fleishman.

1975-76 Durham Huskies Continental Sr. A. Champs — Finalists Ont. Div. — Allan Cup.
Front Row: Gord Becker, Dean Symons, Jim Nixon, Dean Neuman, Larry Schafer, Dave Schafer, Brian Caley
Centre Row: Ron Tanner, Bil Clemens, Ian McCarl, Jim Aitken, Mike Cain, Chuck Niesen, Jerry Herman, Wayne Rawn
Back Row: Bob Becker, Andy Grant, Al Nesbitt, Al Lennox, Brad Deline, Don Neuman, Bob Stoutenburg.

Durham Huskies 1984-85 All Ontario Championship.
Front Row: John Bak, Mark Aitken, Andy Grant, Dean Neuman, George Clarke, Ken Nelson, Ralph Reeves
Centre Row: Paul Rawn, Kelly Koehler, Bruce Marshall, Paul Lahn, Andy Mueller, Doug Zettler, Andy Grant Jr., Paul Nelson, Merv Griffin, Brent Marshall, Virgil McNabb, Brent Sweeney
Back Row: Fred McEachnie, Kevin Eccles, Brad Law, Keith Hopkins, Brent Hopkins, Ken Nixon, Paul Love, Jim Roberts.

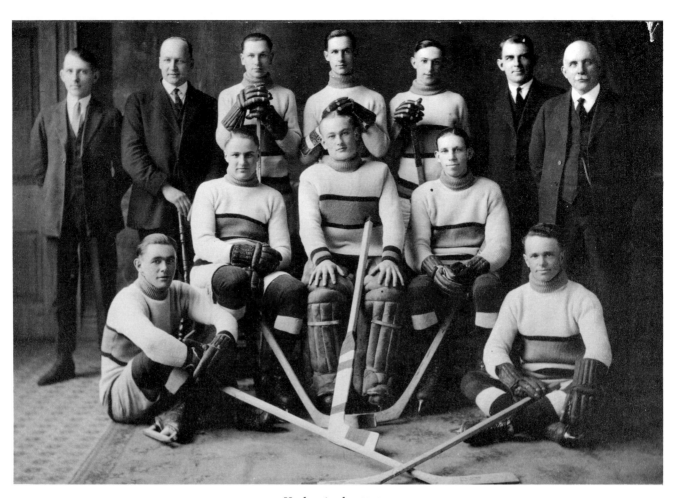

Hockey in the 1920s.
Back Row: Ike Steinacher, Jim McLachlan, I.W. Elvidge, Harry Kress, Gordon Moorhead, Ab Noble, Wm. Calder
Centre Row: Duke Schutz, Punk McDonald, Wm. Vollett
Seated: Clarence McGirr, Cliff Buschlen.

High School Boys — "Durham Aces" Hockey Team.
Back Row: Irvin Elvidge, Cliff Falkingham, Leonard Chumby, Gary Lawrence, Brad Armstrong, John Bell, Bev. Goldsmith, Bill Roberts, Pete Robins, Hiram "Red" Dean.
Front Row: Tom Barker, Ken Clutchey, Harry Styles, Alfred Corbett, Tom Cordick, Jim Roberts, Jim Raeburn, Andy McAuliffe, Murray MacDonald, Morris Caswell.

216

72s/THUNDERCATS

In the early 1970s with the Huskies in the OHA senior league, several good players had no team on which to play. This prompted a group of people, including Don Nearingburg, Joe Detzler, Gord Reaburn and Rose Marie Detzler, to form an intermediate WOAA team. In honour of Durham's centennial the team was called the 72s and for 15 years the team played under this name. The first members of the 72s were:

J.D. Hopkins, Coach	Barry Nixon	Brian Lawrence
Bryon McLean	Ron Matthews	Bruce Vollett
Lloyd Griffin	Bob Hubbard	Bryan Lawrence
Ron MacIntyre	Don Neuman	Andy Grant
Allan Lennox	Maurice Hauver	Jack Sturrock
Butch Graham	Kris Kennedy	Paul Nelson

In 1974-75 the team won the C division of the WOAA — the first such honour for the team.

In 1988 the team name was changed to Thundercats and that year they won the WOAA senior grand championship. Dennis Graham was coach of this team and Tracey Detzler was manager. Team members were:

Gord McInnes	Don Barlow	Randy Reay
William Torry	Scott MacMillan	Jim Nixon, Jr.
Marty Wellwood	Brad Marshall	Mark Taylor
Dave Walton	Dan Sweeney	Rob Reed
Dean Burnett	Rob Traverse	Steven Reay
Brian DeGroote	Dave Nixon	Greg McFadden
Robbin Ferro	Brian Sweeney	Jim Sweeney
Todd Stoddart	Jamie Lindsay	Carl Schafer

In 1990-91 the Thundercats won the Senior A title. They won the grand championship in 1991-92 and 1993-94. Dennis Graham was the coach and Carl Schafer and Randy Reay were assistant coaches. Team members were:

Scott Betts	Bill Speilmacher	Trace Aljoe
Dan Neil	Todd Stoddart	Trevor Heidman
Marty Wellwood	Paul Nixon	Stephen Schenk
Rob LeBlanc	Dave McComb	Jeff Neil
Jeff Verbeek	Ken Nixon	Bob Sullivan
Rob Reed	Stacey Becker	Greg Mighton
Greg McFadden	Terry Whiteside	Shaun Stoddart
Rob Sturrock	Colin MacMillan	

Division Titles were won in the following years: 1974-75, 1978-79, 1981-82, 1986-87, 1988-89, 1990-91, 1991-92, 1992-93 and 1993-94. From the 1988-89 season until now they played in the senior A division. Dennis Graham has been the coach of the Thundercats since 1986.

THE DURHAM FLYERS

In the early 1950s there were several players in Durham who were very good hockey players but did not qualify to play for the Durham Huskies; thus, in 1952 an intermediate team was organized and they played in the Central Ontario hockey league. This team was called the Durham Flyers and included the following players:

Ken Kress	Stan Pust	Ken Cluchey
Alf Corbett	Vern Aljoe	Terry Faulkner

The 1972's.
Back Row: J.D. Hopkins, Barry Nixon, Bryon Lawrence, Bryan McLean, Ron Matthews, Bruce Vollett, Lloyd Griffin, Bob Hubbard, Brian Lawrence, Ron MacIntyre, Don Neuman, Conrad Elvidge.
Front Row: Andy Grant, Alan Lennox, Morris Hauver, Jack Sturrock, Butch Graham, Kris Kennedy, Bob Nelson. Absent: Joe Watson.

Durham Thundercats 1989.

Back Row: Randy Fox (Trainer), Greg McFadden, Dave Walton, Robin Ferro, Dan Sweeney, Brian Sweeney, Rob Reed, Jim Sweeney, Dean Burnett, Todd Stoddart, Rob Traverse, Jamie Lindsay, Steve Reay, Brian Degroote, Carl Schafer (Asst. Coach), Dave Nixon, Tracey Detzler (Mgr.), Tom Eden (Head Trainer), Dennis Graham (Head Coach)

Front Row: Gord McInnis, Don Barlow, Randy Reay, William Torry, Scott MacMillan, Jim Nixon, Marty Wellwood, Brad Marshall, Mark Taylor.

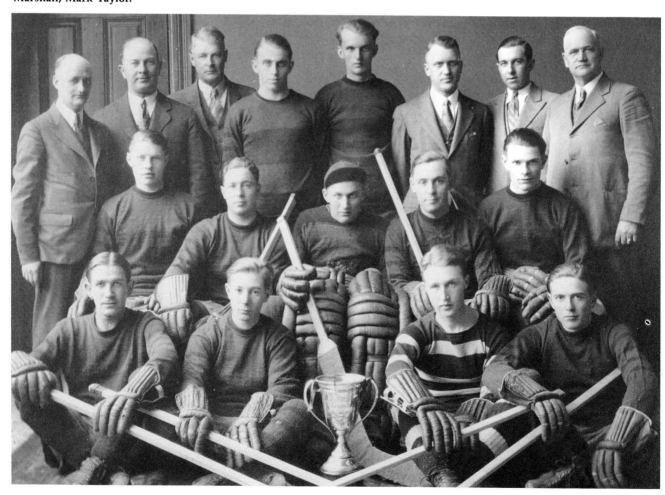

Durham Hockey Club, Junior Northern League Champions 1930-31.
Back Row: R.L. Saunders, V. Noble, H.W. Wilson, F. Murdock, D. Black, R.M. Sparling, N. Ritchie, A. Bell.
Second Row: N. Dean, K. Wilson, J. Schutz, N. McIlraith, E. Tucker.
Front Row: R. McGirr, F. Bolger, B. Irwin, E. Wood.

Norman Bell	Tom Cordick	Tom Kyle
Andy McAuliffe	Murray MacDonald	Don Pust
Jim Duffield	Don Lawrence	Ross MacDonald
Jim Reaburn	Alvin Alexander	Elmer Lake
John Morlock	Dave Nixon	John Morlock
Jerry Tallon	Morris Tschumi	Don Schenk
Norman Tucker	Herb Lantz	Garry Lawrence
Art Aljoe	John Bell	

The Flyers played in the WOAA league in 1953 and 1954.

MINOR HOCKEY

In the first half of the century there was no organized minor hockey as we know it today. There had been juvenile, junior and peewee teams, but it wasn't until the late 1940s that hockey became organized.

In the 1920s and 1930s there were teams that played in the Northern junior league and in 1930 the Durham Team was league champion. Members of this team were:

D. Black	N. Dean	K. Wilson
J. Schutz	N. McIlraith	E. Tucker
R. McGirr	F. Bolger	B. Irwin
E. Woods		

In 1945-46 a Durham-Chatsworth combined team won the OMHA bantam championship. The first such minor hockey honour for Durham. Team members were:

J. Snell	B. McIntosh	D. Wilson
A. Louchs	W. Elder	B. Roberts
J. Bell	E. Aikinson	A. McIntosh
N. Farrow	K. Kress	B. Armstrong
D. Robbins		

In 1948 a Durham-Chatsworth combine juvenile team won the Georgian Bay Division and the WOAA. In addition to the above players, Charlie and John MacDonald, Andy Grant, H. McLelland and Gord McNeil played for this team.

In the fall of 1947, a PeeWee hockey league was formed. This league consisted of boys 12 years of age and under. The executive included Ivan Wood, Lloyd Erwin and Ivan McKechnie. Norman Greenwood and Walter Schafer also played a big part in getting this league started and participated for many years. Service clubs furnished sweaters, equipment and financial assistance. The boys played what is now known as house league and were divided into north, south, east

All-Ontario Bantam Champions 1963-64.
Back Row: Ralph Darroch, Angus Roseborough, Dave Breen, Roger Baskerville, Jim Baskerville, Bill Taylor, Ken Elvidge, Allan Lennox, "Hap" McGirr.
Front Row: Brian Lawrence, Allan Nixon, Barry Nixon, Ross Clark, Bryan Lawrence, Mike Rogers, Paul Aljoe.

1st Midget OMHA Champs for Durham 1980-81.
Back Row: Leonard Eccles, Darryl Mountain, Robin Ferro, Robt. Sullivan, Steve Reay, Michael Robertson, Allan McMann, Paul MacGillivray, Kevin Hopkins, Robbie Barrow, Marvin MacDonald
Front Row: Brian Sweeney, Robt. Stone, Wm. Torry, Robbie Nixon, Scott Eccles, Paul Nixon, Richard Graham.

and west — the dividing line being the railway tracks and Garafraxa Street. This format continued for many years.

In 1949-50 there was a juvenile team called the Junior Aces. In 1951 they were renamed the Flyers and several of the players went on to play intermediate hockey.

An interesting story is told of R. L. Saunders, who had been a referee for 25 years, being asked to come out of retirement to referee a junior game. Mr. Saunders appeared on the ice with a brass hand bell instead of a whistle. This caused much amusement to fans and players.

In 1950 the newly formed Kinsmen Club made the organization of minor hockey one of their priorities and supported them in many ways. After about four years the organization became self-supporting, but it still receives financial support from the Kinsmen and other organizations.

In 1956 minor hockey started to have All-Star or Rep teams as they are now known. In the late 1950s teams became more involved in the Western Ontario Athletic Association (WOAA) and in 1958-59 a midget team won their WOAA division. Walter Schafer was manager of this team and Merv McIntyre was coach.

Team members were:

Les McGirr	Bev Allen	Keith Allen
Larry Schafer	Paul Schutz	Ralph Darroch
Bob Davis	Bill Cook	John Lawrence
Lorne Smith	Bob Becker	Gary Cluley

In 1959-60 the midgets again won the WOAA championship.

In 1963-64 the bantam team won the first Durham WOAA bantam title and went on to be OMHA champions. Ralph Darroch coached this team and Jim Baskerville was manager. Team members were:

Mike Rogers	Barry Nixon	Ross Clark
Allan Nixon	Brian Lawrence	Allan Lennox
Angus Roseborough	Ken Elvidge	Bill Taylor
David Breen	Roger Baskerville	Paul Aljoe
Bryan Lawrence		

In 1965-66 for the first time, a Durham peewee team won the WOAA championship. Bob Braithwaite coached this team and team members were:

Ted Baskerville	Don Neuman	Brian McLean
Niki Koeslag	Bill Braithwaite	Paul Gray
Steve Dempsey	Bruce Vollett	Rick McFadden

The same year a squirt (novice) team also won the WOAA championship — the first for this division. The team was coached by Wilf Lake and managed by Walter Schafer. Team members were:

Don Lantz	Kris Kennedy	Dean Neuman
Lyall McDonald	Joe Dilworth	Andy Grant
Bob Thompson	Jamie Gostick	Bill Elvidge
Jerry Schafer	D. Baskerville	Peter Schwartz

In 1966-67 and 1967-68 the Squirt team won the WOAA championship and the PeeWee team won the championship in 1966-67, 1967-68, 1968-69 and went on to win the OMHA Zone 7 championship in 1969-70. Wilf Lake was coach of the 1969-70 team and Bruce Marshall was manager. Team members were:

Carl Schafer	Mike Caswell	Terry Graham
Dean Hopkins	Ken Dow	Don Marshall
Doug Marshall	Kevin Wight	Tony Lawrence
D. Dennet	Cameron Hynes	John Bell

1981-82 OMHA Midget Champs.
Back Row: Leonard Eccles, Paul Keating, Darryl Mountain, Scott MacGillivray, Paul MacGillivray, Marvin MacDonald, Alan McMann, Murray Robertson, Terry Whiteside, Dave Mauer, Tom Mason
Front Row: Dave Hopkins, Robbie Barrow, Guy Mason, Richard Graham, Robbie Nixon, Robt. Stone, David Eccles.

In the 1971-72 season the peewee and midget teams won the WOAA championship and in 1973-74 the peewee and bantam teams won the WOAA championship.

In 1975 the Durham arena had been condemmed and the minor teams played hockey in Hanover until the 1977-78 season. The Durham minor hockey teams went on to win many more championships. In 1980-81 the Midgets won the OMHA CC championship — the first midget OMHA title for Durham. Coach of this team was Marvin MacDonald and Leonard Scales was the manager. Players were:

Rob Nixon	Darryl Mountain	Mike Robertson
Brian Sweeney	Bob Sullivan	Robbie Barrow
Robin Ferro	Wm. Torry	Richard Graham
Steven Reay	Paul Nixon	Al McMann
Scott Eccles	Rob Stone	Kevin Hopkins
Paul MacGillivray		

In 1983-84 the Midgets won the Silver Stick tournament in Wasaga Beach and came second in the North America Silver Stick tournament in Sarnia. They also won the division championship in a Buffalo tournament. At one point they had won 22 straight games.

1992-93 Pee Wee OMHA Finalists.
Back Row: Dan Elvidge, Trainer, Jim McGillivray, Mark Calder, John Hutchinson, Brad Watson, Jeff McMillan, Chad Woollard, Kelly Atkinson, Joey Bak, Chad Reay, Mike Shields, Willy Hunter, Larry Watson, Manager
Front Row: Evan Hastie, Mike Nixon, Jim Nixon, Coach, Matt Patterson, Andy Grant, Assistant Coach, Brad Doherty, Neil Watson, Chris Wight.

Durham Juvenile OMHA C.C. Champions 1982-83.
Back Row: Jim Stone, Robt. Stone, Dave Hopkins, Paul Nixon, Brian Sweeney, Bill Eden (Stick Boy), Al McMann, Terry Whiteside, Dave Mauer, Robbie Barrow, Randy McNabb, Rusty Hiltz, Dean Neuman
Front Row: Trevor Alexander, Will Torry, Bruce McLaughlin, Robbie Nixon, Bob Sullivan, Tim Peart, Robin Ferro, Dave Walton, Jim Hollands.

In 1987 the WOAA started to record and recognize house league champions and one or more divisions won the WOAA championships in 1988 through 1993.

The following Durham minor hockey players were drafted by Junior A and/or College and NHL teams: Dean Hopkins — London Knights and the Los Angeles Kings; Jerry Schafer — Dixie Beehives, Tier II and North Western Michigan University; Dean Neuman — Oshawa Generals; Michael Schafer — Guelph Platers and Cornell University, New York; Kevin Hopkins — London Knights and Murray Robertson — Windsor Spitfires.

Only one girls' hockey team was organized. This was in the Juvenile division and included:

Julie Fennell	Debbie Nixon	Mary Susan Bell
Cheryl Hopkins	Gwen Ferguson	Kelly Leatham
Janice Nearingburg	Jennifer Player	Cindy Talbot
Corrine Mighton	Fay Nixon	Sherry Love

A very important part of the minor hockey system is the ladies auxiliary. This auxiliary was formed in 1975 with Eileen Mighton as president. Their main function is to hold fundraising events. Max Player contributed much to minor hockey as well, having held the position of treasurer for 27 years.

Pee Wee OMHA Finalists 1991.
Back Row: Dan Elvidge, Bev Eckhardt 2nd Row: Larry Hastie, Scott Eckhardt, Geo. Ramirez, Paul Brown, Chad Brown, Wes Love, David Galbraith, Cody Schenk, Chad Zimmerman, Ken Hollister
Front Row: Ryan Hollister, Aaron Maksymchuk, Matt Tremble, Shawn Baines, Devon Hastie.

CURLING

Curling took place from 1890 until 1908 in the Gara-fraxa Street rink. It was later played in the rink on George Street East, the old cold storage building at the stone plant, and the arena on Saddler Street.

In the early 1960s interest in curling was very strong and a decision was made to build a new curling rink. Art Newell spearheaded this project along with much help from Leonard Vollett, William Wardropper, Cal McAfee, Fred Arnett, Eric Cluley, Art Neff, Vic Blythe, Don MacGillivray and Thomas Watson. Erben Schutz donated the land for the new building for $1.00, Cal McAfee supplied the material for a small percentage over cost and Orville MacDonald built the building. Twenty-five residents put $1,000 each in trust until such time as the building was completed and the Trust Company took over the mortgage. The building fund started with a $150 donation from the lawn bowling club. The rink was completed in 1962 on Kincardine Street and consisted of four sheets of ice, club rooms on two levels and a kitchen and office.

Several championship teams and champions have come out of the Durham Curling club — most notably the following:

1972 — Les Shane, Don Shane, Bob Gray and George Schenk —Ontario Federation of Secondary Schools Association (OFSSA) champions;

1977 — Eric Inthof, Terry McCannell, Don Shane and Gary Deeves, OFSSA champions;

1978 — Eric Inthof, Terry McCannell, Darryl Shane, Brad Lantz and Gary Deeves, OFSSA champions — placing 5th in All Canadian championship;

1986 — Kellie, Shannon and Aryn Tone and Rhonda Watson —Southern Ontario Junior Girls Tankard champions and All Ontario finalists;

1987 — Shannon and Aryn Tone, Eva Linder, Rhonda Watson and Lisa Barclay — CWOSSA champions and CFSSA finalists;

1988 — Shannon and Aryn Tone, Sheri Wilson and Rhonda Watson — Southern Ontario Junior Girls Tankard champions and All Ontario finalists;

1988 — Aryn Tone, Art Field, Kerri Wilson, Sheri Wilson and Heather Aitken — CWOSSA champions and OFSSA champions; and

1990 — Aryn Tone, Sheri Wilson, Kerri Wilson and Josie Wilson — Southern Ontario Winter Games finalists.

An Eight-ender scored at the Durham Curling Rink.
G. Cammidge, G. Dickson, D. Pust, Ulf Petersen.

Edna McLean, Del McGillivray, Helen Whitmore,
Betty Lennox, Catherine Breen, Lois Lang, Adele Schenk,
Helen Watson.

Durham Curling Rink.

FIGURE SKATING

In 1956 the Kinsmen Club sponsored figure skating and from 1957 to 1964 an Ice Carnival was held. After this date the Kinsmen withdrew sponsorship. In 1967 a group of mothers met and again reorganized the club under the sponsorship of the Kinsmen who paid for ice time and expenses.

In 1968 the club joined the Canadian Figure Skating Association, became an organized club with badges and skating tests, and the first Ice Carnival was held — an ongoing event since that time.

In the initial years the mothers and older skaters taught the badge skaters. While the club is now self-supporting and has professional coaches, senior amateurs and amateur coaches, monies are still received from the Kinsmen Bingos. The volunteer work of the executive and mothers deserves much credit — without their work the club could certainly not exist. In the seasons of 1976-1977 when there was no arena available, in order to keep the club going the mothers hired buses to transport the skaters, teachers and mothers to Flesherton.

By 1980 the Ice Carnival was so successful performances were held on Saturday night and Sunday afternoon and this practice has continued.

Guest skaters were: Brian Orser in 1974-1975 when he was starting his skating career, Mark Moore, Curtis Moore, Debbie Horton, Cory Watson, Patricia McNeil, Martin Smith and Michelle McDonald. Smith and McDonald were the Canadian Dance Champions in 1990.

In the beginning, club membership was about 75, but over the years it has approached 200. In 1984 Yvonne Morrison won her Gold Dance, the first such medal for a Durham skater. Others winning this award were:

1989 Cathy Champagne
1990 Patti Jo Schwehr
1991 Sheri Darroch and Leanne Morrison
1992 Kris Pegelo
1993 Kim Darroch and Nichole Schafer

In 1985 the club entered the District Blue Star Inter Club Competitions and won first overall. This was accomplished again in 1986 and from 1989-1992.

In 1987 the Junior Precision Skating Team won Gold at a Central Ontario Sectional Event. From 1991-1993 there was an Adult Precision Team and in those three years the team won one Silver and two Bronze Medals. Durham hosted the Recreation Precision Invitational Competitions in 1993-1994 with over 700 skaters participating.

LADIES SOFTBALL

There have been girls' teams for short times over the past 75 years. In the late 1940s and early 1950s a ladies' team played in a district league. Their coaches were Pete Ramage and Bob Braithwaite. Team members were:

Louise Newell	Jean Howell
Lillian (Collinson) Watson	Shirley (Picken) Torry
Del (Chapman) McGillivray	Madeline (Whitmore) Shay
Yvonne Hunter	Geneva Pratt
D. McCaslin	Janet Cross

Durham Girls Softball Team 1935
"Punk" MacDonald (Coach), Reta Glenholme, Marjorie Middleton, Jean Murdock, Jean Rowe, Kay Wallace, Clara Thompson, Marion House, Freda Ritchie, Mona MacDonald, Peter Ramage (Manager).

BASEBALL

For many years before 1940 baseball was played on any reasonably well-groomed empty field. In the 1940s actual diamonds came into being. A diamond was constructed on the agricultural grounds below the hill. In 1964 this diamond was reconstructed by the Kinsmen Club at a cost of $5,000. In 1967 the lights were installed. A second diamond was built in 1971 and approximately six years later lights were installed, funded mainly by the Recreation Committee and the Kinsmen. In 1989 a third diamond with lights was constructed. This was again funded by the Kinsmen Club and local labour was donated by volunteers.

BASEBALL — The first recorded account of baseball was in 1880. Later there was a report of meetings being held to establish a junior and senior team in the Central league. In the ensuing decades there were various town leagues and in 1956 a town league for men was established by Walter Schafer. This league ran for several years before undergoing changes in format.

In 1977 the town league folded and the Central Ontario Softball League (COSL) was formed. This formation brought to an end two decades of great rivalry among such teams as Kroelher, I.G.A., Hillcrest and Interforest. Since 1982 the Durham Waltons have dominated the league, winning the championship nine times. In 1994 the format has again changed with the COFL being a league of nine teams.

In 1968 the first annual Durham Industrial Tournament was held and in 1993 celebrated its 25th year. Gordon Reaburn has been the convenor since its inception, with Terry Whiteside and Jim Aitken assisting. Monies from these tournaments have gone toward renovations and upkeep of the ball diamonds. Donations have also been made to minor sports.

MINOR SOFTBALL — Before minor softball became organized in the late 1950s and early 1960s, games were being played around town in school yards and vacant lots. In the early 1960s Merv McIntyre, Walter Schafer and Pete Padfield, among others, organized minor ball and Gordon Reaburn has been involved for over 40 years. The first championship gained was in 1974 when the squirt team won the WOAA-AA championship. This team was coached by Gary McNab, assisted by Bev Nixon, and managed by Larry Reay. Championships won over the years are:

1974 — Juvenile — Zone 5 OASA; 1977 Pee Wee Girls — WOAA; 1977 — Pee Wee Boys — WOAA; 1986 — Midget — Major A — WOAA; and 1987 — Mites — WOAA.

In 1993 there were over 200 girls and boys in the minor ball organization.

Baseball Int. "C": OBA Finalists 1957.
Front Row: Bob Braithwaite, Coach, Gary Lawrence, Jim Nixon, John Schafer, Bill Nixon, Alf. Corbett, Jas. Sullivan, Manager
Back Row: Bob Capel, Don Corbett, Roger Goldsmith, Irvine Garvie, Elmer Lake, Stan. Middaugh, Bob Corbett
In front: Cecil Baines, Alan Nixon.

SENIOR BASEBALL (HARDBALL) — After an absence of several years, a hardball team was organized. The executive of this new organization was Wm. Knowles, Harry Kress, J. Grierson, Jim Sullivan, Mel McInnis, Fred O'Brecht, Art Newell, Norman Tucker and Lorne Chumbley. This team played in the WOAA for the next 10 years. In 1949, 1950, 1951, 1952, 1953 and 1954 the team, now called Durham Huskies, won the WOAA grand championship. Team members over these years included:

Andy Schenk	Mid Long	Don Dankert
Jim Huck	John Bell	Bill Sullivan
Bud Weiss	Howard Pollack	Lloyd Irwin
Don Corbett	Bill Russell	Bruce McInnis
Elmer Lake	Bob Capell	Brian May
Al Corbett	Jim Nixon	Bill Nixon
Terry Faulkner	Gerry Strong	Roger Goldsmith
Rob Fawcett	Art Aljoe	Erv Garvie
Charlie Fryer	Ken Jackson	

In 1955 and 1957 the Huskies played in the Bruce league and won the league championship. Players for the 1957 team were:

Bill Nixon	John Schafer	Alf Corbett
Bob Capel	Don Corbett	Roger Goldsmith
Erv Garvie	Elmer Lake	Stan Middaugh
Bob Corbett	Gary Lawrence	Jim Nixon

During the above years Peter Gagnon and James Duffield were benefactors of the team. Bob Braithwaite served as manager with help from Jim Sullivan and Pat Smith.

JUNIOR HARDBALL — In 1950 a junior team named the Cubs was formed. The team was organized by Fred O'Brecht, Jim Duffied, J. Grierson, Tom Barker, Lorne Chumbley, E. Elvidge, Hap McGirr and Dr. Burnett. The players were:

Don Corbett	Alf Corbett	B. Johnston
Roger Goldsmith	Art Aljoe	Gary Lawrence
Tom Cordick	Ken Cluchey	Don Schenk
Terry Faulkner	Dusty Miller	John Bell
Charles Jarrett	Clare Elvidge	Andy McAuliffe
R. Robbins	? Taylor	Brad Armstrong

In 1951 the Kinsmen club sponsored the team and they won the WOAA championship.

In 1954 the Midget Legionaires won the Centre Grey League, having won all their games. Bill Sullivan was the team's coach and John Boyd was the manager. The players were:

Leroy Goldsmith	Allan Boyd	Garry Miller
Bruce Mighton	Larry Scales	Bill Becker
John Schafer	Dan Shubrook	J. D. Hopkins
Jack Lawrence	Gavin Richardson	

In 1958 a junior team coached by Roger Goldsmith and made up of the following players won the Grey Bruce league championship:

Jack Lawrence	Bob Stock	John Schafer
Brad McTavish	Bill Sullivan	Allan Boyd
Larry Reay	Cam Ritchie	Larry Schafer
Bill McFadden	Les McGirr	

The first juvenile hardball championship won for Durham was in 1962 when they became OBA champions. M. McNaughton was the coach of this team and Walter Schafer was the manager. Players were as follows:

Larry Vollett	David Schafer	Ken Walker
Bob Becker	Cecil Baines	Larry Awrey
John Longworth	Bob Davis	Rick Seppela
Bill Matthews	Bev Allen	Monty Falkingham
Butch Griffin	Murray Adlam	

In 1962 the midgets won the Bruce league championship and the juveniles won the WOAA championship in 1963. A pee wee hardball team was formed in 1987 called the Eagles.

LADIES' SOFTBALL — Over the past 75 years there have been girls' teams. Some player names from the 1930s are Thompson, Bell, McDonald, Collinson, Moore, Murdock, Ritchie, Howe, Rowe, Kerr and

Durham Hardball Juvenile Champions 1962.
Only Ontario Ball Championship for Durham.
Front Row: Dave Schafer, Bill Matthews, Bob Davis, Bryan Lawrence, Ken Walker, Larry Vollett, Rick Seppala
Back Row: Mickey McNaughton, John Longworth, Cecil Baines, Murray Adlam, Butch Griffin, Grant Greenwood, Bev Allen, Walter Schafer.
Absent: Fred Allen.

Hahn. In the late 1940s and early 1950s a ladies' team coached by Pete Ramage and Bob Braithwaite played in a district league. Team members were:

Nancy (Bryans) Rawn	Lillian (Collinson) Watson
Dell (Chapman) MacGillivray	Louise Newell
Geneva Pratt	Dorothy McCaslin
Arlene (Roseborough) Lawrence	Yvonne Hunter
Jean Howell	Shirley (Picken) Torry
Madeline (Whitmore) Shay	Betty (Ledingham) Pust

SLO PITCH — In 1982 a men's slo pitch league was formed and the following year a ladies' slo pitch league was organized.

Durham Intermediate WOAA Grand Champions 1951.
Back Row: T. Watson, C. McGirr, G. Reaburn, J. Nixon, R. Goldsmith, R. Capel, I. Garute, B. Wies, B. May, W. Russell, A. Newell, H. Kress.
Front Row: R. Braithwaite, M. Gilson, M. Long, K. Long, P. Gagnon, L. Aurie, A. Corbett, J. Strong, J.B. Duffield.
Bat boys: R. McFadden, L. Aurie.

Durham Intermediate Baseball Team 1950.
Back Row: Andy Schenk, Bob Capel, Bill Russell, Brian May, Art Aljoe, Elmer (Duck) Lake, Ken Russell
Front Row: Mid Long, Bill Sullivan, Don Corbett, Mel McInnes (Coach) Bill Roberts, Bruce McInnis, Dusty "Bud" Weis.
Bat Boy: Bobby McFadden.

1989-90 Walton's.
Back Row: Dave Hopkins, Jim Case, Steven Reay, Richard Hay, Bruce Marshall, Kevin Teeter, Trevor Alexander, Carl Schafer
Front Row: Gary King, John Clark, Paul Nixon, Doug Bell, Randy Reay, Allan Vaughn.

227

Lacrosse Team circa 1930.
Back Row: Fred Murdock, Cyril Becker, Ken Wilson, Wilbur Snell, Fred Benos, Vic Noble, Gunk Wiener, Geo. Hahn
Centre Row: Pete Jamieson, Yank McKechnie, Art McClement, Cliff Moon, Biff Snyder, Punk MacDonald (Coach)
Front Row: ? Wiendorf, Norm Becker, Tim MacIlraith, Hiram Dean, Butch Reese.

LACROSSE

This sport was prominent in Durham before the 1900s and continued into the mid 1930s. It was reported that Durham was one of the earliest and most competitive lacrosse towns in Ontario. Early names mentioned in local newspapers were: Jordan, Demer, Matheson, Lavelle, Munro, Daurent, Theobald, Gagnon, Lenahan, Graham, Pickering, McDonald, Ritchie, Moore, Allan, Wendorf and Briggs. Six Lavelle brothers played lacrosse in Durham with Bill considered one of the best players in Ontario. The teams that played in the first decade of the 1900s were considered the best ever produced in Durham. Members at that time were the Lavelles, Lenahan, Cowan, Pickering and Lawler. These teams won several league and district championships.

In the mid 1920s there was a major dispute with the newly formed Ontario Amateur Lacrosse Association regarding the amateur and professional status of players. The larger towns and cities were making it impossible for smaller centres to compete with their local amateur players. It was the old win at all cost situation and the popular sport gradually died out in the small centres. In 1931 Box Lacrosse (inside) was played for

the first time in Durham, and in 1935 a team played in the new Saugeen League and lost in the league finals.

Lacrosse team Circa 1920.
Back Row: Albert "Sox" Kress, Yok Burnett, Bert McDonald, Irvie Elvidge, Duke Schutz, Clarence McGirr, Cliff Buschlen
Front Row: "Ike" Steinacher, Red Rowe, Bill Snell, Harry Kress, ? Vollett.

RIFLE ASSOCIATION

In April, 1901, a number of citizens of the Town of Durham and vicinity requested Lieutenant Torry to write to the Militia Department requesting steps to be taken for the formation of a Rifle Association. In May of that same year Lieutenant Torry of 4 Company received a copy of a Special General Order relating to the formation of Rifle Associations throughout the country. The requirements of the General Order for the formation of an association were: membership must consist of 40 or more persons and a membership fee of one dollar annually be paid by each member. The government supplied 100 rounds of free ammunition per man, and extra supplies would cost $150 per 100 lbs. Rifles used were to be Lee-Enfields, and these were supplied with certain restrictions.

No further mention appears concerning the Rifle Association in the local newspapers until August, 1903. A meeting was held in the Town Hall and steps were again taken to form an association for South Grey. Mr. J.P. Telford, an ex-Lieutenant, was the driving force behind this latest attempt, and he was voted in as the chairman. Over 100 men joined as members at this meeting. With over 80 names secured, the government grant of rifles and ammunition was increased.

In the 1910 *Durham Chronicle* the South Grey Rifle Association lists the following names as officers who were elected for the year: H.H. Miller, Honorary President; Robert Torry, Honorary Vice President; J.P. Telford, President; J.G. Hutton, M.D., Secretary; John Kelly, Treasurer; Wm. Ramage, Captain; D.B. Jamieson, Lieutenant. Committee of Management: W.F. Rolph, W.C. Vollett, P. Ramage, J. Johnston, A.D. Browning, and J.F. Grant. Range Officers: Wm. Ramage, D.B. Jamieson, J.P. Telford, J.G. Hutton and R. Torry.

Shooting matches were held between individual members of the South Grey Association and against members of other outside teams. Prizes were given for the marksmen who could shoot the highest scores within the following ranges: 300, 500 and 600 yards. The rifle range was located north of McGowan's Upper Dam in Saugeen Park. A sign regarding the site of the rifle range is situated in the first clearing above the dam of the present Saugeen Conservation Park.

This organization carried on operations in the Town of Durham for a number of years.

SAUGEEN BICYCLE CLUB

The Saugeen Bicycle Club was formed in the 1880s. The following officers were elected for the 1897 season: President, David Jamieson, M.D.; Vice President, N. W. Campbell, P.S.I.; Secretary, G.W. Jones; Captain, J.F.Evans; First Lieutenant, A. Galbraith; Second Lieutenant, J.M. Sutherland; Bugler, Jas. Carson; Consul., Jas. R. Gun. Good Roads Committee: J.A. Hunter, A.H. Jackson, J.C. Elliott, N.W. Campbell, Thos. Brown, W. Irwin and C. Ramage. Club runs were held on the first and third Thursday of each month. Bicycle races took place on occasions such as Dominion Day, etc.

The club at times became very vocal in showing its displeasure to the town officials concerning the dangerous condition of the streets in Durham — not only from the cyclist's point of view but also from the pedestrian's.

The following letter appeared in the *Durham Review*, May 13, 1897:

> "To the Editor.
> The Saugeen Bicycle Club wants to speak a piece.
> We want to ask why a bridge built only last summer should be so warped by the frost as to make it a nuisance to every one who has occasion to travel over it.
> Perhaps if some of our town fathers in the council had occasion to pass over that bridge half a dozen times a day on a bicycle with the momentum that is gained by a descent of the hill, and were nearly pitched into the river in doing so they would bestow some little attention on it. Hoping this may have some little effect in straightening things out. We remain, Yours respectfully, Saugeen Bicycle Club. We Want Good Roads."

A notice appearing in the newspaper of the day warns of a condition commonly suffered by cyclers.

The Bicycle Nose

The bicycle nose is the latest development resulting from the bicycle craze. The dust from the road accumulates in the top part of the nostril, having been driven there by the bicyclist's rapid movement through the air, and a doctor's help has to be obtained as a remedy. It must be remembered that the roads had not been paved at this time in Durham's history.

QUOITS

Another early sport in Durham was the game of Quoits. At first the game was played using flat iron rings. The object was to throw the ring over an iron peg in the ground several feet away. Many of the pioneers had a quoit bed in their backyards where they could play a game or two in the summer evenings with their neighbours or friends. As horses became more common in the pioneer village, horseshoes were substituted for the iron rings because they were so plentiful and used ones were of little or no value. Although the game is called Horseshoes today it was still called Quoits for many years.

On August 14th, 1925, a number of horseshoe enthusiasts met in the Public Library and formed the Durham Quoit Club. The officers were: J.N. Murdock, Thomas Moffat, D.C. Town, James McLachlan, C.

Elvidge, Charles Moffat, John McQueen, H. Heagill, John Moffat, John Aldred, William Bourne and Samuel Chapman. The club played in the little Town Park just south of the Town Hall. A small membership fee was charged to cover the expenses of putting in six new pitching beds and installing electric lights so that the game could be played at night.

Several townsfolk would often be seen walking to the park in the evening to watch the games, visit with their friends and neighbours, and gather all the news. It was really a time of relaxation and recreation — there were few radios and no television in those days to provide entertainment. It is not known when the Quoit club ceased to exist but it is believed to have been in operation for ten years or more.

Mayor Floyd Lawrence officially opens horseshoe pits.

There has always been some horseshoe played in Durham. During the 1980s the game's popularity was renewed and in 1991 a new Horseshoe Club was organized with a membership of 40 men and women, and with Larry Dyer as president. Mayor Floyd Lawrence officially opened the new horseshoe pits in June of that year. Many members came from the Durham Legion and the Curling Club. The club installed eight pits next to the Curling Club so that the Horseshoe Club could use the Curling Club's services and amenities, including a happy hour at the club after the game. After a heavy rain the sand in the pits is like quicksand, and a few men have sunk to their knees if they slipped into the pit.

In recent years the club's standouts have been: Wayne Sharpe, Virgil McNabb, Dan Neuman, Madge Sharpe, Doug Schwehr, and Dorothy Milligan.

BOXING

The summer of 1938 saw great activity in the field of boxing in Durham.

Durham Review, June 16, 1938: "Arrangements are being made to hold a boxing tournament in the Durham Rink early in July when Durham's now-famed boxer, Jack O'Sullivan, better known as Dick Atkin,

will participate in the main bout, a 10 round affair. Jack is the Golden Glove Heavyweight Champion of New York State at 195 pounds. Dick's father is a local blacksmith."

The July 14, 1938, issue of the same paper reports that approximately 1,100 spectators witnessed the big boxing tournament in Durham Rink which started with four preliminary bouts between local boys. Floyd Kearns and Joe Noble were opponents in four one-minute rounds; Kearns got the decision. Geo. Atkin was knocked out by Henry Carwell of Flesherton. The next bout featured Gordon Greenwood of Town and Jim Armstrong of Hutton Hill; this was an excellent bout with Gordon Greenwood declared winner. The fourth bout was between Gordon McDonald and Stan Falkingham; McDonald got the decision.

The main bout was between Jack O'Sullivan and Leroy Barrow of Detroit, a tall young Negro of six feet four inches, weighing in at 225 pounds. Barrow was a first cousin of Joe Louis, heavyweight champion of the world, and one of his sparring partners. O'Sullivan won the fight on a split decision.

The August 25th edition of the *Durham Review* reported that some 1,300 fans crowded into the Durham Rink to witness a return grudge fight between Jack O'Sullivan and Leroy Barrow. In this fight O'Sullivan was the clear winner.

The September 22nd issue of the *Review* advertised another boxing tournament in the Durham Rink for September 23rd. The main bout would be between Jack O'Sullivan and Ollie Smith of Syracuse, N.Y. (The newspapers published following this event are missing so no account is available.)

In 1939 Jack O'Sullivan fought British Empire Champion Tommy Osbourne in Toronto, knocking Osbourne out in the sixth round. Dick Atkin was also a strong swimmer, competing in several marathons; he swam Lake Erie in, at that period, record-breaking time.

Another boxer, Billy Hadfield, came to town about this time and worked with "The Durham Athletic Club." He only stayed a short while in Durham, leaving to box out of the Maple Leaf Boxing Club in Toronto; he went on to win a Canadian Boxing Championship.

Another Durham boy, Mr. Alfie Phillips, son of Bert Phillips, presented a programme of diving at the 1935 Durham Old Home Week Reunion. Alfie was born in Durham when his father was in business here some years ago. He is the champion diver in Canada and has represented Canada at the Olympic games. (*Durham Chronicle*, August 15, 1935.)

LAWN BOWLING

Joseph Brown built a hockey rink on George Street at Kincardine Street in 1908. The following year he established Lawn Bowling Greens to the south of the rink. At first there were only a few greens, but as interest and membership grew more greens were created. The greens were generally maintained by the club members, and at one time they were known as some of the best bowling greens in this part of the province. Over the years many quality tournaments were regularly held and many Durham homes today still contain prizes won.

In 1930 Mr. John Hunter of Durham's Lawn Bowling Club was a member of the Canadian team that travelled by steamship to Melbourne, Australia. Included in the competition were teams from Suva, New Zealand, Australia, and Canada.

In 1937 a bowling team of H. Cross, W.S. Hunter, W.C. Pickering, and Dr. T.H. Sneath, played against a South African team. The score was 27 to 7 for the South Africans — a team that was only defeated three times in their three-week tour of Canada.

When the curling rink was erected on Kincardine Street South, Mr. Erben Shutz donated a lot beside it for Lawn Bowling Greens. However, the membership of the Lawn Bowling Club was too small to manage the extensive cost of establishing new greens and the lot was never used. Bowling continued at the original greens until 1964.

Some names of prominent male bowlers were: Goodchild, McKechnie, Sneath, Lloyd, Ritchie, Cross, Hunter, Smith, Tucker, McGirr, Henry. Some women's names mentioned in a 1937 *Durham Chronicle* included: Mrs. H. Cross, Mrs. C.H. Darling, Mrs. S. Dargavel, Miss W. Blythe, Mrs. G. McKechnie.

**Norman and Myrtle Tucker,
winners of Fursman Trophy in Hanover 1959.**

TENNIS

The first mention of tennis in Durham was that of private courts on residents' lawns. One of the earliest of these was owned by Mr. J. Hunter in Upper Town. Eventually there were several others.

A Tennis Club was formed in 1932 and the following year the Club built hard courts on Mill Street North just west of the old Public School. Over the years many tournaments were held; and in addition the tennis club also sponsored a great number of fund-raising dances — these were a feature of the social season. The date of the club's demise is unknown, but it was still in operation in the early 1940s. During the 1950s attempts were made to reorganize the club but these were unsuccessful.

First tennis in Durham. Hunter lawn Upper Town.

In the late 1970s a new Tennis Club was formed, and the following year the Club Site Committee approached town council regarding a court site. At first the council did not approve the application but, after much deliberation and perseverance, a site was chosen and approved at the eastern end of George Street just south of the Saugeen River and McGowan's millpond. The estimated cost for the first phase of construction was $12,000, of which the Kinsmen donated $5,000, Wintario granted $6,898, and the Club raised the balance. Construction began in July, 1978, and on August 26th the courts were officially opened with a celebration at which players from the Ontario Lawn Tennis Association were present. Credit for the undertaking goes to Larry Vollett, Peter Fallis, Heather Baxter, Kris Milne, Bob Martin, Norman Marshall and Don Pust.

SOCCER CLUB

From 1880 to 1900 Durham had both senior and junior soccer clubs and they played against clubs in neighbouring communities. After 1900 soccer gradually died out in favour of lacrosse. In 1982, with the help of Manuel Ramirez, soccer was organized. At this time there was no executive and no committees had been set up. In that year there were only enough players (22) for one team and they were all different ages.

Every year the sport gained in popularity and by 1986 the club decided it was time to have a proper playing field. Up to this time they were playing at Durham District Community School, St. Peter's & St. Paul's School and at Saugeen Valley Elementary School. None of these fields were of adequate size or condition.

The estimated cost of a field was $15,000 with the club deciding to raise half. A grant was received from the Province (ONIP). Through the fund raising efforts of the club, the money was raised and in 1987 the field was readied thanks to a lot of support from Ross Taylor, the Town of Durham and the local municipalities. Many extra hours were also donated by the Soccer Club members.

In 1987 President Manuel Ramirez started the Midwestern Ontario Soccer League for adults and in that first year the Durham club placed second. By this time the minor soccer had grown to 140 registered members.

Soccer has grown from an exhibition status in this area to a point where the Durham Soccer Club has teams in a local House League, a Saugeen League from Flesherton to Kincardine and a Five County League for the older players. Unfortunately, Durham doesn't have a men's team in the Midwestern Ontario Soccer League at the present time, but a number of the seasoned Durham veterans play with the Saugeen Oldtimers.

Over the years Durham has become well known also for its very competitive girls' teams — an area that continues to grow.

SNOWMOBILING

An early snowmobile in Durham was a Model T Ford car which Dr. D.B. Jamieson had converted for winter travel. It had two skiis on the front and two drive tracks on the back. These were placed the same distance apart as sleigh runners so that they would follow the beaten track on back roads. This innovative vehicle greatly increased the speed with which the doctor could respond to calls for help in the rural areas, but it was nothing like what is known as a snowmobile today.

Snowmobiling had its beginning in Durham and area in 1969. Then, as now, the sport depended on having a reliable dealer close by for service and repairs. Skidoo, made by Bombardier, was a major player then and when the craze hit Durham, the yellow and black machines dominated the scene.

Clarence and Elsie Caldwell supplied many a first-time sledder with a machine from their dealership in Egremont Township. They soon outgrew this location and moved out to Highway 6 where they built the

facility now occupied by Kelly Joe's. Durham has its own dealer, Steve Kerr of Snowmobiles Unlimited, for sales and service, and many a stranded snowmobiler has been treated to a good dose of old fashioned hospitality here. Early snowmobilers used to head out to Homestead and Watra Resorts on Friday and Saturday nights. There were a few fun torchlight parades as well. The Trailblazers organized into a club in the early 1970s charging one dollar for membership. When the price quickly rose to two dollars, the grumbles started but the club survived this, and went on to become a well organized group contributing to the community in several ways.

One of the major areas in which the Club has worked has been in contacting landowners and securing permission for the trail system in the winter. Installing small bridges and culverts, signing and removing dead trees, and the like, has kept the members busy in both spring and fall each year.

Other Clubs organized in the area, and in 1975 several joined together to form The South Grey Snowmobile Trail Association. As an association, they purchased a SV252 Bombardier grooming machine to groom trails. Groom they did, and this first machine groomed a trail from Durham to Fergus and east to Grand Valley. Now four large groomers work the system.

The Trailblazers also sponsor Driving Training classes ensuring that youngsters have a thorough knowledge of the machine's operation. These instructors are carefully trained and issue MTO licences to successful graduates of the course. Allan Trafford is the current Trainer and has graduated all his trainees, an achievement of which the club is proud.

In 1985 it came to the attention of the Trailblazers that the Durham Ambulance Service did not have the appropriate equipment to rescue injured skiers or snowmobilers from remote locations. The club arranged for the purchase of this equipment and presented it to the Ambulance Staff.

The Trailblazers, respectful of our heritage, also contributed to the refurbishment of the Old Town Hall, a building which serves the community well. From 1979-1989 the club organized and sponsored the Snow Fest, the February Winter Carnival. Proceeds from these Carnivals were presented to the Durham Arena in the form of kitchen equipment and microphones, and to the Durham Library to assist with the purchase of a microfilm reader. Today there are 260 members including members from several southern Ontario communities who come to the Durham area to snowmobile and spend their tourist dollars. The trail system that the Association maintains from Fergus through Durham is host to hundreds of sledders every winter thus contributing to the area's winter economy.

Today Durham sledders have hundreds of miles of trail at their doorsteps and enjoy many pleasant hours in the beautiful countryside.

Snowmobile Trail Rides are often organized on behalf of different organizations — in the early years for minor hockey, and more recently for the Canadian Diabetes Association.

RINK RACES

A Durham newspaper reports that the first foot races for 1910 were held in the rink on Tuesday evenings in June, and these would draw large crowds who loved to watch the young men compete for prizes. Races consisted of the one mile open, one mile, one-half mile open, three-mile relay, and the five mile open. Boys would come to Durham from other towns and villages around the district to compete with the local lads.

The boys from Swinton Park were in excellent shape and gave the local chaps a real run for the prizes. These out-of-towners came in first in every event in which they competed. Some of the boys running for Durham were Roy Vickers, ? Henry, E. McKenna and Vernon Elvidge.

One Mile Open — R. Crawford, 1st; R.J. McMulty, 2nd; E. McKenna, 3rd. Time 4.48.

One Mile, Boys — V. Elvidge, 1st; S. Levine, 2nd. Time 5.33.

Three Mile Relay — McNulty, Crawford and Black, 1st; McKenna, Vickers and Henry, 2nd. Time 14.54.

One—half Mile Open — Crawford, 1st; McNulty, 2nd; E. McKenna, 3rd; Time 2.20.

Five Mile Open — W. Black, lst; V. Elvidge, 2nd. Time 26.53.

OTHER SPORTS

VOLLEYBALL — In 1980 Michelle Walls was a member of the Canadian Women's Volleyball team which competed in the Silent Olympics in Cologne, Germany.

TRACK AND FIELD — In 1984 Paula Robison at 16 years of age won the silver medal in the Legion Ontario javelin finals. In 1985 Paula won gold in the OFSSA javelin competition and bronze in shotput and in 1986 Paula won gold in javelin, shotput and discus competitions at CWOSSA and silver in javelin at the provincial championships. Craig Harrison in 1978 competed in the Canadian Special Olympics in Regina and won a gold medal in bowling and a bronze for the 100 yard dash.

RINGETTE — A girls' team was organized and played for several years in the 1980s.

MEN'S BROOMBALL — Durham had a team in the late 1960s and the early 1970s.

LADIES' BROOMBALL — In 1984-85 Durham had a team and Dean Atchison was named coach of the year and Darlene Coleman was named rookie of the year.

BADMINTON — A club operated for a short time in the mid 1950s.

LANE BOWLING — In 1962 a bowling alley was built on the south east corner of Bruce and Chester streets but because of a lack of bowlers the building was sold to the Royal Canadian Legion.

AWARDS — The Mike Weichel Award was presented annually by the WOAA to the person in the area deemed by the WOAA to be the greatest contributor to sports. In 1963 Anna Greenwood won this award; in 1967 Walter Schafer won, and in 1980 Larry Reay won.

LADIES' HIGH SCHOOL HOCKEY — In the 1920s and 1930s girls' hockey teams were organized.

HOCKEY — An industrial league was organized in 1972. The first industrial league tournament was held in 1978. In 1982 an old timers team was organized for players 35 and over.

SOFTBALL — In 1994 Michael Nixon was honoured by the Ontario Minor Softball Association for pitching a perfect game while playing for Hanover PeeWee B's in 1993. Ryan Hollister has been on five Ontario minor softball championship teams while playing with teams from Harriston and Owen Sound.

NAMES OF NOTE IN SPORTS

PETER GAGNON

Peter Gagnon, together with Frank Irwin, organized hockey in Durham, played lacrosse and financially supported all areas of sports.

ROSS TAYLOR

Ross Taylor served on the executive of minor hockey for many years, on the executive of Durham Huskies for 27 years and was manager of the Huskies for six years. He was a member of the Kinsmen club for 38 years with 35 years of perfect attendance. He spends countless hours for the betterment of all sports, working through the Kinsmen club and in his personal time. He is always involved in community work in Durham and for Durham.

BOB BRAITHWAITE

Bob Braithwaite managed the Huskie Sr. baseball team for nine years, managed the Huskie hockey team from 1947-1961 and was a club executive member from 1965-1975. He served on the executive of minor hockey for 16 years and coached for four years. He was a charter member of the Kinsmen club with 26 years perfect attendance. Working through the Kinsmen club and in his personal time, he has spent many hours on the promotion of sports in Durham.

IRVING ELVIDGE

Irving, or Irvie as he was called, apparently did not learn to skate until the age of 13 but quickly became an expert. It is known that when he wasn't in the local rink he was practicing on the river and ponds.

In the 1920s Irvie played on a Junior, Intermediate and Senior Team, all in the same year. The length of the season depended on ice and weather conditions and often he played every week night.

In 1936 he was a member of the Durham OHA Intermediate "B" Championship team.

In 1938 he played with the Owen Sound Trappers and this team was an OHA Intermediate "A" finalist.

In the late 1930s Irvie retired from playing hockey but kept returning to the ice as late as the 1947-1948 season to assist teams which were short of players and talent. From 1948-1960 he was coach of the then called Durham Huskies.

In 1962 Irvie was awarded the OHA's highest honour. At a presentation in the Royal York Hotel in Toronto he was given a gold hockey stick lapel pin. He always wore this pin on his suit jacket. While involved with the Huskies he played on one OHA Championship team, and coached two OHA Champions and three WOAA Championships. Irvie also at one time played lacrosse and was an avid fisherman. After retiring from coaching he continued to help teams with his expertise and many sporting teams were recipients of his financial assistance.

WALTER SCHAFER

Walter Schafer's participation in sports began in the 1940s and continued over 40 years. He was involved with minor hockey, minor hardball and softball and the Huskies executive. He was a member of the Recreation Committee and in 1956 started the Softball Town League.

In 1967 he was honoured by the WOAA when he received the Mike Weichel Award presented annually by the WOAA to the person in the area whose contribution is greatest in sports.

GORD REABURN

Gord Reaburn has been a member of the Recreation Committee for many years, was associated with minor ball for 40 years and with the Town League softball and Industrial Tournament for 25 years.

JIM NIXON

As a young boy Jim played minor hockey in Owen Sound and at the age of 13 was talented enough to play Junior "B" with the Owen Sound Greys. Later, he played on occasion with the Owen Sound Mercurys while still a junior.

In 1950 Jim came to Durham to play with the Huskies and his association with this team lasted almost 30 years. During that period Jim either played on, or coached, six OHA championship teams. In the 1950s Jim played on the Huskies hardball team. During this time the team won five WOAA Championships, two Bruce League Championships and three OBA Finalists.

In later years Jim has coached the Hanover Barons of the Junior "C" League. Under his leadership this team won one Ontario Championship and were three time finalists.

Jim also played several years in the town softball league and in old-timers hockey. He is an excellent golfer. Jim was associated with seven Ontario championships and nine finalists.

BEV NIXON

Bev was an umpire for 42 years and a referee for 30 years. Bev started umpiring minor baseball in Owen Sound at the age of 12. Over the years he has umpired minor baseball, industrial leagues, inter-city fastball, senior fastball and baseball for the WOAA, OBA and COSL.

Bev was invited one year to officiate at the Canadian championships in Thunder Bay. He continued to attend umpiring school and has also been an instructor. Bev was president of the Durham Umpiring Association and area umpire-in-chief until 1991.

When Bev Nixon came to Durham to play hockey, he decided that refereeing was his game rather than playing. He refereed minor hockey initially, kept upgrading his "cards" and eventually worked OHA junior and senior, with a couple of NHL tryouts. In the mid '80s he decided that hockey's fast pace was more than he could handle, and he retired.

He has been president of the WOAA and Minor Hockey. To say Bev has been colorful in his umpiring career would probably be an understatement. Who else would toss five of his brothers off a ball diamond in one game?

Lawn Bowling Tournament 1950s.
Left: **Raymond McGirr;** *Right:* **Art Newell.**

Ententainment

The first record on any organized entertainment in what is now Durham is found in Belden's *1880 Illustrated Atlas of Grey County.* Referring to Archibald Hunter's log British Hotel, it says: "The entertainment here offered was of course of a rather primitive character." Many of the early societies provided entertainment for the pioneers. The Orange Lodge 1855, St. Andrew's Society 1856, Agriculture Society 1858, churches and school, all made their contribution in this area. There was also dancing to the music of one or two violins. The Mechanics Institute, organized in 1858, provided book reviews and debates

Around 1860 a man by the name of Adam Cranston moved to the Durham area. When he became ill, and went blind as a result of his illness, because he had a wife and family to support he turned to his greatest asset, an extensive training in vocal music. For many years he conducted music classes and gave private voice lessons and his contribution to the community added greatly to its enrichment. Later, he moved his family to the United States.

Over the years there were other teachers of vocal music in Durham, and as a result there always seemed to be a group of excellent singers available for solo

Masonic Ball Dance Card 1876.

for its members and occasionally for the public. One such debate was "Resolved that Love carries a man to greater extremes than Ambition." The affirmative was upheld by Mr. D. Jackson and the negative was taken by Mr. H. Rowswell. In the March 23, 1866 *Durham Standard* is an advertisement for a "zographicon of Bunyon's Pilgrim's Progress and nearly one hundred other pictures to be shown at the Orange Hall, admission 15 cents and 10 cents." At this time the Anglican Church was canvassing for money to replace the church bell. The owner of the exhibit donated half of his profit to the church to assist in paying for the bell.

Music played an important role as entertainment for the pioneer community, especially vocal music.

work or choral singing.

The first Durham Choral Society was formed in 1901 by Mrs. W.L. Newton, wife of the Baptist minister. She was a very gifted organist and choir director. Her community choir consisted of over 50 voices; the choir presented two or three concerts a year in the Town Hall with the proceeds going to some worthy cause, usually the Durham library. While in Durham she also gave an organ recital of classical music which was well received. After the Newtons left town in 1910 there was a void in the direction of the choir. In 1914 Mr. J. Arthur Cook of Mount Forest took over as choir director and again concerts were held in the Town Hall. This was during World War I so the songs were patriotic and the concert proceeds went to humanitarian relief. Three soloists who sang with this group were Miss Zeta Black, Miss Margaret Hunter and Mrs. A.W.H. Lauder.

Durham Carnegie Library.
Old Mechanics Institute behind at right.

Bathing beauties in their bathing suits in the Saugeen River.

Christmas Concert 1895.
Mary Sharpe, Bird Parker, May Saunders, Grace Barclay, Hilda Parker, Etta Fox, Inno Davidson, Flo Limin, Marie Douglas, ?, ?, Jessie Laidlaw, Clara Aljoe, Essel Laidlaw, Bertha Sparling, Ada Limin, Emma Harvey, Santa Claus John Livingston.

Nautical Knot 1914-1918 at the Town Hall.
Back Row: Mrs. J.H. Harding, Frances Kelly, Edna Limin, ?, Mrs. David McAuliffe, Stella McAuliffe, Georgina Lawson, Nan Gun, ?, Alice Ramage.
Second Row: Peter Ramage, Lily Walker, Jack Stedman, Mrs. A.W.H. Lauder, Miss Black, J.H. Harding, Vaddi Caldwell, ? McAuliffe, Inno Davidson, ? McAuliffe, Earl McDonald.
Front Row: Reta Irwin, ?, Margaret Ewen, ? McAuliffe, Frankie Burnett, Martin Lauder, Jean Morlock, ? McAuliffe, Flora Belle Nichol.

Entertainment at the Fall Fair.

Knox Church Social Circa 1908.
Back Row: Allie (McGowan) McCracken, Margaret Edge, Mrs. W.H. Smith, Susie (McKinnon) Burgess, Jane (Kelsey) Gloin
Front Row: Marion Calder, Jean (McGowan) Breen, Berta (Milne) Barlow, Mary McKechnie.

MECHANICS INSTITUTE/ DURHAM PUBLIC LIBRARY

Mechanics Institutes were organized to provide their members with lectures, classes, reading rooms and a lending library. The first mention of the Durham Mechanics Institute was a report in the February 17th, 1860 edition of the Durham Standard of the second annual meeting of the Durham Mechanics Institute held in the old schoolhouse. Therefore, it was organized very early in 1858, or late in 1857. The officers for 1860 were: John Miller, President; Peter Watson, 1st Vice President; James Brown, 2nd Vice President; J.W. McDonald, Librarian; James Brown, Secretary-Treasurer. The directors were: Thomas Jones, Thomas Gray, William Boyle, S.L.M. Luke, James Jones, Donald McKenzie, James Edge.

It was moved by G. Jackson and seconded by T. Gray that subscribers pay the dollar per annum membership dues in advance and that shareholders using the library shall pay 25 cents per annum in advance, that the secretary-treasurer be authorized to purchase books up to the value of $50 at six months credit, that the books would be selected by the president and directors and also that the treasurer pay the librarian the rate of 25 cents per attendance at the library.

The March 23, 1860 edition of the same paper reports that a large collection of books by the most popular authors of the day had been added to the library of the Mechanics Institute. In addition, Messrs. Watson, Legate and McDonnell had all severally given interesting and instructive lectures and others were expected to follow.

The government gave the Mechanics Institutes a grant to encourage the development of work being carried on by the Institutes, but in 1859 the grant was discontinued, and it was possibly in 1863 that this organization ceased to exist due to a lack of funds. By 1867 there was only a handful of Mechanics Institutes still operating in Ontario and the grants were reinstated. The early Mechanics Institute (library) was in Upper Town.

At the urging of Dr. James Gun, a public meeting was called on November 4th, 1873, in the Durham council room for the purpose of reorganizing the Durham Mechanics Institute. Those in attendance agreed that a Mechanics Institute and Library association should be reorganized in Durham consisting of an unlimited number of subscribers each purchasing one share to the value of one dollar, and that a committee, consisting of Messrs. Wm. Jackson, J.H. Hunter, F. McRae, H.J. Middaugh, A. Butters and Dr. James Gun, take names and subscriptions of shareholders and report to a meeting of subscribers to be held a week later. At this subsequent meeting it was found that 101 subscribers had purchased shares. The Board of Directors appointed was: President, George Jackson; 1st Vice President, Rev. Wm. Park; 2nd Vice President, J.H. Hunter; Treasurer, Walter Hastie; Secretary, Dr. James Gun; Committee: D.C. McDonell, John Jack, Thomas Smith, W.R. Rombough, James Jones and John Franks.

The first home of the Mechanics Institute is not known, but when the new Town Hall building was completed in 1875, it was moved into the council chambers where it remained until 1888. In that year David Jackson, Jr., mayor of the Town of Durham, erected a building for a library on land which he owned just north of the Presbyterian Church. Some years later he deeded the building and land to the town. The Carnegie Library was built on the east side of this lot in front of the old library. The Mechanics Institute purchased the lot north of the library.

Part of the Mechanics Institute's mandate was to provide adult education courses free to its members, and any person who was not a member could attend the classes by paying a yearly fee of 50 cents. The

Institute hired a competent teacher and night classes ran for several weeks during the winter. It is interesting to note that English Grammar, English Composition and Arithmetic were always offered and it appears that these courses were very popular. It is likely the men (no ladies) taking them had little or no opportunity to obtain a formal education during their early years when they should have been in school but were unable to attend. Other subjects were also offered. In 1881 the Mechanics Institute held adult night classes in English Grammar, English Composition, Arithmetic, Mensuration, Penmanship, Bookkeeping, Principles of Mechanics and Freehand Drawing.

In 1893 some of the daily publications made available to the public in the Reading Room were The Globe, The Empire and the London Times. In 1895 the name Mechanics Institute was changed to Durham Public Library.

Over the years many organizations in town presented concerts in support of the Mechanics Institute or Library. Two of these were the Durham Drama Club and the Durham Choral Club which both presented several concerts. The Mechanics Institute also held debates, skits and other entertainment to which

Pocahontas Concert in Durham 1924.
Front row, left to right: Mary Pickering, Jimmy Henderson, Jean Grant, Jack Lauder, Marjorie Noble, Gordon Grant, Elsie Hunter, Norman McIntyre, Louise Jamieson.
Second row, left to right: Clarence Robinson, Peter Ramage, Martin Lauder, Miss Margaret Hunter, organist and director, Alice Ramage, Winnie Blyth, Allie McGowan, Sadie McDonald, Florence Kerr, Esther McComb, Beulah Stonehouse, Jessie Bell.
Third row: left to right: Arthur Derby, Harold McKechnie, George Bell, Vaddie Caldwell, Mrs. A.W.H. Lauder, Thomas Bell, Mrs. J.H. Harding, Mrs. Moore McFadden, Mrs. Guy Kearney, Mrs. Rev. W.H. Smith, Mrs. D.B. Jamieson, Wm. (Bill) Vollett, John D. McKechnie, Leonard McComb.
Back row, left to right: J.H. Harding, Stewart MacArthur, Moore McFadden, John McGirr and ?.
Mrs. Bert Stonehouse should be in the group somewhere, since she was a member of the choir for many years.

the public was invited. The most energetic and grandiose of these productions was The Temple of Fame which was produced by the young people in Durham, mostly ladies. It was presented for three nights in the Town Hall and even the standing room was sold out. Admission was 25 cents.

The *Durham Chronicle* edition of April 1, 1897 gives in part the following account:

"The scenic appearance of the stage, and its tasty arrangement of everything connected with it, is the most conclusive evidence of the aesthetic character for which our young people are noted far and wide.

The costumes, one and all, were made right here in Durham, and each in itself was a perfect poem of artistic neatness.

The plan of the play may be outlined as follows: A crown is to be given away by a goddess, who sends forth a summons to all to present their claims. Queens, princesses, artists, heroines, patriots, etc., etc., respond to the call. The goddess listens patiently to each one's plea and at the close she places the crown on the head of The Mother, whose object in life is to "live for those who love her" in the belief that "the hand that rocks the cradle rules the world." We must say in conclusion, that we feel our inability to do justice to this highly intellectual, classical and historical entertainment.

THE TEMPLE OF FAME — CAST OF CHARACTERS

Albani — Miss N. Meredith
Barbara Frietchie — Miss B. MacKenzie
Bridget O'Flannigan — Miss N. Parker
Canada — Miss Aggie Bull
Chorus — Misses MacGregor, A. Hughes, Crawford, Anderson, Blackburn, Hunter, Parker, Munro and J. Laidlaw
Cleopatra — Miss F. Meredith
Elizabeth of England — Miss E. McKenzie
Empress Josephine — Miss Arrowsmith
Flora McDonald — Miss Alice (Allie) McRae
Florence Nightingale — Miss L. MacKenzie
Florence Nightingale Guards — Messrs Castell and Evans
Francis Willard — Miss M. Cameron
Goddess — Mrs. ? Holt
Goddess Guards — Messrs. Finlay Graham and Douglas Sutherland
Grace Darling — Miss McCracken
Guards for Joan of Arc — Wm. Harris, Thos. Carson
Harriet Hosmer — Miss Mary Large
Helen of Troy — Mrs. Jas. Gun
Heralds — W. Lauder and Jones
Hypatia — Miss G. Pomeroy
Ike — Lauder Buchan
Isabella of Spain — Miss Carson
Jephtha's daughter — Miss H. Anderson
Joan of Arc — Miss M. Gun

Josiah Allen's wife — Miss Aggie McRae
Mariam — Miss Maggie Harris
Mariam's maidens — Misses Davidson, Kress, Limin, Grant and Maggie and Mamie Hunter
Martha Washington — Miss M. Bull
Mary Queen of Scots — Miss L. Anderson
Mrs. Mucklebackit — Mrs. Walter Buchan — A Scotch fish woman
Mrs. Partington — Miss Stewart
Mother — Mrs. Rev. Kitching
Mother Goose — Miss M. Elvidge
Orchestra — Messrs. Parker, W. Vair, M. Sutherland, R. Meredith and Arthur Parker
Pages — Masters Brad Jamieson and Bertie Mockler
Pocohontas — Miss Collier
Portia — Miss Harris
Ruth, a Bible Character — Miss M. Wallace
Sappho — Miss McIntyre
Sister of Charity — Miss Vollet
Tabitha Primrose — Miss Annie McKenzie
Thomas Jefferson — G. Wright
Tirzah Ann — Miss G. McRae
20th Century Girl — Miss Nellie Swallow
Xantippe Wife of Socrates — Miss E. Blackburn"

In 1898 photographer Browne of the Elite Studios in Durham made a donation to the library of a large framed picture of all those who had taken part in the Temple of Fame. This picture was rescued from the library basement a few years ago, was framed by Susan and David's of Durham and is now hanging upstairs in the library.

In 1903, encouraged by a $100 grant to the Library from the Town Council, the library directors rented a new store downtown, built by J.M. Hunter, and moved most of the Public Library books and all of the magazines and daily newspapers, into the new quarters. Librarian C. Elvidge, assisted by carpenter, E. Kress, had shelves in position and books put in place. It was thought that this move would increase the library membership, but the increase did not materialize, and the library moved back to the original building a few months later.

In 1911 the taxpayers voted to establish a Carnegie Free Library in Durham which would be known as Durham Free Library. A cheque for $8,000 was received from the Andrew Carnegie Foundation to pay for the construcction of a new library building. Trustees appointed to oversee the construction of the new edifice were: Reverend Dr. Wm. Farquharson, John Kelly, John Graham, Chas. Ramage, Thos. Allan, Wm. Irwin and Mayor Black. The site chosen was on Garafraxa Street in front of the old library. Mr. Hugh McDonald was awarded the contract for the building. On November 11, 1911, the cornerstone was laid by Dr. D. Jamieson and the building was completed in July, 1912. The brickwork was done by Mr. Hugh McDonald, the carpentry by Mr. George Kress and the painting by Mr. B.H. Willis.

Second production of the Temple of Fame in the rink.

The old library was used as an overflow classroom from 1912 to 1916. It was later utilized as a storage and service depot for the Public Utilities Commission and was demolished circa 1970.

The library basement has had many varied uses. During World War II it was an overflow classroom, and in 1968 and 1969 it housed the kindergarten class of the Saugeen Valley Elementary School. The basement has been a voting station, courtroom, lecture hall, and many local organizations have used it for meetings, even church services. From 1978 to 1991 the Durham Art Gallery was located there. When the Art Gallery moved out, the Children's and Young Adults' department was moved to the lower floor.

Librarians:
J.W. McDonald
Alex Robertson (10 years)
H.H. Miller
? Winterbourne
A.H. Jackson
Mrs. ? McRae
Wm. Gorsline
A. Davidson
C.C. Elvidge (34 years)
Mrs. S.F. Dargavel
Miss Margaret McGirr (22 years)
Mrs. Wm. Sullivan
Mrs. Phyllis Dickson
Mrs. Lori Roberts
Mrs. Dorothy Smith (15 years)
Mrs. Marlaine Elvidge
Present Librarian Assistants:
Janet Gardiner
Sharon Davis

DURHAM LITERARY ASSOCIATION

The Durham Literary Association was formed in 1867 with William Jackson as President. A constitution was drafted by Mr. ? McCabe, Rev. Wm. Park, and Mr. A. Cochrane, and approved by the Association. The group soon became known as the Durham Literary and Mutual Improvement Association. Meetings were held weekly for the members and once a month the public was invited to attend.

The meetings consisted of a reading, essay or book review, vocal and instrumental music, and, of course, a debate. The debates covered a wide range of subjects such as "Whether is Possession or Pursuit of an Object — the most conducive to happiness," E. Orchard taking the affirmative, and C. Privat the negative. After January, 1883, this organization became known as Durham Literary and Debating Society.

In 1899 the young men of Durham once again formed a Young Men's Society for Literacy with Mr. N.W. Campbell as Chairman.

BRASS BAND — 31st BATTALION/CITIZENS

Early newspaper articles seem to suggest that a brass band was started as early as the year 1860. Mention is also made that the band in Durham was reorganized in 1870. No information appears again until the year 1881.

In that year a notice appeared in the *Grey Review* announcing a meeting to take place at McAlister's Hotel to organize a Brass Band. The band, however, was not officially formed until 1885. It was known as the 31st Battalion Band. For many years the band led the Grey Battalion as it left for camp and on other official occasions. The band won many prizes at tournaments around the Province and played at the Toronto Exhibition. The band held Grand Carnivals at the rink in town. These were in the form of masquerade parties, and many prizes were given for the best costumes and the fastest skaters. Prizes were handed out by Mayor Wm. Calder, H.H. Mockler and F. Search. Some of the prize winners were as follows: Pearl Warner, Fred Glass and Edith Allan. Boys' race winners under 14 years of age were Mac Saunders and Foster Saunders.

The first band leader was Professor ? Konold; some later leaders were Richard Parker, James Oldfield, Fred Peel, J. Hawthorne, Bill Johnston, George Wright and H.D. McIntyre.

Members of the first band were: J.P. Telford, J.R. Gun, W. Vair, R.W. Meredith, Arthur Jackson, A. Vollett, Jack Hunter, R. Macfarlane, John Smith, J. Kress, Tom Brown, E. Elvidge, Arch. Robertson, Joe Brown, Bob Lawson and Nat Horn.

A resolution by the officers of the 31st Battalion Band was passed in February, 1899, and the Battalion Band was moved to Owen Sound. The Regimental grant went with it and there was then concern that the Town of Durham would be left without any band of its own, but after a period of reorganization, a new Citizens Band was formed.

The Town of Durham supported this band by contributing the sum of $100 in 1911. Some of the members of this group were as follows:

Sandy McIntyre	Bob Colville
A. Whelan	Bob Henderson
Tom Carson	George Yiirs (Bandmaster)
Frank Bunce	W. Lake
Bert Saunders	Pete Ramage
Frank Irwin	R. Whitmore
G.R. Padfield	N. Ritchie

In 1912 the Durham Furniture Company took over the Citizens Band and pledged a grant of $500 annually for a leader, provided the Town Council continue its annual grant of $300 to the band. The band was run by a committee consisting of town citizens and representatives from the furniture company. In donating the annual grant of $500, the company wanted the band to be run strictly on a business-like basis. The furniture company did not expect any monetary return but hoped that by helping to finance it they would in turn be improving the quality of life in Durham for their own employees and the townsfolk in general. There were approximately 20 band members at this time; the Bandmaster was Mr. M. Wilson.

The band was still going strong in 1935, but World War II decimated its ranks, and it ceased to operate. Some of its members and instruments eventually found their way into the Grey and Simcoe Regimental Band.

In 1952 Mr. John Jarratt organized a Town Band which included both boys and girls. Rhys Padfield, Sr., gave $20 towards the repair of one of the instruments which the town still had on hand; Rhys had played for

31st Regimental Band 1910 Durham.
Front Row: Alex T. McComb, Nat (Kelly) Horn, Geo. Stinson, A. McClocklin, ? , Ray McCracken, Earl McDonald, E. Wright, John McGirr, W.R. McGowan.
Back Row: Chas. Rantz, Peter Ramage, John McDonald, Caldwell Marshall, Geo. Wright (bandmaster), C. Cowan, Herb Wright.

the Durham Town Band years before. Instruments owned by the town were valued at $1,000. Frankie Banks and Harry Mann loaned three cornets and one alto horn to the group. The band President was Bill McLeish; Vice president, Elizabeth Schaefer; Secretary, Marilyn Darroch; Treasurer, Andy McAuliffe; and Press Correspondent, Alan McGillivray.

Some of the younger members of the group, and the instruments which they played, were as follows: Rhys Padfield and John Darling — alto horn; John Schaefer — clarinet; Eileen Wilder, Bruce Catton, Shirley Watt and James Vasey — clarinets; Bill McLeish — baritone horn; Bill Neff — trombone; Charles Coutts — bass horn; and Allan MacGillivray on drums.

GRAND CONCERT !

In the Town Hall, Durham, on

Thursday Evening, May 4, 1905
Under Auspices of the Durham Fire Dept.

~PROGRAMME~
Part I.

1. Chairman's Address ....Dr. Hutton
2. Piano Solo.... ....
3. Solo—"In May Time" (Dudley Buck).................Dr. Brown
4. SCENE FROM "HAMLET"—A Hall in the Castle.
   Claudius, King of Denmark—Mr. Thos. McClocklin.
   Gertrude, Queen of Denmark—Mr. E. C. McClocklin.
   Polonius, Lord Chamberlain—Mr. E. D. McClocklin.
   Hamlet, Son of the late and Nephew of present King—Mr H H Mockler
5. Solo—"When the Heart is Young".................Miss King
6. Song—Selected................Master Harry Roos, the boy singer
7. Solo—Selected.... ....Miss B. Crawford
8. Recitation, From "The School for Scandal."...........Miss Koenig
9. Solo, "That is Love".... ....Mr. J. S. Drysdale
0. SCENE FROM RICHARD III,—London ; A Street ; Meeting of the Brothers
   Clarence on his way to the Tower
   Richard, Duke of Gloster—Mr. H. H. Mockler.
   George, Duke of Clarence—Mr. E. D. McClocklin.
   Guard (over the Duke of Clarence)—Mr. E. C. McClocklin.
   Lord Hastings(who has just been released from the tower)—Mr T.Mc
   [Clocklin

Part II.

Violin Solo....................................Master Edward Roos
Solo—"The Flight of Ages"...........................Miss Jean Brown
Solo—"Island of Dreams" (Adams)...................Dr. Brown
SCENE FROM RICHARD III.—The Tower ; Clarence's Dream ; The Murder
   George, Duke of Clarence—Mr. E. D. McClocklin.
   Sir Robert Brakenbury (Lieut. of the Tower)—Mr. H. H. Mockler.
   1st Murderer—Mr. Thos. McClocklin.
   2nd Murderer—Mr. H. H. Mockler.
Solo—Selected.... ....Miss G. King
Song....................................Master Harry Roos
Recitation—Selected...................................Miss Koenig
Solo—"The Scottish Emigrants' Farewell"...........Mr. J. S. Drysdale
SCENE FROM J SHERIDAN KNOWLES' COMEDY—The Love Chase.......
   Time—The Gainsborough Period
   Sir Wm. Fondlove (a choleric old Baronet)—Mr. E. D. McClocklin.
   Trueworth, his Friend (who is used to Sir William's eccentricities)—
   [Mr. H. H. Mockler

Doors open at 7.30, Concert to begin at 8 o'clock, sharp.
ADMISSION, 25c.   —   —   RESERVED SEATS, 35c.

Concert for Fire Department.

CIVIC HOLIDAY
-- AND --
FIREMENS' BENEFIT
PICNIC !

The Annual Picnic under the auspices of the Citizens of Durham
for the benefit of the
~ DURHAM FIRE BRIGADE ~
WILL BE HELD IN THE
Agricultural Grounds, Durham,
— ON —
Thursday, Aug. 10th,
— 1899. —

Prizes will be given as follows:
CALITHUMPIANS:
Most Original Outfit, 1st, 75c., 2nd, 50c. | Best Comic Character, 1st, 75c. 2nd, 50c.

RACES:

Bicycle Race, Boys under 16 years : 1st, Valuable Set Bicycle Fittings, 2nd, Pr. Cuff Buttons, value, $1 00	Egg and Spoon Race : 1st, Book, value .. .. $1 00 2nd, Silver Match Holder.
Bicycle Race, Open : 1st, Pr. Gent's Kid Gloves, 1 00 2nd, Christy Stiff Hat, 75	Goat Race : Pair Gloves, ... 1 00
Bicycle Race, Girls, 1st, Gold Brooch, ... 1 50 2nd, Fancy Lady's Belt & Tie, 1 00	Sack Race : 1st, Pair Kid Gloves, ... 1 00 2nd, Silver Pepper Duster.
Foot Race, 200 yards, Men : 1st, Pr. Gent's Ev'g Slippers, 1 00 2nd, Durham Review one yr., 1 00	Dog Race : 1st, Whip, 75c. 2nd, Cash, 50
Foot Race, 100 yards, Men : 1st, Smoking Set, ... 1 00 2nd, Chronicle one year. 1 00	Catching the Jingler, Cash, ... 50 Dancing :—Best Lady Dancer, beautiful Lamp Shade and Butter Dish.

Cricket Match—Palmerston vs. Durham.   Wickets pitched
at 2 P. M.

Hose Reel Race :   Prize, Gold Medal valued at $10.00.
Lacrosse Match.—An exciting Lacrosse Match will be played
on the Grounds..

Evening Concert in the Town Hall at 8 p. m.

Admission to Grounds, including Refreshments, 25 cents.
Ladies and Children 15 cents.

"GOD SAVE THE QUEEN."
DURHAM. AUG. 5TH, 1899.   CHRONICLE PRINT.

Firemen's Picnic.

THE DURHAM DRAMATIC CLUB

PRESENT

Shakespeare's Famous Comedy

"The Merchant ? ? of Venice"

(AS PRODUCED BY EDWIN BOOTH.)

"And at the last, ten thousand crowns
They offered him to save:
Gernutus said, 'I will no gold,
My forfeit I will have.'"

—The Ballad of Gernutus.

CAST OF CHARACTERS

The Duke of Venice..................Mr. R. McCracken
Antonio, the Merchant of Venice.......Mr. T. H. McClocklin
Bassanio, friend to Antonio.........Mr. E. D. McClocklin
Gratiano \
Salarino | Venetian Gentlemen,..........Mr. J. F. Grant
Solanio | Friends to Antonio and Bassanio. ....Mr. R. Hughes
Salerio /   {Mr. T. W. Maylor
Lorenzo in love with Jessica.........Mr. Jas. McClocklin
Shylock, a rich Jew..................Mr. H. H. Mockler
Tubal, a Jew, his friend.............
Launcelot Gobbo, the clown, servant to Shylock...........Mr. L. Buchan
Old Gobbo, his father................
Leonardo, Page to Bassanio.........Master Alfred McClocklin
Balthazer, Page to Portia ....Master Albert McClocklin
Portia, a rich Heiress...............Miss E. A. Mockler
Nerissa, her friend and Companion....Miss M. A. Munro
Jessica, daughter of Shylock.........Miss Jessie Laidlaw
Magnificoes of Venice, etc...........................

SCENE—Partly in Venice, and partly at Portia's villa, named Belmont, on the adjacent main-land.

PERIOD—The sixteenth century.

TIME OF ACTION—A little more than three months.

"The hunted fox, the tortured wild-cat, loves its young—the despised and persecuted race of Abraham love their children. . . . When the day comes, and I ask my own, then what hear I but dammed Jew, and the curse of Egypt on your tribe."—Scott.

SYNOPSIS

ACT I—SCENE 1—Venice, the Rialto.
SCENE 2—Belmont, a room in Portia's House.
SCENE 3—Venice, the Rialto.

ACT II—SCENE 1—Venice, a street in front of Shylock's house.
SCENE 2—The Rialto.
SCENE 3—Venice, a street in front of Shylock's house.

ACT III—The Rialto.

ACT IV—Belmont, a room in Portia's house.

ACT V—Venice, a Court of Justice.

Note.—The play ends with the Court Scene in accordance with Booth's version, the subsequent scene not being practical in the original.

Merchant of Venice.

DRAMATIC CLUB

In 1878 the Durham Dramatic Club was formed under the direction of Mr. J. Lewis. Very little is known about Mr. Lewis' background except that he had considerable acting and directing experience. He was determined to develop a group in Durham which would share his enthusiasm for this art form and he was fondly known around town as Professor Lewis.

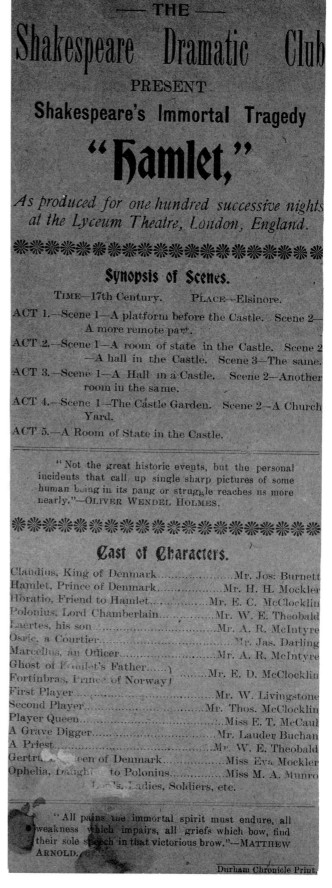

—— THE ——

Shakespeare Dramatic Club

PRESENT

Shakespeare's Immortal Tragedy

"Hamlet,"

As produced for one hundred successive nights at the Lyceum Theatre, London, England.

Synopsis of Scenes.

Time—17th Century.   Place—Elsinore.

ACT 1.—Scene 1—A platform before the Castle.   Scene 2—A more remote part.

ACT 2.—Scene 1—A room of state in the Castle.   Scene 2—A hall in the Castle.   Scene 3—The same.

ACT 3.—Scene 1—A Hall in a Castle.   Scene 2—Another room in the same.

ACT 4.—Scene 1—The Castle Garden.   Scene 2—A Church Yard.

ACT 5.—A Room of State in the Castle.

"Not the great historic events, but the personal incidents that call up single sharp pictures of some human being in its pang or struggle reaches us more nearly."—Oliver Wendel Holmes.

Cast of Characters.

Claudius, King of Denmark...........Mr. Jos. Burnett
Hamlet, Prince of Denmark...........Mr. H. H. Mockler
Horatio, Friend to Hamlet...........Mr. E. C. McClocklin
Polonius, Lord Chamberlain..........Mr. W. E. Theobald
Laertes, his son...................Mr. A. R. McIntyre
Osric, a Courtier...................Mr. Jas. Darling
Marcellus, an Officer...............Mr. A. R. McIntyre
Ghost of Hamlet's Father......\
Fortinbras, Prince of Norway/......{Mr. E. D. McClocklin
First Player.......................Mr. W. Livingstone
Second Player......................Mr. Thos. McClocklin
Player Queen.......................Miss E. T. McCaul
A Grave Digger.....................Mr. Lauder Buchan
A Priest...........................Mr. W. E. Theobald
Gertrude, Queen of Denmark..........Miss Eva Mockler
Ophelia, daughter to Polonius.......Miss M. A. Munro
Lords, Ladies, Soldiers, etc.

"All pains the immortal spirit must endure, all weakness which impairs, all griefs which bow, find their sole speech in that victorious brow."—Matthew Arnold.

Durham Chronicle Print.

Hamlet.

TOWN HALL, DURHAM

Under the auspices of the Public Library the Durham Dramatic Club will present Oliver Goldsmith's most clever comedy

"She Stoops to Conquer"

Originally produced at "Covent Garden" Mar. 15, 1773, and ever since holding first place among comedies of the eighteenth century.

SYNOPSIS

ACT I

SCENE 1.—A room in Mr. Hardcastle's house. My Lady's Troubles—An old fashioned husband and a mischievous son.

SCENE 2. The "Three Pigeons" Inn. Tony Misleads the Travellers.

ACT II

SCENE. A room in Mr. Hardcastle's house. Hastings and Marlow make themselves at home—Hardcastle dumbfounded—The most modest young man alive—Tony's plan.

ACT III

SCENE. The same. Father and daughter disagree—Tony steals the jewels—Marlow's mistake—She stoops to conquer.

ACT IV

SCENE. The same. Mr. Hardcastle loses patience—Marlow discovers his mistake—Mrs. Hardcastle prevents the elopement—Tony has a bright idea.

ACT V

SCENE 1. The same. Sir Charles and Hardcastle at fault—Kate promises to convince them.

SCENE 2. The back of the garden. Tony Drives Hard. Mrs. Hardcastle is subdued at last.

SCENE 3. Hardcastle's house. Marlow declares his attachment and sees a great light—Tony sets all to rights—"Bless you my children."

"If comedy forsake us, they'll turn us out and no one else will take us."
David Garrick's Prologue to the play.

CAST

SIR CHARLES MARLOW, an English gentleman....Mr. M. McFadden

YOUNG MARLOW, the modestest young man alive..Mr. H. H. Mockler

HARDCASTLE, a lover of antiquity ... . Mr. E. D. McClocklin

HASTINGS, friend to Marlow.....................Mr. A. Robertson

TONY LUMPKIN, step-son to Hardcastle ......Mr. T.H. McClocklin

DIGGORY, servant to Hardcastle...................⎫
                                                  ⎬ Mr. L. Buchan
STINGO, landlord of "The Three Pigeons"..........⎭

ROGER, another servant of Hardcastle.............Mr. W. Buchan

JEREMY, valet to Young Marlow...............Mr. Jas. McClocklin

MRS. HARDCASTLE, a fond mamma with a craze for fashions....Miss E. A. Mockler

MISS HARDCASTLE, her daughter...............Miss M. A. Munro

MISS NEVILLE, cousin to Tony......... ....Miss J. Laidlaw

DOLLY, maid to Miss Hardcastle...................Miss C. Jackson

She Stoops to Conquer.

The Grey Review of August 1, 1878, states that the Dramatic Club presented its first entertainment in the Town Hall and gave a very good performance.

The Dramatic Club continued to present two or three major performances a year and under the able direction of Professor Lewis, the actors and actresses improved greatly in their art and were able to present more difficult works. This also required a more complicated wardrobe, and the Dramatic Club began to acquire men's and women's period costumes and wigs, as well as stage properties, and by 1900 they had assembled a large collection of both.

In 1904 a group of the Dramatic Club wished to present a Shakespeare play, and at the urging of Mr. H.H. Mockler a Shakespeare Club was formed. That first year Shakespeare's Hamlet was performed. Although the first performance did not produce the attendance hoped for, it was praised for its excellence. The Mayor and Council highly lauded the efforts of the Club in their beautification of the Opera House (Town Hall). Other Shakespeare presentations by this Club were: The Merchant of Venice, Julius Ceasar, MacBeth and Richard III.

MOVING PICTURES

On January 3, 1901, Durham had its first moving picture show which was held in the Town Hall. Moving pictures were shown on a screen and the sound was supplied by phonograph. This entertainment was conducted by Gray Brothers.

In 1910 a group called the Carey Brothers appeared on a number of occasions during the year to packed halls. The entertainment provided consisted of a number of interesting and instructive moving pictures, as well as several illustrated songs. The brothers would return on a yearly basis.

In the Durham Chronicle edition of November 14, 1912, a Mr. David Allan is reported to be fixing up the Mockler store in order that it might be used as a moving picture theatre. Mockler's store was later A.A. Aljoe's Store on Garafraxa Street East between Lambton and Saddler Streets. There was another theatre in operation at the time and there was concern that the town would be unable to support two similar businesses. The cost of a license from the Town to run a Movie House was $25 and the cost of a provincial license was $75.

By the year 1914 a Mr. Willoughby was running a motion picture theatre in Durham called the Star Theatre. This theatre had packed houses nearly every night. The Photo-Drama of Creation was presented in limelight views and motion pictures and was explained throughout by the use of a couple of phonographs. Motion picture reels were seen regularly and a Miss Whittaker of Ceylon would often render a solo at the performances. In October of 1914 the theatre changed its name to the Happy Hour Theatre. A notice in the June 1, 1922 edition of the Durham Chronicle stated that the Veteran Star Theatre will run only Friday and Saturday nights until further notice due to poor attendance. Mel Cordick showed movies in the 1940s in the Town Hall.

The last film theatre in Durham opened in August of 1948. Billed as South Grey's most modern theatre, it was owned and operated by Mr. Delbert Holley, who named it the Dell Theatre. This business was located where the "Foodtown" grocery store is now situated on Garafraxa Street West between Lambton and George Streets.

In 1949 Mr. Holley hired Mr. Edward Goss as his assistant and under his guidance a very successful promotion called Foto-Nite was started and became a weekly feature at the Dell Theatre. Every Wednesday a name was selected from the eligible entries and if the person whose name was called responded, he or she was offered a large cash amount for his or her photograph. It was not necessary, however, to produce a photograph until one week after the person's name was selected. It was announced from the stage that all a person had to do to be eligible for the prize money was to register his or her name and to be at the theatre on Foto-Nite, or Attendance night, which was Tuesday of each week. The prize started each time at $50. If no one received the prize, it was increased by $10 each time. One of the winners who presented his 8 x 10 inch photo was Elmer Lake. Mr. Lake won $150.

Losers were Mr. Stanley Brown and Mr. Mel Calder who were not in attendance on the night their names were drawn from a box containing the names of those persons present that night. The four contestants engaged in various contests and a winner was usually determined by judging who had received the loudest audience applause. The amateur contestant winner would receive a prize and in turn the person whom he or she represented in the audience would also win. The amateur contestants at one particular Foto-Nite were Elizabeth Schaefer, Jalna Sharpe, Dan Shubrook and Freddie Illingsworth. The four sang and Dan Shubrook was acclaimed the winner.

whom he or she respresented in the audience would also win. The amateur contestants at one particular Foto-Nite were Elizabeth Schaefer, Jalna Sharpe, Dan Shubrook and Freddie Illingsworth. The four sang and Dan Shubrook was acclaimed the winner.

Mr. Holley leased the theatre and adjoining Coffee Shop in May, 1951, to Mr. Goss who then ran it for a number of years. In 1956 it was taken over by Mr. Bev. Wiggins who had originally started working in the theatre as an usher and then had become the projectionist. Mr. Wiggins ran the business successfully for a number of years and added many inventive ideas to the original Foto-Nite format.

Especially interesting was the featuring of local bands and other acts in talent contests which took

Dell Theatre 1953.

place on the theatre stage between the first and second shows.

Sadly by 1961 the advent of Television was just too much competition for this beautiful theatre. Attempts to sell books of tickets by Mr. Wiggins and Mr. Jaffy Elvidge in an effort to keep the theatre going as a viable operation were not successful, and as a result the building was eventually sold to Mr. Stanley Mc-Afee, who turned it into a grocery store, thus ending an era in Durham.

THE GRAMOPHONE COMES TO DURHAM — 1897

A Grand Concert was held in the Town Hall for everyone to hear the Gramophone Machine that "talks talk." This concert was presented under the auspices, and for the benefit, of the Durham Orchestral Club. The programme consisted of songs by the most celebrated singers and music by the best bands and instrumentalists in America as delivered by the gramophone. Selections by the Orchestra and other local talents were also presented. The admission was adults 15 cents, children ten cents.

DURHAM HIGH SCHOOL FIFE AND DRUM BAND 1930-1940s

The members of this band were: Mr. ? Muir, Bill Levi, Dan Armstrong, Frank Ritchie, Ray Hopkins, George Braithwaite, Bob Milne, Dave Allen, Dave Aljoe, Thos Ritchie (Leader), Bill McGirr, Clarence Hargrave, Fred Roseborough, and Donald Kennedy.

PATRIOTIC CLUB

The Durham Patriotic Club was first organized in the year 1900 with the following officers: Honorary President, Dr. D. Jamieson; President, J.P. Telford; Secretary, W.S. Davidson; Treasurer, R.J.S. Dewar; Committee of Man., J.A. Hunter, R. MacFarlane Jr., E. McClocklin and W.D. Elliott. The club presented a series of concerts for the purpose of raising money for the National Patriotic Fund, which was used to supply relief of the wives and children of Canadians who were serving at that time in the Boer War in South Africa.

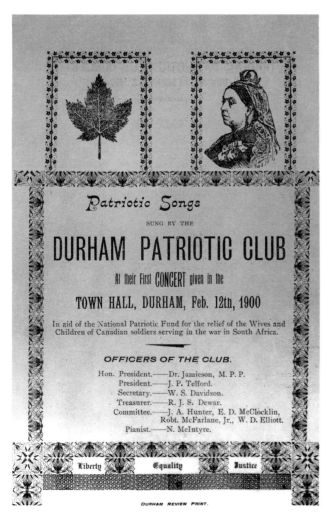

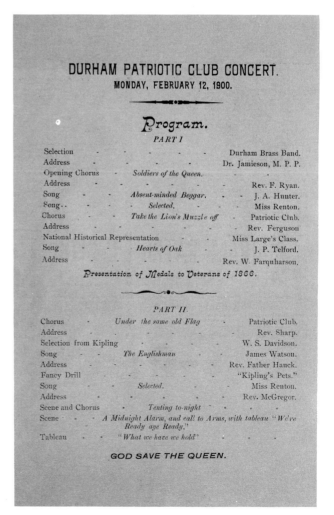

Patriotic Club.

CHAUTAUQUA FESTIVAL PROGRAMME COMES TO DURHAM

An association was formed by some progressive citizens of Durham to sign a contract with the "Chautauqua Company." The Chautauqua Company was a large international company which produced entertainment and educational lectures and concerts. Local organizations could negotiate to bring in a series of such concerts. For several years these Chautauqua programmes were presented all across Canada and the United States. Mr. P. Ramage was the secretary of the local association and other members were: J.P. Telford, Rev. E.S. Moyer, Dr. W.C. Pickering, Dr. ? Hutton, W.A. McGowan, J. Kelly, M.J. Bolger, R.H. McWilliams, E.A. May, J.J. Smith, and G.H. Mistele.

The purpose of the Chautauqua Company was to stimulate an atmosphere of community development by presenting dramatic and musical productions as well as other efforts from the theatre. In western Canada, where the "Chautauquas" were well-known, concerts drew large crowds from up to 20 or 30 miles away. Local Associations made money from the Chautauqua Company by collectively purchasing several hundred dollars in tickets, and then selling them to the public at a higher price. Net profits were a donation to charity. The first afternoon and evening the townsfolk were entertained by the Hampton Court Singers who did a How-do-you-do miscellaneous musical programme. In the evening the same group presented their famous Elizabethan programme in the costumes of Elizabeth's Court. On the second day the Lyceum Arts Club Orchestra of Chicago entertained. The third afternoon Captain W.H. Hindley of Winnipeg, one of Canada's most noted preachers, lectured on The Nation's Needs, followed in the evening by a performance by the Kaffir Boys. Profits from the series went to the local Red Cross and Patriotic Society.

DANCE/DRAMA CLUB

In the early 1950s Elizabeth McIlwain, a Scottish lady, ran the Dance/Drama Club in various locations around town. The classes were held in the afternoon, when school had ended for the day, and on Saturday mornings during the fall and winter. Classes were conducted in the rudiments of dance, including the basic steps in ballet, and the national dances of Scotland. The children ranged in age from four to fourteen. At least two or more times a year the club presented performances upstairs in the Town Hall theatre. The programmes were musicals which combined the dance and drama arts. Piano accompaniment was provided by Mrs. M.C. MacInnes, the backdrop for performances was painted by Joseph Marquis, and special lighting was under the direction of William Hewitt. These performances were full scale productions with costumes made by the children's parents.

Some of the students who took part were as follows:

June Sleeper	Carol Sewell	Marilyn Peart
Clive Elvidge	Margaret Hopkins	Kit Darling
Dennis Greenwood	Sharon Aljoe	Mary Lee MacDonald
Betty Jean Duffield	Shirley Hargrave	Carole Hopkins
Faye Arnett	Mary Lou McComb	

Old Home Week 1935.

The Durham Lacrosse Club

requests the company of yourself and ladies

at an

Informal Dance

to be held in the

Town Hall, Durham

Thursday, March 22nd, 1928

Dancing from 9.00 to 1.00

Gentlemen, $1.00; Extra lady 25c.

J. N. Murdock, Pres.   B. Jamieson, Secretary

Durham Lacrosse Dance Card 1928.

BACHELOR'S BALL

During the 1800s the bachelors of the town gave a number of balls during the year on Friday evenings in the Town Hall. The usual attendance was about 50 couples. Music was furnished by Mr. ? Collett of Allan Park, and Mr. T. Horn acted as floor manager. Those present always enjoyed themselves until an early hour on the Saturday morning.

DURHAM GIRLS TRUMPET BAND

In 1949 John Jarrett approached the school board with regard to starting a school band. He was given permission plus a small donation. In the 35 years which followed the Durham girls boosted their home town in cities and towns across Ontario and parts of the U.S.A.

The first appearance of the Durham Girls Bugle Band was on November 11, 1949. By means of bake sales and other money raising projects the girls had managed to raise money for a few instruments, but no uniforms. The band entered its first competition in 1950 at the Waterloo Band Festival. Over the next few

years the band's popularity grew and the members became a familiar sight at all area parades in their blue blazers, white pleated skirts, white blouses, tams and saddle shoes. In 1954 the name was changed to the Durham District High School Girls Trumpet Band. The band won third prize at Waterloo in 1953, second prize in 1954, first prize in 1955, and then first prize for four consecutive years, a feat that has never been duplicated.

During the late 1950s the band travelled to the U.S.A. where they won several championships. Mr. Jarrett left Durham in the fall of 1960 and the band did not enter competitions that year. The band at this time came under the direction of Mr. Lambertus Verwell. In 1964 it was taken over by Mr. Dave Baxter. Membership increased and a corps of little majorettes was started.

The band was hit with a crisis in early 1968 with the phasing out of the Durham District High School and it appeared that the band would be taken over by the neighbouring school and consequently disappear. However, the band was reorganized and became known as the Durham Girls Drum and Bugle Corps. The 30 band members undertook numerous jobs and money raising projects to stay alive. They did indeed stay alive and again became one of the most recognized junior drum corps in Canada.

D.H.S. Bugle Band 1950 — Charter Members.
Back Row: Donna Lunn, Jean Weir, Flora Marshall, Mary Mortley, Jalna Sharpe, Eileen Wilder, Shirley Watt, Marilyn Wilson, Jessie Bell, Lorna Peart, John Jarratt (Bandmaster)
Middle Row: Gwen Wilson, Janet Cross, Joan March, Edythe Crutchley, Ann Jarratt, Jean McLachlan, Mary Lawrence, Betty McGowan, Margaret Bryan
Front Row: Jean Morrison, Marie Koeslag, Darlene McCracken, Catherine Elvidge, Edna Weppler, Jessie Crutchley, Dorothy Manus, Elizabeth Schafer.
Missing: Joyce Moore, Nadine Blyth, Mary Miller, Janet Leonard, Sheila Darling.

In 1969, under the direction of a former member, Gayle Magwood, the band members practiced twice a week and it was decided that they were again ready to enter competition. Funds were raised for transportation and upon entering the first competition in ten years, the corps walked off with the Provincial Novice Championship, recording a mark of 84, the highest mark given during the entire competition that year.

In 1972 there were 60 members ranging in age from five year old Kelly Magwood to 19 years. The corps was primarily self-supporting, backed by the strong spirit of the town residents.

In the 1970s the corps continued to march in parades, at Ontario Place and various other events. They also continued to compete in Ontario, New York State and Pennsylvania.

In 1980 the corps hosted the Circuit "C" Championships and, in conjunction with a Durham Girls Day, members from previous years paraded, along with the founder of the corps, Mr. John Jarrett. From 1981 to 1983 the corps competed successfully in the Individual Competitions bringing home gold medals in Colour Guard, Brass and Percussion. During the 1982 Durham Home Coming the corps hosted a successful Durham Girls Reunion. Gayle Magwood and Eileen Mighton greatly appreciated the recognition given them as directors at this time.

In 1984, with the decline of membership and the prospect of having to face much larger corps in the circuit, a decision was made to disband the corps.

DONKEY
BASEBALL

These baseball games were a highlight of the summer months in the 1940s and 1950s. The teams consisted of players in colourful uniforms mounted on the backs of donkeys. A regular baseball game was played with all players exhibiting the skills used in a normal game, but with the added challenge of riding on donkeys while performing these skills. Both the players and the donkeys toured the countryside on a regular circuit. In later years the ball games were played using local persons on one team in opposition to the touring team. In the middle 1950s the Kinsmen Club and the Rotarians got together to play donkey baseball against each other to raise money for crippled children. The match was billed as — The Keen Clever Kinsmen led by Captain Tom Watson (if the donkey can't carry Tom, he'll carry the donkey) versus the Rough Riding Rotarians led by Captain Bill Leonard (dismounted from the last game, Bill still has a couple of hoof prints where they don't show). Bowman Jamieson pitched for Rotary and Fred O'Brecht received.

LOCAL PLAYS

Over the years there have been many plays and pageants presented in the Town Hall by various Durham organizations. From 1910 to 1920 the Anglican Young People's Association each year presented a comedy play. During the 1930s the Presbyterian Young People's Society also presented plays yearly. In 1937 the Imperial Order of the Daughters of the Empire presented a coronation pageant entitled Behold Your King. The Durham High School held commencement exercises in the Town Hall each year to honour graduates and to present proficiency and other awards. The major entertainment at this annual function was a play presented by the high school students. Other organizations have also produced many concerts in which the principal performers were local citizens.

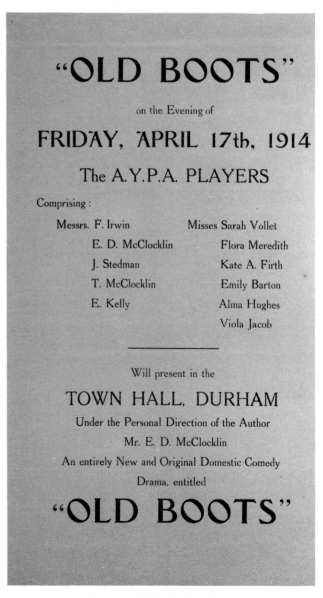

"Old Boots" AYPA Production.

OPEN SATURDAY NIGHTS

During the 1930s and 1940s the Durham merchants kept their establishments open late on Saturday night from about the first of May until the end of September. In this period in history there were nearly ten times as many people in the Durham area carrying on farming operations as there are now. When the farmers came to town on Saturday night they would deliver a can or two of cream and a crate of eggs to the creamery and then would hunt for a place to park. If they arrived late a parking space could not be found within two blocks of Garafraxa Street. From Smith's garage to the Saugeen River the sidewalks were a mass of slowly moving people, both town and rural, strolling along and visiting their neighbours, relatives and friends — up one side of the street and down the other side. Around ten o'clock the town folk started to go home and the rural folk would begin to do their shopping. Some merchants said they transacted almost as much business between ten p.m. and eleven p.m. as they did during the remainder of the day. Eventually the popularity of this social evening disappeared and the merchants closed their shops at the usual time.

HORSE-RACING

The first mention of horse-racing in Durham was recorded in the *Durham Standard*, May 18, 1866.

> *"Durham Race Course — Active exertions have been put forth of late to bring this course into good condition. It has been ploughed, levelled, the stones picked off, and seeded down. No doubt is entertained of its being in first class condition for the coming races."*

Horse-racing in Durham has been poorly documented, but it is known that it was a popular sport with horse lovers and fanciers for at least more than a century. For many years the local Fall Fair sponsored horse-races.

During the 1880s a Turf Club was formed in Durham. A track was built at the fall fair grounds and racing was held on all special occasions such as Dominion Day. Horses from town and the surrounding area were trained for these events. There was great excitement generated in the area for these races and, although there is no documented mention of wagers being placed on the outcome, betting probably occurred. For instance, on the back of a very old postcard belonging to Jack Breen is the message: "Hope you can make it to the horse races on Saturday because I need some one to bet with."

In 1898 a Dominion Day race was won by Baby Boy that made the mile in two minutes forty seconds and was owned by Robert Scott of Durham. Mr. Knapp's famous runner Springbok took second prize in the

Butch Graham and Keith Waples.
Keith Waples was named Citizen of the Year for 1973.

open run, although it was said after the race that he would have placed first with a good start and a rider about two pounds lighter.

Around 1950 Lance Rumble established a stable of well bred hackney horses on the Durham Road East. He showed his horses at the major Canadian and American horse shows and won many coveted awards. Some years later Keith Waples bought the same property and established his stable of Standardbred horses. Keith Waples was the first person to drive a Standardbred horse in Canada that paced the mile in under two minutes. In 1972 he won the North American Standardbred's most prestigious crown "The Little Brown Jug" with a horse called Strike Out.

"POOL" WITH A CAPITAL P COMES TO DURHAM

A pool and billiard room was opened up in the old Standard Bank premises in 1911. Many of the town's citizens expressed opposition to the opening of this new establishment. The Public Houses, which sold liquor, were being closed down at this time because it was thought that they were a cause of evil. The playing of pool was a form of recreation which was gradu-

Boats transporting young gentlemen and their lovely lady friends (with white parasols) about in the water.

ally taking the place of the Public Houses and no use of liquor was involved. However, there was concern that the young people would be betting on these games and that they might also neglect their chores in order to play them.

The Town Council fixed a yearly license fee of $200 for the first table and $100 for each additional table. These figures were thought to be so high that no one would want to undertake this venture; however, the new owners paid $400 in advance and put in three tables. In April of 1912 the pool room managers appeared before the Town Council to ask that the seven o'clock closing hour on Saturday nights be extended to eleven o'clock as on other open evenings. A request was also made for three more tables at the same license fee of $400. The council gave the consent for the extension of the Saturday closing hour, but denied the request for more tables.

The thought of the day was that these pool halls would not survive very long.

Durham still has a Pool and Billiard room which has been operated for many decades in a very orderly fashion — first by Mr. Alex Hastie and then by his son, Graham.

BATHING IN TOWN

During a four year period between 1900 and 1904 the Town of Durham had a problem with the indecent conduct of boys and young men bathing in the river within the town limits during the daylight hours in the summer months. This was actually a daily occurrence. The Town Council was forced to take action on the matter in 1904 after it had received many complaints from the townsfolk.

Bathing was restricted within the town limits between the hours of 5 a.m. and 8:30 p.m. with the passing of a By-law. Those found guilty of breaking the by-law would be prosecuted. If the boys and young men had kept under cover such action, according to the council, could have been avoided.

FIZ BIZ

Mr. J.A. Darling, who operated an Ice Cream parlour, employed the services of the George Yiirs orchestra. This orchestra played at his establishment on Wednesday and Saturday evenings. Mr. Darling was credited for his progressiveness and his endeavours to supply the young people of Durham and vicinity with good wholesome amusement and refreshments at small cost.

SKIFFING ON THE SAUGEEN

In olden days rowboats and canoes would be rented on a warm Sunday by young men of the town from Mr. J. Brown, who had decided that the calm and placid

waters of the Saugeen River above the McGowan Milling Company's dam could be turned into a miniature Venice. During the summer of 1910 and for a few years after, Mr. Brown, with Mr. McGowan's permission, operated a line of skiffs, in order that Durham's mariners could enjoy boating and kindred amusements. Eventually a wharf and boathouse were built for his use. This venture enjoyed the support of the people, and many picnics were held during the summer at this location, during which a ride in a skiff would be part of the event.

Canoeing on the Saugeen.

THE CANADIAN ART AND COLLECTABLE SHOW AND SALE

In 1981 the Canadian Art and Collectable Show and Sale began in the town of Durham with five exhibitors. Of great interest in the 1984 show was the introduction of the Ted Xaras Tomorrow's Memories Series plates. The first plate, called Tomorrow's Memories, depicted the C.P.R. railway bridge in Durham with the Knechtel Mill in the background. Other plates in the series which depicted scenes of Durham and the surrounding area were: Furniture for the Nation, which features the Kroehler Furniture factory; From Tiny Acorns, with a scene from the Interforest plant; and Pit Run — The Gravel Story, which shows the Durham Stone and Paving plant yard.

The show ran until 1988 in Durham and became such a success that it outgrew local facilities and had to be moved north to the city of Owen Sound, where it was held until 1991. From then until the present it has been relocated at Kitchener, Ontario, in the Kitchener Memorial Auditorium. There are 60 different exhibitors at present, and interested people come from all over Canada and the United States to view beautiful displays of paintings and collectors' plates, etc., and also to take advantage of the opportunity to make purchases for their own private collections.

BANJO COMPETITION

Canadian National Open Banjo Competition 1974-1983.

For nine years the sounds of banjo music, from bluegrass to classical, filled the air on a July weekend in the town of Durham as musicians vied for the honour of being named the Canadian National Open Banjo Competition Grand Champion. At a suggestion made by Mr. Bev. Wiggins, the Durham Kinette Club took on this project as a fundraiser for the arena.

To facilitate all banjo types three categories were established in the open competition: five-string, tenor and plectrum. Ladies and Junior classes were also available for those not wishing to compete in the Open. Players and audience came from various parts of Canada and the U.S.A.

With the exception of the year 1975, when Durham was without an arena and the facilities at Varney Speedway were used, all activities took place at the Durham Arena, with camping facilities set up below the hill at the fair grounds. In 1976 there were 21 competitors and 1,000 spectators.

Area businesses and interested citizens generously provided the banjo-shaped keeper tropies, and the name of the annual Grand Champion was engraved on a large trophy donated by Ross and Marion Buchner of Durham I.G.A. Cash prizes were also awarded. Several organizations manned food booths and supplied meals donating 50 per cent of their proceeds to the arena.

Long after the close of each evening's events, the sound of banjos could still be heard as the players continued to play in their campgrounds.

THE DURHAM ART GALLERY

In 1978 a group of insightful seniors met to discuss the establishment of an art gallery in the Town of Durham. Eventually, with a New Horizons government grant and with money contributed by individuals, foundations and corporations, they persuaded the town to allow them to refurbish the lower floor of the Library building so that it could accommodate a Gallery. Over $30,000 was spent in providing washrooms and a kitchen and in repairing the deplorable condition of the Library space. This was a benefit both to the Gallery and the Library. Indeed, William Fahey, who was chairman of the Gallery group and previously of the library board, had been responsible for reviving the Carnegie Library and bringing its operation into some sort of order.

Incorporated and fully under way by 1980, the Gallery began modestly. With a focus on the visual arts (musical concerts and poetry readings were also introduced), its mandate was to provide an accessible cultural resource for future generations of the area. It soon developed a reputation for presenting quality programmes, and its opening in 1980 by the then Lieutenant-Governor Pauline McGibbon gave it a kind of official approval. With its acceptance for funding by the Ontario Arts Council it became in that same year the smallest art institution to hold public gallery status.

Norman and Myrtle Tucker, winners of Old Tyme Waltz at Durham Centennial, Verna Sharpe on right.

Fishing in the Saugeen.

Until 1990 the Gallery occupied the Library space. At that time the Town and the Library had informed the Gallery that the space was required for Library expansion. The town, to compensate for the Gallery loss and for the money it had put into the building, offered them a property on the old railway line. At that time, however, the Gallery was in no position to build. To play for time and continue their operation they rented a downtown storefront.

After over a year in expensive rented spaces the Board realized it would have to build or perish.

After a feverish eight months of planning, the Board, along with a strongly participating membership, approved a building project. The offer of land, which had first been made a few years before by the then Mayor Gordon McLean, was reaffirmed. The building design was generously provided by David Oldford. By January, 1993, the Gallery was able to move into the nearly completed building situated at the east end of the Heritage Bridge and across the road from the old Knechtel Mill. All of this was financed entirely with private rather than public funds.

During its first 15 years the Gallery and its various Boards and directors have been responsible for, and instrumental in, promoting many ventures: A performing arts group, film society, the Herb Fair, the exchange with Durham, England, the arena mural, Saugeen Music Society and the Wood Show. The Wood Show has since then given the Gallery much needed support.

The Gallery has averaged some ten exhibitions a year since 1981. It is a member of the Ontario Association of Art Galleries and a recipient of support from the Ontario Arts Council, The Ministry of Culture and Recreation and the Canada Council. People from around the world have been to see its exhibitions.

Durham Art Gallery.

The original New Horizons Group was as follows:

Wm. Fahey, Chairman   Arthur and Carol Bonnett
Kelly Koehler   Edna Tolley
Stuart Foden   Audrey Hunt
Adele Wilson   Gertrude Hewitt
Wm. Morlock   Joyce Gamble
Marg and Jim Williamson

Since that time there have been many Boards and many employees. Debbie Bryans, Jo Ann Monk, Catherine Campbell and Donna Miller were among the first. Sarah Brown was the first Curator/Director followed by Gordon Hatt, Ann Pappert, Bean Epp, Dyan Jones and Freyda Odonahae.

SAUGEEN BACH CHOIR

Michael Schmidt, the founder of the choir, came to Canada from Germany in 1983. He received his early musical training at the Waldorf Schools in Germany and conducted his first orchestra at the age of 17. He played in several orchestras and chamber groups in Germany, where he founded and conducted a Youth Orchestra. Michael purchased Glencolton Farms (Firth Homestead) north-east of Durham, Ontario. He brought with him a profound love of music and a determination to encourage this appreciation in Saugeen Country.

The Saugeen Bach Choir sings sacred choral music. The choir has performed from Owen Sound to Toronto, Kincardine to Meaford, and in several other area towns. A concert tour in Germany in May, 1988, was a highlight of the choir's history.

The choir began in September, 1984, when a small group of interested singers began practising at Trinity Anglican Church in Durham. Under Michael's leadership, the choir grew in both numbers and ability during the following months. The first choir performance was at the Nine Lessons and Carol Service in Trinity Anglican Church, December, 1984. The choir sang Christmas music as well as excerpts from W.A. Mozart's Twelfth Mass. With the new season, membership reached nearly 100 singers.

Michael Schmidt and Mr. Herman J. Maes of Ayton, Ontario, together conceived the idea of an annual Saugeen Bach Festival. The first festival took place in April, 1985. It was then that the Saugeen Bach Choir and Orchestra made its first major appearance, singing three Bach Cantatas. In the fall of 1985 the choir presented three full house performances of Handel's Messiah.

The Saugeen Musical Society is a registered non-profit organization supported by interested volunteers, who look after the administrative detail. Various church boards have been generous in allowing the use of their facilities for the performances over the years. Throughout the years the choir's membership has ranged between 60 and 80 members.

Some of the guest performers have included: The Kitchener-Waterloo Symphony Orchestra, the Laurier Singers, Bach-Collegium Orchestra, the German Chamber Orchestra, Guelph Chamber Choir, Kitchener-Waterloo Philharmonic Choir, Dufferin Choral Singers, and the Kitchener-Waterloo Chamber Orchestra.

In 1993, due to a heavy schedule of business, Michael handed over his conductor's baton to John Wervers, a Shelburne music teacher who trained as a conductor in Salzburg, and who had joined the Choir as a singer.

That same John Wervers decided to make the Festival a platform for promising young talent such as: Sylvain Landry, a tenor from Quebec, Alyson Leyton-Brown, a 14 year old pianist, Shelagh Tyreman from Hanover, and the Children's Choirs from Southampton and Owen Sound.

The 10th Saugeen Festival season in 1994 was celebrated in an exceptional fashion. The Festival opened on Good Friday, April 1st, at Trinity Lutheran Church in Ayton. The Saugeen Bach Choir sang Requiem by Gabriel Faure, accompanied by the Kitchener-Waterloo Chamber Orchestra. Soloists were: Theresa Thibodeau and John Medina. Rehearsal accompanist was Alexander Damyanovich. The finale was held in St. Matthew's Evangelical Lutheran Church in Hanover, on Sunday, May 15. The Saugeen Bach Choir, the Dufferin Choral Singers, and the Orangeville District Secondary School Concert Choir joined for this concert. The programme was Lord Nelson Mass by J. Haydn (1732-1809), and Gloria by Antonia Vivaldi (1680-1743). The accompaniment was by the Kitchener-Waterloo Chamber Orchestra, with John Wervers conducting. Soloists were: Theresa Thibodeau, Soprano, Allyson McHardy, Alto, and John Medina, Bass. Classical music is surely thriving in rural Grey-Bruce, Saugeen Country.

Durham and District Pipe Band.
Back Row: **Bob Dickson, Dave Dixon, Bill McMeekin, Ross Clark, Colin Hill, Elmer Clark, Raymond Collins, Reid Johnson**
Front Row: **Ian Dison, Ron Schwevaier, Brad Fraser, Bob Pettingill.**

THE WOOD SHOW

Mr. Herb Miller, a woodworker and the founder of Welbeck Sawmill Ltd. located near Durham, was also the founder and promoter of the Wood Show in Durham. He also has been a lifetime supporter of community projects. He felt the Wood Show would not only provide a showcase for the talented men and women who work in wood, but would also bring tourists, visitors and much needed revenue into the area.

Durham, and indeed the whole of the Saugeen Valley, has a strong connection with woodworking, which began with the pioneers. Many of those original woodworking industries still exist today. As well, there are also an amazing number of talented individuals in this area who do woodworking (furniture design and making, bird carving, turning, small wooden crafts and household items, canoes, etc.).

The first show was staged in August of 1984. The nine-person Board of Directors serve on a volunteer basis throughout the year. During the actual weekend of the show over 300 volunteers from the community are utilized. The show manager is the only fulltime salaried position.

The format of the first year's show consisted of two areas: Commercial Booth Space and the Juried Woodworking Competition. In the first years of the show, the Durham Art Gallery was involved with the competition side of the show. The booth space was rented to woodworking machinery and tool suppliers as well as to craft people who produced unique custom-made wooden goods.

Quickly the show expanded to include live free Seminars which ran every other hour throughout the show. Some of the topics covered over the years have been: Chip Carving, Bird Carving, Relief Carving, Scroll Saw Techniques, Furniture Building, Birch Bark Canoe, Marquetry, Violin Making, Carousel Horse Carving, Tole Painting on Wood, Intarsia, Model Airplane Building, Parquetry, etc.

Those giving the Seminars were all well recognized in their particular area of expertise. They came from Durham, Flesherton, Toronto, Windsor, Kitchener, Illinois, British Columbia, and England, just to mention a few. In recent years guest woodworkers have been featured at the show. Many of these guests have won international awards for their work.

Other show features have been the Loggers Sports Event, which brought in lumberjacks from the Ottawa valley, and a chainsaw carver from British Columbia who demonstrated how to turn a log into a beautiful eagle, bear, etc.

Bob Hastings, a woodworking teacher from Southampton, had the idea of staging a Children's Workshop. Bob sets up the programme and trains the volunteers to help. In 1990 the first children's workshop was held for ages five to eleven. This was a huge success.

In 1993 a Women's Workshop was added and almost 600 women went through the programme with nearly 1,000 children at their own workshop. The Women's Workshop will be expanded in 1994 because many women had to be turned away in 1993. The Show has grown to have an attendance of 20,000 plus each year.

The Wood Show endeavours to: give the talented men and women who work in wood a showcase to show and sell their work; encourage excellence in woodworking through the juried competition; honour our heritage in wood; bring visitors, and thereby revenue, into our area; give the whole family who attend the show a good time..

In the first ten years the Wood Show has donated over $100,000 to various community organizations and facilities. This show would not be possible, however, without the volunteers who assist at the show, and, therefore, this is truly a community event.

SAUGEEN VALLEY CONSERVATION AUTHORITY PARK

On March 16, 1950, the Saugeen Valley Conservation Authority was established by an Order-in-Council of the Ontario government. Over the next few years surveys and studies were made of the Saugeen watershed to determine how best to protect the rivers, streams and land within the Saugeen area. These studies included protection and conservation of the rivers, streams and forests, including flood and pollution control, as well as improved land use and provision for recreational facilities.

During the 1950s, the Wm. Knetchel Mill Ltd. (middle dam) had trouble with the water power and converted the mill to electricity. It is reported that after this change had been made Arthur Neff and C.M. Elvidge approached A.J. Metzger, owner of Knetchel's Mills, to see if he would donate his property in Durham for use as a park. In 1959 Mr. Metzger donated his water rights, including a large block of land north of the river consisting of 35 acres, to the town of Durham for the sum of one dollar. The town donated this land to the SVCA for a park and the Authority purchased another 123 acres along the river between Durham and Concession 2 E.G.R Glenelg Township, for $52,800. The Ontario government built a new flood control dam west of Knetchel's mill which is operated by SVCA.

Several organizations, including Kinsmen, Rotary and Legion, have helped by donating time and finances to convert the wilderness north of the river into a beautiful park with fine recreational facilities. The first task was to cut out the brush and underbrush in order to make paths, roadways and open spaces. This work was assisted by the residents of Camp Oliver, a minimum security institution in Glenelg township for boys who ran afoul of the law.

The conservation area serves both watershed residents and visitors. The property's two campgrounds, containing 214 sites, are open to the public from Victoria Day holiday to the Thanksgiving weekend. During 1985 almost 5,000 campers visited the conservation area. During the early part of the summer season, the majority of campers originate from within an hour's drive of the area. By the mid-summer, the majority of campers come from the wider area. Facilities and services include 60 hydro and water serviced sites, shower/washroom building, trailer sanitary dumping services, pull-through campsites, group camping areas (by reservation), picnic and playground areas, with a pavillion, and two beach areas for swimming, fishing and small craft boating. In the summer, the area hosts a variety of community activities including an annual fish derby, swimming lessons and family reunions. During the winter months, the area is used by local cross country skiers. For many decades swimming lessons have been given for both children and adults at the Upper Dam.

Entrance to the Durham SVCA Park.

DURHAM FLOOD CONTROL

As a result of historical flooding, a study was commissioned by the SVCA in 1975 to determine Regional Storm (Hurricane Hazel) floodlines and develop an associated protection programme for the Town of Durham. While floods of the magnitude created by Hurricane Hazel are only theoretical to town residents, the destructive capabilities of the Saugeen are only too familiar. Over the past 100 years, damages have ranged from the loss of mill dams and a railway bridge to the almost annual flooding of adjacent properties.

From the study, a high priority was placed on the construction of a 1,100 foot earthen dike along the river in the easterly section of the town. A majority of the project was completed by private contract, with the exception of the "gobimat" erosion protection, which was installed by SVCA staff.

With the completion of the dike, an area extending from the project site to the town's main street has been protected from flooding. The cost of the project, undertaken in 1977, was $90,000.

DURHAM'S LOWER DAM

While the Lower Dam is just one of three such structures crossing the Saugeen River within the Town of Durham, its existence provides unique benefits to both the SVCA and the community. From the Authority's perspective, the dam helps to retard the upstream buildup of "frazil" or slush ice. When allowed to build, the ice is capable of creating a natural dam which, in the past, has caused winter flooding in downstream portions of the town. The municipality views the structure and reservoir as an integral part of its riverside park belt, stretching almost the entire length of the town from the conservation area to the community centre grounds. The water level maintained in the reservoir also ensures that the Lambton Street-Highway #4 bridge abutments are not exposed to river erosion. Through a cost benefit analysis undertaken by the Authority in 1978, rehabilitation works were chosen over the construction of a replacement weir.

The 1981 works, costing $90,000, included the pressure grouting of cavities under the apron of the dam, the replacement of the original concrete wingwalls with gabions, the installation of a walkway and the filling of scours in the channel, immediately upstream and downstream of the structure.

In co-operation with the town, the Authority is also proposing additional channel improvements downstream of the Lower Dam, as a means of further reducing the buildup of frazil ice.

This park is a wonderful asset to the town of Durham and its existence attracts thousands of vacationers to the area each year.

Fishing in the Saugeen River.

Last day of swimming lessons at Middle Dam 1994.

Durham Pipe Band 1949
Delbert Aicheson, Bob Lunn, Gordon Aicheson, Delbert Haw, Angus McCormick, Cam Millman, Elmer Clark, Cal Gray, Joan Roseborough, Jack Lunn and Carman Roseborough.

Boating on the middle dam.

John Hunter 8th from right, one of Canadian team at international bowling tournament in Melbourne, Australia, 1930.

Pavilion at Upper Dam.

Children's playground in Saugeen Valley Conservation Park.

Council Highlights Since Incorporation

No. 48.] **BILL.** [1872.

An Act to incorporate the Town of Durham and to define the limits thereof.

WHEREAS the inhabitants of the unincorporated village of Durham, in the Townships of Bentinck and Glenelg, in the County of Grey, have by their petition, represented that the said village has a population of fourteen hundred or thereabouts, and that the population of the said village is increasing and will be further augmented by the early construction of railways and other causes, and in order to enable the inhabitants to make and carry out certain necessary improvements, and in compliance with a resolution passed by a public meeting, duly convened, to consider the matter of incorporation, and numerously attended, it is desirable that the said village be incorporated as a town; and it is expedient to grant the prayer of the said petition;

Therefore Her Majesty, by and with the advice and consent of the Legislative Assembly of the Province of Ontario, enacts as follows:—

1. On and after the passing of this Act the inhabitants of the said village of Durham shall be, and they are hereby constituted a corporation or body politic, under the name of the "Corporation of the Town of Durham," apart from the said Townships of Bentinck and Glenelg respectively, in which it is situate, and shall enjoy all the rights, powers and privileges enjoyed by incorporated towns in the Province of Ontario, and exercised by the council thereof under the existing municipal laws of the said Province, which are hereby made applicable thereto, but only so far as the same are not inconsistent herewith.

2. The said town shall comprise and consist of the following farm lots, with such parts thereof as are laid out and known as the Durham town plot, or otherwise, that is to say, the second and third divisions of lot number twenty-four and lots numbers twenty-five, twenty-six and twenty-seven in the first concession from the Garafraxa Road, in the Township of Bentinck, in the County of Grey, and the second and third divisions of lot number twenty-four and lots numbers twenty-five, twenty-six and twenty-seven in the first concession from the Garafraxa Road, in the Township of Glenelg, in the said County of Grey.

3. The said Town of Durham shall be divided into three wards to be called North Ward, East Ward, and West Ward:

(1.) North Ward shall be composed of the second and third divisions of lot number twenty-four in the first concession from the Garafraxa Road, in the Townships of Bentinck and Glenelg respectively, and so much of lot twenty-five in the said first concessions and Townships of Bentinck and Glenelg respectively as lies north of Chester Street, in the Durham town plot;

48

Act of incorporating the Town of Durham.

The council highlights from 1872 to 1972 were compiled by J.B. Duffield and are taken from the Durham Centennial Historical Review 1872-1872. The History Committee has completed them to date.

First meeting of Durham Town Council — March 29, 1872. Held in Dalglishes Hall, Alexander Cochrane, Mayor, Archibald McLellan-Reeve, Councillors: East Ward, J.H. Middaugh, W.R. Rombough. A.C. McKenzie. West Ward: George Russell, Donald McKenzie, John H. Smith. North Ward: Harry Parker, William Anderson, John Cameron.

Rules for the guidance of Council were read by the Mayor and adopted. Samuel E. Legate was appointed Treasurer — Salary $12.00 per year. John Moody was appointed Assessor, salary $20.00 per year. John Rowland was appointed Constable or Messenger of Council Salary $20.00 per year.

Licenses held by Bentinck and Glenelg be turned over to Town. These covered the British Hotel, Royal Exchange, Durham Hotel, Cattle-Yard Hotel. Shop licenses within the Town Limits be issued at $50.00 each for such merchants as deal in liquors. Town funds to be deposited in the Savings Bank. Mayor's Auditor Wm. Jackson. Council Auditor Joe Brown. Council met a deputation in the interests of a Railway.

April 16, 1872 Committee appointed to examine and report on suitable site for monthly Fairs. Donald McDonald was appointed Constable.

May 17, 1872 The Mayor was instructed to proclaim May 24th the Queen's Birthday and the sum of $10.00 was allotted the Committee to provide public amusements.

May 21, 1872 Special meeting to consider Railway matters. Council gave a bonus of $15,000 to the Wellington, Grey and Bruce Railway for an extension of their line into Durham.

May 28, 1872 Council ordered Poll Tax rolls to be prepared and given to the Tax Collector for collection of said tax.

Abstract Statement
Receipts and Expenditure of the Town of Durham

For the Year Ending Dec. 31st, 1898,

RECEIPTS

Balance on hand last audit	$4572 65
Taxes collected from Rates of 1897	77 93
Taxes collected from Rates of 1898	5984 09
Non-resident Taxes collected in 1898	56 63
Arrears of Taxes collected in 1898	13 10
Rent of Town Hall	76 75
Market fees from Dec. 1st, 1897 to Dec. 1st, 1898	208 04
Dog Tax	71 90
Licenses	302 23
County grant, Roads and Bridges Equivalent	35 08
Debentures	18777 00
Loan on Notes	4000 00
Loan not Specified	144 00
Magistrate's Fines	23 00
	$34342 40

EXPENDITURE

Salaries and Allowances	$ 590 75
Printing, Advertising and Stationery	100 43
Insurance	25 00
Fire, Water and Lights	346 13
Law Costs	8 00
Roads and Bridges	883 17
Charity	102 78
Debentures under By-law 67	18510 04
Interest Coupons	2453 14
Interest on Notes in Bank	51 00
County Rates	340 80
School Account	1553 83
Royal Art Paving Company	4025 00
Grant to Band	50 00
Miscellaneous	32 96
Balance in Bank	5269 37
	$34342 40

Abstract Statement

Showing RECEIPTS and EXPENDITURE of the TOWN of DURHAM on Account of PUBLIC and MODEL Schools for Year Ending Dec. 31st, 1898.

RECEIPTS

Amount of balance last audit	$748 06
From Township of Bentinck	35 72
From Township of Glenelg	34 29
Amount of estimate from Town	1553 83
Provincial grant to Public School	159 00
Provincial grant to Model School	150 00
Provincial grant to Continuation Classes	100 00
County grant to Model School	150 00
Non-resident, Pupils fees for Public School	65 30
Model School fees from Pupils	105 00
High School Examination fees	5 79
	$3106 99

EXPENDITURE

Teachers' Salary due for 1897		$ 21 66
Teachers' Salary due for 1898		2281 47
Caretaker Salary balance for 1897		10 83
Caretaker's Salary for 1898		130 00
School Supplies		47 06
Heating Buildings		69 48
Printing		12 00
Gravelling Walks		10 75
Sundries		95
Debentures Redeemed under By-law 208	$184 00	
" " under By-law 283	102 31	286 31
Interest Coupons under By-law 208	$34 85	
" " under By-law 283	10 49	45 34
Balance in Bank		191 14
		$3106 99

August 27, 1872 Circus licensing by-law was passed.

October 29, 1872 A petition to the Legislature asking for a separation of the County of Grey, and the selection of the Town of Durham as the County Town.

October 30, 1872 Dog Tax By-law passed.

November 12, 1872 and December 31 By-law #14 granting $20,000 to the Railway was introduced and finally passed.

January 24, 1873 Committees appointed for first time.

October 27, 1873 By-law regulating the "Assize of Bread" and preventing the use of deleterious materials in baking bread.

March 19, 1874 That Agricultural Hall be put in shape to be used as a school until better premises are provided for such purposes.

March 19, 1874 Wooden sidewalks were ordered for Garafraxa Road.

March 3, 1875 First stove and pipes for Town Hall cost $9.80.

June 5, 1875 County rates amounting to $457.38 were paid.

Plaque mounted on the Town Clerk's office commemorating the founding of Durham.

J. Lenahan's house on Albert Street East.

September 1, 1875 The Oddfellows rented the Town Hall for one night at $2. Road work (statute labour) was commuted at 50 cents per day.

July 5, 1876 Sidewalk to be laid from Garafraxa Street to school to be made 4 feet wide, to be laid on sound cedar timber and covered with sound 2 inch hemlock plank.

January 20, 1879 The Council newly elected consisted of Mayor, H.J. Middaugh, Reeve, Gilbert McKechnie, Councillors, Norman McIntyre, James Burnett, Richard Horn, Robert S. Bull, W.A. Anderson, Hugh Rose, Henry Storrey, and Robt. McFarlane. The Review Office was given the printing for the year in competition with the *Chronicle*.

March 5, 1879 Among other accounts paid at this meeting is one for splitting 5 cords of wood $1.50. At this same meeting $25,000 in debentures was authorized to the Georgian Bay and Wellington Railway.

August 6, 1879 Twelve dollars was spent to make the hill on Queen Street between George and Chester Streets more passable for teams. $30.00 for improvements to Lambton Street and $20.00 for improvements on George Street.

July 6, 1880 By-law granting $7,000 to Georgian Bay and Wellington Railway passed. $4.00 was authorized to be spent on Albert Street and $10 for grading Countess, Lambton and George.

November 1, 1880 First record of Welfare $1.50 per week was allowed for a needy case.

August 1, 1881 Presbyterians of Knox Church rented lower hall for religious services for $1.00 per meeting.

October 3, 1881 By-law to raise money for County rate passed $228.97 (1 mill) Total Town Assessment shown as $237,514.00. By-law to raise money for expenses of Town $475.02 (2 mills). By-law to raise money for school purposes 7-3/8 mills ($1,814.00). By-law to raise money for Railway purposes 6 mills ($1,410.00).

January 16, 1882 New Council: David Jackson, Mayor, Gilbert McKechnie, Reeve, Councillors, W.A. Anderson, Harry Storrey, Richard Horn, John Robertson, A.C. McKenzie, J.H. Brown, R.K. Bull, Norman McIntyre, James Burnett.

July 10, 1882 $5,000 was set aside to build new bridge on Lambton Street.

March 12, 1883 Thos. H. Easton appeared as Clerk — Tender of J.C. Dunsmoor accepted to build bridge on Lambton Street for $1,500.

May 17, 1883 Several Councillors (including all those from the North Ward) apparently forfeited their seats by absence from meetings and the Mayor was authorized to exercise his Warrant to call a new election to fill said seats. The election or nomination was held but the new Councillors did not take the Oath of Office until August 6. New sidewalk ordered built from Mill Street to Durham Road.

November 5, 1883 Professor Morgan rented Town Hall at $1.25 per night to conduct a singing class.

February 10, 1890 Rail Electric Light Company given right of way through Town. Council got five lights for $215.00 per year of 300 nights.

March 7, 1890 $1,6700 to School Board for construction of Model School. Auditors were paid $6.00 each for auditing 1889 accounts.

April 7, 1890 $1.25 per week for a woman and $1.50 per week for a man who need welfare. Petition presented to Ottawa through Dr. David Jamieson to have mail clerk on G.T. Railway.

April 7, 1890 3-foot sidewalk to be installed east side of Bruce Street, Lambton to George Streets. Lockup, at cost of not more than $15.00 be built in corner of Town Hall. Recommendation that indigents be sent to Poor House unless we can get them taken care of in Town for not more than $2.00 per week.

January 3, 1890 Several streets in Town were provided with gravel sidewalks, some on only one side of street. Also crossings to the Hotels, British and Durham. Meeting called by Orangeville Mayor to discuss rebate of bonus paid to Toronto Grey & Bruce Railway. Attended by Mayor Laidlaw.

January 19, 1891 Notice of Motion re by-law to prevent cattle roaming at large during certain hours.

March 2, 1891 South Street from Railway to College Street declared closed and conveyed to Agricultural Society.

April 6, 1891 $100.00 to be spent for poles to carry Bell Telephone wires through Town (Mount Forest to Flesherton). Public meeting called to discuss purchase of fire engine.

April 3, 1893 License fee of $50.00 be set for a shooting gallery in the Town.

August 14, 1896 Report from medical Officer of Health regarding "infectious Tonsillitis" was read. Dr. Gun complained also that the Saugeen River was being used as a sewer to the endangerment of people using the river for drinking water and swimming, etc. (So they were having a pollution problem 75 years ago).

November 2, 1896 Gravel 10 cents per load 25 cents per yard. There does not appear to have been a Reeve from 1899 to 1907.

Back Row: John Murdock's friends
Front Row: A Mr. Lavelle and friends 1910.

Harding's Hardware Store before the 1929 fire.
J.H. Harding, Jane McLean. At the window at the back of the store were chairs where customers could rest.

January 11, 1897 Wm. Calder elected Mayor; George Sparling, Reeve. Report from Dr. Gun that epidemic was cleared up — 80 cases, 3 deaths. 100 lbs. flour $2.40.

March 4, 1897 Town Council passed By-law exempting taxation for 6 years for any one building a house, etc., of the value of $700.

May 18, 1897 2" Hemlock plank $6.00 per M.

June 6, 1898 First granolithic sidewalk laid — 9-7/8 per sq. ft. This was a busy year with sidewalks being petitioned for extending from the north end of Garafraxa St. to bridge over the Saugeen also from Lambton St. bridge to station crossing.

March 6, 1899 Offer 10 years free taxes and free site for any firm employing 25 hands establishing in Town.

January 8, 1900 Mayor elected Wm. Laidlaw — only 3 councillors Mr. Lock Elvidge and Mr. A.S. Hunter — and later T.R. Whelan April 2, 1900.

May 6, 1901 Wood up to $1.80 per cord — wages still $1.00 per day. Mr. Burnett offered 10 acres of his property for $2,800, being site for Portland Cement Company. Albert and Elgin Streets closed from South Street to Elgin Street for Cement Company.

January 13, 1902 Norman McIntyre elected Mayor. Gas Company given permission to lay gas pipes.

1903 More sidewalks laid — George and Bruce to Saddler.

June 1903 New bridge on Lambton cost approximately $2,000 including retaining walls.

January 11, 1904 During this year a great many more streets were given sidewalks (granolithic). Wage rates seem to have gone up to $1.50 per day.

December 5, 1904 Board of Works instructed to purchase snow plow for cleaning sidewalks.

April 24, 1905 After fire at Furniture Factory, Town received insurance to cover $10,000 loan.

May 8, 1906 Memorial to Sir Wilfred Laurier, Prime Minister, asking that his Government prohibit the sale, manufacture or importation of cigarettes, cigarette tobacco, cigarette papers or wrappers.

September 1, 1906 Deputation sent to Montreal re C.P.R. extension to Southampton.

October 4, 1907. In the month of October there was a smallpox case and the resulting care and quarantine cost $118.20.

November 18, 1907 By-law #532 authorized Council to take local Option vote.

October 4, 1909 Junior Hockey team granted use of Town Hall free.

November 1, 1909 Resolution asking Government to submit a vote to the electorate favoring Government and Municipal ownership and operation of telephone lines, long distance and local.

June 6, 1910 Richie Bros. awarded contract to build Clerk's Office and weigh scales.

June 6, 1911 By-law giving power to establish Continuation School. Band received grant on condition they play free concerts in summer months. Invitation from Rev. Hartley to Council to attend Coronation service June 22 accepted with thanks.

June 22 accepted with thanks.

March 4, 1913 Negotiations started with Post Office Department to sell old Town Hall site.

April 7, 1913 Board of Works to recommend method of preventing floods in town.

July 14, 1913 Town Hall moved to present site for $350 by Reuben Rogers.

December 1, 1913 Council petitioned Hydro Electric Commission of Ontario to build Electric Railway from Guelph to Owen Sound.

June 1, 1914 By-law making Wednesday afternoon and evening the closing day for the merchants. Thursday night open night.

December 7, 1914 Town Hall free use granted for holding a patriotic concert.

January 11, 1915 A.S. Hunter, Mayor, Wm. Calder, Reeve. Ed. McClocklin refunded rent of Town Hall for Patriotic Concert. Durham Choral Society refunded rent of Town Hall for Patriotic Concert.

March 9, 1915 Mayor and Clerk authorized to sign Contract with H.E.P.C.

March 22, 1915 $2,000 additional grant to High School Board to complete new building.

May 7, 1915 Mr. McIntyre sold his Electric Plant to Town for $3,800.

June 29, 1915 Council ordered a flag for Clerk's office.

July 10, 1915 Offer of Durham Furniture Co. Ltd. to supply street lights accepted.

October 18, 1915 $500 granted to Imperial Red Cross fund.

December 5, 1916 Provincial Government assessed all municipalities 1 mill on the assessment for war purposes.

August 6, 1917 Clerk appointed to act between farmers requiring help to take off crop and volunteers in the Town who would take this work.

April 1919 Daylight Saving Time approved from April 13 to October 1. Man and team 50 cents per hour — labor 27-1/2 cents per hour.

January 10, 1921 Petitioned government to build post office delayed by war. Band received $25 monthly. Memorial Committee formed.

November 1921 Council expressed their opinion that wives of property owners should be granted a vote. November 1926 Debentures for addition to High School approved $25,000.

April 4, 1927 Grant of $70 made to Hockey Team.

August 15, 1927 I.O.D.E. granted $75 to help pay cost of wiring Town Hall.

April 2, 1928 Men's Club, Knox Church, offered to equip playground behind Town Hall for the children. Offer accepted.

August 13, 1928 Councillors present receive $2 each. Pavement and sewers By-law passed and bid $45,000 and $13,000 be accepted — Main Street.

August 26, 1929 Council approved paving on Lambton and Bruce Streets, Lambton from bridge to C.N.R. tracks, Bruce from Lambton to C.P.R. tracks, Lambton from Garafraxa east to overhead bridge.

December 9, 1929 Council paid bills from Owen Sound, Hanover and Mount Forest fire brigades for help given during Main Street fire. W.B. Vollett, Clerk for 27 years, died. Hugh Rose appointed.

April 14, 1930 Offer of $1,200 from I.O.D.E. accepted to change and rehabilitate Town Hall.

May 5, 1930 Site for C.P.R. station approved — old station destroyed by fire.

November 3, 1930 $25,000 grant from Provincial Relief Fund obtained to apply on installation of waterworks.

April 6, 1931 By-law passed to regulate Miniature Golf in Town. Problem of transients needing overnight accommodation. Council will take steps to provide such accommodation.

April 13, 1934 New 20 ton scales purchased. Rob Roy Mills burned April 26. Council promised utmost co-operation with Old Home Week Committee.

October 1, 1934 Council bought corner lot — Garafraxa and George for $390. Cleaning up the lot and beautifying it as a Park would be part of our winter works program. Government ordered all relief to be made on a cash basis. Council objected but complied in order to get subsidy.

April 1936 Council appointed Committee to work with Hockey Club executive re banquet celebrating the 1936 Intermediate 'B' Championship of Ontario. Council decided they would present a wrist watch to each member of the hockey team and the Executive. Banquet held June 19. Council were guests.

December 15, 1936 Boxing Day declared a Public Holiday.

January 10, 1938 The year was predominantly spent in dealing with Welfare applications — the whole Council being the Welfare Committee. The usual other business, roads, fire & lights, etc., was dealt with and the cash balance at the end of the year amounted to $25,093.89. This represented the 1938 taxes for expenditure in 1939. A record collection of pre-levy taxes. The tough attitude taken by Council toward able-bodied men applying for relief contrasts strangely with the present Government regulations in this matter. It would appear that the Councillors were rugged he-men embued with the old spirit of the pioneers who looked after their own obligations. At the same time they were dealing with an existing condition and as in the past no one was allowed to starve or be in actual want.

May 1939 Committee of Council appointed to confer with Committee organized to recognize the visit of the King and Queen.

May 20, 1939 Council granted to Band for new uniforms, music, etc. $150. Special train taking school children and others to Guelph where special accommodation will be provided so that all will see Their Majesties.

1940 During the period 1935 and in the following years Council business was conducted by Committees. Chairmen of each standing committee presenting a report to the regular monthly Council meeting and having their report approved including their expenditures.

June 14, 1940 New Union Jack purchased for Clerk's office. Town Hall free to any organization doing war work.

July 8, 1940 Deputation waited on Council advocating creation of a Civil Guard as recommended by Provincial Government. J.B. Duffield was asked to take command at the request of the Returned Soldiers organization and the Town Council Committee appointed to make some recognition to all who enlisted from the Town for active service.

October 17, 1940 Medical Officer of Health, Dr. R. Burnett, granted leave of absence for the duration of his enlistment in the R.C.A.F.

January 15, 1941 W.S. Hunter, Reeve, elected Warden of Grey County and Council held a banquet in his honour.

May 5, 1941 War Savings Certificate drive went well over the quota. Council formed Committee to promote Victory Bond drives. Visits of military units to the Town are very successful.

December 1, 1941 Insurance agents association formed and all Town insurance will be handled by this association. McGowan's Mill burned. During the war period the whole Council seemed to be imbued with a sense of urgency. All expenditures were held to a bare minimum, grants were made to various patriotic organizations. Tag days approved for such organizations as the Chinese Relief Fund, the Victory Committee, Navy League, etc. Church services were organized by Council for a Day of Prayer and pre-Victory Bond campaigns. Members of Council were representing Council on most war committees. A Ration Board with Peter Ramage the Executive Officer was formed.

March 1, 1943 Committee organized to welcome soldiers back home after service overseas. Rotary Club requested grant to assist in purchasing a skating rink for public use. Permission to hold Tag Days given to

Joe Snell — worked as a handy man around town until he was over 90 years old.

1948 Town Council in the council chambers at the clerk's office.
Back Row: Charles Graham, Stanley McAfee, Bowman Jamieson, Gordon Greenwood, Clerk.
Front Row: Dr. Gordon Grant, G.R. Padfield, Mayor, Lawrence Chapman, Reeve, Arthur Neff.
Absent: R.S. Ball.

the Navy League, Chinese Relief Fund, Rotary Club,. Canadian Legion, Red Cross Society.

January 10, 1944 Wage rates for town employees raised to 40 cents per hour.

February 21, 1944 Rehabilitation Committee formed to deal with returning soldiers needing work after discharge.

January 8, 1945 Harry Kress, Mayor; C.M. Elvidge, Reeve. Reception Committee for returning service people formed with Council represented on Committee. Effort made to have new industries located here — limited success, candy factory in Queen Street Church, etc.

October 1945 Rings ordered for returned service personnel and arrangements made with Legion for presentation ceremony and reception dance.

November 5, 1945 Harry Scott, long time (14 years) Chief of Police, resigned for personal reasons.

February 1946 Decision made to purchase new pumper for Fire Department

April 1, 1946 Frank Ilingworth appointed Police Chief. Garbage collection inaugurated.

March 1947 Wage rate for town employees at 50 cents per hour.

June 1947 Delbert Holley given permission to erect and operate a movie theatre.

September 2, 1947 Rotary Club given permission to erect wading pool in Park.

October 6, 1947 Wages of town employees raised to 55 cents per hour.

April 1948 Town employees wages raised to 60 cents per hour.

September 1948 Recreation Committee formed. County Assessor set the date for the Court of Revision and exercised some control over the decisions of that Court.

January 4, 1949 Lambton Street bridge condemned and sold for scrap to Lackie Bros. Council raised its own fee to $4.00 per meeting.

October 1949 Foot bridge installed for pedestrians on Lambton Street to cost $500 (considerably reduced when bill presented).

December 5, 1949 Council decided to help form Saugeen Valley Authority. Mayor A.C. Neff appointed to represent the Town.

September 5, 1950 Durham Road repaired at bridge — Durham Crushed Stone thanked for their contribution. Council was represented at meetings setting up High School District.

November 1951 Lambton Street Bridge opened by Hon. George Doucett.

May 1952 Council expressed themselves as being in favor of the erection of a new Public School. Council discussed earwigs and tent caterpillars. Kinsmen thanked for the signs installed at the entrances to the Town. Huskies Hockey team presented with jackets and crests to commemorate their Ontario Championship.

June 1952 By-law setting up Community Centre was passed. Chief Dickens resigned, Ted Zimmer appointed.

September 8, 1952 Factory strike became a "Law & Order" issue. As police protection was not adequate, Council requested aid from Provincial Police.

February 1953 Strike ended.

April 1955 Parking By-laws passed, also By-law to erect stop signs, etc., also taxis to be licensed and regulated.

April 4, 1955 Fire Alarm Siren installed in place of factory whistle.

May 2, 1955 Wages of Board of Works employees raised to 90 cents per hour.

January 10, 1956 Fire protection agreements were signed by adjoining townships.

June 4, 1956 Trailer By-law passed.

December 17, 1956 Chief Berger resigned, Constable Ward appointed Chief. Council raised their salaries to $5.00 per meeting.

February 18, 1959 Recently acquired Park was put under a newly formed Parks Commission who transferred same to Saugeen Valley Authority. Park on north side of river donated by Alvin Metzger of Knechtel Milling Company.

October 1959 Maple Leaf Veneer requested water service from the Town. Reeve Ab McRonald of Bentinck and Harry Kress formed a deputation to Toronto to investigate the possibility of Durham supplying water to Bentinck and Bentinck supplying same to the Veneer Plant.

June 5, 1961 Twin Pines building for senior citizens on Bruce North. Sewage installation under discussion and information gathered.

August 3, 1961 Council agreed to provide $40,000 for erection of new P.U.C. building repayble annually. LCBO requested to open Liquor Store as a result of recent plebiscite.

November, 1961 2 year term approved by electors.

February 5, 1962 Request for approval of extension to High School granted. Water line to Hospital approved.

March 5, 1962 Bell Telephone given consent to lay underground wires. Considerable discussion at several meetings re garbage, new hospital and installations of sewers and disposal plant, separate school, Planning Board.

June 11, 1962 New Fire Truck purchased cost about $15,000. Council invited to attend opening of new bowling alley. Twin Pines apartments opened.

November 1962 Gas Company given permission to install lines in Town. After many meetings and discussions a By-law was passed authorizing Mayor and Clerk to sign agreement with Bentinck Township re water supply for Maple Leaf Veneer.

December 3, 1962 Council raised its salary to $13.00 per meeting for 13 meetings.

1964 Alterations to eastern end of Highway #4 link approved. A great deal of the Council's time was taken up during this year by correspondence with the OWRC regarding sewers, the acquisition of land for the treatment lagoon, consultation with the engineers regarding this, setting water rates and other charges to pay for the operation and amortization of the cost. New sidewalks were also laid on the Main Street after considerable haggling with property owners. Garbage, crossing guards, road foreman also took up their share of Council's time. Special meetings were the order of the day. Nursing Home opened in old Hospital building.

April 5, 1965 Preliminary steps taken to engage professional planner to produce plan for the Town.

December 8, 1965 Engineers asked to prepare 5 year plan to reconstruct streets torn up by the sewer installation.

Plaque commemorating the Durham Road at entrance to SVCA Park.

April 18, 1966 Parking meter by-law given third reading. Fringe benefits re OHSIP and OMSIP granted employees.

May 1, 1966 Three days June 30, July 1 and 2 set aside as Canada Centennial Days in the Town of Durham. As a result of a visit by two representatives of the Ontario Police Commission, it was decided to set up a Police Commission in place of the Police Committee of Council. Considerable discussion regarding a south-west Grey Board of Education were taking place at meetings with both School Boards and eventually on receiving satisfactory adjustments of debenture debt, the Council reluctantly resolved to accede to joining this new Board of Education.

July 1966 Process of proposition to extend the sewers to the Hospital started. This is a very urgent matter, so after usual due process the extension was actually built in 1968.

December 12, 1966 Town Weigh Scales closed.

March 6, 1967 After several deputations voicing objections to Parking Meters, Council had the O.M.B. dismiss our By-law covering this installation. Flood conditions below lower dam very bad.

May 1, 1967 County Assessment established by County.

September 11, 1967 Council appalled by the increased education costs under the new S.W. Grey Board of Education. Some action on Low Rental Housing — plans and requirements presented to Council and approved.

January 8, 1968 Twin Pines taken over by Ontario Housing. Fire Agreements signed with adjoining municipalities. Provincial Residential Property Tax reduction instituted. Survey of river by S.C.V.A. engineer to plan abatement of spring flooding.

May 6, 1968 Mayor reported that hockey activity during past winter has put Arena Commission on sounder financial position than it has been for years. Committee appointed to recommend suitable recognition. Marathon Realty accepted offer for triangle of land opposite Town Hall, which has been used for parking and will now permit George Street to be deviated, eliminating sharp corners.

September 1968 County Board of Education established with Durham and Normanby represented by one member.

December 16, 1968 James Sullivan elected to represent Normanby and Durham on County Board. Protest meeting re Hospital held in High School Auditorium. Packed house listened to fervid oratory and all agreed that the Provincial Department of Health had better change its mind. Eric Winkler, M.P.P., assured meeting that the Durham Hospital was safe and would continue to operate as in the past.

January 3, 1970 Garbage collection given to private contract, $12,500 for two years. This obviated the necessity of Council enacting controlling by-law. Old Post Office building purchased by Town and redecorated and re-planned to be used for Town Clerk's Office and Council Chamber.

May 21, 1969 First meeting of Council in new Building. Dead elm trees discussed and program to cut down and remove same was approved. Dead maples included.

August 10, 1969 Plaque commemorating opening of Durham Road a hundred years ago located at northern entrance to S.V.C.A. Park officially opened.

January 3, 1970 Garbage collection given to private contract $12,500 for two years.

May 4, 1970 Official request made to D.H.O. to renew Garafraxa Street bridge. Clerk appointed Lottery Licensing Officer.

June 29, 1970 C.N.R. Station to be removed as it has not been in use recently.

Town Council 1970.
Back Row: Bev Wiggins, Wm. Wardropper, Roger Goldsmith, Don Pust, Elmer Clark
Front Row: Anna Koehler, Ken Macdonald (Mayor), Harry Kress (Reeve), Edgar Patterson (Clerk).

January 22, 1971 Ralston Purina plant totally destroyed by fire. Council investigating possibility of aid to owner in rebuilding.

February 8, 1971 Special meeting to discuss above held and possible Provincial grants were outlined. Eric Winkler, MPP, promised all possible aid. Senior Citizen housing again before Council and further inquiry will be made to Ontario Housing Corporation. Widening and rebuilding of Garafraxa Street bridge promised a year ago was discussed. Consulting Engineer will contact Department. Cemetery turned over to Town and Board appointed to administer same. Centennial Celebrations to be held August 5 to August 9, 1972.

June 11, 1971 Committees appointed for Centennial Week.

July 5, 1971 Dog Catcher renamed Canine Control Officer. The Dump renamed Sanitary Site.

Runaway truck coming down Durham Hill went through front of Yirr's Jewellery store. One pedestrian was killed.

October 29, 1971 Council decided to change 2-year term to one year in 1972 so that Municipal Elections will coincide with County Board of Education Election date.

November 7, 1971 Middaugh House apartments and stores totally destroyed by fire. Council held meeting to discuss demolition of dangerous walls, which must be done soon as traffic has to be rerouted around the remains of the building. Owner assured Council that this would be done immediately.

December 6, 1971 Council raised Council fees to Mayor $800 per annum; Councillors $400 per annum; Chairman Board of Works an extra fee of $200. 1972 Council (by acclamation) Mayor K.L. MacDonald; Reeve W.H. Kress; Deputy-Reeve Albert Wilton; Councillors, Jas. Baskerville, B. Marshall, Orv. MacDonald, Ron Murdock, Ross Thompson, and Tom Watson.

January 10, 1972 Contract let to rebuild #6 Highway from Lambton Street north to town limits including new bridge over the Saugeen River. Tender price was $317,904.

February 7, 1972 A special meeting was called to commemorate the first Durham council meeting one hundred years before on March 29, 1872. Reeve Kress and Councillors Thompson and Murdock arrived in formal attire including top hats.

May 1, 1973 OMB approval given for proposed sanitary sewer system.

March 2, 1973 Council voted to support Rotary Club in repairing the wading pool to the extent of $2,000.

May 7, 1973 The sum of $300 granted to the Horticulture Society for work done in the park.

October 16, 1973 A special meeting was called to discuss the newly created regional municipality that had stolen the name of Durham.

November 5, 1973 Council and community saddened by the sudden death of J. Edgar Patterson, the town clerk.

February 4, 1974 The town engineer reported to council that an error had been made in their estimates on the proposed water reservoir and the size would have to be increased from 300 MIG to 500 MIG.

May 21, 1974 The town lost the court case re the name of Durham. An appeal was recommended.

November 8, 1974 Traffic lights were installed at the junction of #4 and #6 Highways at a cost of $9,871.

February 17, 1975 Manager of Saugeen Valley Conservation Authority presented flood plain maps. Council moved to study flood control measures for the town. Council decided to have two regular meetings each month. Council decided to install parking meters. Authorization given to Save Durham's Name Committee to appeal to Supreme Court.

May 12, 1975 The minister of labour reported it would allow no operation of the Arena after the first snowfall in fall of 1975.

July 7, 1975 Town purchased properties required for roadway between Credit Union and Creamery.

January 5, 1976. Report from Canadian Open Banjo Competition showed profit of $1,076.

Council decided to demolish old arena and build new one on the old site.

Council decided to build a Fire Hall, Police Station and Board of Works garage on George Street east of the Town Hall.

March 7, 1977 Bluebird bus purchased from Wilmer Vollett for use of Girls' Trumpet Band.

June 6, 1977 Census of Durham confirms Durham's population at 2,501.

June 30, 1977 Official opening of new arena set for July 17, 1977.

September 6, 1977 Council approved Dyking system for Upper Dam.

Town changed all signs to metric.

February 20, 1978 Town decided to buy a new fire pumper truck at approximate price of $47,500.

April 17, 1978 Town plans to fight the Provincial government plan to close the Registry Office.

August 9, 1978 A stripper was purchased to place lines on the street.

December 18, 1978 Council approved construction of steel walkway over Upper Dam.

September 17, 1979 The Council endorsed and supported arrangements for visit of the Lieutenant Governor the Honourable Pauline McGibbon to officially open the Durham Art Gallery October 4, 1979.

February 18, 1980 Mayor Wiggins objected to the increased honorarium for council and donated his increase of $600 to cover cost of visitors from Durham, England. Councillor Gordon MacLean also donated his $400 increase toward the twinning of the two Durhams.

May 5, 1980 A tender was accepted for the demolition of the old Fire Hall and Police Station halfway up the hill.

October 6, 1980 A letter was read from the Chamber of Commerce from the Netherlands in which they sent a charter of friendship and 1,000 bulbs to be planted in thanks for the Canadian servicemen who helped liberate Holland.

January 19, 1981 Council purchased a Crest with Coat of Arms for the Town of Durham.

July 4, 1982 Councillor Taylor reported that sandblasting and painting of the water tower was completed at a cost of $21,850.

August 9, 1982 Council published an open letter of appreciation to the Durham and District Old Home Week Committee and all others who worked to make the celebration a success.

Old Home Week 1972.

September 20, 1982 An invitation was received by Council to attend the sod turning ceremony for the new 100 bed Home for the Aged.

October 4, 1982 A letter from Peter Fallis was read regarding a bond for $1,000 that was registered in 1890 against the Calder Block for work to be done on the property. A letter was sent to Peter Fallis that the bond has been satisfied in full, all of the improvements required within a period of 2 years from the 13th of February, 1890, have been made to the satisfaction of Council and therefore the bond is void. Judith Gray was appointed Clerk-Treasurer, effective September 1, 1983.

October 3, 1983 A by-law was passed for construction of a heliport at Durham Memorial Hospital.

February 13, 1984 County Council assumed road maintenance and storm sewers for the Durham Road.

October 31, 1984 Rockwood Terrace was officially opened October 31, 1984.

August 12, 1985 Council approved the purchase of C.P.R. bridge from Knights of Sauble Beach and accepted from Canadian Pacific Railway the gift of the C.P.R. right of way through town with legal costs to be paid by the town.

March 3, 1986 County Council requested photographs of former Wardens of Grey County from Durham, namely George Jackson, Wm. Calder, Allen Bell, Wm. S. Hunter, Harry Kress.

August 5, 1986 The clerk was directed to inform the author of a letter of complaint re exotic dancers and male strippers at the hotel that such dancers are no longer employed at the hotel.

October 6, 1986 Council appointed a building official, plumbing inspector and standards officer.

November 3, 1986 The property owned by the town at the north-east corner of Saddler and College Streets was designated as a soccer pitch.

June 15, 1987 Council informed that Durham Legion had approved full funding for the illumination of McGowan Falls.

August 18, 1987 Ball Park Pavillion officially opened.

May 15, 1989 Council donated the former C.P. Railway land between Elgin and Albert Streets to the Durham Art Gallery.

July 19, 1989 Water was in short supply and an emergency was declared that prohibited all outside use of water.

October 2, 1989 The Town accepted the donation of a clock , to hang on the outside of the Municipal Building, from Durham Legion Branch #308 in honour of the Branch's 50th Anniversary.

April 2, 1990 Council passed by-law requiring the installation of water meters in buildings within town.

August 10, 1991 Durham, co-operating with 7 other municipalities, built an airport in Brant Township. It was opened on August 10, 1991.

September 3, 1991 A by-law was passed to authorize the operation of a transit system for the disabled.

December 2, 1991 Mayor Lawrence presented a cheque for $30,000 to Gordon MacLean of the Hospital Board as Council's 1991 donation to the hospital's x-ray fund.

It was noted that the Registry Office was closed and a motion was passed to have it designated as a heritage property

February 17, 1992 Discussion of closure of Kroehler Manufacturing Company and its impact on Durham.

April 6, 1992 Council set up ad hoc committee to "Save the Factory" with the mayor and reeve as members from council.

April 20, 1992 The mayor reported that arrangements had been made by a group of local investors to keep the factory open under the name of Durham Furniture Company.

May 12, 1992 Park Business College moved into Saugeen Press building.

June 15, 1992 The Town of Durham accepts with thanks the Heritage Walkway Bridge as constructed and landscaped by the Durham Bridge Committee and that said committee now be dissolved.

July 13, 1992 Mayor Lawrence thanked all those who had made "the 1992 Homecoming" a success.

December 15, 1992 The Board of Works has recommended that Norvair's colour Commodore Blue be adopted as Durham Blue and used on all vehicles, buildings, etc.

December 20, 1993 The Town agrees in principal for the use of the sewage treatment plant for treatment of leachate from a proposed composting operation by Seeley and Arnill aggregates.

MAYORS OF DURHAM

1872 — Alexander Cochrane	1921 — Thos. Allan
1877 — Walter Harris	1923 — J.L. Smith
1879 — H.J. Middaugh	1925 — J.N. Murdock
1882 — David Jackson	1930 — Oliver Hunter
1884 — Alex Cochrane	1931 — J.N. Murdock
1886 — H.W. Mockler	1933 — Harry Kress
1887 — David Jackson	1936 — W.A. McDonald
1890 — Wm. Laidlaw	1938 — Allan Bell
1893 — Thomas Brown	1941 — James B. Duffield
1894 — J.W. Mockler	1943 — Oliver Hunter
1895 — Wm. Laidlaw	1945 — Harry Kress
1897 — Wm. Calder	1947 — G.R. Padfield
1900 — Wm. Laidlaw	1949 — A.C. Neff
1901 — Wm. Calder	1952 — R.S. Ball
1902 — Norman McIntyre	1954 — J. Frank Irwin
1904 — A.S. Hunter	1957 — R.S. Ball
1907 — Wm. Calder	1960 — Marion Calder
1909 — Wm. Laidlaw	1963 — K.L. Macdonald
1911 — Wm. Black	1968 — J.B. Duffield
1915 — A.S. Hunter	1970 — K.L. Macdonald
1917 — Wm. Laidlaw	1975 — Bev. Wiggins
1919 — G. McKechnie	1980 — Gordon MacLean
1920 — J.F. Grant	1986 — Floyd Lawrence

DURHAM REEVES

1873 — Duncan McDonald
1874 — Geo. Jackson
1885 — David Jamieson
1887 — Gilbert McKechnie
1890 — J.H. Brown
1895 — Wm. Gorsline
1897 — Geo. Sparling
From 1897 to 1907 there was a new system used, therefore no reeves were elected in those years.
1907 — L.P. Saunders
1910 — Wm. Calder
1916 — A.A. Catton
1917 — Wm. Calder
1919 — A.A. Catton
1920 — Wm.Calder
1923 — A.B. Currie
1924 — Wm. Calder
1926 — Allan Bell

1932 — Allan Bell, Warden
1933 — W.S. Hunter
1941 — W.S. Hunter, Warden
1943 — C.M. Elvidge
1948 — S.T. Chapman
1953 — J.H. McQuarrie
1954 — Marion Calder
1957 — W.H. Kress
1965 — W.H. Kress, Warden
1972 — Albert Wilton, Deputy, a new position
1975 — Neil Benninger
1977 — Clive Elvidge
1979 — Carol Lawrence
1989 — Bill McDonald

Bryson Morlock. Note Garafraxa Street is not paved but a cement sidewalk crosses the street.

DEPUTY REEVES

1975 — A. Wilton
1979 — Glen Marshall

1989 — Ross Taylor
1992 — Elmer Clark

Durham Town Council 1994
Front Row: Deputy Reeve Elmer Clark, Mayor Floyd Lawrence, Reeve Bill McDonald
Back Row: Ross Thompson, Harley Berry, Isabelle Schierz, Art Hand, Wayne Mighton, Gord Reaburn.

Durham's first fire brigade 1895 in front of C.L. Grant's store at Durham Road West and Garafraxa Street.

William Price's Carpet Store after the fire in 1979.

Middaugh House after the fire in 1971.

The McIntyre Block following the fire in 1929.

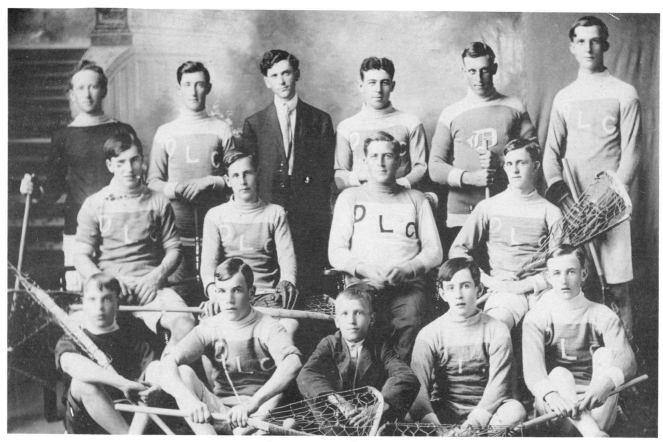

Lacross team early 1900s.
Back Row: Ted McKenna, H. McEachnie, G.S. Burnett, Fred Falkingham, J. Vollett, Roy Calder
Centre Row: Jim Allen, Vern Elvidge, Howard MacDonald, Lou Lavelle
Front Row: Fred Laidlaw, Mac Saunders, Fred Saunders, J.C., Lenahan, Bob Saunders.

Kinsmen donate improvements to the ball diamond 1963.
Bob Braithwaite, Jim Flewelling, Ken MacDonald, Mayor, Ross Taylor, Glen Budd, Jack Lawrence.

Durham Presbyterian Church Choir 1909

Organist: Miss B. McKenzie
Soprano: Mrs. A.H. Jackson, Misses Margaret Hunter, Mamie Munro, S. Burnett, Maggie Young, L. Lauder, T. Oliver
Alto: Mrs. Buchan, Mrs. Stonehouse, Mrs. J. Fraser, Miss J. Ireland
Tenor: J.P. Telford (centre, leader), Peter Ramage
Bass: Geo. Sinclair, W. Nichol, Dr. J.F. Grant, J. Roberts, John Burgess
(Three absent)

~DIED:~

On Friday, September 1st, 1899,

Archibald McKenzie.

~~~

~ THE FUNERAL ~

Will leave his late residence, for the Durham Cemetery, on Sunday, Sept. 3rd at 2 p. m. sharp.

Friends and acquaintances will please accept this intimation.

Durham, Sept. 1st, 1899.

John McKechnie Jr., clerked all his life in Durham stores, mainly in the drug store. He was affectionately called 'Drug Store Johnny.'

275

Garafraxa Street looking south, 1900.

Boating on the Saugeen.

One of Durham's first bands in a parade at Garafraxa and Lambton. Circa 1890.

INDEX

McDonald, Gordon, 230
McDonald, Howard, 84
McDonald, Hugh, 75, 240
McDonald, J.W., 238, 241
McDonald, John, 242
McDonald, Katharine, 72, 192
McDonald, Lyall, 220
McDonald, Michelle, 224
McDonald, Mrs. H., 115
McDonald, Sadie, 117, 239
McDonald, Thomas, 94
McDonald, William, 122, 189, 271
McDonnel, Duncan, 15, 238, 239
McDonnell, J.W., 8
McDonnell, Maude (Kress), 172
McDonnell, Mrs. W., 115
McDougald, Colin, 15, 209
McDougall, Duncan, 125
McDougall, Warren, 31
McEachnie, Fred, 215
McEachnie, H., 274
McEachnie, Ivan, 23, 139
McEwen, Rev. E.J., 42
McFadden, Bobby, 227
McFadden, Clara (Alexander), 116
McFadden, Greg, 217, 218
McFadden, Moore, 153, 239
McFadden, Mrs. Moore, 239
McFadden, R., 226
McFadden, Reg., 114
McFadden, Rick, 220
McFadden, Terry, 26
McFadden, Thomas, 47
McFadden, W.J., 22
McFadden, Wm., 108
McFadyen, Martha, 75
McFarlan, Allen, 15
McFarlan, Geo., 15
McFarlan, Robert, 15
McFarlan, Robt., 15
McFarlane, Archie, 7, 67, 167, 206
McFarlane, David B. (Allen), 67, 206
McFarlane, James, 206
McFarlane, Lorna, 32
McFarlane, Robt., 111, 261
McGarry, 177
McGibb, Isabella Cranston, 40
McGibbon, Pauline, 115, 253, 270
McGillivray, Alan, 243
McGillivray, Del (Chapman), 223, 224
McGillivray, Don, 30, 212
McGillivray, Donald Gordon, 103
McGillivray, Jim, 221
McGillivray, Ken, 29
McGillivray, Marianne, 29
McGillivray, Russell, 120
McGillivray, Ted, 122
McGirr, 231
McGirr, Allie, 107
McGirr, Andrew, 49
McGirr, Annie, 117
McGirr, Bill, 23, 247
McGirr, Binnie, 19

McGirr, C., 226
McGirr, Chrissie, 117
McGirr, Clarence, 110, 213, 216, 228
McGirr, Cliff, 212, 213
McGirr, Elsie, 110
McGirr, Ernest, 152
McGirr, Eunice, 123, 158
McGirr, Gordon, 120, 122, 209, 212
McGirr, Harper, 178, 211
McGirr, Isabelle, ii, 277
McGirr, James, 15, 43, 91
McGirr, Jas., 15
McGirr, Jennie, 158
McGirr, John, 46, 107, 239, 242
McGirr, L., 152
McGirr, Les, 220
McGirr, Margaret, 123, 241
McGirr, Mrs. A., 31
McGirr, Mrs. Thomas, 112
McGirr, Raymond (Hap), 210, 212, 213, 218, 219, 225
McGirr, Raymond, 120, 213, 214, 234
McGirr, Thomas, 91
McGirr, William, 105
McGoey, Rev. J.S., 53
McGowan, 252
McGowan, A., 119
McGowan, Allie, 239
McGowan, Arthur, 97, 130
McGowan, Betty, 32, 249
McGowan, Bobbie, 95
McGowan, Elsie, 36, 110
McGowan, Jean, 33, 129
McGowan, Joan, 31
McGowan, John, 22, 110, 128, 129, 130
McGowan, Mary, 29
McGowan, Ottilie, ii, 77, 89, 116
McGowan, Robert, 88, 95, 127, 129, 132
McGowan, Robert S. Jr., 128
McGowan, W.R., 100, 132, 189, 242
McGowan, Wallace, 45, 97, 128, 130
McGowan, Wm. A., 153, 248
McGrade, Patrick, 75
McGrade, Thomas, 75
McGrath, Michael, 153
McGregor, E., 116
McGregor, Rev. Wm., 42
McHardy, Allyson, 255
McHugh, Rev. F.J., 53
McIllwain, Elizabeth, 248
McIlraith, Christine, 36
McIlraith, I.S., 36, 47
McIlraith, Mary, 117
McIlraith, N., 218, 219
McIlraith, Stewart, 22, 28
McInnes, Gord, 217, 218
McInnis, Bruce, 225, 227
McInnis, Gord, 218
McInnis, Mel, 225, 227
McInnis, Sally, 30
McIntosh, A., 219
McIntosh, Bill, 210, 214, 219
McIntyre, 240, 264, 273
McIntyre, A., 207

McIntyre, David, 15
McIntyre, H.D., 242
McIntyre, Jessie, 98
McIntyre, Malcolm, 15, 173
McIntyre, Merv, 220, 225
McIntyre, N., 86
McIntyre, Norah, (Stewart), 23
McIntyre, Norman, 15, 136, 164, 172, 174, 208, 239, 261, 263, 271
McIntyre, Norman P., 98
McIntyre, Sandy, 242
McKay, Frank, 94
McKay, George, 77
McKay, Hugh, 15, 77, 201
Mckechnie, Ivan, 219
McKechnie, 231
McKechnie, Allan, 75
McKechnie, Fred, 213
McKechnie, Gilbert, 15, 55, 58, 81, 109, 141, 142, 146, 147, 183, 261, 271, 272
McKechnie, Harold, 97, 111, 186, 191, 208, 239
McKechnie, Hilda, 158
McKechnie, J., 65
McKechnie, J.C., 20, 24, 25, 27
McKechnie, John, 15, 45, 63, 80, 120, 127, 128, 131, 146, 147, 153
McKechnie, John C., 26
McKechnie, John D., 239
McKechnie, John Jr., 275
McKechnie, Margaret, 146
McKechnie, Marjorie, 24, 26
McKechnie, Mary, 238
McKechnie, Mrs. G., 115, 231
McKechnie, Mrs. N., 109
McKechnie, N.G., 65
McKechnie, Neil, 15, 43, 127, 140, 146, 147
McKechnie, Neil G., 131
McKechnie, Percy, 94
McKechnie, Velma, 74
McKechnie, Yank, 211, 228
McKee, David, 15
McKelvey, John, 75
McKenna, E., 233
McKenna, Ted, 208, 274
McKenzie, A.C., 15, 58, 80, 259, 261
McKenzie, Annie, 240
McKenzie, Archibald, 15, 73, 75
McKenzie, B., 275
McKenzie, David C., 206
McKenzie, Donald, 41, 238, 259
McKenzie, E., 154, 240
McKenzie, Edie, 117
McKenzie, Edith C., 21
McKenzie, Flora, 15
McKenzie, Laura C., 20
McKenzie, William L., 206
McKerracher, Donalda, 20
McKessock, Bob, 156, 183
McKinnon, Charles, 184
McKinnon, L., 12
McKinzie, James Geo., 15
McKinzie, Rod, 15
McLachlan, A., 136
McLachlan, Alex, 7
McLachlan, Cam, 211

McLachlan, James, 229
McLachlan, Jean, 249
McLachlan, Jessie, 185
McLachlan, Jim, 211, 216, 29
McLaren, A.F., 142
McLaren, John, 58
McLaughlin, Bruce, 222
McLean, A.J., 107
McLean, Anna, 23
McLean, Brian, 217, 220
McLean, D., 77
McLean, Don, 31
McLean, Edna, 107, 223
McLean, Jane, 263
McLean, Jennie, 117
McLean, John, 15
McLean, Mrs., 15
McLean, Scott, 33
McLeish, 55
McLeish, Bill, 243
McLellan, Archibald, 15, 259
McLelland, H., 219
McLeod, A., 44, 154
McLeod, Rev. D., 44
McMann, Al, 220, 221, 222
McMeekin, Bill, 255
McMeekin, Robert W., 94
McMillan, Miss, 18, 177
McMillan, Donald, 75
McMillan, E.D., 15
McMillan, Jeff, 221
McMullen, James, 58
McMullen, Jean, 123
McMullen, Jim, 122, 212
McMulty, R.J., 233
McNab, A.B., 39, 73, 75, 79, 106, 183, 201
McNab, Anna, 15
McNab, Gary, 225
McNab, Hugh, 44
McNabb, Hugh, 43
McNabb, Neil, 77
McNabb, Randy, 222
McNabb, Virgil, 212, 214, 215, 230
McNair, Rev. Robt., 45
McNally, Margaret, 110
McNally, Stanley, 94
McNamara, Dolores, 34
McNaughton, Don, 27
McNaughton, Emily, 26
McNaughton, H.E., 111, 124, 226
McNeil, Gord, 219
McNeil, Patricia, 224
McNemara, Mary, 75
McNichol, David, 183
McNulty, 233
McPhail, Agnes, 183
McPhail, Lachlin, 75
McQuarrie, J.H., 272
McQueen, Don, 24, 26, 110
McQueen, Grace, 47
McQueen, Jean, 30
McQueen, John, 230
McRae, Aggie, 240
McRae, Alice (Allie), 240
McRae, F., 238
McRae, G., 240
McRae, Mrs., 109, 241
McRae, Rev. J.A., 42

BIBLIOGRAPHY

Grant, J.F. — Historical Review of Durham, 1935

McGirr, Isabelle; MacDonald, Hector — A Historical Review of the Town of Durham, 1958

Sharpe, I.B. — Durham Centennial Historical Review, 1972

Belden, H. & Co. — Illustrated Atlas of the County of Grey, 1880

Smith, W.W. — Gazetteer and Directory of the County of Grey, 1865-66

Marsh, E.L. — A History of the County of Grey, 1931

Davidson, T. Arthur — A New History of Grey County, 1972

Churchill, A.G. — Poetical Directory of Businesses in Mount Forest, Neustadt, Durham, Owen Sound

Magazine of Industry of the Owen Sound Herald, Descriptive and Illustrating Grey County, 1911

Stewart, E.H. — Reverend Alexander Stewart, 1991

Durham Presbyterian Jubilee Souvenir, 1859-1909

Department of Planning and Development, Ontario: Upper Saugeen

Valley Conservation Report, 1953

Durham Municipal Council Minutes

Durham Red Cross Memorial Hospital Minutes

Durham Red Cross Society Minutes

South Grey Agricultural Society Minutes

The Durham Standard 1858-1866

The Durham Chronicle 1866 to 1994

The Grey Review 1878 to 1896

The Durham Review 1896 to 1942

The Durham Citizen 1990 to 1994

The Toronto Daily Star

The Owen Sound Sun-Times